Minicomputers

Hardware, Software, and Selection

Udo W. Pooch

Texas A&M University

Rahul Chattergy

University of Hawaii

MINICOMPUTERS

Hardware, Software, and Selection

West Publishing Company

St. Paul   New York   Los Angeles   San Francisco

Cover photograph courtesy Intel Corporation

Copyright © 1980 by WEST PUBLISHING COMPANY
50 West Kellogg Boulevard
P.O. Box 3526
St. Paul, Minnesota 55165

Printed in the United States of America

Library of Congress Cataloging in Publication Data

Pooch, U. W.
    Minicomputers: hardware, software, and selection.

    Includes bibliographical references and index.
    1. Minicomputers. I. Chattergy, R., joint author.
II. Title.
QA76.5.P633   001.6′4′04   79-24692
ISBN 0-8299-0055-1

*Once in every person's life comes an experience
that casts its glow over all the years after.*
BILL MOONAN *provided me with such an experience.*

Udo W. Pooch

Contents

Preface

In the last several years, numerous books have been published on various aspects of minicomputer technology. However, the treatment of the overall functional operation of a minicomputer has been largely confined to studies of specific minicomputers, or groups of minicomputers, available on the current market. Such presentations, while valuable, are often confusing to the reader or, alternately, invoke a negative interest. When a wide range of minicomputers is presented, none can be treated in detail so the material often appears to be a long list of briefly presented topics. The reader may react negatively to a specific brand of minicomputer, and, on that basis, reject the material presented. In contrast to the above approaches to minicomputer technology, this book offers a much more thorough analysis of the functional operation of a minicomputer than heretofore presented.

After a brief introduction to minicomputers in Chapter 1, Chapter 2 develops the design considerations and functional architecture of a minicomputer system. The minicomputer is presented as a set of functional components, each of which is described in terms of block diagrams and an operational language developed specifically for that purpose. Instruction formats and addressing modes are described in Chapter 3. Although the material presented in Chapters 2 and 3 assumes no prior knowledge of hardware, it is more meaningful to a reader with a basic understanding of the design of digital systems.

The basic concepts of minicomputer interfacing are developed in Chapter 4 in a rather unique presentation. Functional designs for a generalized programmed I/O controller, an interrupt I/O controller, and finally a direct memory access controller are developed. These generalized concepts are then used to develop specific functional controller designs for a selected set of peripheral devices. The authors feel that the approach and material presented in Chapter 4 will not be found in any other text on minicomputer technology.

Minicomputer programming concepts are presented in Chapter 5. The reader is guided through machine mnemonic programming and assembler language programming. Numerous examples are presented to aid the reader in understanding the basic concepts involved in programming a minicomputer. The reader who is familiar with minicomputer programming may skip Chapter 5 without loss in continuity.

The rapid rise in the use of minicomputers can be explained by the readily available applications for small computers and by the relatively low cost of minicomputer hardware that makes many applications economically feasible. With these developments in mind, a discussion of the status of minicomputer software is presented in Chapter 6. The current "mini" environment affects software differently, depending on what type of software is involved. For purposes of discussion, software is broadly treated as five distinct categories. The first category, basic support software, is composed of a collection of programs and routines for interfacing the user and the hardware more easily and quickly in the solution of user problems. Such items as assemblers, compilers, program debugging aids, and arithmetic operation routines are discussed. The second category, high-level languages, is discussed in terms of detailed analysis of assemblers, compilers, and interpreters. The third category, utility software, consists of data conversion programs, extended mathematical subroutines, specially developed packages for detecting and identifying hardware faults, floating-point arithmetic routines, general-purpose input/output device handlers, and various kinds of scientific subroutines. The fourth category, operating system software, is composed primarily of the programs and routines specifically required by the hardware to produce the functions and capabilities of the minisystem itself. Such items as executives, loaders, and controllers are discussed in this category. The fifth category, application software, is composed of programs and routines designed specifically to solve user needs. The user's needs are as diverse as imagination allows. Examples in any minicomputer installation range from dedicated process control to general-purpose service bureau usage. The status of each software category is discussed in detail.

Chapter 7 presents microprogrammed minicomputer organization using a simple microprogrammed computer as the vehicle. The relationship between microprogramming hardware and software are explored. Specific examples of microprogrammed minicomputers are presented to indicate the variety of microprogrammed organizations currently available.

Today's minicomputers offer the user a flexible and large array of equipment at very attractive prices. Along with the attractive prices, come numerous claims that each manufacturer's product is the "ideal" computer for every user's needs. These claims are extremely difficult to substantiate since standardization in minicomputer nomenclature is essentially nonexistent. In Chapter 8, the authors present, discuss, and at times express their own views on factors that they feel are important in the selection of a minicomputer. Thus, the discussion of minicomputer selection centers around the following topics: specifying requirements, defining the application, comparing characteristics, preliminary screening, and techniques available for final evaluation.

The authors feel this textbook may be used by a variety of readers. If the reader is totally unfamiliar with minicomputers, all the chapters should be read and studied in detail. However, if the reader is familiar with minicomputers, Chapter 5 might be omitted. Finally, the material presented is suitable for a seminar at both the junior and senior undergraduate levels, as a graduate-level course in the area of minicomputer systems, for the researcher contemplating the use of a minicomputer or "blue collar" system, and lastly, for the computer scientist desiring an in depth knowledge of the field.

Udo W. Pooch
Rahul Chattergy

Minicomputers

Hardware, Software, and Selection

1

Introduction

1.1 Introduction to Minicomputers

Minicomputers represent one of the fastest growing segments of the computer market. The rapid increase in the use of minicomputers can easily be explained by the readily available applications for small computers, and by the relative low cost of the computer's hardware that makes many applications feasible. The decrease in cost of the minicomputer with the accompanying increase in performance is largely due to the use of *integrated circuit (IC)* technology and *medium-scale integration (MSI) devices*, faster and cheaper memory, and modular designs.

DEFINITION: *Integrated Circuit (IC)* refers to sets of discrete circuit components fabricated onto a single piece of substrate called a chip. Integrated circuits are grouped into four major categories:

- SSI (small-scale integration)—circuits with no more than 12 gates per chip.
- MSI (medium-scale integration)—circuits with more than 12 but fewer than 100 gates per chip.
- LSI (large-scale integration)—circuits with more than 100 gates per chip.
- VLSI (very-large-scale integration)—circuits with approximately 1000 gates per chip.

The minicomputer is a highly successful attempt to encapsulate a lot of computing capability into a small system. The prefix "mini-" refers to such features as physical size, processing capability, minimum available configuration, price, and software support. (Figures 1-1-1 and 1-1-2 are

1

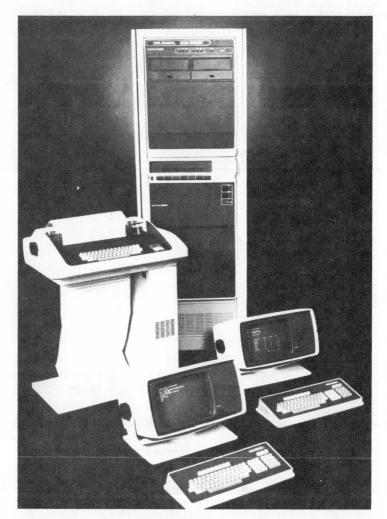

FIGURE 1-1-1. Data General's NOVA® 3 Computer System. Features a 16-bit computer system architecture, a disk operating system, high-level languages (e.g., BASIC, FORTRAN IV, ALGOL), and a full line of peripherals. (Reprinted by permission of Data General Corporation. Copyright © 1977, 1978 Data General Corporation, Westboro, Massachusetts.)

example systems.) In terms of these features, most minicomputers can be described as low-cost, high-speed, short-word-length computers, with the following characteristics:

· A central processing unit (CPU) to perform arithmetic and logical operations
· A memory (usually with a minimum of 4096 words) to store data and programs
· A memory cycle time ranging from 400 nanoseconds (ns) to 5 microseconds (μsec)

2

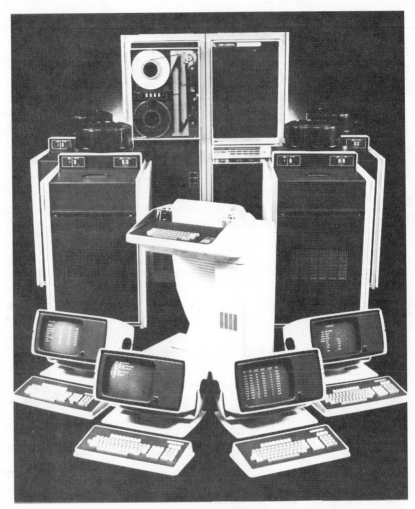

FIGURE 1-1-2. *Data General's ECLIPSE® Computer System. Shows the full line of system hardware. The ECLIPSE® system features COBOL, RPG II, and Business BASIC along with extended memory options and a wide range of peripheral equipment. (Reprinted by permission of Data General Corporation. Copyright © 1977, 1978 Data General Corporation, Westboro, Massachusetts.)*

- Word lengths ranging from 8 to 32 bits
- Small physical size ranging from 30 to 200 lbs, with low power consumption, and single-phase 115V, 60 or 50 Hz
- Environmental conditions requiring little more than reasonable temperature and humidity
- Main memory expansions ranging from 4–128K (K = 1024) words
- Instruction sets ranging from 20–200 instructions
- An input/output (I/O) system to permit the user to enter commands and data, receive answers, and control information (usually including a switch register and a teletypewriter (TTY) interface)

· Additional I/O equipment, such as disk and tape units, line printers, cathode ray tubes (CRTs), and card readers and punches
· A price range of $2500–7500

In response to a broad range of applications, minicomputer systems are designed around a highly flexible and modular standalone system. This system is usually composed of minimum hardware modules—a central processing unit, small core memory, and a teletypewriter for input and output (see Chapter 4)—with a variety of optional hardware modules that can be incorporated to produce systems tailored to a user's requirements. With the optional hardware modules attached, most minicomputers are quite impressive, powerful, and not so "mini."

Because manufacturers sell different configurations, it is very difficult to compare minicomputers by price alone. A user must understand the particular application and consequent restrictions and requirements placed on the minicomputer. Required execution times, storage capacities, costs, delivery date, local and vendor-supplied software capabilities, reliability, interfacing capabilities, and peripherals also need to be considered. While many user specifications may be directly translated into desired hardware options, this translation requires a knowledge of both hardware and software, and the relative costs of tradeoffs that must be made (see Chapter 8).

Minicomputers can provide capabilities that allow them to be adapted to almost any application. However, because of its usual small core memory capacity, limited instruction repertoire, and limited number of peripherals, a minicomputer is somewhat less flexible and more difficult to program (see Chapter 3). Several application areas where these small-scale general-purpose minicomputers have replaced special-purpose (possibly hardwired) controllers or even large-scale computer systems are:

· Information storage and retrieval
· Data concentration
· Process control
· Message switching and communications control
· Data acquisition
· Data display
· Graphics

1.2 Motivation for Minicomputers and Their Use

Potential for improved production and services at lower cost through automation and computerization is rapidly being achieved, especially with the recent and continuing developments in minicomputers. In the past, the progress toward full automation in industrial production and services has been slow due to the economics involved. This hurdle is rapidly being overcome because of inexpensive minicomputer systems. Hence, many previously neglected applications are now economically feasible.

The rapidly expanding market and application areas for minicomputers are producing a typical feedback system with the manufacturer, the user, and industry in its loop. The more production, the lower the cost and price per unit; the more applications, the larger the software program library resources available for new uses and applications; the wider the customer base, the broader the peripherals, interfaces, and application program resources (see Chapter 4).

Tolerances, precision, and mass production in all phases of industry continue to increase. Application of digital control systems for machinery are showing an accelerated upward trend. The need for services for small businesses and professions is growing and is becoming economically feasible for implementation by computers. In many application areas, computer automation offers distinct advantages over manual techniques in succinctness, cost effectiveness, and accuracy (see Chapter 8).

The large, centralized computer, of course, is not being displaced, but rather augmented by dedicated front-end minicomputers. These minicomputers form system components of hierarchical and distributed systems.

Minicomputers find applications where large computers were never cost-effective, e.g., control of research and general-purpose laboratory instrumentations, connections to industrial processes and manufacturing equipment, dedicated field research labs, and even classroom activities.

Minicomputers are so inexpensive in an economic sense that they offer an opportunity for computerization without a large capital investment. Because of their extreme modularity and flexibility, these computers can exist in a variety of configurations, completely tailored to a user's application, and more important, to available resources. (An example of such a system is given in Figure 1-2-1.)

FIGURE 1-2-1.   *Texas Instruments' 990/4 Packaged Minicomputer System. Texas Instruments' packaged minicomputer system with video display screen and keyboard, hard disk with 10 megabytes of storage, and the 990/4 computer. System is packaged in desk-top enclosure. (Reprinted by permission of Texas Instruments.)*

1.3 Applications

Instead of considering the uses of minicomputers for very specific applications (see Chapter 6), consider their use in the following environments:

· Standalone processing system
· Dedicated computer system
· Research tool
· System component in hierarchical and distributed computer systems
· Timeshared computer system

As a *standalone processing system*, the minicomputer is a self-contained unit ranging from a minimum configuration of a CPU, small memory, and ASR-33 teletype for input/output, to a large comprehensive computer system with disks for external storage and multiple input/output devices. Similarly, the corresponding software range from a simple basic software system to a large disk-based operating system, with control for real-time processing and priority interrupted background processing. The basic software system provided by the computer manufacturers usually includes an assembler, different types of loaders, input/output handlers, editors, and diagnostic programs.

As a *dedicated processor*, the minicomputer is usually interfaced directly to the control or monitoring device, acquiring data, analyzing data, and subsequently communicating results to the controlled equipment. This use of the computer is readily adaptable for product or environmental testing, process control monitoring, and/or control of data acquisition. Dedicated processors can acquire data from a multisource environment, analyze and respond to data, and prepare files to be shared by many users (see Figures 1-3-1 and 1-3-2).

As a *scientific research device*, the minicomputer can interface, control, and respond to many instruments; acquire data from several sources, and perform complex analytical functions. It operates analogously to a standalone system whenever real-time functions are not performed. The software, possibly including a real-time operating system, is specifically oriented to the desired application.

A minicomputer can also function as a *system component* for a large computer system. As a system component, its primary functions are preprocessing for the larger computer and handling data communications among any number of terminals. In this environment the minicomputer can also be used as a load-leveling processor, performing many functions on its own and calling on the larger system only when problems too complex or large arise. These systems can be very efficient, with each component, especially the minicomputer, performing those functions for which it is best suited.

More and more minicomputers are being used as *small timesharing systems*. Because of cost and size, a timesharing minicomputer is economically feasible for a number of users, eliminating the expense of communication lines to a large-scale timesharing service.

6

FIGURE 1-3-1.   *Hewlett-Packard 1000 System Model 30. (Reprinted by permission of Hewlett-Packard.)*

FIGURE 1-3-2.   Hewlett-Packard 1000 System Model 45. Combines RTE-IV Operating System, the new F-Series computer, the HP 2648 graphics terminal, and the HP 7906 20M-byte disk. (Reprinted by permission of Hewlett-Packard.)

1.4 Hardware Design

The basic minicomputer organization consists of a central processing unit (CPU), a memory module, an input/output module, and a control console. The design of minicomputers is flexible and modular, allowing a variety of hardware options to be incorporated to produce a system specific to a user's requirements. A typical block diagram indicating the relationship of these modules, as well as the flow of data, instruction, and control logic is presented in Figure 1-4-1.

The organization of the central processing unit is quite similar to that of larger systems. Essentially, the module contains several registers designed to contain one word of data each, an arithmetic/logic unit (ALU)

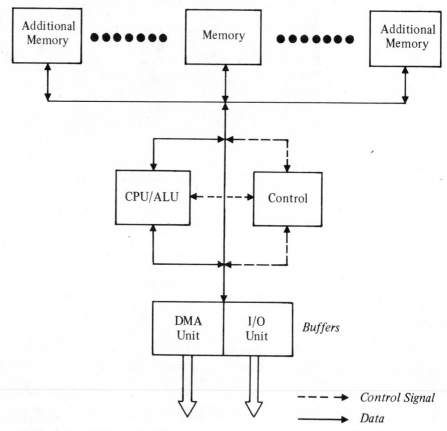

ALU: Arithmetic/Logic Unit
CPU: Central Processing Unit
DMA: Direct Memory Access
I/O: Input/Output

FIGURE 1-4-1. *Basic minicomputer organization, with optional memory units, I/O and high-speed I/O buses. Direction of arrows indicate information flow.*

capable of logical and arithmetic operations, a storage unit, and connections to one or more data buses, providing paths for the transfer of data and access to core memory.

Most minicomputers are single address, binary arithmetic machines, with negative numbers expressed in twos complement notation. The 16-bit minicomputers use one word instructions, which may be expanded to two for full addressing capability or for the inclusion of additional data. The 8-bit minicomputers use two 8-bit words for an instruction, and are similarly expandable with the addition of one to three words.

Core memory for most minicomputers is organized into 1, 2, 4, 8, 16, and 32K-word modules (K = 1024) with maximum core sizes of 64K and 128K words, although sometimes limited to 16K or 32K by the format of the instruction and the addressing techniques used. The typical word size ranges from 8, 12, 16, 24, to 32 bits, with *memory cycle times* from 0.5 to 5 microseconds (1 μsec = 10^{-6} sec).

DEFINITION: *Memory Cycle Times* involves access times and cycle times. Access time is the time required to read out any randomly selected word from memory. Cycle time is the minimum time interval required between the initiation of two successive, independent, memory operations.

Short word length, a characteristic of minicomputers, has reduced cost because fewer bits per word are required in memory, registers, adders, and transfer paths, compared to the longer word lengths found in the more expensive and larger machines. Minicomputers rarely require the longer word lengths for data simply because major minicomputer applications, such as process or machine control, data collection, and data communication, seldom require word lengths of more than 16 bits. In those applications requiring longer data word lengths, the problem of a 16-bit data word is circumvented by programmed multiple precision. This larger precision obtained by programming is of course a tradeoff to performance. It would appear that short word lengths create problems in instruction formats because of the limited addressing capabilities; however, ingeniously developed addressing techniques have helped to provide extremely powerful instructions in a short word length. Some of these addressing techniques are discussed at length in Chapter 3. Nonetheless, performance is sacrificed because some of these addressing techniques require an additional memory access for the determination of an effective address.

Instruction formats for minicomputers having one or two operational registers typically contain 4- or 5-bit operation codes, a 3-bit addressing mode, and 8 or 9 bits of memory address. The addressing modes provide one or more combinations of addressing and indexing techniques that are used to completely determine the *effective address* (see Chapter 3) of the data to be transferred to or from core memory. Whenever an effective address is required, it is obtained either from the contents of a register (if available), the second word of an instruction, or through expensive additional memory accesses.

9

DEFINITION: *Effective Address* is the final computed address from which an opcode or data is retrieved from memory. This address may be an absolute value contained within the instruction, the value contained in the program counter plus or minus a relative branching offset, or an address computed by going indirectly to the final location by means of an intermediate stopping point.

Another important consequence of short word lengths is a limited instruction repertoire. Minicomputers, in their basic or sometimes extended configurations, do not provide for floating-point arithmetic, decimal arithmetic, searching instructions, or byte manipulating instructions. Fixed-point multiply and divide are frequently provided in a basic configuration by software routines, although hardware multiply/divide options are not uncommon.

Data, instructions, and control signals are transferred among memory, the CPU, and other modules by way of a bus. Quite often one or more *direct memory access (DMA) channels* may also communicate with memory and I/O controllers over this same bus. (A complete discussion is given in Chapter 4.) Conflicts that arise over access to memory between the CPU and memory and the slower modules, such as DMA to memory, are settled by *priority assignments*, usually in favor of the slower components. Multiport architecture is considered to be a luxury for minicomputers and is very rarely found.

Though minicomputer manufacturers provide one or two optional memory protect/parity bit(s), the design trend is to preclude this option because the extra bit(s) would require enlarging the data paths and widths of registers resulting in unfavorable cost/performance ratios.

Another characteristic that differentiates the minicomputer from its larger relatives is the number of programmer accessible registers. Many minicomputers have one or two accumulators with one or two index registers, although there are several computer designs that provide multiple general-purpose registers (e.g., PDP-11, NOVA®), and some that provide no registers at all (e.g., PDC-808). Except for very small minicomputers, the low cost of integrated circuit *scratch pad* memories (or control storage) will favor design of minicomputers with multiple-register organization.

DEFINITIONS: *Direct Memory Access Channels* refer to memory addressed space that is used to hold data to be used by some I/O device. These spaces require a unique address, some data pattern or bit string, and some form of control, usually called a DMA controller.

Priority Assignments refer to the assignment of preferences of one media or device over another. Usually this type of requirement stems from the requirement to allocate resources in an effective and efficient manner.

Scratch Pad, the nickname given to CPU memory, pertains to the information that the CPU holds only temporarily.

1.5 Software Systems

The very aspects of minicomputers that make them attractive (i.e., adaptability to a wide range of applications, relatively low cost) have also acted as constraints on minicomputer software developments. Thus, the basic software supplied with the initial hardware consists of only the minimum software modules necessary to support the basic hardware functions. The adaptability to a wide range of applications substantially increases the variability required in the general-purpose software. A further complication arises from the multiplicity of configurations that can be assembled from the products of different vendors. The ready-made software provided by the minicomputer vendors in support of whatever basic hardware configuration can be classified into three distinct categories: basic support software, operating system software, and applications software.

The *basic support software* comprises a collection of programs and routines for interfacing the user and the hardware. The minimum software modules which are provided for even the smallest configuration include assemblers, loaders, mathematical utilities, program debugging aids, and input/output utilities.

The *operating system software* comprises primarily the programs and routines that insulate the user from the complexity of managing the hardware and software resources of the system. A typical operating system provides I/O control, interrupt management, data and program management, library support, and job scheduling, but at the expense of a larger configuration (i.e., memory, random access devices).

Applications software comprises the programs and routines designed specifically to solve user problems in the user's environment. This category is the most diverse, with examples ranging from dedicated process control to the general-purpose service bureau user. Extensive discussions on all aspects of minicomputer software appear in Chapter 6.

1.6 Future Trends

The stage for potential growth of the minicomputer has already been set. The factors of (1) modularity and interchangeability of units within product lines; (2) compatibility of software between product lines; and (3) expandable memory will occupy the major efforts of the minicomputer manufacturers. The major limitations for increased applications of the minicomputer will be in the amount of education provided by the computer industry, the limitations on capital investment, and the incursion of microcomputers.

Microprogramming will play an ever significant role in future minicomputer systems. The advantages of microprogramming are greater flexibility, more regular structure, and lower development costs. Although the basic hardware of minicomputers may be similar in organization, its architecture can differ greatly due to the flexibility afforded by micropro-

11

gram control. These microprogrammable minicomputers will incorporate such features as push-down stacks, elaborate interrupt handling capabilities, plus such additional instructions as multiply, divide, multiprecision, and floating-point operations. Powerful instructions, heretofore found only in expensive computers, such as moves, searches, translates, and floating-point operations, will be implemented in minicomputers. Input/output channels other than high performance DMA channels will also take advantage of adaptive line controlling control. In data communication applications, I/O channels will be capable of handling data line protocol procedures, error checking, encoding, and code translation.

The microprogram organization of minicomputers will allow computer architecture to be tuned for particular applications. A basic architecture and instruction set may have add-on capabilities which enhance the throughput and cost performance for a specific application such as mini-timesharing, data communication, laboratory automation, or process control. Individual users will tailor their minicomputer for a particular application by writing their own microprogram—either by adding to their basic architecture, or by creating their own architecture from the basic microprogrammable hardware. Extension and applications of microprogramming is the subject of Chapter 7.

Great improvements can be anticipated in the implementation of new and better software to accommodate additional areas of application. As a programming aid, it is expected that a large computer will be used to translate from high-level languages to the mini-machine language (cross-compiling) and, therefore, create greater flexibility in programming. More and more implementation of COBOL, or subsets of COBOL, will be devised for special applications in the business environment. And, finally, operating systems will be created that can (with improved and enlarged memories) ease the burden of program management.

PROBLEMS

1. Draw and define a functional block diagram of a typical minicomputer.

2. Define the following terms:
    a. Minicomputer
    b. CPU
    c. Standalone processing system
    d. Software
    e. Time-sharing
    f. Cycle time
    g. Scratch pad
    h. Instruction
    i. Word
    j. Integrated circuit

3. Discuss and compare absolute address, indirect address, and effective address.

4. Discuss *briefly* the application of minicomputers.

5. Discuss *briefly* differences and similarities between standalone systems and a dedicated computer system.

6. What is a time-shared system?

7. Name and discuss briefly at least two current periodicals whose primary purpose is to inform professionals about the minicomputer industry.

PROJECTS

Pick any two minicomputers and discuss in detail:

1. Their instruction set organization with regard to:
   a. Address modes
   b. Branching capabilities
   c. I/O handling instructions
   d. Interrupt capabilities

2. Architectural differences with regard to:
   a. Programming model
   b. Technical specification comparisons
   c. I/O handling capability
   d. Mathematical capability (fixed, integer, vs. floating-point hardware or software)
   e. Ancillary hardware requirements, for example:
      · Bus structure
      · Clock requirements and timings
      · Multiplexers
      · Serial/parallel port devices
      · RAM/ROM requirements

3. Language availabilities and software:
   a. Compilers, interpreters, incremental compilers
   b. Assemblers, linkers, loaders
   c. High-level languages vs. lower-level languages

4. Operating systems:
   a. Tape vs. disk
   b. Batch vs. time-shared

2

Functional Description of a Computer

2.1 Introduction

All complex systems can be described from two different viewpoints, the functional viewpoint and the structural viewpoint. These two descriptions are called the functional level description and the structural level description, respectively. Both the functional approach and the structural approach reduce a complex system to simpler subsystems, but they use different criteria. In the functional approach, the overall function of the system is subdivided into subfunctions. In the structural approach, the exact structure of the complex system is inspected in great detail and the system is broken down to simplify its implementation. Fortunately for many complex systems both approaches generate the same subsystems; the functional approach identifies the functions of the subsystems, while the structural approach provides the means to implement the subsystems.

The overall function of a computer is to process information or data following a set of processing instructions, called a *program*. Therefore, a computer must have a storage unit for storing the information to be processed and the instructions that constitute a program. This storage unit is called the *memory unit (MU)* of a computer. The processing of information is carried out by a *central processing unit (CPU)* which fetches instructions and data from the MU and returns the results to the MU for storage. Two subsystems of the CPU are: the *arithemetic/logic unit (ALU)* that performs the arithmetic and the logic operations on the data fetched from the MU, and the *control unit (CU)* which synchronizes and supervises all operations in the computer. Finally, communications with the outside are carried out by means of the *input/output unit (IOU)* via suitably designed interfacing subsystems. Various types of information, such as data, instruction, and

14

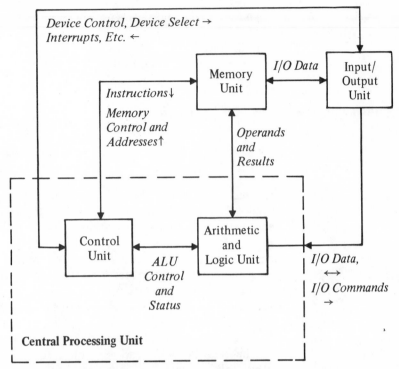

Device Control, Device Select →
Interrupts, Etc. ←

FIGURE 2-1-1. *Functional diagram of a computer.*

control information, are exchanged by these units through information
transmission paths, called *buses*. This functional description of a computer
is shown in Figure 2-1-1 and illustrated in Figure 2-1-2. The structure is

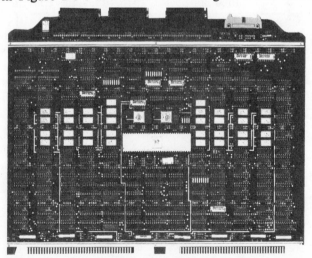

FIGURE 2-1-2. *Texas Instruments' 990/5 processor—a single-board
unit based on the TMS 9900 chip which is shown at the center of the
circuit board. Introduced in February 1979, the 990/5 is the central
processor for Texas Instruments' DS 990 Models 1 and 2 minicomputer
systems. (Reprinted by permission of Texas Instruments.)*

15

somewhat idealized and shows far too many buses than are commonly used. The following sections provide functional descriptions of each of the subsystems in detail except for the I/O system which is discussed in Chapter 4.

2.2 Functional Subsystems of a Computer

2.2.1 The Memory Unit

The *memory unit* of a computer is designed as a hierarchy for reasons of economy. The *primary memory* is the portion of the MU that is directly accessible from the CPU. The rest of the MU is called *secondary* or *auxiliary memory;* information must be transferred from the secondary memory to the primary memory before it can be accessed by the CPU. The primary memory of a minicomputer is made either from arrays of magnetic cores or from arrays of semiconductor storage cells using large-scale integration (LSI) technology. The secondary memory consists of magnetic disk and/or magnetic tape storage facilities.

The smallest unit of information in a computer is a binary digit, called a *bit*. The smallest unit of addressable information is normally a string of eight bits called a *byte*. Using the bit as the fundamental building block, all other units of information result in a *byte* and/or a *word*. The primary memory in the MU can be thought of as a linearly ordered array of words as shown in Figure 2-2-1, where each word is identified by a unique number called its *address*. In order to fetch information from the MU or store information in it, the address of the word containing the information must be specified. Since any word addressed at random in the primary memory can be accessed by the CPU in the same fixed period of time, the primary memory is often called a *random access memory (RAM)*.

Address	Byte 1	Byte 0
54		
55		
56		
57		
58		
59		

Word (heading spanning Byte 1 and Byte 0)

FIGURE 2-2-1.   A segment of the linearly ordered primary memory. (Each word consists of two bytes.)

2.2.2 The Central Processing Unit

The principal function of the *arithmetic and logic unit (ALU)* of a computer is to perform arithmetic and logic operations on data or *operands* fetched from the primary memory or in registers in the ALU. The arithmetic operations may consist of addition, subtraction, multiplication, and division. The logic operations may consist of AND (conjunction), inclusive OR (inclusive disjunction), exclusive OR (exclusive disjunction), and NOT (complementation) of Boolean algebra. A table summarizing the definitions, laws, and rules of Boolean algebra is included in Appendix A.1, since Boolean algebra is the basis upon which computer technology and its uses have been built. A second table, in Appendix A.2, displays the logic symbols used to represent the logic operators used in logic design. Furthermore, ALUs also carry out left and right shifts and rotations of strings of bits.

An ALU requires some local storage for storing operands fetched from the primary memory and for the results of the performed operations. This storage is provided by arrays of semiconductor storage cells called *registers*. One such register used by an ALU is called an *accumulator* and it normally stores one of the operands at the beginning of an operation by an ALU. At the end of the operation the original contents of the accumulator are replaced by the results of the operation. Figure 2-2-2 shows the functional diagram of an ALU.

The *control unit (CU)* is of central importance in the operation of a computer. It controls the sequence of execution of the instructions fetched from the primary memory, and synchronizes the operations of all other units in the system. Therefore, the basic functions of the CU are twofold. First, it must locate instructions in the primary memory in the proper sequence. Second, it must decode each instruction and generate the required control and timing signals for the other units in the system. To locate instructions in the memory, the CU uses a register called a *program counter (PC)*. When

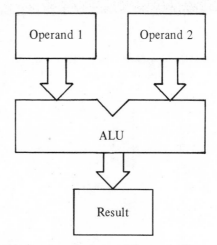

FIGURE 2-2-2.   *Functional diagram of an ALU.*

17

properly managed, the contents of the program counter are always the address of the word in the primary memory containing the next instruction to be executed. Instructions fetched from the primary memory are stored in a register, called the *instruction register*. The CU decodes or interprets the contents of the instruction register by means of hardware logic circuits or microprograms (discussed in Chapter 7), and generates the required control and synchronization signals to complete the execution of that decoded instruction.

The CPU usually contains other registers for computing addresses of stored operands and these will be introduced later in connection with the various addressing schemes.

2.3 Functional Operation of the Memory Unit

The primary memory of a computer, accessible from the CPU, consists of three basic storage components: the *memory address register (MAR)*, the *memory data register (MDR)*, and the physical memory itself (see Figure 2-3-1). The address of the word in the memory containing the required information is transferred from one of the registers in the CPU (normally the program counter while fetching instructions) into the MAR. The contents of the word in the memory addressed by the MAR are then transferred into the MDR which can be accessed by the CPU.

For a store operation, the contents of the MDR are transferred to the word of the memory addressed by the MAR. Fetching information from the memory is also known as the *memory read* operation and storing information in the memory is called the *memory write* operation.

As mentioned in Section 2.1, transfer of information among registers in the CPU and the MAR or MDR is carried out via information transfer paths called buses. This transfer operation is denoted by:

$$[A] \xrightarrow[\text{BUS}]{} B$$

which means that the *contents of the A-register* are transferred to the B-register via a bus.

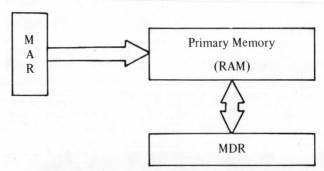

FIGURE 2-3-1.   *Addressing of primary memory.*

TABLE 2-3-1.   Read Memory Cycle

Step	Transfer Operation	Description
1	AI $\xrightarrow{\text{BUS}}$ MAR	Address information is transferred from the CPU.
2	$[M_{[MAR]}] \xrightarrow{\text{READ}}$ MDR	Contents of addressed location are read into MDR, forcing all bits of $M_{[MAR]}$ to 0.
3	$[MDR] \xrightarrow{\text{REWRITE}} M_{[MAR]}$	Information in MDR is rewritten into memory.
4	$[MDR] \xrightarrow{\text{BUS}}$ CPU	Information in MDR is transferred to the CPU.

The primary memory of a computer can be of two types: memory with *destructive read-outs* and memory with *nondestructive read-outs*. This is usually transparent to users since they buy a memory system, and not components of a memory. In the first case the contents of the word read out to the MDR are destroyed in the process of reading. Thus, these contents must be regenerated or restored before the contents of the MDR are changed, in order not to loose the information stored in the word. *Destructive read-out memory* is made of magnetic core material. With a *nondestructive read-out memory*, there is no need to restore the contents of the word read since these contents are not altered in the process of reading. The time required to read information out of a word in the primary memory is called the *read memory cycle*. The sequence of operations performed during the read memory cycle of a destructive read-out memory is shown in Table 2-3-1, where AI denotes address information from the CPU, M denotes the primary memory, and $M_{[MAR]}$ denotes the word in M addressed by the MAR. Steps 2 and 3 in Table 2-3-1 represent the actual read operation, namely the read-restore activity of the destructive read-out memory. Since the restoring activity is essentially a write operation, the whole cycle is also known as a *read/write (or read/regeneration) memory cycle*.

The time required to store information in a word of the primary memory is called the *write memory cycle*. The write memory cycle for a destructive read-out memory is operationally similar to the read memory cycle with one exception. During the read portion of the cycle, the information read from the addressed word is blocked from entering the MDR and is simply lost. The effect of the read portion is to clear all bits of the addressed word to zeros. The sequence of operations performed during the write memory cycle of a destructive read-out memory is shown in Table 2-3-2. The time required for a read/write memory cycle is called the *memory cycle time* and the time required to select and read a word is called the *access time*. The memory cycle times of typical minicomputer destructive read-out memory units range from 650 to 8000 nsec with an average around 1 μsec. Approximately half the cycle time is access time, although for some minicomputers, access time may account for two-thirds of the cycle time.

19

TABLE 2-3-2.   *Write Memory Cycle*

Step	Transfer Operation	Description
1	AI $\xrightarrow[\text{BUS}]{}$ MAR	Address information and information to be stored are transferred from the CPU.
	DATA $\xrightarrow[\text{BUS}]{}$ MDR	
2	$[M_{[MAR]}] \xrightarrow{\text{READ}}$ LOST	Clear out old information from addressed location, zero all bits.
3	$[MDR] \xrightarrow{\text{WRITE}} M_{[MAR]}$	Contents of MDR are written into memory location.

For *nondestructive read-out* primary memory constructed of semiconductor devices, the contents of a word do not change with a read operation. Hence there is no need for a read/restore or clear/write operation during a memory cycle. The sequence of operations performed during the read and write cycles of a nondestructive read-out memory is shown in Table 2-3-3.

A third type of memory, the *read-only memory (ROM)*, is often used to form part of a primary memory of a minicomputer. The words in an ROM contain information that is stored permanently during the fabrication of the ROM. Once set up, the contents of the words of an ROM cannot be changed later without physically destroying the ROM. The ROMs in minicomputers are used to store fixed sequences of instructions that occur very frequently

TABLE 2-3-3.   *Read and Write Cycles for Semiconductor Memory*

	Read Cycle	
Step	Transfer Operation	Description
1	AI $\xrightarrow[\text{BUS}]{}$ MAR	Address information is transferred from the CPU.
2	$[M_{[MAR]}] \xrightarrow{\text{READ}}$ MDR	Memory location is read. Contents of the location are unaffected.
3	$[MDR] \xrightarrow[\text{BUS}]{}$ CPU	Information in MDR is transferred to the CPU.
	Write Cycle	
Step	Transfer Operation	Description
1	AI $\xrightarrow[\text{BUS}]{}$ MAR	Address information and information to be stored are transferred from the CPU.
2	$[MDR] \xrightarrow{\text{WRITE}} M_{[MAR]}$	Information in MDR is written into memory location.

TABLE 2-3-4.   Read Cycle for a ROM

Step	Transfer Operation	Description
1	$AI \xrightarrow[BUS]{} MAR$	Address information is transferred from the CPU.
2	$[ROM_{[MAR]}] \xrightarrow{READ} MDR$	Addressed ROM location is read, its contents are unaffected.
3	$[MDR] \xrightarrow[BUS]{} CPU$	Information in MDR is transferred to the CPU.

in applications and also in microprograms (see Chapter 7). A variety of ROM called a *programmable ROM (pROM)* is also used sometimes in primary memory design. The contents of the words of a pROM can be stored after fabrication but not by the CPU as in the case of an RAM. Since an ROM may only be read, its functional operation includes only the read cycle which is shown in Table 2-3-4.

Like semiconductor random access memory, read-out of an ROM is nondestructive, requiring no restore operation. Depending on the type of ROM employed, access times vary from 2 to 450 nsec.

2.4 Functional Operation of the Arithmetic and Logic Unit

The heart of the arithmetic and logic unit (ALU) consists of a *binary adder* whose function is to add two binary numbers and generate their sum. The rules for binary addition are discussed in Appendix A.3. A simple binary adder, called a *full adder*, can add two bits and a carry bit at a time and generate the carry bit for the next two bits. The bits can be fed into a full adder, one pair at a time, from shift registers. The combination is called a *serial adder* (see Figure 2-4-1). Other binary adders can add all the corresponding pairs of bits of the two binary numbers simultaneously, passing the

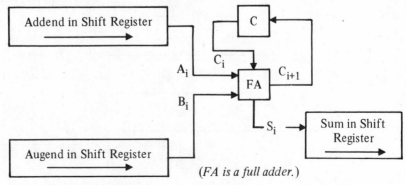

(*FA is a full adder.*)

FIGURE 2-4-1.   *Operation of a serial adder.*

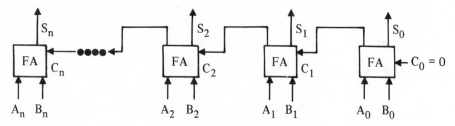

(*FA's are full adders; C_n's are carry bits*)

FIGURE 2-4-2.   *Operation of a parallel adder.*

carry bits along from column to column. These binary adders are called *parallel adders* (see Figure 2-4-2). Parallel adders are much faster than serial adders in the execution of addition. Some minicomputers use a combination of serial-parallel adders. The parallel adder adds four pairs of bits simultaneously and bits are shifted into it in groups of four from the addend and the augend operands. Increased use of integrated circuit technology has made parallel adders economical to use and they are used exclusively in most modern minicomputers.

A parallel adder needs two registers to hold the two numbers being added, with one of them usually the accumulator mentioned in Section 2.2.2. The sum generated is also stored in the accumulator by transferring it via a bus. The functional diagram of a binary adder is shown in Figure 2-4-3.

As explained in Appendix A.3, in most minicomputers subtraction is performed by representing negative numbers in signed twos complement form and by adding the minuend to the twos complement of the subtrahend. Thus, the same parallel adder is used to perform subtraction by adding circuits to generate twos complement of the subtrahend (see Figure 2-4-4). SUB = 1 generates twos complement, while SUB = 0 does not.

The *multiplication* operation involves multiple additions of the multiplicand to itself, with appropriate shifting before addition. The multiplication of two *n*-bit numbers produces a 2*n*-bit result which would overflow a

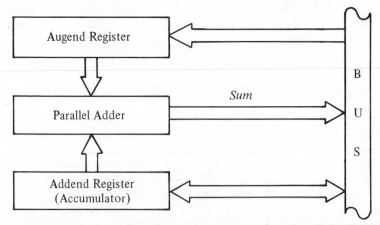

FIGURE 2-4-3.   *Functional diagram of an adder with associated registers and bus.*

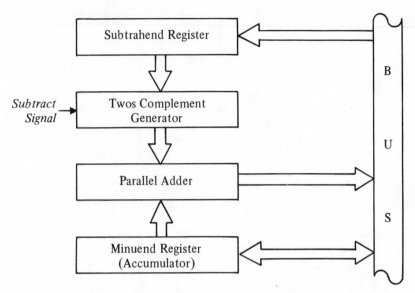

FIGURE 2-4-4. *Functional diagram of a combined adder/subtracter.*

single n-bit register. Therefore, an additional n-bit register is included in the arithmetic unit to store $2n$-bit products. This register, sometimes denoted by Q, stores the lower half of the product. The upper half of the product replaces the multiplier in the accumulator.

During multiplication, the accumulator holds the multiplier, and another adjacent input register (B) holds the multiplicand. As the product is formed the lower half of the product is placed in the Q-register and the upper half in the accumulator. Figure 2-4-5 illustrates the extension of the arithmetic section to handle multiplication. Functionally, multiplication is represented by:

$$[B] \times [A] \xrightarrow[\text{BUS}]{} \text{Accumulator, Q}$$

Division involves the repeated subtraction of the divisor from the dividend with appropriate shifting, yielding a quotient and a remainder. No additional registers are required for division. Since division is the inverse of multiplication, a double-word dividend is divided by a single-word divisor to produce the quotient and the remainder. In division, the double-word dividend is contained in the accumulator and the Q-register (lower half in the Q-register), and the divisor is contained in the B-register. As the quotient and remainder are formed, the quotient is placed in the accumulator, and the remainder in the Q-register. Functionally, division is represented by:

$$\frac{[A,Q]}{[B]} \xrightarrow[\text{BUS}]{} \text{Accumulator}$$

$$\text{Remainder} \xrightarrow[\text{BUS}]{} Q$$

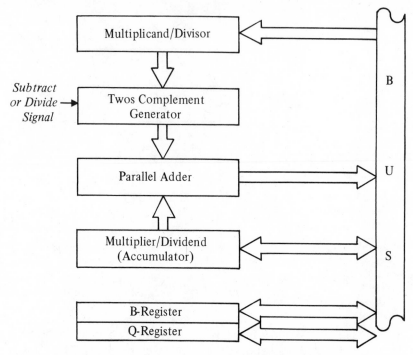

FIGURE 2-4-5. *Functional diagram of a multiplier/divider.*

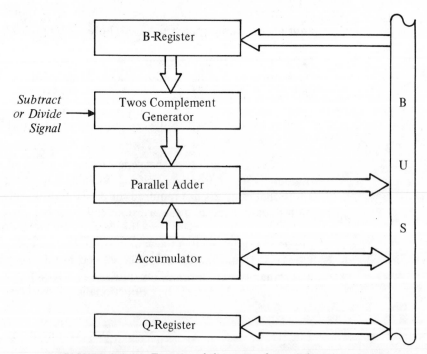

FIGURE 2-4-6. *Functional diagram of an arithmetic unit.*

Figure 2-4-6 shows the functional diagram of an arithmetic unit commonly found in minicomputers. In this unit, arithmetic operations are performed between the contents of the accumulator and the contents of a specified memory location. For each instruction, the B-register contents are retrieved from memory during the operand fetch part of the instruction cycle. The B-register receives one operand from the memory via the bus. The other operand is stored in the accumulator.

$$[MDR] \xrightarrow[BUS]{} B$$

Register-to-register arithmetic instructions require that the Q- and B-registers be addressable like the accumulator. On some minicomputers hardware multiply and divide are options at extra cost. If the minicomputer does not have this option, multiplication and division must be implemented by software subroutines. *Software multiply/divide* operations are on the order of 50–100 times slower than *hardware multiply/divide*. If a user's application requires many multiplication and division calculations, the hardware multiply/divide feature should be seriously considered.

The logic unit of an ALU performs *logic operations*, such as AND and OR, between two operands. These logic operations are performed on pairs of corresponding bits of the two operands with no interactions among bits in different columns. Logic operations between two operands can be carried out by simultaneously transferring the corresponding pairs of bits through appropriate logic gates. Figure 2-4-7 illustrates the AND operation

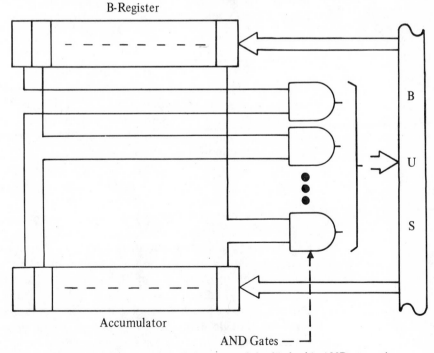

FIGURE 2-4-7.   *Functional diagram of the bit-by-bit AND operation.*

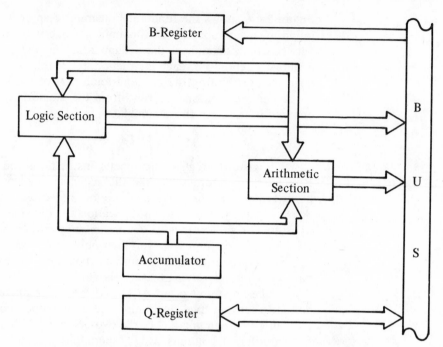

FIGURE 2-4-8. *Functional diagram of a typical arithmetic logic unit.*

between the contents of the B-register and the accumulator on a bit-by-bit basis. Functionally the logical AND operation is represented by:

$$[B] \wedge \text{Accumulator} \xrightarrow[\text{BUS}]{} \text{Accumulator}$$

where ($\wedge$) is the symbol used for the logical AND. Figure 2-4-8 provides a functional diagram of a typical ALU of a minicomputer. For logic operations, signals from the control unit transfer the contents of the registers to the logic section, and for arithmetic operations they are transferred to the arithmetic section.

2.5 Functional Operation of the Control Unit

The basic operations of a control unit (CU) consist of fetching instructions from the primary memory in the proper sequence specified by a program, decoding the instructions, and computing the addresses of the operands needed (if any) and generating the control and timing signals necessary for the execution of the instructions. The time spent to complete these operations for a single instruction is called an *instruction cycle*. An instruction cycle is divided into three parts: (1) instruction fetch and decode, (2) address computation and operand fetch, and (3) instruction execute. During the first part of the cycle, a CU is said to be in the instruction *fetch state*. During the last two parts it is in the instruction *execute state*.

As mentioned in Section 2.2.2, the CU uses a register called a *program counter (PC)* or instruction counter to locate instructions stored in the primary memory. Normally the instructions of a program segment are stored in consecutive words of the primary memory. Hence, to keep track of these instructions it is only necessary to load the program counter with the address of the first instruction and then to increment it by a suitable value. Often it becomes necessary to jump from one program segment to another stored in different parts of the primary memory. In these cases the program counter is not incremented but reloaded with the address of the first instruction in the destination program segment.

Instructions fetched from the primary memory by the CU are stored in a register called the *instruction register (IR)*. The contents of this register are decoded by the CU by means of either hardware logic circuits or microprograms (see Chapter 7) to generate the required control and synchronization signals. In most minicomputers, instructions are coded in the one-address format shown in Figure 2-5-1. The *opcode* is a string of bits that

FIGURE 2-5-1.   *One-address instruction format.*

identifies the operation to be performed, while the address part gives the address of the word containing one of the operands. The other operand is assumed to exist in the accumulator. The cross-hatched part of the instruction contains extra bits used in augmenting the addressing technique and these are discussed in detail in the next chapter. Figure 2-5-2 shows the functional diagram of a simple CU.

When the control unit enters the fetch state, the contents of the PC are transferred into the MAR. A memory read cycle is performed, retrieving the contents of the word at the specified address, which is transferred from the MDR to the IR. This completes the fetch operation. While in the IR, the instruction opcode is decoded by *hardwired logic circuits:*

ENTER FETCH STATE

$[PC] \xrightarrow[\text{BUS}]{} MAR$

$[M_{[MAR]}] \xrightarrow{\text{READ}} MDR$

$[MDR] \xrightarrow[\text{BUS}]{} IR$

DECODE OPCODE

EXIT FETCH STATE

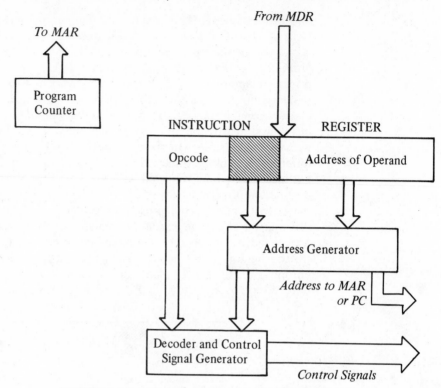

FIGURE 2-5-2.   Functional diagram of a simple control unit.

DEFINITION: *Hardwire-Logic* refers to logic designs for control or problem solutions that require interconnection of numerous integrated circuits formed or wired for specific purposes and relatively unalterable. Hardwired interconnections are usually completed by soldering or by printed circuits and are thus hardwired in contrast to software solutions achieved by programmed mini- or microcomputer components.

The duration and the sequence of operations performed during the execute state depends greatly on the type of instruction being executed and the type of addressing technique used. The execution of a very simple instruction, such as load accumulator (AC), with mnemonic opcode LDA and direct addressing of the operand is:

Decode: DECODE OPCODE

$[IR]_{OPCODE} \xrightarrow{\text{DECODE}} LDA$

EXIT FETCH STATE

ENTER EXECUTE STATE

$$[IR]_{ADDRESS} \xrightarrow[BUS]{} MAR$$

$$[M_{[MAR]}] \xrightarrow{READ} MDR$$

$$[MDR] \xrightarrow[BUS]{} AC$$

$$[PC] + 1 \longrightarrow PC$$

EXIT EXECUTE STATE

Illustration of an add instruction, where the contents of the word addressed by the instruction is added to the contents of the accumulator follows:

DECODE OPCODE

$$[IR]_{OPCODE} \xrightarrow{DECODE} ADD$$

EXIT FETCH STATE

ENTER EXECUTE STATE

$$[IR]_{ADDRESS} \xrightarrow[BUS]{} MAR$$

$$[M_{[MAR]}] \xrightarrow{READ} MDR$$

$$[MDR] \xrightarrow[BUS]{} B\text{-}REGISTER$$

$$[ACCUMULATOR] + [B\text{-}REGISTER] \xrightarrow[BUS]{} AC$$

$$[PC] + 1 \longrightarrow PC$$

EXIT EXECUTE STATE

2.6 Bus Structure

The function of a control unit is to supervise and synchronize the transfer of information among the other units of a computer. In the process of this transfer, information is transformed and the result of this transformation guides the future of the information transfer process. Electrical transmission lines that provide paths for the transfer of information are called data-flow circuits, bus circuits, or simply *buses*. A bus structure identifies the transfer paths available among the various units of a computer. One such bus structure was shown in Figure 2-1-1 where the arrows represent individual buses. The types of information that move along these buses are identified next to each bus.

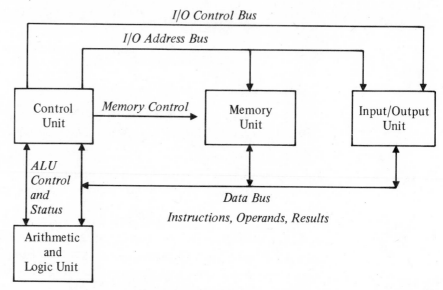

FIGURE 2-6-1.   *Shared bus structure.*

An alternate bus structure is shown in Figure 2-6-1, fundamentally different from that shown in Figure 2-1-1. In Figure 2-6-1, the device select code that selects one among many input/output registers in the I/O unit shares the same bus used by address information (*address bus*) used to select memory locations. The implication is that the input/output registers are treated as extensions of the primary memory and this is known as *memory-mapped input/output*. There is also a single *data bus* shared by different types of information shown in Figure 2-6-1. Control information is transferred by a separate *control bus*. Comparing these two bus structures we come to the obvious conclusion that the number of buses and their interconnections influence the number of concurrent information transfers within a computer. The structure shown in Figure 2-1-1 is somewhat idealized and shows far too many buses than are commonly used. However, a bus structure similar to that shown in Figure 2-6-1 is used by a popular minicomputer (Digital Equipment Corporation's PDP-11).

Functionally buses are shown by lines along which information is transferred. However, inside a computer, information is coded into strings of bits. These bits can be transferred, either one at a time using a single transmission line, or in parallel using a dedicated transmission line for each bit. The former approach is more economical in terms of the number of transmission lines used compared to the latter, but it is also slower than the latter. Most modern minicomputers use a dedicated transmission line for each address bit and each data bit. Thus, a bus in reality consists of several parallel transmission lines called bus lines. Each bus line requires a driver, a receiver, a cable, a connector, and electrical power for operation. The structural details of these devices, however, are quite beyond the scope of this text.

DEFINITION: *Memory Mapped I/O* refers to the scheme of utilizing some specific address within the allowable address space of the computer. As an input or output port, this technique is most amenable to systems that have limited memory space and relatively few input or output devices to service.

Although large-scale integration of electronic circuits has reduced the cost of such components as memory units and ALUs, buses with their associated electronics are still quite expensive. Hence, to reduce hardware costs, buses are normally shared by several components. Internal buses within a component such as an ALU are also shared by devices such as the B- and Q-registers, PC, AC, IR, and the parallel adder. When several devices share a common bus, it is necessary to isolate the input and the output signals of each device from the bus when the device is not using the bus. Devices whose output signals can be isolated from a shared bus are called *tri-state devices*. Again, the electronics used to implement such isolation are beyond the scope of our discussion. However, all such devices have a *load signal* and an *enable signal*. The load signal is used to transfer data from the bus into the device and the enable signal is used for transferring data in the opposite direction. The control unit generates and synchronizes these signals for the proper operation of each device under its control.

DEFINITION: *Tri-state* refers to the ability of a device to take on three events. These states are:
a) On
b) Off
c) High impedance
The third state, high impedance, is the state that, when activated, effectively switches that device out of the circuit. The high impedance state may be activated through an enabling signal external to that device.

2.7 Functional Description of Minicomputers

This section contains functional descriptions of several popular minicomputers. This is only to illustrate the variations in computer designs and not meant to be all inclusive.

2.7.1 HP 2000 Minicomputers

A functional diagram of a Hewlett-Packard minicomputer is given in Figure 2-7-1 and illustrated in Figures 2-7-2 and 2-7-3. The central processing unit has a bank of five registers. The M-register is used as the MAR for the memory unit and the T-register acts as the MDR. The P-register acts as the program counter and the A- and B-registers act as two accumulators. The

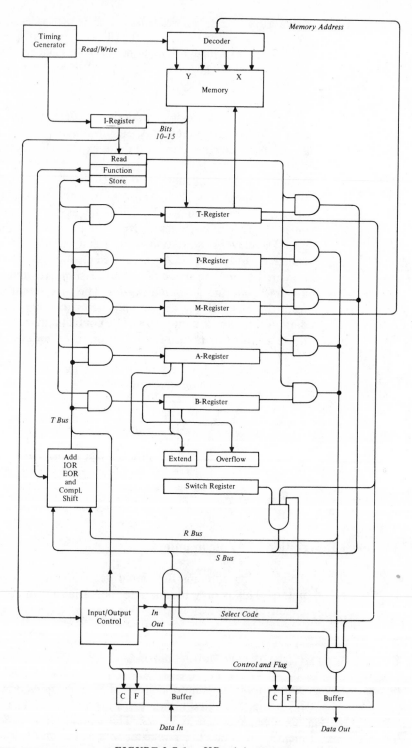

FIGURE 2-7-1.   HP minicomputer.

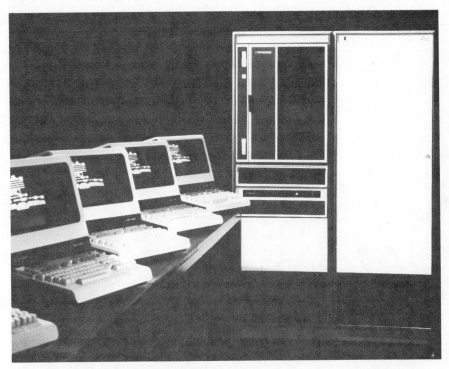

FIGURE 2-7-2. *Hewlett-Packard 2000 access system. (Reprinted by permission of Hewlett-Packard.)*

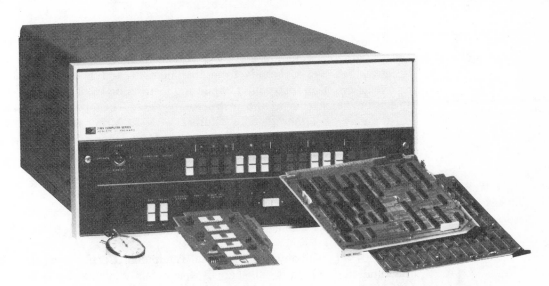

FIGURE 2-7-3. *Programmable dynamic mapping system for the Hewlett-Packard 21 MX minicomputers. Expands the address space, yet retains the 650-ns cycle time. (Reprinted by permission of Hewlett-Packard.)*

33

main reason for providing two accumulators is to obtain faster and more flexible arithmetic operations.

The two operands needed for the arithmetic and logic operations are transferred to the arithmetic/logic unit via the R- and S-buses. The results of the operations are transferred back to the registers via the T-bus. The R-, S-, and T-buses are shared by the five registers in the central processing unit.

2.7.2 DEC PDP-8 Minicomputer

A functional diagram of the Digital Equipment Corporation (DEC) PDP-8 minicomputer is shown in Figure 2-7-4, and illustrated in Figure 2-7-5. The system consists of a processing unit, a control unit, and a memory unit; all of which communicate by means of a common bus called OMNIBUS.

PC is the program counter; CPMA is the central processor memory address register, i.e., the MAR. MB is the memory buffer register, i.e., the MDR. AC represents the accumulator and MQ is the multiplier/quotient register. MQ contains the multiplier at the beginning of a multiplication and the least significant half of the product at the conclusion. At the start of a division it contains the least significant half of the dividend and at the conclusion the quotient.

2.7.3 Varian 620/L Minicomputer

Figure 2-7-6 shows a functional diagram of a Varian 620/L minicomputer. The L- and W-registers are respectively the MAR and the MDR. The A-register is the accumulator and the P-register is the program counter. The R-register receives operands from the memory and holds them during the execution of an instruction, while the instruction itself is stored in the U-register which acts as the instructor register. The operands in the R-register may be either data or address words. During multiplication or division operations, the R-register holds the multiplicand or the divisor. The B-register serves as an extension to the accumulator during multiplication and division.

2.7.4 DEC PDP-11 Minicomputer

In the PDP-11 minicomputer of Digital Equipment Corporation, the CPU, MU, and the I/O units all share a single bus called a UNIBUS™. A functional diagram of the CPU is shown in Figure 2-7-7a. In addition to performing all arithmetic and logic operations, the CPU also arbitrates priorities of use for the shared bus. It has sixteen general-purpose registers which can be used as accumulators, index registers, or stack pointers (see

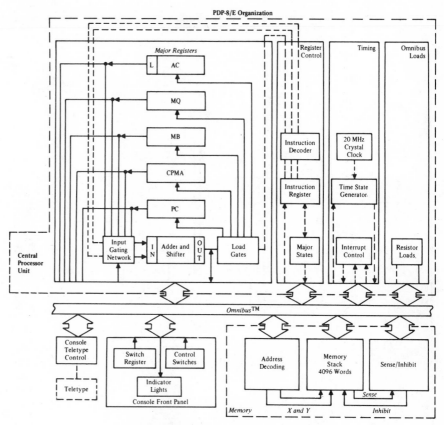

FIGURE 2-7-4.   *DEC PDP-8 minicomputer.*

FIGURE 2-7-5.   *Digital Equipment Corporation's PDP-8. Features a 12-bit word. (Reprinted by permission of Digital Equipment Corporation.)*

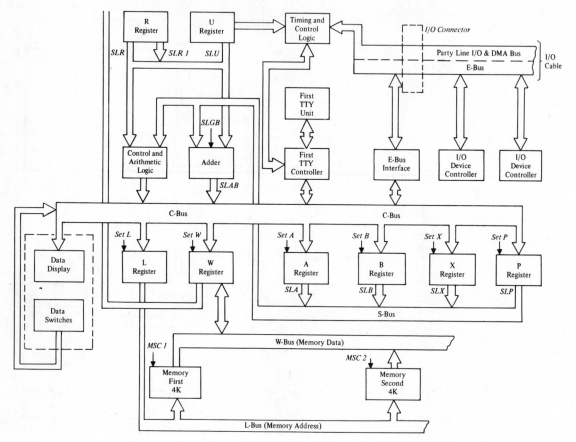

FIGURE 2-7-6.   *Varian 620/L minicomputer.*

Figure 2-7-7*b*). The CPU is directly connected to the general-purpose registers, the shared bus priority arbitration unit, and high-speed semiconductor memories.

2.8 Sequencing of Operations

The timing for sequencing operations inside a minicomputer is controlled by a digital clock, called a *master clock*. The primary memory of most minicomputers consists of magnetic core with destructive read-out properties, although refresh semiconductor memories are becoming popular. The primary memory operates continuously in a read/write memory cycle where the duration of a memory cycle may vary from 0.5 to 2.0 μsec. During the read operation, the contents of the word addressed by the MAR are transferred to the MDR and all the bits in the word in the memory are reset to zero. During the write operation, the contents of the MDR are written back

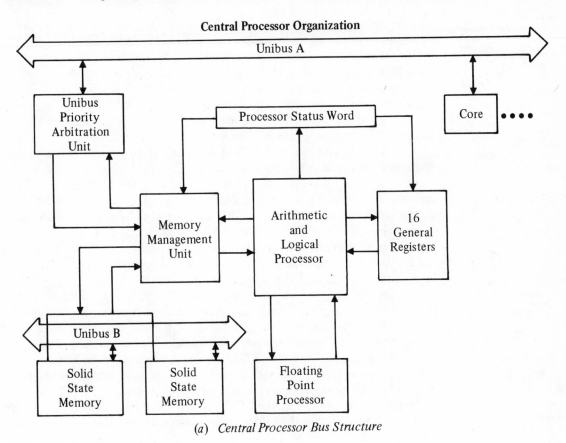

(a) *Central Processor Bus Structure*

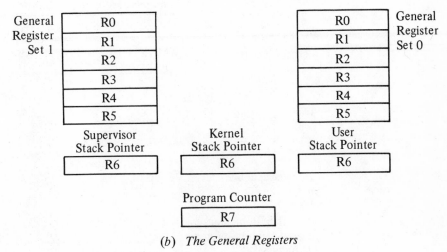

(b) *The General Registers*

FIGURE 2-7-7.   *DEC PDP-11 minicomputer.*

into the word addressed by the MAR. On occasions during a read operation, the contents of the addressed memory word are prevented from entering the MDR and are thus discarded permanently. All the bits in the addressed word are still reset to zero and the overall effect is that of clearing the addressed word in memory. The time period of the master clock is much smaller than the duration of a memory cycle and may vary from 0.1 to 0.45 μsec. Thus, the master clock divides a memory cycle into several subintervals and various CPU operations are carried out in these subintervals.

The CPU and the MU in most minicomputers operate concurrently, and communication between these two units is synchronized by the master clock. The CPU communicates with the MAR and the MDR at the proper instants in a memory cycle and these time instants are specified by the master clock. At other times the CPU can carry out its own internal operation independent of the MU. Table 2-8-1 shows the sequence of operations carried out to execute a single-word instruction which stores the contents of the accumulator in memory. The address of the memory word involved is given directly as part of the instruction.

The MU continuously executes a memory cycle, i.e., a read/write or a clear/write operation in sequence. After decoding the opcode, the control unit in the CPU decides whether to allow a read operation or a clear operation to start. The read and write memory operations are adequately separated in time to allow the CPU to set up the contents of the MAR and the MDR. At the beginning of a fetch state, the CPU transfers the contents of the PC to the MAR and requests a memory read operation. While the MU carries out a read operation, the CPU waits. Then, during the following write operation, the CPU transfers the contents of the MDR to the IR and decodes the opcode. Before the MU starts its next memory cycle, the CPU transfers

TABLE 2-8-1. Execution of a Single-Word Store Instruction

Sequence of Operations	CPU Operations	MU Operations
Fetch instruction	[PC] ⟶ MAR	
	↓	Read Memory
Transfer instructions and decode	[MDR] ⟶ IR	Write Memory
	↓	
Transfer address	[IR] $\xrightarrow[\text{ADDRESS}]{}$ MAR	↓
Transfer data and clear memory	[AC] ⟶ MDR	Clear Memory
	↓	↓
Write data in memory and generate address of next instruction	[PC] + 1 ⟶ PC	Write Memory

TABLE 2-8-2. Execution of a Single-Word Fetch Instruction

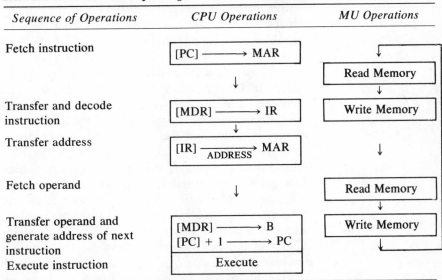

Sequence of Operations	CPU Operations	MU Operations
Fetch instruction	[PC] ⟶ MAR	Read Memory
Transfer and decode instruction	[MDR] ⟶ IR	Write Memory
Transfer address	[IR] ⟶ MAR (ADDRESS)	
Fetch operand		Read Memory
Transfer operand and generate address of next instruction	[MDR] ⟶ B [PC] + 1 ⟶ PC	Write Memory
Execute instruction	Execute	

the address of the memory word from the IR to the MAR and requests a clear operation. While the MU clears the addressed memory word, the CPU transfers the contents of the AC to the MDR. During the next write operation in the memory cycle, the CPU generates the address of the next instruction in the PC.

Table 2-8-2 shows a similar sequence of operations carried out to execute a single-word instruction which fetches an operand from the memory. Since the exact nature of the instruction is not discussed, the execute state of the CPU is shown in an abbreviated form.

SUMMARY

A minicomputer is composed of three functional units: the memory unit, the processing unit, and the input/output unit. The processing unit is made up of an arithmetic and logic unit and a control unit. The purpose of the memory unit is to store data to be processed and instructions for processing data. For reasons of economy, the memory unit is designed to be hierarchical and the portion of the memory unit directly accessible to the processor is called the primary memory. The unit of storage in the primary memory is known as a word. A word stores a string of bits or binary digits, the length of which varies among different computers. Words in primary memory are uniquely identified by their addresses. The time required to access the contents of any word in primary memory is independent of the address of the word, and hence, is often called a *random access memory*. If the contents of the words in a random access memory are assigned permanently during the manufacturing process, it is called *read-only memory*.

The arithmetic and logic unit in the processor performs all the elementary operations on operands received from the primary memory. The control unit fetches and interprets instructions from the primary memory and synchronizes and controls the operations of all other units according to these instructions. The input/output unit, discussed in Chapter 4, communicates with the environment outside the computer. The processor has a limited amount of local memory for storing instructions, operands, results, and addresses; and this memory consists of easily accessible registers. The program counter stores the address of the instruction to be fetched from the primary memory and the instruction register stores the instruction itself while it is being executed by the control unit. Accumulators store operands fetched from the primary memory and results of operations.

The different units in a digital computer are connected to each other by means of information transmission lines, called buses. The arrangement of buses, or bus architecture, differs from one computer to another and has a subtle influence on the overall system. The bus architecture determines the type of elementary operations that can be performed simultaneously and determines the speed of execution of instructions. It also determines the accessibility of one unit from another. Too few buses create the problem of efficient time-multiplexing or sharing of buses and priority of bus use. Too many buses increase the cost of hardware. Several bus architectures have been shown and discussed in the previous sections, with tradeoff descriptions regarding bus architectures given in Chapter 7.

PROBLEMS

1. What are the basic functional units of a computer?

2. Explain the meanings of a bit, a byte, and a word. What is the purpose of an address of a word?

3. What is a random access memory? What are the uses of an MAR and an MDR?

4. What are the functions of an ALU? What are the uses of an accumulator?

5. What are the uses of a program counter and an instruction register?

6. Show the read/write operations of an RAM incorporating an MAR and an MDR.

7. Explain the differences between a serial adder and a parallel adder.

8. Show the functional diagram of an arithmetic unit.

9. What is an instruction cycle? Explain the sequence of operations that occur during an instruction cycle.

10. What is a bus? Explain with a diagram how a shared bus structure operates.

11. Show by means of diagrams how the operations of a destructive read-out MU are synchronized with the operations of a CPU.

12. Compare the advantages and disadvantages of the following minicomputer design alternatives:
    a. Asynchronous vs. synchronous timing
    b. Parallel vs. serial data transfer
    c. Parallel vs. serial arithmetic
    d. Hardware arithmetic options vs. software arithmetic

13. Discuss the main design considerations for a minicomputer if internal processing speed is of primary importance.

14. Is it possible for a minicomputer to communicate with a device that is faster than the processor? Explain your answer.

15. Why should the design criteria of an I/O processor match the criteria of the CPU?

16. Discuss the advantages a single-bus computer organization has over a multibus organization.

17. If the trend in minicomputer design is toward the elimination of internal hardware registers—all to be replaced by memory registers—how is the loss, if any, of performance justified?

18. How does the control unit decide what the next operation is to be?

19. How does the control unit distinguish between an instruction and data? Is it possible to execute a data word by mistake?

20. Discuss several application areas and their influence on CPU designs.

21. What characteristics differentiate memory locations from other internal CPU registers?

22. What are the important characteristics to be considered in the selection of a memory system?

23. Compare and contrast different memory systems in terms of their advantage and contribution toward the overall computer system design.

24. Describe the different accessing methods or modes to memory.

25. What advantages does asynchronous memory have over synchronous memory? What disadvantages?

26. Why has the addition of ROM to a typical minicomputer not enhanced the computer's performance? What changes would be needed to take advantage of this ROM?

27. Why bother to incorporate ROM for a minicomputer if it is not microprogrammable?

28. Discuss several examples of ROM applications in which RAM would not do.

29. How does parity checking effect the cost of a memory system, if an extra parity bit is included in the actual word size?

30. What are the advantages/disadvantages of LSI memories?

31. What is meant by refreshing semiconductor memory? How does this effect the CPU performance?

32. What would be the advantages, if any, of an overlapped instruction fetch while the previous instruction is in its execution cycle?

33. What are the basic memory cycles? Describe the operational sequences for random access memory (RAM) read/write.

PROJECTS

1. Describe, discuss, and differentiate between:
   a. 2D memory
   b. 2 1/2D memory
   c. 3D memory

2. Are there other symbolic means for describing the actions of a computer than presented in this chapter? If so, discuss and describe.

3. Describe, differentiate, and give specific examples of:
   a. Memory-mapped I/O
   b. DMA
   c. Dedicated input/output port locations

3

Instruction Formats and Addressing Modes

3.1 Introduction

The functional organization and operation of minicomputers and their sub-systems have been discussed in Chapter 2. Similar organizations and princi-ples of operations are valid for some large computers as well. However, the examples, at the end of Chapter 2, clearly point out that the CPUs of minicomputers use only a few registers and the number of independent buses are also severely limited. There are other limitations in the design of mini-computers which are discussed here.

3.2 Minicomputer Design Considerations

The cost of minicomputers can be significantly reduced by reducing the size of the primary memory—not only by reducing the number of words in the primary memory but also by reducing the number of bits per word. A word in the primary memory contains either an instruction or data. Thus, the instruction format and the data format directly influence the number of bits per word. The following sections discuss the instruction formats and the data formats for minicomputers, culminating in a discussion on the choice of the word length, i.e., the number of bits per word. Note though that due to the rapid advances in large-scale integration technology, the size of the primary

43

memory of a minicomputer should increase in the future without any appreciable increase in cost. The major hardware costs will then come from packaging, power supplies, and mechanical peripherals.

Another important design consideration for a minicomputer centers around the number of hardware executable instructions provided. This is called the problem of the *instruction set* design. By limiting the size of the instruction set, the design of the control unit can be simplified, resulting in a reduction of cost. Hence, most minicomputers in the past had much smaller instruction sets compared to the conventional large computers. However, microprogramming can be used in a cost-effective manner to create a large instruction set (see Chapter 7).

3.2.1 Instruction Formats

The most general format of an instruction in a computer is shown in Figure 3-2-1. The *opcode* is the binary coded identification of the instruction to be executed. The addresses of the two operands of the instruction and the address of the word for storing the result are specified. Finally, the address of the word containing the next instruction is also given. This is called a *four-address instruction format*. Since all the addresses and the opcode must be converted to strings of bits, the number of bits in the word that stores such an instruction will be quite large.

Opcode	Address of Operand 1	Address of Operand 2	Address of Result	Address of Next Instruction

FIGURE 3-2-1.   *Four-address instruction format.*

Normally instructions are stored in consecutive words in the primary memory and the address of the next instruction is contained in the program counter. The result of the operation can be temporarily stored in the accumulator prior to storing in the primary memory and, therefore, it is not necessary to specify the address of the word assigned to store the result in the instruction format. These considerations result in a shorter *two-address instruction format* shown in Figure 3-2-2. Some large computers are designed using the two-address instruction format exclusively.

The two-address instruction format can be further simplified by assuming that one of the operands is already available in the accumulator. In this case, it is only necessary to specify the address of the other operand as

Opcode	Address of Operand 1	Address of Operand 2

FIGURE 3-2-2.   *Two-address instruction format.*

44

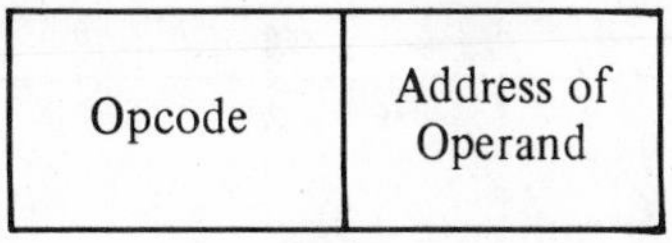

Opcode	Address of Operand

FIGURE 3-2-3.   *One-address instruction format.*

shown in Figure 3-2-3. This is called a *one-address instruction format*. Most minicomputers use this instruction format for reasons of economy. Note though that this reduction in the size of the instruction format is obtained by increasing the number of instructions required to carry out an operation. This normally implies an increase in the time required to complete an operation and in the storage requirement of a program. For example, consider the problem of adding the contents of the words 57 and 58, storing the sum in the word 59, and fetching the next instruction from the word 16. Let ADD, LDA, and STA denote the mnemonic opcodes for addition, loading, and storing the accumulator, respectively. The four-address instruction format results in:

$$\text{ADD 57, 58, 59, 16}$$

while the two-address instruction format generates:

$$\text{ADD 57, 58}$$

$$\text{STA 59}$$

And finally, the one-address instruction format generates:

$$\text{LDA 57}$$

$$\text{ADD 58}$$

$$\text{STA 59}$$

3.2.2 Data Formats

The most fundamental unit of data in a computer is the nonnegative binary integer or fixed-point binary number. The binary number system has only two digits, the 0 and the 1. A string of binary digits or *bits* denoted by b_{n-1}, . . . , b_2, b_1, b_0 represents a number given by:

$$b_{n-1} \times 2^{n-1} + \cdots + b_2 \times 2^2 + b_1 \times 2^1 + b_0 \times 2^0$$

where b_i is either 0 or 1 for all i. For example, the bit string 10011010 is the binary representation of the number:

$$1 \times 2^7 + 0 \times 2^6 + 0 \times 2^5 + 1 \times 2^4 + 1 \times 2^3 + 0 \times 2^2 + 1 \times 2^1 + 0 \times 2^0$$

$$= 128 + 16 + 8 + 2 = 154$$

45

TABLE 3-2-1.   Largest Number Stored as a Function of Word Length

Length of Word in Bits n	Largest Storable Positive Number $2^n - 1$
8	255
12	4095
16	65535
18	262143

Suppose a word in the primary memory of a computer is n-bits long. Then the largest positive number that can be stored in the word is given by a string of n ones, which equals $2^n - 1$. Table 3-2-1 shows the largest positive numbers that can be stored in a word of n bits for values of n in the range commonly found in mini- and microcomputers.

To perform useful arithmetic operations, it is also necessary to be able to store negative integers in a word. The leftmost bit in a word is commonly used to denote the sign of the number; a zero represents a positive number while a one represents a negative number. For a word of n bits, b_{n-1} is the sign bit and $b_{n-2}, ..., b_0$ stores the magnitude of the number. This format is commonly known as the *sign/magnitude representation* of numbers. For an 8-bit word:

$$b_7 \; b_6 \; b_5 \; b_4 \; b_3 \; b_2 \; b_1 \; b_0$$

$$0 \; 1 \; 1 \; 0 \; 0 \; 1 \; 1 \; 1$$

represents the decimal number $+103$, where the sign bit $b_7 = 0$ represents the plus $(+)$ sign, and:

$$1 \; 1 \; 1 \; 0 \; 0 \; 1 \; 1 \; 1$$

represents -103, where $b_7 = 1$ represents the minus $(-)$ sign.

In most modern minicomputers, magnitudes of negative numbers are represented using the *twos complement system*. The reason for the adoption of the sign/twos complement system over the sign/magnitude system is that the design of the arithmetic unit becomes very simple in the former system. If B is a binary number of n-digits, then its twos complement is given by $2^n - B$. Arithmetic operations using the twos complement system are discussed in Appendix A.3.

There is a simple way to obtain the twos complement of a binary number, given by a bit string. Starting on the right-hand side, find the first 1 in the bit string. Complement every digit in the bit string after the first 1 from the right. For example, the twos complement of 103, whose bit string is shown above, is:

$$1 \; 0 \; 0 \; 1 \; 1 \; 0 \; 0 \; 1$$

Note that the sign digit b_7 has become 1 which signifies that this is a negative number. As another example consider the number 52 whose binary representation using 8 bits is:

$$0\ 0\ 1\ 1\ 0\ 1\ 0\ 0$$

and consequently -52 in twos complement system is given by:

$$1\ 1\ 0\ 0\ 1\ 1\ 0\ 0$$

The two data formats discussed so far are used to represent integer numbers. Real numbers are represented in terms of a mantissa and an exponent similar to the scientific notation of real numbers. For example, real numbers, such as -0.00053 or -9.231, are written in scientific notation as -0.53×10^{-3} and -0.9231×10^1. In scientific notation, -0.53 and -0.9231 are called the *mantissa* and the power of 10 used is called the *exponent*. In a computer, both the mantissa and the exponent are coded into binary strings. Different minicomputers allow different numbers of bits for the mantissa and the exponent. Figure 3-2-4 shows the different formats used by different minicomputers for storing numbers. For greater precision, most minicomputers use multiple words to store real numbers.

For example the Hewlett-Packard and the Varian 620/L minicomputers use 16-bit words for integers (see Figure 3-2-4a). Bit 15 is used to store the sign, and negative numbers are represented in twos complement form. The largest positive integer that can be stored is $2^{15} - 1 = 32767$ and the smallest negative integer is $-2^{15} = -32768$. Figure 3-2-4b shows the double-word format used by the Hewlett-Packard computers for storing a signed 23-bit mantissa and a signed 7-bit exponent (in twos complement form if necessary).

FIGURE 3-2-4a.   *Integer formats for the Hewlett-Packard and Varian 620/L minicomputers.*

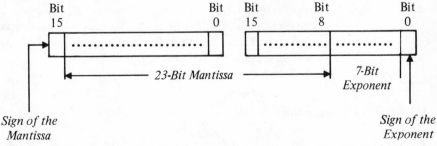

FIGURE 3-2-4b. *Double-word format for the Hewlett-Packard minicomputer.*

3.2.3 Choice of Word Length

The number of bits in a word in the primary memory is called the length of the word. The words in the primary memory contain data and instructions, where each instruction contains an opcode and, in most cases, at least an address for one operand. Therefore, the length of a word has important implications for the precision of data, the size of the instruction set, and the number of directly addressable words in the primary memory.

The length of a word determines the number of bits used to store integer numbers, and hence it directly affects the numerical precision in fixed-point computations. The addresses (nonnegative integers) of words containing operands are represented by binary numbers in the address field of an instruction format. The number of bits in a word assigned to store addresses determines the number of distinct addresses that can be generated, and consequently the number of directly addressable words in the primary memory. If K bits of an n-bit word are used to store addresses of operands, then 2^K distinct addresses are possible. The number of bits in a word used to store opcodes determines the number of distinct opcodes that can be generated, and consequently limits the total number of possible instructions in the instruction set. The number of bits in a word also influences the width of buses, registers, and adders, and thus has serious effects on the overall design and the speed of operation of a computer.

As an example, suppose the primary memory is required to contain 16K words, where 1K equals 1024 words. Since $2^{14} = 16K$, it is necessary to have at least 14 address bits in a word to be able to directly address every word in the primary memory. If the instruction set is required to contain at most 128 instructions, then it is necessary to allow at least 7 bits for coding the opcodes, since $2^7 = 128$. An extra 3 bits are usually needed to specify the *mode* of addressing, discussed in detail in the following sections. Thus, the length of a word in this case must be at least $14 + 7 + 3 = 24$ bits. A double word of 48 bits can then be used to provide sufficient precision in computations.

The length of a word in most popular minicomputers varies from 12 to 16 bits. The DEC PDP-8 minicomputers use words of 12 bits, whereas Hewlett-Packard, Varian 620/L, NOVA®, and DEC PDP-11 use words of 16 bits. The basic design problem of a minicomputer architect is to code a useful instruction set in short words while providing enough addressing bits to directly address a sufficiently large section of primary memory. The types of instructions in a typical minicomputer and the various addressing modes are discussed in the following sections.

3.3 Types of Instructions

The design of an instruction format, as noted in the previous section, represents a compromise between the creation of a reasonably large *instruction set* and a sufficiently large *address space* of directly addressable memory locations. Various combinations of the following approaches are used to achieve this compromise:

1. Address expansion schemes called addressing modes
2. Multiple-word instructions
3. Variable-length opcodes
4. Multiple registers in the processing unit

Various addressing modes are discussed in detail in a later section. The format of a single-word instruction using one of many possible addressing modes is shown in Figure 3-3-1a. A few bits (typically 2 to 3) of the word are used to specify the mode of addressing. The most commonly used multiple-word instructions are double-word instructions whose format is shown in Figure 3-3-1b. Part of the first word contains the opcode and all the bits of the second word are used to specify an address. The obvious disadvantages of this approach are the extra storage and the extra memory access required to fetch the address word. Variable length opcodes are used since not all instructions need to access memory for an operand. For example, typical input/output instructions address only registers in the processing unit and the input/output unit. Normally 7 to 8 bits are sufficient for this purpose and the rest of the bits can be used to specify opcodes for input/output instructions (see Figure 3-3-1c). Finally, memory accessing for operands and the consequent need for long address fields can be reduced by storing

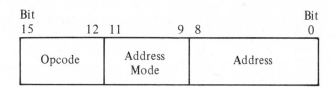

FIGURE 3-3-1a.   Single-word instruction with 16 bits per word.

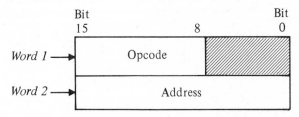

FIGURE 3-3-1b.   Double-word instruction using 16 bits for address.

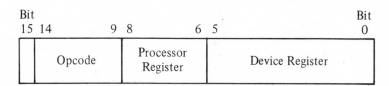

FIGURE 3-3-1c.   Format of input/output instruction.

49

operands in multiple registers in the processing unit. This approach requires a large number of instructions for register-to-register operations but fewer bits in the address field for addressing registers. Usually from two to sixteen registers available in the processing units of minicomputers can be addressed by instructions.

The rest of this section contains descriptions of specific types of instructions found in the instruction sets of most minicomputers.

3.3.1 Memory Reference Instructions (MRIs)

3.3.1.1 Memory Reference with Registers. With several registers in the CPU, memory reference instructions (MRIs) are required to load and store operands, and to perform arithmetic and logic operations between the contents of a register and a word in memory. The results of the operations are usually placed in the register involved in the operation, destroying its previous contents. Typical MRIs with register references may be described by the following operational equations:

$$Load: \quad [\text{Memory Location}] \xrightarrow[\text{BUS}]{} \text{Register}$$

$$Store: \quad [\text{Register}] \xrightarrow[\text{BUS}]{} \text{Memory Location}$$

$$Arithmetical\ or\ Logical:$$
$$[\text{Register}] \sim [\text{Memory Location}] \xrightarrow[\text{BUS}]{} \text{Register}$$

In the operational equations shown above, square brackets [ ] denote "contents of" and $\sim$ represents an arbitrary arithmetic or logic operation. The formats of memory reference instructions that address registers are shown in Figures 3-3-2a and 3-3-2b.

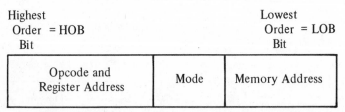

FIGURE 3-3-2a.   *Single-word MRI with register reference.*

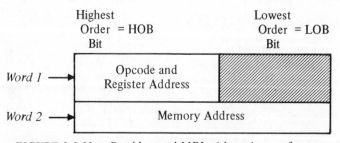

FIGURE 3-3-2b.   *Double-word MRI with register reference.*

50

3.3.1.2 Memory Reference without Registers. Some minicomputers have MRIs that do not address any registers. For example, an increment memory and replace instruction increments the contents of a specified word in memory; its functional equation is of the form:

$$[\text{Memory Location}] + 1 \xrightarrow[\text{BUS}]{} \text{Memory Location}$$

In writing computer programs it often becomes necessary to repeatedly execute a set of instructions with different data. Frequently it also is necessary to break the normal flow of control and branch to a different set of instructions called a subroutine. Such branches are carried out by means of *unconditional jump* and *subroutine jump* instructions. These instructions are described by the following operational equations:

Unconditional Jump:
$$[\text{Address field of instruction}] \xrightarrow[\text{BUS}]{} \text{Program Counter (PC)}$$

Subroutine Jump:
$$[\text{PC}] + 1 \xrightarrow[\text{BUS}]{} \text{Memory Location}$$

$$[\text{Address of Subroutine}] \xrightarrow[\text{BUS}]{} \text{PC}$$

In the above instructions, the addresses are usually "effective" addresses which will be discussed in Section 3.4 on addressing modes.

3.3.1.3 Byte Manipulation Instruction. A 16-bit word length computer contains exactly two 8-bit bytes. Sometimes the user may want to handle operands in byte units rather than in 16-bit word units; for example, in manipulating *ASCII (American Standard Code for Information Interchange) characters* for the line printer or teletype, or other byte-oriented input/output devices.

Byte-oriented MRIs allow byte operands to be accessed one at a time. For example, load and store byte instructions allow the user to load and store half the contents of a specified register using either the left- or right-hand byte of a memory location. Figure 3-3-3a illustrates a byte instruction format.

Load Left-/Right-Hand Byte:
$$[\text{Memory Location}]^{\text{LH/RH}} \xrightarrow[\text{BUS}]{} \text{Register}^{\text{RH}}$$

Store Left-/Right-Hand Byte:
$$[\text{Register}]^{\text{RH}} \xrightarrow[\text{BUS}]{} [\text{Memory Location}]^{\text{LH/RH}}$$

where the LH/RH represents the left-hand or the right-hand byte of the referenced location or register. Bytes are usually loaded into or stored from the rightmost 8 bits of a register.

Highest
Order = HOB
Bit

Lowest
Order = LOB
Bit

Byte Opcode	Register Address	Address Mode	Address

FIGURE 3-3-3a.   *Single-word byte instruction.*

HOB

LOB

Opcode	Bit Field	Address Mode	Address

FIGURE 3-3-3b.   *Single-word bit instruction.*

3.3.1.4 Bit Manipulation Instructions.

The ability to use the 16 bits of a word individually as status indicators, flags, or bit maps can greatly aid certain programming applications. For example, the 16 bits of a designated status word could be used to indicate when 16 motors are to be turned on or off, by assigning one motor to each bit position. When a motor is turned on, its associated bit is set to 1, otherwise it is reset to 0.

Bit manipulation instructions allow the individual bits of a memory word to become operands. Typical bit instructions allow a specified bit to be set to 1, reset to 0, or tested. Figure 3-3-3*b* illustrates a bit instruction format.

Using operational equations, the typical bit instruction may be described as follows:

Set/Reset n^{th} *Bit:* [Memory Location] $\sim \left\{{1 \atop 0}\right\}_n \xrightarrow[\text{BUS}]{}$ Memory Location

Test n^{th} *Bit:* Test^n: [Memory Location]

causes:

$$[PC] + k \xrightarrow[\text{BUS}]{} PC$$

where $\left\{{1 \atop 0}\right\}$ represents the set/reset activity on bit n of the addressed location, and Test^n: denotes the logical testing of the value of bit n, producing a skip of k words ($k = 2$ or 3) if the tested condition is true.

3.3.1.5 Register File Instructions.

In certain situations, it is necessary to save the contents of all addressable registers, called a *register file*, and later to restore them. For example, when the CPU recognizes an *interrupt request* from an external device, the current operating environment should be saved before the interrupt is serviced, and then later restored.

DEFINITION: *Interrupt Request* refers to the condition when a control line emanating from an external device forces the interrupt request line of the processor to set the interrupt request bit within its status register (sometimes referred to as status word, program status word, status, or other terms).

A number of minicomputers have register file instructions that allow the entire set of addressable registers to be stored in contiguous memory locations by a single- or double-word memory reference instruction. The counterpart to the store file instruction is the load file instruction, which loads the entire register file from the contents of a set of contiguous memory locations. The size of the register file determines the effectiveness of these instructions. For 8 to 16 registers, they can greatly speed up the interrupt servicing process. If the register set consists of 4 or fewer registers, they are probably not needed. Figure 3-3-4 illustrates a register file instruction format where R_a and R_b $(a < b)$ define the range of registers affected by the load or store register file instruction. Typical register file instructions are described by the following operational equations:

$$\textit{Load Register File:}\quad [n\text{-Memory Locations}] \xrightarrow[\text{BUS}]{} n\text{-Registers}$$

$$\textit{Store Register File:}\quad [n\text{-Registers}] \xrightarrow[\text{BUS}]{} n\text{-Memory Locations}$$

where n-contiguous memory locations as well as n-contiguous registers are involved.

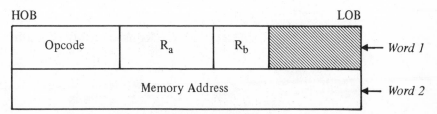

FIGURE 3-3-4. *Double-word register file instruction format.*

3.3.2 Register Reference Instructions

If a minicomputer design demands minimal use of memory reference instructions, this may be achieved by maximizing the use of register operate and change instructions, also known as register reference instructions (RRIs). A machine in which this design philosophy prevails will have most data manipulations occurring in the register file. Hence, it is important that the computer provide adequate instructions for register-to-register operations and register modification operations.

3.3.2.1 Register-to-Register Instructions. Register-to-register operation instructions allow the programmer to perform arithmetic and logical operations and register transfer operations between two specified registers of the register file. Typically, one register is referred to as the source register, while the other as the destination register. In an operation involving two registers, the contents of the destination register is replaced by the result of the operation. The contents of the source register remains unchanged. Figure 3-3-5 shows the format of a typical register-to-register instruction.

Typical register-to-register instructions are described by the following operational equations:

$$\text{Arithmetic and Logical: } \begin{bmatrix} \text{Source} \\ \text{Register} \end{bmatrix} \sim \begin{bmatrix} \text{Destination} \\ \text{Register} \end{bmatrix} \xrightarrow[\text{BUS}]{} \text{Destination Register}$$

$$\text{Transfer: } [\text{Source Register}] \xrightarrow[\text{BUS}]{} \text{Destination Register}$$

In both the memory reference with register instructions, and register-to-register instructions, the typical arithmetic operations involve addition, subtraction, multiplication, and division. The logical operations typically involve the Boolean instructions for **AND**, **OR**, and sometimes the exclusive **OR** (**XOR**).

Besides arithmetic, logical, and transfer instructions, some minicomputers provide register-to-register compare and shift instructions. Compare instructions may result in either a change in the program counter, or a change in the state (a 0 changed to a 1 or a 1 changed to a 0) of some status bit of a CPU program status register. Compare instructions may be described by:

$$\text{Compare: } [\text{Source Register}] \text{ .CMP. } [\text{Destination Register}]$$

causes:

$$[PC] + k \xrightarrow[\text{BUS}]{} PC$$

or:

$$[\text{Status Register}] \text{ .CMP. } \begin{Bmatrix} 1 \\ 0 \end{Bmatrix}_n \xrightarrow[\text{BUS}]{} \text{Status Register}$$

where .CMP. represents a compare operation (e.g., equal, not equal), and $\begin{Bmatrix} 1 \\ 0 \end{Bmatrix}_n$ is a set/reset operation on bit n of a status register.

HOB		LOB
Opcode	Source Register	Destination Register

FIGURE 3-3-5. *Single-word register-to-register instruction format.*

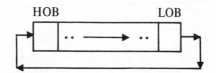

FIGURE 3-3-6a. Rotate right operation.

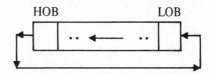

FIGURE 3-3-6b. Rotate left operation.

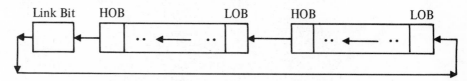

FIGURE 3-3-6c. Double-word rotate left operation.

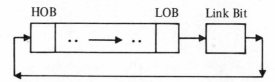

FIGURE 3-3-6d. Rotate right including link bit.

Shift and rotate instructions are useful in programming multiplication and division operations and in selecting a string of bits in a register for further operations. The results of a shift or rotate instruction may be put back in the source register or placed in a separate destination register. *Logical rotate* operations involving a single register are shown in Figures 3-3-6a and 3-3-6b. In case of a right rotation, all bits in the register are shifted one place to the right and the LOB is rotated into the position of the HOB. The operation of a left rotation shown in Figure 3-3-6b should be self-evident. Two registers can be combined into a single rotate operation by linking them together via an extra flip-flop, called a *link bit*, *carry bit*, or *extend bit*. Functionally, such a rotation is shown in Figure 3-3-6c. Link bits can normally be preset to either a zero or a one and then combined with a register in a rotate operation as shown in Figure 3-3-6d.

Left and right *logical shifts* are special cases of left and right rotations. In case of logical shifts, the bit shifted out of one end of a register is lost and a zero bit is shifted in at the other end. Some minicomputers provide left and right *arithmetic shifts* to facilitate modulo two arithmetic operations. For left arithmetic shifts, the sign bit, i.e., bit 15 remains unchanged, bit 14 is shifted out and lost, and a zero bit is shifted in bit 0. For right arithmetic shifts, bit 15 remains unchanged and is copied into bit 14 and bit 0 is shifted out and lost.

3.3.2.2 Register Change Instructions.   The register change instructions affect the contents of a single designated register. Typical register change instructions allow the programmer to increment a register, *swap* (or exchange) register bytes, and clear a register.

In some minicomputers, the increment, decrement, complement, and swap register byte instructions are between a source and a destination register, and therefore would qualify as register-to-register instructions. However, in this discussion they are treated as register change instructions. They are described as:

$$\textit{Register Change:} \quad \text{Op:[Register]} \xrightarrow[\text{BUS}]{} \text{Register}$$

where Op: represents any of the above noted register change operations.

3.3.2.3 Immediate Instructions.   Immediate instructions are a special type of register change instructions available only on some minicomputers. In an immediate instruction, the referenced operand is part of the instruction word itself. In other words, the address field of the instruction contains the immediate operand.

Immediate instructions usually allow the programmer to load a specified register with some fixed value, to add or subtract a fixed value to a register, or to perform some logical operation between a fixed value and a register. They are described by the following functional equations:

$$\textit{Arithmetic and Logical Immediate:}$$
$$\text{[Register]} \sim \text{Immediate Operand} \xrightarrow[\text{BUS}]{} \text{Register}$$

$$\textit{Load Immediate:} \quad \text{Immediate Operand} \xrightarrow[\text{BUS}]{} \text{Register}$$

Figure 3-3-7 illustrates the format of immediate instructions.

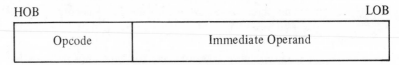

HOB   LOB

Opcode	Immediate Operand

FIGURE 3-3-7a.   *Single-word immediate instruction.*

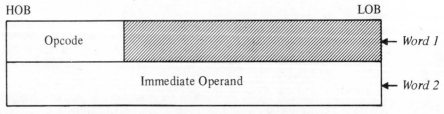

FIGURE 3-3-7b.   *Double-word immediate instruction.*

3.3.3 Special Instructions

Every minicomputer has a group of special instructions, some of which are necessary for the machine to be useful and others which are added by the designers to give the machine added flexibility. Some of these special instructions are discussed here.

3.3.3.1 No-Operation Instruction.   The No-Operation (NOP) instruction just causes the program counter to be incremented by one. Program execution then continues with the next sequential instruction. Operationally, this is represented as:

$$No\ Operation:\quad [PC] + 1 \xrightarrow[BUS]{} PC$$

What good is an instruction that just advances the PC? Since the NOP instruction requires an instruction cycle, a fixed time is required for its execution. The fixed time increment may be used to create time delays in the sequential execution of a program. In fact, *a software timer* may be created by stacking a series of NOPs in a loop so that they are executed a fixed number of times. In some minicomputers, an NOP is not included in the basic instruction set since an NOP can always be simulated by other instructions which do not affect the contents of the register file in the CPU. For example, a simulated NOP is generated by an instruction that adds a zero to the contents of some register in the CPU.

3.3.3.2 Halt Instruction.   The *halt* (HLT) instruction stops program execution until the program is manually restarted from the console switches. Usually the halt occurs after the PC is advanced to the next instruction address. A halt terminates all input/output operations that may be in process before its execution. Operationally, the halt may be represented as:

$$Halt:\quad [PC] + 1 \xrightarrow[BUS]{} PC;\quad CPU\ stops$$

In some minicomputers the halt instruction is part of the I/O instruction set, while in others it is a special instruction or a control instruction. Instead of a halt instruction some minicomputers have a wait instruction in the instruction set. Execution of a *wait* causes the processor to cease operation except for I/O using direct memory accesses and interrupt operations. If an *interrupt occurs*, or the computer is manually restarted from the console, program execution continues. The operational equation is:

$$Wait:\quad [PC] + 1 \xrightarrow[BUS]{} PC;\quad CPU\ idles$$

The wait instruction is not as "final" as the common halt instruction.

3.3.3.3 Read Console Data Switches.   The status (setting) of the console switches can be read and the 16-bit result transferred to a specified register or memory location. This allows a program to read data during execution using only the console data switches. Operationally, this instruction is described as:

Read Data Switches

Register Reference: [Data Switches] $\xrightarrow[\text{BUS}]{}$ Register

Memory Reference: [Data Switches] $\xrightarrow[\text{BUS}]{}$ Memory Location

The read data switches instruction gives the programmer a way to manually enter binary information into a program. Such data might, for example, control what test module is to be executed next.

3.3.3.4 Memory Protection Instructions.   There are several memory protection schemes currently in use in minicomputers. Two of these schemes, word protection and block protection, are common enough for consideration here.

The *word protection scheme* requires an additional bit in every memory word. This bit, like the word parity bit, is transparent to the programmer during normal instruction execution. However, when this bit is set to one, an attempt to write into the protected word location causes a memory protect violation to occur. This violation may generate an internal interrupt or set a processor status flag, or both. Special instructions allow the memory protection bit to be set or cleared under program control.

Word Protection

Set Protection: Protect Bit $\xrightarrow[\text{BUS}]{}$ Set

Clear Protection: Protect Bit $\xrightarrow[\text{BUS}]{}$ Cleared

The second memory protection scheme, *block protection*, allows the programmer to create protected partitions or blocks of core. In some minicomputers, the size of the protected partitions are fixed, whereas in others the protected regions may be partially specified. For example, blocks of 128, 256, 1K, or 2K words may be declared protected.

To implement block protection an extra bit in each word is generally not required. Instead memory protection registers may be used to declare a protected area in memory. Special instructions allow the programmer to set memory protection registers thereby defining the protected area. Attempting to store a word into a protected region produces a storage protection violation, causing some predefined processor action.

In general, memory protection instructions are used by systems programmers involved in the development of a software operating system where it is necessary to protect the system from the user programs.

3.3.3.5 Double-Precision and Floating-Point Instructions.   A *double-precision fixed-point operand* is usually a signed or unsigned quantity represented by

58

at least two computer words. Furthermore, most minicomputers in their standard configuration do not have standard hardware supporting such double-precision arithmetic. Such hardware is often provided as an optional expensive supplement, if at all. As a result of this expense most double-precision instruction sets are implemented through single-precision software. In other words, the single-precision instructions are used to write subroutines that perform the double-precision operations. A typical set of fixed-point double-precision instructions or routines provide for addition, subtraction, multiplication, and division.

A double-precision instruction executes about ten times slower than the corresponding single-precision instruction. A software double-precision routine requires approximately 20 to 50 instructions, with execution times from 50 to 500 microseconds. If an application requires double-precision accuracy and is time-limited (or constrained), the user should carefully examine the double-precision capabilities of any machine under consideration.

A double-precision signed integer operand has 31 data bits (for a 16-bit word machine) which allow for the representation of any positive number up to $+2^{31} - 1$ and maximum negative value of -2^{31}. To provide for even greater range and accuracy some minicomputers have triple-precision fixed-point arithmetic routines to manipulate triple-precision (3-word) numbers. However, this multiprecision fixed-point arithmetic is awkward to use because programmers must perform their own scaling and maintain their own factors. Floating-point arithmetic is a much more satisfactory approach.

A *floating-point single-precision* operand is represented by two words in a minicomputer, just as the double-precision operand. However, as noted earlier, the floating-point format sacrifices some of the precision afforded by a double-precision representation for a much greater range in magnitude. The actual decimal range depends on the chosen floating-point representation, but can be approximately $10^{\pm 75}$. A commonly used representation was shown in Figure 3-2-4b.

For the rapid manipulation of floating-point operands, also referred to as *real numbers*, a floating-point instruction set is required. Until recently, most minicomputers provided software floating-point subroutines to manipulate real-number operands, due to the high price of the optional floating-point hardware. With the current trend of using microprogrammed control units, floating-point instructions may be microprogrammed and thus become available at a much lower cost.

Most floating-point instructions or routines assume that all nonzero operands are normalized, i.e., the leading digit of the fraction is nonzero, and all nonzero results are returned normalized. Floating-point operations are usually supplied for addition, subtraction, multiplication, and division functions.

The format for floating-point instructions depends on the individual manufacturers. The potential user of a minicomputer should consult each vendor regarding the floating-point instruction set, and to determine whether it is standard or optional hardware, or software supplied routines. Hardware supplied floating-point instructions greatly speed up the execution of programs. Depending on the application, a minicomputer with standard

59

floating-point hardware should be given a higher evaluation in comparative analyses.

This concludes the discussion of the typical and more useful instruction types found in minicomputers. For a given minicomputer, the reader should consult the reference manual for a description of the instruction set and individual instruction formats. Input and output instructions are discussed in Chapter 4.

3.4 Addressing Modes

Since all minicomputers have some instructions with a limited addressing range, it is necessary to consider various addressing modes used by designers to augment the limited address space of directly addressable memory locations. The *effective address* of an operand is its true address in memory and the effective address calculation in all minicomputers takes the form expressed by the following formula:

$$EA = X + D \qquad (3.4.1)$$

where EA is the final effective address of the word in memory, D is the address given in a single-word MRI, and X is a full-word address whose value depends on the addressing mode selected. Since, in general, D may have either a positive or a negative value, the sum expressed in Equation 3.4.1 is assumed to be algebraic. The address given by D is often referred to as a *displacement*.

3.4.1 Direct Addressing

If the address bits in the instruction format alone provide the effective address of the operand in memory, then the addressing mode is called *direct*. In this case $X = 0$ in Equation 3.4.1 and $EA = D$, where D is interpreted to be a nonnegative integer. Since there are only a few address bits in a single-word instruction of a minicomputer, only a few words in the memory can be directly addressed. If the address field in a single-word instruction contains m bits, then words with addresses from 0 to $2^m - 1$ can be directly addressed. For example if 4 bits of a 16-bit word are used for the opcode, then at most $2^{12} = 4096$ words in the memory are directly addressable. However, as will be seen later, not all of the remaining 12 bits are usually available for direct addressing. The range of direct addressing can be increased by using double-word instructions where all the bits of the second word are used to address memory. However, this approach increases instruction storage, and, due to multiple memory accesses, increases execution time.

3.4.2 Indirect Addressing

In a double-word instruction, the first word stores the opcode and the second word stores the address of the operand. In principle, the address of the operand can be stored in any word of the memory and not necessarily in the second word of the double-word instruction. However, in this case the first word of the instruction must store the address of the word that stores the address of the operand. This can be easily implemented since the first word stores only the opcode and hence has some bits left over for storing an address. However, precaution must be taken so that the processor does not interpret the address in the instruction word as a direct address of a word containing the operand, but rather as the address of a word containing the address of the operand. This mode of addressing is called *indirect addressing*. A special bit in the instruction format is used to differentiate between a direct and an indirect address of the operand.

The details of indirect addressing are illustrated in Figure 3-4-1. A double-word instruction is shown in Figure 3-4-1*a* where the second word contains the address of the operand. The addresses are all given in the decimal number system for ease of understanding. Figure 3-4-1*b* shows the address of the operand stored in word 69. The address field of the instruction word contains the address 69. A special bit in the word, called the *indirect address bit*, is set to 1 to denote indirect addressing. After testing and determining the indirect address bit to be 1, the processor treats the address

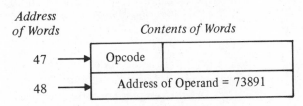

FIGURE 3-4-1a.   Double-word instruction.

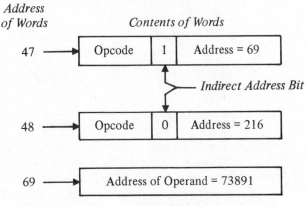

FIGURE 3-4-1b.   Format of indirect addressing.

69 to be the address of the word containing the address (73891) of the operand. Word 48 contains another instruction whose indirect address bit is set to 0. For this instruction, addressing is direct and word 216 contains the operand. If the operand stored in word 73891 is transferred to some other word, the bit pattern of the address in word 47 need not be changed at all. Only the contents of word 69 needs to be changed to show the new location of the operand in the memory.

Double-word instructions can now be thought of as a special case of indirect addressing. Although indirect addressing increases storage and execution time for instructions, it is essential in many cases such as in addressing paged memory. Paging of memory will be discussed later.

3.4.3 Program Relative Addressing

In the *program relative addressing mode*, the contents (D) of the address field of the instruction is treated as a signed integer, and added to the contents of the program counter (PC). If the value of D is negative it is stored in twos complement form. A special bit in the instruction is set to 1 to denote program relative addressing. This form of addressing can be combined with both the direct and the indirect mode of addressing. In the *direct address mode*, the effective address of the operand is given by:

$$EA = [PC] + D \tag{3.4.2}$$

where the addition is interpreted as an algebraic addition.

In the *indirect address mode*, the effective address is:

$$EA = M_{[[PC] + D]} \tag{3.4.3}$$

where $[PC] + D$ is the address of the word in memory (M) that contains the effective address of the operand.

As an example, suppose the instruction being executed is stored in word 523 of memory as shown in Figure 3-4-2. The instruction is assumed to be a single-word MRI with 8 bits in its address field. The contents of the program counter is 524, the address of the next instruction. Of the 8 bits in the address field, one bit is used to denote the sign of the address D. The largest value of $D = 2^7 - 1 = 127$, while the smallest value of $D = -128$. Hence, in the direct address mode, the current instruction can address any word in the range of 396–651.

3.4.4 Base/Index Addressing

The program relative addressing mode is limited in the sense that the effective address of the operand is computed relative to the contents of the program counter. This limitation is removed if, instead of the program counter, a register from the register file in the CPU is used for the computation of the effective address. Registers used in this manner are called *base* or

62

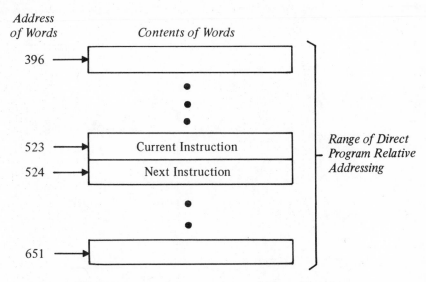

Address of Words

Contents of Words

396

523 — Current Instruction

524 — Next Instruction

651

Range of Direct Program Relative Addressing

FIGURE 3-4-2.   *Direct program relative addressing.*

index registers. If R denotes such a register, then the effective address computation is given by:

$$EA = [R] + D \qquad\qquad (3.4.4)$$

When operands are addressed such that the same instruction can operate on different data each time it is executed, the addressing mode is called *indexing* and the R-register in Equation 3.4.4 is called an *index register*. *Indexed addressing mode* is shown in Figure 3-4-3 where the instruction stored in word 735 uses direct addressing to address the first operand stored in word 2037. The contents of the index register R is zero and the effective address is 2037. In Figure 3-4-3*b*, the contents of the index register has been incremented by one. The effective address is now 2038 and the same instruction in word 735 operates on the second operand stored in word 2038. Operations shown in Figure 3-4-3*c* should now be obvious.

In the *base displacement address mode*, the base register contains the address of the first instruction in the program segment being executed. All other addresses computed are relative to the address of the first instruction and are given by displacements with respect to the address of the first instruction. This address mode allows a program segment to be moved from one part of the primary memory to another, without extensive modifications to the contents of the address fields of the instructions in the program. This type of movement of program segments in memory is called *relocation* and is used for efficient utilization of memory.

Indexed addressing can be combined with the indirect addressed mode to provide powerful addressing techniques for systems programmers. If indexing is used before *indirection* (indirect addressing computation), it is called *preindexing*. On the other hand, if it is used after indirection, it is called *postindexing*.

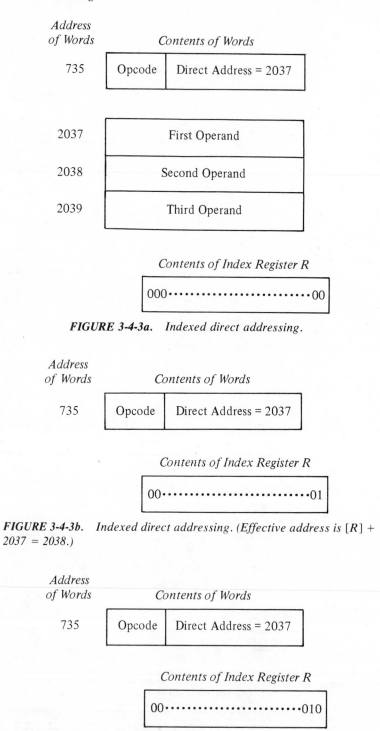

Address of Words   *Contents of Words*

735 | Opcode | Direct Address = 2037 |

2037   First Operand

2038   Second Operand

2039   Third Operand

Contents of Index Register R

000 · 00

FIGURE 3-4-3a.   *Indexed direct addressing.*

Address of Words   *Contents of Words*

735 | Opcode | Direct Address = 2037 |

Contents of Index Register R

00 ·01

FIGURE 3-4-3b.   *Indexed direct addressing. (Effective address is [R] + 2037 = 2038.)*

Address of Words   *Contents of Words*

735 | Opcode | Direct Address = 2037 |

Contents of Index Register R

00 ·010

FIGURE 3-4-3c.   *Indexed direct addressing. (Effective address is [R] + 2037 = 2039.)*

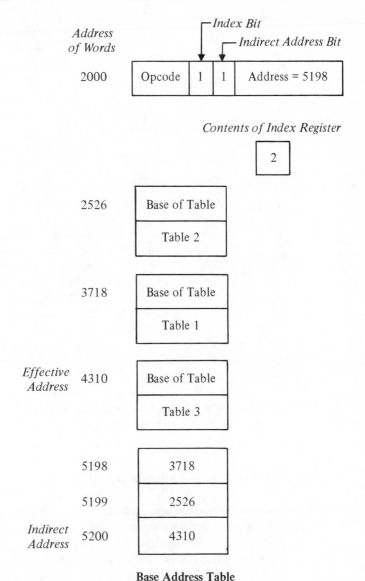

Base Address Table

FIGURE 3-4-4.   Preindexed addressing.

Preindexing is a useful technique for accessing words in memory via multiple base addresses as shown in Figure 3-4-4. This figure shows three tables of information stored in three different parts of the memory. The addresses of the bases of these tables (2526, 3718, and 4310) are stored in consecutive words of the base address table. The starting address of the base address table (5198) is stored in the instruction format. With preindexing, indexing is done first and this gives the indirect address of $5198 + 2 = 5200$. The contents of the word 5200 gives the effective address 4310, which is the address of the first item in the third table.

65

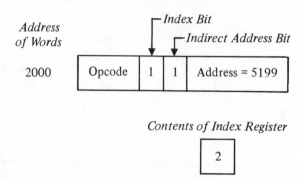

FIGURE 3-4-5. *Postindexing with program relative addressing.*

Preindexing allows the programmer to retrieve the first item of a table. To retrieve subsequent items it becomes necessary to modify the contents of the base address table. This is undesirable if tables of items are shared by many users. To allow a programmer to "walk through" a table it becomes necessary to use the postindexing technique shown in Figure 3-4-5. The instruction specifies an indirect address which is the address of the word 5199. This address is used to retrieve the contents of the word 5199 which is 2526, the address of the first item in table 2 (see Figure 3-4-4). Adding the contents of the index register (2) to 2526 results in 2528, which is the address of the third item in table 2.

Minicomputers with index registers normally provide preindexed addressing. Very few of the current minicomputers provide postindexing. Together they can provide the assembly language programmer with addressing techniques that vastly reduce the programming effort.

3.4.5 Autoindexed Addressing

Several minicomputers provide special memory words called *autoindex locations*. When an autoindex location is indirectly addressed, its contents are automatically incremented or decremented and then used as the effective address. Autoindexing normally provides only preindexing in the indirect address mode. Autoindexing always requires an extra memory access as in the case of indirect addressing. However, since autoindexing is automatic with MRIs using the indirect access mode, no extra opcode bit is needed in the instruction word. Ordinary indirect addressing is not possible with the autoindex locations in the memory.

3.5 Paging

In many minicomputers a set of contiguous memory locations that can be directly addressed by a single-word MRI in the base/displacement mode is called a page. Primary memory is thought of as a collection of such pages for programming purposes. A page of memory is a logical concept and does not in any way imply a physical fragment (or block) of memory. Memory is addressed in terms of pages and words within a given page, in order to use short address fields for addressing large memory.

Within a given page in memory, words are addressed relative to the address of the first word on the page. The most significant bits of the address of the first word of a page are held in a register called a *page register*. The least significant bits from the address field (displacement) of an instruction are concatenated (combined into a contiguous string of 0s and 1s) to the contents of the page register to generate the effective address of the operand.

As an example, consider a memory of 2K words logically subdivided into 8 pages of 256 words each, as shown in Figure 3-5-1a. To address the entire 2K memory it is necessary to use 11 bits, but any word within a page can be addressed by only 8 bits, relative to the first word of that page. Figure 3-5-1b shows how the 43rd word on page 4 can be addressed using a page register. Bits 8–11 of the page register contain the most significant bits (0100) of the first word on page 4. This is often called the *page address*. The address of the word given by the address field of the instruction is 42. The bits in the address field of the instruction register are concatenated with the bits in the page register to form the effective address of 1066. Thus, the paging scheme shown allows the user to address any word in a 2K memory with only 8 bits in the address field of a single-word MRI.

In some paged memory minicomputers, programs are segmented and stored on pages. An instruction on a given page can address any word on

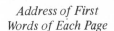
Address of First Words of Each Page

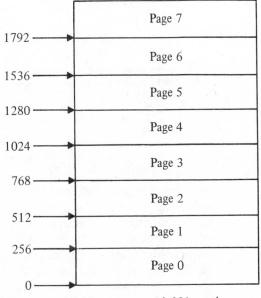

FIGURE 3-5-1a.   *Paged 2K memory with 256 words per page.*

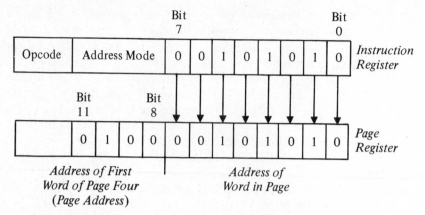

FIGURE 3-5-1b. *Computation of the effective address in paged memory.*

that page or any word on page zero. A special bit in the instruction format decides whether the addressed word is on the same page (current page) or on page zero. Words on pages other than the current page or page zero are addressed by indirection through page zero. Such an instruction format is shown in Figure 3-5-2. Since the page selection bit is 0, the address of the MRI is used to address the corresponding word on page zero. Since the indirect address bit is 1, the contents of the word on page zero is used as the effective address of the operand of the MRI.

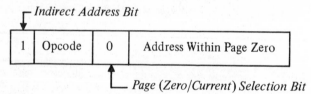

FIGURE 3-5-2. *Accessing a word on a page other than the current page.*

SUMMARY

An important consideration in the design of a minicomputer is the selection of the word length. This choice is intimately related to the selection of the instruction format and the precision of data. The most commonly used word length has come to be 16 bits and the memory reference instructions use the single address format. Different techniques have been developed to balance the number of instructions in the instruction set against the number of addressable words in the primary memory. These include multiple-word instructions, multiple registers in the processing unit, variable length opcodes, and addressing modes. Multiple-word instructions using n-bits per word can directly address 2^n words but require more storage and execution time due to the extra memory accesses. Multiple registers in the processor can reduce the total number of memory reference instructions and thereby reduce the number of bits used for their opcodes. This normally increases the number of bits available for addressing. Also, register reference instructions use fewer bits for addressing allowing large numbers of such instructions.

The major addressing modes are direct and indirect. The latter form of addressing is useful in accessing tables of data and in linking different program segments. Address modification techniques are based on the computation of the effective address by the addition of the displacement given in an instruction to the contents of a specified register. These techniques include base/displacement addressing, program relative addressing, and indexed addressing. The latter form of address modification can be combined with indirect addressing to obtain preindexing and postindexing. These addressing schemes are useful for selecting tables of data and retrieving data sequentially from a selected table.

The major categories of instructions are the memory reference instructions and the register reference instructions. The first set at least must include load and store instructions and branch instructions for program flow control. For ease of programming, it may also include some data processing instructions. The second set normally includes all arithmetic and logic processing instructions involving only the registers in the processor. Various special instructions are also provided to simplify the job of programming.

PROBLEMS

1. What are the major design considerations in reducing the cost of minicomputer hardware?

2. Describe the different instruction and data formats.

3. Discuss the factors affecting the length of a word in memory.

4. What is the largest unsigned binary integer that can be stored in a word of length n? Compute the values of this integer for $n = 4, 6, 8, 12,$ and 16.

5. List all the signed binary integers that can be stored in a 4-bit word using sign/twos complement representation. Show the binary as well as the decimal representations.

6. What are the major classes of instructions in an instruction set? What is the difference between a memory reference instruction and a register reference instruction?

7. Show the instruction formats of a single-word and a double-word instruction.

8. List the techniques that can be used to expand the address space of an instruction.

69

9. What is the effective address of an operand?

10. Show by means of examples the techniques of direct and indirect addressing. Compare the two in terms of storage and memory access requirements.

11. Show by means of examples, program relative and base/displacement addressing techniques. What is program relocation and how does base/displacement addressing assist in relocation?

12. Show by means of examples preindexing and postindexing.

13. How does paging assist in expanding the address space? How is a page register used to form the effective address? How can operands on a different page be accessed via page zero?

14. Using the operational language, functionally describe the hardwired trap sequence for a minicomputer that stores the program counter in the trap location, and then branches indirectly through the next location to the interrupt service routine.

15. Using operational language, describe the instruction cycle for the following instruction types:
    a. Load instruction
    b. Store instruction
    c. Output instruction
    d. Add to register instruction
    e. AND to register instruction

16. Is a program location (PC) register necessary in a relative-address machine? What takes its place?

17. Suppose you have an 8-bit single address minicomputer, what is the minimum number of instructions you would need to add two numbers in 16K memory? Outline the actual steps required for this addition.

18. If indexed addressing provides the capability to address all of memory, why have any other addressing modes?

19. Devise an addressing technique or combination of addressing techniques which would allow the construction of a minicomputer with a 12-bit word length and 32K locations. How could a transfer instruction specify any arbitrary location in memory with a 12-bit instruction word?

20. Propose an instruction format for a 16-bit minicomputer. Provide for indexing, relative, direct, and indirect addressing. Make the instruction format as effective as possible.

21. Suppose you have a minicomputer with a 12-bit word length. Treat it in order as a single address, double address, and table address processor, and devise your own allocation for operation codes and addresses. Consider the restrictions imposed by word length, address length, and operation code length.

22. What are the minimum components of an instruction word? If an instruction contains an operand address, why is this address normally shorter than the maximum capacity of memory?

23. How is a binary subtraction carried out in the sign/twos complement number system?

24. What effect, if any, does relocation have on memory designs?

25. Why bother to implement memory relocation on a minicomputer system? Explain and give examples.

PROJECTS

Assume:

1. You have a 16-bit minicomputer

2. You required a rich instruction set

3. It is required to have addressing modes of:
    a. absolute
    b. relative
    c. indirect (single level)
    d. indexed with absolute
    e. indexed with indirect

4. It is desired to have:
    a. at least two accumulators
    b. program counter
    c. at least one index register
    d. other registers, as required

5. Memory spaces for at least 65,535 words of 16 bits

6. Variable word length instruction set

Outline at least one approach to the design of such a machine with respect to the instruction set, word length, and bit patterns. Do not attempt to design the entire system.

4

Minicomputer Interfacing— Input/Output Protocols, Instructions, Programs, and Controllers

4.1 Introduction

The usefulness and wide applicability of a minicomputer is largely due to its ability to communicate with a variety of peripheral devices such as analog-to-digital converters, digital-to-analog converters, display devices (e.g., CRTs), control systems, and various types of transducers. These devices are made by many different manufacturers, and each type of device has its own special input/output requirements. This makes it difficult for the designer of a minicomputer to anticipate all possible input/output requirements and to build these capabilities into the processor. The input/output design problem is solved by establishing some well-known and commonly used *protocols* for communication with the minicomputer. These protocols will be discussed in subsequent sections. Every device that needs to communicate with a given minicomputer must do so by following one of the protocols acceptable to the minicomputer. The special input/output requirements of a device are handled by a separate *device controller* whose design is independent of that of the minicomputer.

72

4.2 Bus Arrangements for Input/Output

Minicomputers and peripheral devices communicate with each other via a shared *input/output bus*. In most minicomputers the input/output bus is separate from the bus connecting the MU to the CPU and is often called a *party line*. A general arrangement of a minicomputer and its peripheral devices are shown in Figure 4-2-1. This figure implies that logically each device has the same access rights to the input/output bus. Physically, however, the devices are often connected in a *daisy-chain* scheme shown in Figure 4-2-2.

The input/output bus is composed of anywhere from twenty to over a hundred individual transmission lines, each of which is dedicated to the transmission of a specific type of information. These transmission lines can be categorized into five groups, each discussed below.

1. *Data Lines*. The data lines are used to transmit binary coded data between the CPU and a device controller. Usually the number of data lines is equal to the number of bits in a word. The data lines are commonly bidirectional, i.e., they can transmit data either from the CPU to the device controller or vice versa. However, even with bidirectional lines, data can be transmitted only in one direction at a time. Character-oriented devices normally cannot accept a full word of data from the CPU. Such devices are connected only to a subset of the data lines over which binary-coded character data are sent and received by

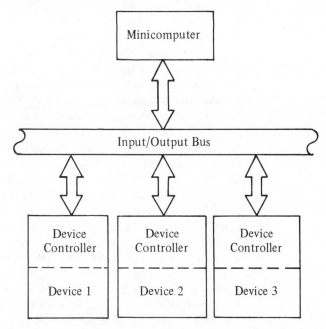

FIGURE 4-2-1. Minicomputer and devices connected via an input/output bus.

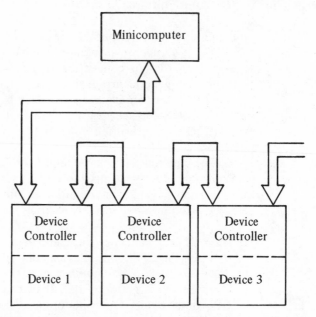

FIGURE 4-2-2. *Daisy-chain connection of devices via the input/ output bus.*

the CPU. Within the CPU, the data lines are logically connected to one of the registers in the register file, frequently to the accumulator.

2. *Control Lines.* Sharing of a bus among the CPU and the device controllers requires a certain amount of coordination. The information necessary to coordinate the transmission of data on the data lines is transmitted over the control lines. Typically such control information consists of, for example, identification of the operation (input or output) and synchronizing signals from the CPU to the device controllers. Control lines are generally unidirectional, i.e., they transmit information in only one direction. Within the CPU, the control lines are logically connected to the control unit that interprets and executes instructions.

3. *Device Address Lines.* The various devices on the input/output bus are identified by their addresses. Commands from the CPU to the device controllers are accompanied by the address of a unique controller, and this address is transmitted over the device address lines.

4. *Command Lines.* The command lines are used by the CPU to transmit a specific operational instruction to a device controller, such as backspace a tape unit, etc. In some minicomputers, commands are also transmitted over the data lines.

5. *Interrupt Lines.* A commonly used communications protocol allows a device controller to interrupt the CPU with requests for service. (This protocol is discussed in detail in a later section.) These interrupt requests are transmitted over the interrupt lines.

FIGURE 4-2-3. *Network interconnections among Hewlett-Packard 1000 Computer Systems are possible at a higher level than ever before, with HP Distributed System/1000 Software and Firmware (DS/1000). (Reprinted by permission of Hewlett-Packard.)*

In some minicomputers (such as DEC's PDP-11) the CPU, the memory unit (MU), and the device controllers all share a single bus for transmitting and receiving information illustrated by the system of Figure 4-2-3. Such a *shared bus scheme* is shown in Figure 4-2-4. Any unit attached to the

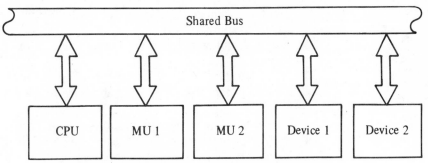

FIGURE 4-2-4. *CPU, MUs, and devices sharing the same bus.*

shared bus and capable of sending data on it can become the *bus-master*. Any unit capable of receiving data from the bus can become the *bus-slave*. Any bus-master can transmit data to any bus-slave without CPU intervention. The CPU or MU acts as a bus-master or bus-slave depending on whether the unit is transmitting or receiving information. In this shared bus system, registers in the device controllers are addressable like the words in the MU or the registers in the register file of the CPU. Hence, the CPU does not need any special input/output instructions; any memory reference type instruction can be used to transfer data to a device. This arrangement also allows the device controllers to directly communicate with each other without CPU intervention. However, this type of activity requires that each device controller be capable of performing complex logic functions somewhat like the CPU.

4.3 Communication Protocols

Minicomputers generally use three different types of communication protocols to communicate with the peripheral devices. If the input/output operation is synchronized and controlled by a program executing on the CPU, it is called a *programmed data transfer*. If the input/output activity is synchronized and controlled by the device controller, it is called a *program-interrupt data transfer*. Most minicomputers also allow a third protocol called the *direct memory access* (*DMA*) technique. The first two protocols are discussed here while the DMA is discussed in detail in the next section.

4.3.1 Programmed Data Transfer Protocol

A programmed data transfer between the CPU and a device controller is performed by an input/output instruction in a program executing on the CPU. An input/output instruction is used to perform the following operations:

1. Send a command to the device controller instructing it to take some specific action.
2. Receive and test the status (busy, idle, out-of-service) of a peripheral device.
3. Transmit data from the computer to a peripheral device (data output).
4. Transmit data from a peripheral device to the computer (data input).

A flowchart of the programmed data transfer protocol is shown in Figure 4-3-1. Prior to initiating a data transfer operation, the CPU tests the status of the device. If the device is busy, the CPU executes a loop and continues to test the status periodically. When the device becomes idle, the CPU initiates a data transfer by an input/output instruction.

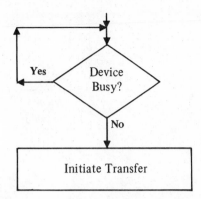

FIGURE 4-3-1. *Programmed data transfer by the CPU.*

The two phases to the execution of an input/output instruction are the *select phase* and the *execute phase*. A typical input/output instruction format is shown in Figure 4-3-2. During the select phase, the CPU puts the address of the device selected on the address lines. The opcode is decoded by the CPU to generate the appropriate control signals for the device controller. The input/output bus transmits the address and the control signals to all the devices. Only the device controller of the addressed device responds to these signals. During the execute phase, the command and data (if any) is transferred by the CPU to the device controller's internal registers. The device controller then sets its status register to indicate it is busy and starts to execute the command received from the CPU. The hardware used to carry out a programmed data transfer is shown in Figure 4-3-3.

The input/output instruction is stored in either the memory data register (MDR) or transferred to the instruction register (IR). The opcode is decoded to generate the control signals. The address and the command are put on the appropriate lines of the input/output bus. The data is normally stored in the accumulator. Programmed data transfer protocol needs the following four types of input/output instructions.

1. *Commands to Device Controller.* Commands are used by the CPU to direct the addressed device controller to initiate some operation on the device, such as backspace a tape unit. The decoded opcode generates the proper control signal, informing the addressed device controller that a command will be transmitted to its internal register by the CPU over the command lines. Upon receiving the command, the device controller decodes it and activates the peripheral device. The instruction format of such an input/output instruction is shown in Figure 4-3-2.

Opcode	Address of Device	Command to Device Controller

FIGURE 4-3-2. *Instruction format of a typical input/output instruction.*

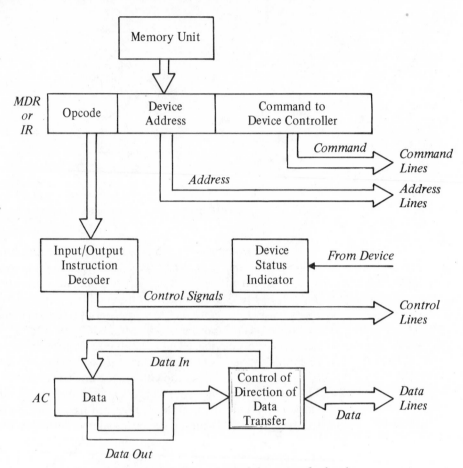

FIGURE 4-3-3. *Programmed data transfer hardware.*

2. *Test Device Status*. This instruction allows the program executing on the CPU to test the status of an addressed device. The status of the device may be idle, busy, or out-of-service. The CPU initiates a data transfer only when it determines that a device is not busy carrying out another operation. The instruction format is shown in Figure 4-3-4.

3. *Data Input Instruction*. This instruction transfers a data word from the addressed device to the CPU. The decoded opcode of the instruction sends a read control signal to the device controller, and in response it puts the data word from its internal register on to the data lines. The CPU transfers the data word from the data lines into its internal register.

Opcode	Address of Device	Send-Status Command to the Device Controller

FIGURE 4-3-4. *Instruction format to receive and test status information of a device.*

78

Opcode	Address of Device	Input or Output Command to Device

FIGURE 4-3-5. *Instruction format to transmit data over data lines.*

In some minicomputers, the CPU is informed of the availability of a data word on the data bus by a read request signal from the device controller. The instruction format is shown in Figure 4-3-5.

4. *Data Output Instruction.* This instruction transfers a data word from the CPU to an internal register of the addressed device controller. The decoded opcode of the instruction sends a write control signal to the device controller while the CPU puts the data word on the data lines. In response to the write signal, the addressed device controller transfers the data word from the data lines into its internal register. The instruction format is shown in Figure 4-3-5.

4.3.2 Program-Interrupt Data Transfer Protocol

Programmed data transfer protocol, as described in the previous section, does not, in general, make efficient use of the CPU time, and is not capable of handling all input/output situations properly. For example, suppose an output device is busy when the program on the CPU wants to transmit some data. In this case, the CPU has to loop, waiting for the device to become idle. If the average execution time of an instruction on the CPU is one microsecond and the device takes one millisecond to finish its operation, the CPU could have executed a thousand instructions if it did not have to wait for the device. Furthermore, suppose a device's internal buffers are almost full with incoming data and it needs the CPU to transfer this data into the memory so as not to lose data due to *buffer overflow*. In this case, the device cannot wait for the program executing on the CPU to execute a data input instruction. The *program-interrupt data transfer* protocol is designed to eliminate the deficiencies of the programmed data transfer protocol.

In the interrupt mode of data transfer, the device controller initiates a data transfer operation by interrupting the execution of the current program on the CPU and requesting CPU aid in data transfer. The execution sequence of the CPU in this case is shown in Figure 4-3-6. To operate in the interrupt mode, a minicomputer must provide a *hardware interrupt system* that can do the following:

1. Register an interrupt signal from the device controller to the CPU.
2. Enable or disable the mechanism that allows an interrupt signal to be registered.
3. Provide a priority structure to resolve contention problems among simultaneous interrupt signals.
4. Allow the interrupting device controller to identify itself by its address.

79

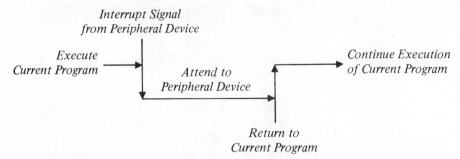

FIGURE 4-3-6. *Execution sequence of the CPU under interrupt mode of data transfer.*

A simple hardware scheme to achieve 1) and 2) is shown in Figure 4-3-7. The *enable flip-flop* shown in the figure is controlled by program instructions. An interrupt enable instruction executed by the CPU sets the output of the enable flip-flop to one. This action opens the AND gate through which the interrupt signal from a device controller comes into the computer. When the interrupt signal arrives, it sets the output of the *interrupt flip-flop* to one and this is how the interrupt signal is registered with the CPU. Arrival of a subsequent interrupt signal resets the enable flip-flop output to zero and closes the AND gate. This action disables the interrupt mechanism and prevents any other interrupt signal from registering. The program that services that particular device then decides when to enable the interrupt mechanism again. The CPU can also disable the interrupt mechanism by sending an interrupt disable signal (shown in the figure) to reset the enable flip-flop.

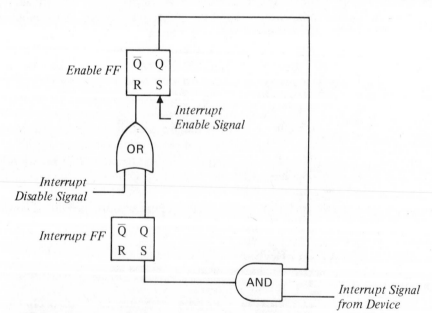

FIGURE 4-3-7. *Interrupt enable/disable mechanism. (See Appendix A.2 for a summary of the SR flip-flop.)*

This is necessary, for example, when a CPU is executing a double-word instruction, an input/output instruction, or a shift or rotate instruction.

In general more than one peripheral device communicates with the minicomputer by using the *interrupt protocol*. Thus, the minicomputer is faced with the problem of resolving contention among several simultaneous interrupt signals. The most primitive way of handling multiple interrupt signals is to pass them all through an OR gate before they arrive at the interrupt flip-flop. In this scheme, the CPU knows of the occurrence of an interrupt but does not know which device or devices sent the interrupt signals. Each device controller has a *flag flip-flop*, which is set when the controller generates an interrupt signal. Upon receipt of an interrupt, the CPU branches to and executes a program that queries the device controllers in some order till it finds the first controller with its flag set. The CPU then services the request of that device controller. This scheme is shown in Figure 4-3-8.

The priorities of service among the device controllers depend on the order in which they are queried and hence are built into the interrupt query program. This scheme requires less hardware but is time consuming. The whole interrupt mechanism must be disabled as soon as and as long as any interrupt signal is pending, and low priority interrupt services cannot be preempted by higher priority interrupts occurring at a later time. Sometimes all the outputs of the flag flip-flops are transferred to an *interrupt storage register* in the CPU, which is either tested bit by bit or used as an indirect address to the first instruction of a service routine.

The response time of this scheme for handling multiple interrupts can be considerably reduced if the software program is replaced by a hardware *interrupt search ring* shown in Figure 4-3-9. In this system, when no interrupt signal is present, the binary counter continuously cycles through its normal counting sequence. When the output signal from the counter reaches an AND gate where an interrupt signal is present, the output of that gate sets an interrupt request flip-flop, which in turn stops the binary counter. The output of the binary counter, when it has stopped, can be used as the address of the device controller requesting service. After an interrupt has been

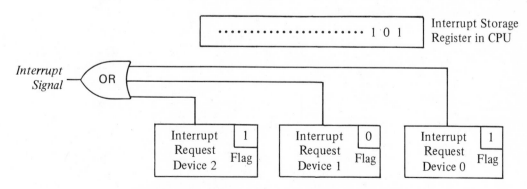

FIGURE 4-3-8.   *Simple scheme to handle multiple interrupt signals.*

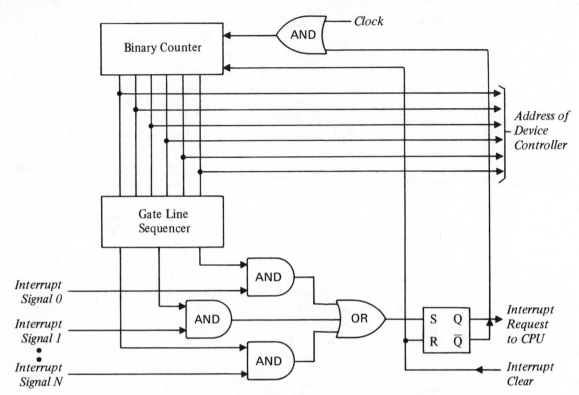

FIGURE 4-3-9. *Searching system to Identify interrupting device controller. (See Appendix A.2 for a summary of the SR flip-flop.)*

serviced, an interrupt clear signal resets the request flip-flop and the binary counter, and the whole cycle is repeated.

As discussed earlier, it is sometimes necessary for the CPU to disable the entire interrupt system. In system programs, it often becomes necessary to disable only a selected set of interrupts. This is done by means of *mask flip-flops* as shown in Figure 4-3-10. Mask flip-flops can be set and reset by instructions executed by the CPU. When a mask flip-flop is reset to zero, the corresponding flag signal, if present, is effectively masked from the interrupt query program.

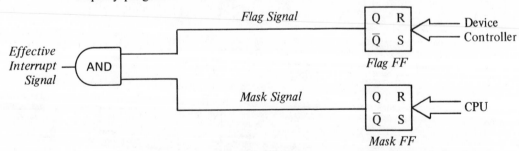

FIGURE 4-3-10. *Selective disabling of interrupts by mask flip-flops. (See Appendix A.2 for a summary of the SR flip-flop.)*

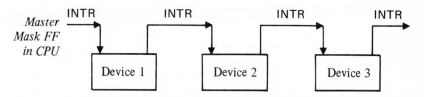

FIGURE 4-3-11.   Priority determination by a daisy chain.

A commonly used scheme for assigning priorities of service to devices is to chain them together as shown in Figure 4-3-11. When the *daisy chain* shown in the figure is enabled by the CPU, an interrupt request signal (INTR) is sent through the chain by a *master mask flip-flop.* Any device requesting service from the CPU traps the INTR signal and stops it from proceeding further down the chain. After trapping the INTR signal, the device controller can request an interrupt. Thus, devices toward the beginning of the chain by their position have higher priorities than devices toward the end of the chain.

A simplified version of the logic circuit used to trap the INTR signal is shown in Figure 4-3-12. An interrupt signal from the device controller is received by the CPU only if the controller can set the request flip-flop. Setting the request flip-flop is controlled by setting the mask flip-flop (set by

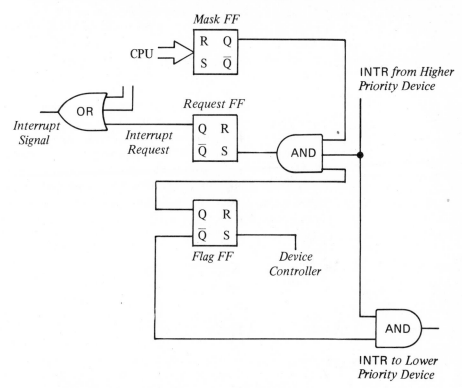

FIGURE 4-3-12.   Trapping of the INTR signal. (See Appendix A.2 for a summary of the SR flip-flop.)

83

the CPU) and the INTR signal received from a higher priority device. If the INTR signal is not received from the higher priority device, the request flip-flop cannot be set. The flag flip-flop is set by the device controller when it needs service from the CPU. The setting of the flag flip-flop closes an AND gate and prevents the INTR signal, when it arrives, from entering a lower priority device. If the daisy chain is not disabled by resetting the master flip-flop, a higher priority interrupt can preempt a lower priority interrupt being serviced by the CPU. By disabling the entire chain after service of an interrupt has begun, the CPU can prevent this from happening. This choice is exercised by the programmer by using suitable instructions in the service routine.

Before the start of the fetch phase of a new instruction, the CPU tests the interrupt flip-flops of all the daisy chains in order of priority. If interrupts are pending, it sends an interrupt acknowledgement signal (INTA) to all the devices of the selected chain. Upon receiving the INTA signal, the interrupting device controller puts the address of a memory location on the data lines. The CPU uses this address as an indirect address and branches to the first instruction of the interrupt service routine for that device. Such an interrupt system, where each device controller provides a separate memory address for each interrupt service routine, is called a *vectored interrupt system*.

As an alternate scheme of interrupt handling, the CPU may branch by indirection to the first instruction of a general interrupt service routine. This routine then queries the device controllers and selects the service routine to be executed by the CPU. This is normally called a *polled interrupt system*.

Every time a program executing on the CPU is interrupted, the contents of the program counter are saved so that the program can be properly resumed after servicing the interrupt. In general, the contents of the register file are also saved to prevent the loss of intermediate results. This action can either be taken automatically by the hardware or done under program control. The contents can either be stored in a stack or in an arbitrary, but carefully remembered, memory region. The saving and restoring of register contents are considered *overhead* since they do not contribute to any useful computation. This overhead can be completely eliminated by using a large register file built of integrated circuits. Such a file can provide multiple register groups for use by service routines and the interrupted program. When an interrupt occurs, a hardware pointer automatically selects a unique register group. With the cost of hardware reducing, this technique may be feasible for use in minicomputers in the future.

4.4 Direct Memory Access Data Transfer Protocol

The interrupt protocol as discussed in the previous section allows a device controller to operate at its own speed. Whenever necessary, the device controller interrupts the CPU for service. Since servicing an interrupt involves a certain amount of overhead on the part of the CPU, too many

84

interrupts may make it difficult for the CPU to get any useful computation done. Consequently devices that cause fewer interrupts per unit of time are given higher priority over those that do not. This means that the slower peripheral devices, such as line printers, have higher priority over faster devices such as disks and drums. Another reason for giving higher priority to slower devices is that, in order to get a reasonable volume of data transferred per unit time, they must be kept operating as much as possible.

Drums and disks usually transfer large blocks of data at one time. If they use the interrupt protocol, where the transfer of each word is followed by an interrupt, they will generate a large number of interrupts. Since they have lower priority, many of these interrupts will not be promptly serviced by the CPU. Data transfers with drums and disks are time-critical operations in which an unattended interrupt can cause long delays in the completion of the transfer operation. Due to the time-critical nature of the transfer operation, if the CPU attends to these numerous interrupts promptly, very little time will be left to do any useful computation because of the overhead involved in servicing interrupts. Minicomputers also have to interface with real-time systems in which an unattended interrupt may result in permanent loss of data.

To avoid these problems it is necessary to have a communications protocol whereby high-speed devices can communicate with the memory without too much delay and too much overhead on the part of the CPU; the *direct memory access (DMA) data transfer protocol* is such a scheme. The initiation of data transfer using the DMA protocol is done under program control and termination is achieved in the usual manner by means of an interrupt which involves CPU overhead. Completion of the transfer of each unit of data is also followed by a service request signal from the device controller. However, the CPU does not service these requests by saving the contents of all registers and then branching to a service routine. It simply suspends the execution of the current program and devotes one machine cycle in transferring data between the memory unit and the device controller via the MAR and the MDR. Upon completion of this transfer the CPU resumes execution of the original program where it left off. This activity is usually called *cycle-stealing* by the device controller and is shown in Figure 4-4-1.

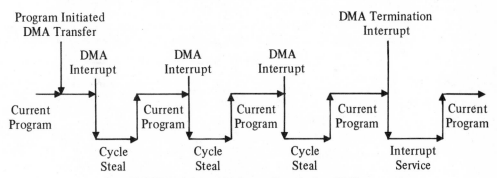

FIGURE 4-4-1. *Cycle stealing during DMA operation.*

Data transfer in the DMA mode is initiated under program control and can be terminated by a program interrupt action. Obviously, if the DMA mode is used to transfer one word of data at a time it will not be much of an improvement over the program-interrupt mode of data transfer. Therefore, DMA is almost exclusively used to transfer blocks of data between the memory and a high-speed peripheral device. To initiate a DMA block transfer, the program specifies the address of the first word in the block, the total number of words in the block, and the direction of the transfer (input or output). The DMA controller has a *current address counter* and a *word counter* (see Figure 4-4-2) which are initialized by the program with the starting address of the block in memory and its length in words. The DMA controller also has a data register to store the data being transferred.

When a DMA controller is ready to transfer data, it sends a cycle-steal request to the CPU. If the CPU grants a cycle-steal, the DMA controller transfers one word of data via the MAR and the MDR. It also increments the contents of the current address register and decrements the contents of the word counter by one. When the contents of the word counter reaches zero, the block transfer is terminated. The DMA controller then requests a program interrupt and the CPU executes a service routine that completes the block transfer process.

The *DMA request bus line* (DMAR) is serially attached to each DMA device controller on the input/output bus. Each controller receives the DMAR signal and passes it on to the next controller if it does not desire a DMA cycle-steal. The DMAR signal is trapped by the first controller requesting a DMA cycle-steal. The priority of a DMA controller is there-

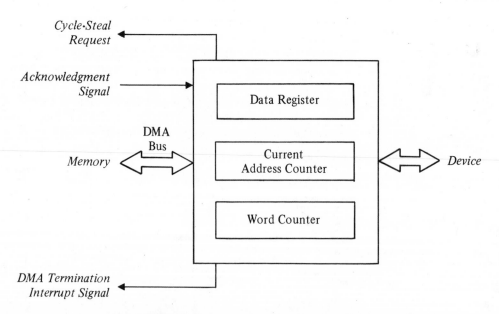

FIGURE 4-4-2. *Functional description of a DMA controller.*

fore dependent on its position in the daisy chain of DMA controllers with respect to the starting point of the DMAR signal.

At the start of each instruction cycle, the CPU control unit polls all controllers, both DMA and non-DMA, for cycle-steal and interrupt requests. If a DMA and a non-DMA controller have requested interrupts, the DMA request is honored first. All DMA cycle-steal requests are given the highest priority. This is necessary since the higher speed DMA device should not be forced to wait for a slower speed non-DMA device because there is a danger that the DMA controller might lose data. However, all DMA transfers occur in one memory cycle, hence the non-DMA device interrupt is locked out only a few instruction cycles at most. In general, there is little danger that the service of lower speed devices will suffer significantly because of higher priority DMA cycle-steals, but contention does occur nonetheless.

4.5 Input/Output Instructions

Every minicomputer instruction set contains input/output instructions to select and operate peripheral devices. This means that another instruction format is required for input/output, with its own instruction bit-code combination. Since no two types of computers have identical input/output architectures, their input/output instructions are likewise dissimilar. In fact, minicomputers probably differ more in their input/output architecture and instructions than in any other respect.

Input/output data may be routed through an accumulator, a general-purpose register, or directly in and/or out of memory. Most minicomputers provide these capabilities via their input/output instructions. In general, all input/output data transfers are initiated by the programmer, i.e., under program control. The single exception might be a status input initiated by some external event in an environment, such as a process alarm condition. Once input/output is initiated by the program, it may proceed under program control (programmed I/O) or peripheral control (interrupt I/O). The choice is up to the programmer in most situations; however, some peripheral devices are constrained by controller design to operate in only one or the other of the two modes. All input/output instructions must specify at least three items of information:

1. Direction of data transfer (input or output)
2. Identification of the device to be used
3. Identification of the CPU register or memory location to be used in the data transfer

Probably the most popular approach is to specify the input/output operation by the opcode bits of the instruction word, and to use 6–8 bits of the instruction word to select the device via a preassigned device code. The remaining bits of the instruction word are then used to specify an ac-

I/O Operation Specification	CPU Register ID	Peripheral Device ID

FIGURE 4-5-1. *Register-reference input/output instruction format.*

cumulator or a general-purpose register from the register file. This format is illustrated in Figure 4-5-1.

If 6 bits are allocated for device codes, then $2^6 = 64$ different devices can be addressed. A 6-bit device code is more than adequate for most minicomputer applications. Most minicomputer users cannot afford, much less use, 64 devices. In fact, 64 devices on an input/output bus would probably have signal propagation delay problems in the device controllers farthest from the CPU.

The register referenced in the input/output instruction receives the data on an input, and holds the data prior to an output operation. All data transfers initiated by this instruction format go through a register in the register file and it is therefore referred to as *register input/output.*

A second approach to input/output specification uses a memory reference instruction to point to a single- or double-word memory location, the bits of which select the device, specify the data transfer operation, and provide the memory address for the data being transferred. The input/output MRI may itself be in single-word or double-word format as illustrated in Figure 4-5-2.

The memory reference I/O instruction itself does not specify a particular input/output or control operation. Instead the effective address from the instruction is used to fetch *control word(s)* from memory. The control word(s) specify the operation and all the parameters defining the operation to be performed. The format of a double-word control word is shown in Figure 4-5-3. The *address field* (first word) specifies the memory address of a data value to be used in a single-word data transfer operation. Alternately, the address field may specify the starting address of a data area to be utilized in a direct memory access (DMA) block transfer over a data channel. The *area*

I/O Opcode	Address Mode	Address of Control Word

FIGURE 4-5-2a. *Single-word memory reference input/output instructions.*

FIGURE 4-5-2b. *Double-word memory reference input/output instructions.*

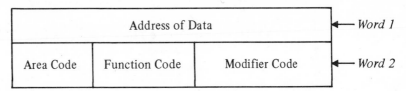

FIGURE 4-5-3. *Format of a control word referenced by a memory reference input/output instruction.*

code specifies the device affected by the operation, such as the fourth line printer. The *function code* specifies the transfer or control operation to be performed. Typically, this is one of four operations: sense operational status, test condition of control operation, input (read) a single-word or data block, and output (write) a single-word or data block. Finally, the *modifier code* provides additional details about the input/output operation not provided by the area or function code fields.

In both the programmed and the interrupt mode of data transfer, the status of the device involved must be sensed before an input/output instruction is issued by the CPU. A *sense status instruction* in the input/output instruction set allows a program to determine the status of the device involved in the data transfer operation. The instruction may produce a branch or a skip in response to the sensed status. Alternately, it may only retrieve a device status word which must be tested by subsequent instruction(s) and have the appropriate action taken. Sense instructions would have the same general format as shown in Figure 4-5-1.

Finally, an input/output instruction is needed to control the operating condition of a peripheral device, for example, to rewind a magnetic tape or to move the tape forward one record. Control may be effected by transferring a control word to the device using the output instruction. Alternately, control may be implemented by using specific bits in the input/output instruction word, such as the register specification bits.

Four basic types of input/output instructions have been identified, input (read), output (write), sense or test status, and control. The operational equations of these instructions are:

Input (read):

$$\text{Register-Reference: [Device Register]} \xrightarrow[\text{BUS}]{\text{I/O}} \text{Register}$$

$$\text{Memory-Reference: [Device Register]} \xrightarrow[\text{BUS}]{\text{I/O}} \text{Memory Location}$$
$$\text{(DMA)}$$

Output (write):

$$\text{Register-Reference: [Register]} \xrightarrow[\text{BUS}]{\text{I/O}} \text{Device Register}$$

$$\text{Memory-Reference: [Memory Location]} \xrightarrow[\text{BUS}]{\text{I/O}} \text{Device Register}$$
$$\text{(DMA)}$$

Sense/Test Status:

$$\text{Sense Status: Device Status} \xrightarrow[\text{BUS}]{\text{I/O}} \text{Register/Memory Location}$$

$$\text{Test Status: Device Status} \xrightarrow[\text{BUS}]{\text{I/O}} \text{CPU,}$$

$$\text{causes [PC]} + \text{K} \longrightarrow \text{PC}$$

A branch or skip next instruction occurs if the tested condition is true.

Control:

$$\text{Register-Reference: [Register]} \xrightarrow[\text{BUS}]{\text{I/O}} \text{Device Control}$$
$$\text{Register}$$
$$\text{Memory Reference: [Memory Location]} \xrightarrow[\text{BUS}]{\text{I/O}} \text{Device Control}$$
$$\text{Register}$$
$$\text{Direct-Reference: CPU} \xrightarrow[\text{BUS}]{\text{I/O}} \text{Device Controller}$$

The input/output instruction set must include special instructions to allow the programmer to enable or disable global and selective interrupt control, i.e., control the interrupt system. The exact mechanism employed varies from one minicomputer to another. For the present discussion assume the computer has 16 interrupt levels, with each device controller hard-wired to one level although several may share the same level. Let each bit of a 16-bit CPU *interrupt register* control one level. If a bit is set to 1, the interrupts corresponding to that level are enabled; and if cleared to 0, the interrupts are disabled. Thus, by loading the interrupt register with a 16-bit word having selected bits set or cleared, the programmer may selectively control peripheral device interrupts. Loading all 1s enables all device interrupts; loading all 0s disables all device interrupts (global control). The interrupt system can be controlled by using a set interrupt register instruction, and its state sensed by using a sense interrupt register instruction. Either the register-reference or memory-reference instruction schemes may be used. Functionally, these operations may be described by:

Set Interrupt Register:

$$\text{Register-Reference: [Register]} \xrightarrow[\text{BUS}]{} \text{Interrupt Register}$$

$$\text{Memory-Reference: [Memory Location]} \xrightarrow[\text{BUS}]{} \text{Interrupt Register}$$

Sense Interrupt Register:

$$\text{Register-Reference: [Interrupt Register]} \xrightarrow[\text{BUS}]{} \text{Register}$$

$$\text{Memory-Reference: [Interrupt Register]} \xrightarrow[\text{BUS}]{} \text{Memory Location}$$

90

The instructions that control the interrupt system are normally assumed to be part of the input/output instruction set. Hence, the instruction formats given in Figures 4-5-1 and 4-5-2 are still valid.

4.6 Input/Output Programs

As mentioned earlier, minicomputers differ more in their input/output architectures and instruction sets than in any other respect. This makes it difficult to write detailed illustrative input/output programs that cover the data transfer operations of the most popular minicomputers. Furthermore, since details vary from one machine to another, details are virtually useless in understanding the overall principles of operation. Hence, input/output programs are illustrated in this section by means of flowcharts and general input/output instructions discussed in the previous sections.

1. *Programmed data transfer.*
   The flowchart of a programmed data transfer operation (Figure 4-6-1) illustrates a programmed data input operation. It can be trivially modified for a programmed data output operation.
2. *Program-interrupt data transfer.*
   The flowchart of a program-interrupt operation (Figure 4-6-2) assumes that the interrupt service routine saves and restores all register contents in the CPU. Since all other interrupts are disabled upon acknowledging the current highest priority interrupt, the service routine can execute without further interruption. If the service routine enables the interrupt system, it can be interrupted by a higher priority interrupt. The test interrupt request operation occurs in the control unit of the minicomputer, and is not accessible by the programmer.
3. *Direct memory access data transfer.*
   The flowchart of a direct memory access operation (Figure 4-6-3) should be self-explanatory, in view of the discussion in Section 4-4.

4.7 Data Transfer Techniques

Data are transferred between the data register in the CPU and the data register in the device controller via the data lines with the help of timing pulses transmitted over the control lines. Two modes of data transfer from the data lines into the registers are shown in Figures 4-7-1a and 4-7-1b where the data register consists of N flip-flops. In Figure 4-7-1a, the registers are first cleared by a clear control signal generated by the input/output instruction, and then the bits on the data lines are *strobed* into the flip-flops by a strobe control signal. In Figure 4-7-1b, the flip-flops are not cleared by a separate control signal. The bits on the data lines are strobed into the

91

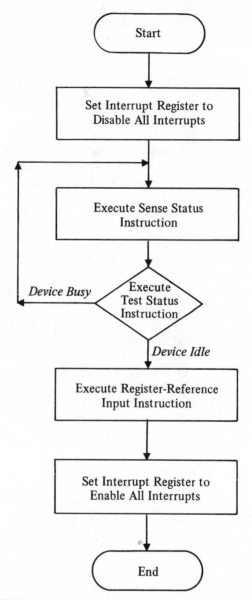

FIGURE 4-6-1. *Flowchart for programmed input operation.*

flip-flops by means of a single control signal. This method of data transfer is called a *jam transfer* and requires slightly more hardware but fewer control signal pulses. In some situations, such as with digital-to-analog converters, the clearing of the flip-flops followed by a wait for the strobe signal, interferes with the proper operation of the device; jam transfer eliminates this problem.

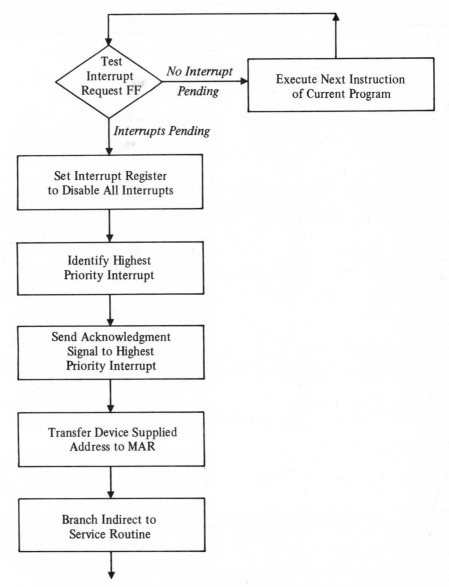

FIGURE 4-6-2. *Flowchart of program-interrupt data transfer operation with vectored interrupt.*

4.7.1 Data Output Operation

A data transfer operation from the CPU to the device controller is shown in Figure 4-7-2. The data register in the CPU is assumed to be the accumulator. The input/output instruction contains the address of the device which is transmitted to the address decoder of the device controller. The opcode part

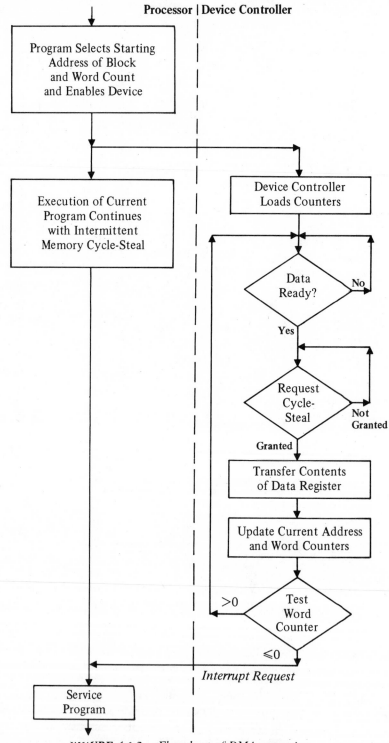

FIGURE 4-6-3. *Flowchart of DMA operation.*

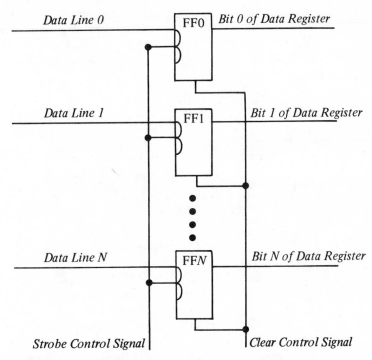

FIGURE 4-7-1a. *Clear-and-strobe method of data transfer. (SR flip-flops are commonly used.)*

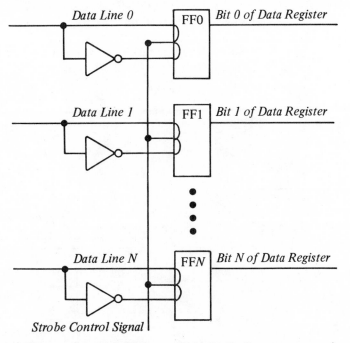

FIGURE 4-7-1b. *Jam transfer method. (SR flip-flops are commonly used.)*

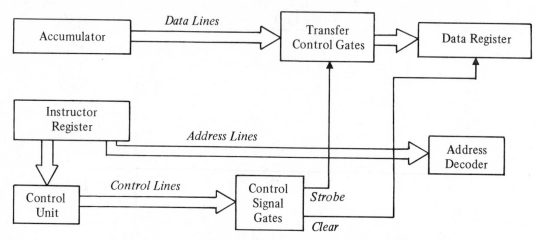

FIGURE 4-7-2. *Data output operation.*

of the input/output instruction is decoded by the control unit in the CPU to generate the clear and strobe control signals. The data, address, and control signals are transmitted to all the device controllers; only the addressed device controller responds to the control signals. To complete the data output operation, first the accumulator is loaded with the data stored in the memory. Then, an output instruction is executed with the selected device address in its address field.

4.7.2 Data Input Operation

A data transfer operation from the device to the CPU is shown in Figure 4-7-3. The input/output instruction generates a *gating signal* which puts the

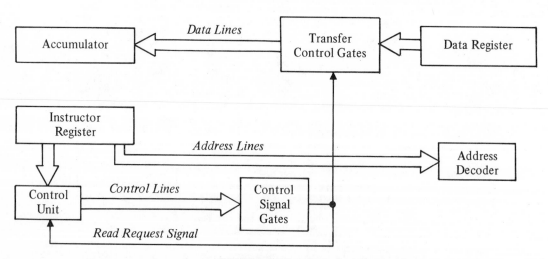

FIGURE 4-7-3. *Data input operation.*

contents of the data register of the addressed device on the data lines. The CPU then strobes the bits on the data lines into the accumulator. This strobe signal is either generated internally by the control unit in response to a specific bit in the instruction register or sent to the CPU by the device controller in the form of a read request signal.

4.8 Operation Synchronization

Since the CPU and the devices operate at different rates, their operations must be carefully synchronized during data transfers. With the programmed data transfer protocol, this is done by the CPU sensing the status of the device before initiating a data transfer operation. With the program-interrupt data transfer protocol, the device controller provides synchronization by means of interrupt requests.

Figure 4-8-1 shows the sense status operation performed by the CPU. The control unit in the CPU sends a control pulse and an address to select the device controller. This control pulse, called a *sense status signal,* is passed through an AND gate controlled by the status flag flip-flop and returned back to the control unit. If the status flag flip-flop output is zero, the sense status pulse is blocked at the AND gate. Otherwise, if the status flag flip-flop output is one, indicating an idle device, the sense status pulse passes through the AND gate and increments the program counter by one as shown

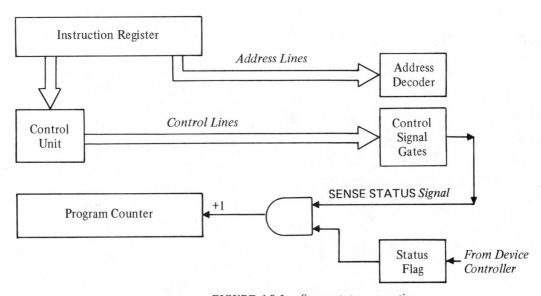

FIGURE 4-8-1. Sense status operation.

in Figure 4-8-1. The following program shows how this operation can be used to properly initiate a data transfer operation:

10   SENSE STATUS
            GO TO 10
            START DATA TRANSFER

As long as the status flag flip-flop output is zero, the instruction GO TO 10 is executed forming a loop that repeatedly senses the status of the device. Once the status flag flip-flop output becomes one, the program counter is incremented by one and the GO TO instruction is skipped. This starts the data transfer operation.

Figure 4-8-2 shows the interrupt request and acknowledgment operation. If a device requests an interrupt, the interval control unit traps the INTR signal coming from a higher priority device and generates a set interrupt signal. The clock in the CPU sends a periodic pulse to the interrupt request flip-flop. If a set interrupt signal is present from the device controller and is not masked off by the CPU, then this clock pulse sets the interrupt request flip-flop. When the CPU decides to service this interrupt, it sends an interrupt acknowledgment signal over the control lines. Upon receiving the acknowledgment signal, the address generator of the device controller allows the address of the service routine in memory to be put on the address lines.

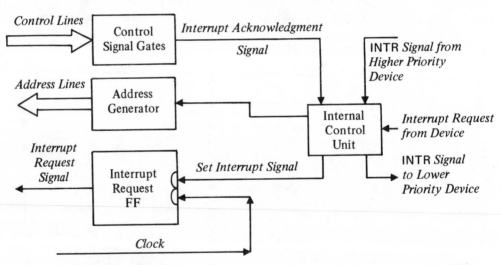

FIGURE 4-8-2.   *Interrupt request and acknowledgment operation. (SR flip-flops are commonly used.)*

4.9 Device Controllers

Three basic communications protocols are discussed in earlier sections: programmed data transfer, program-interrupt data transfer, and direct memory access data transfer. The following sections discuss the functional design

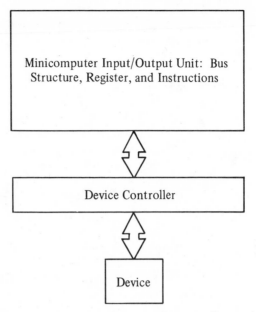

FIGURE 4-9-1. *The role of the device controller in the input/output interface.*

of the *input/output interfaces* which utilize these three modes of data transfer. Each minicomputer has a general-purpose input/output unit represented by its input/output bus structure, associated registers, and instructions. Each peripheral device has its own unique input/output requirements; the responsibility of matching these requirements to those of the input/output unit of the minicomputer lies with the device controller. This role of the device controller is depicted in Figure 4-9-1.

4.9.1 Functional Organization of a Device Controller

Device controllers that use either the programmed data transfer protocol or the program-interrupt data transfer protocol are very similar in their internal organization. The functional organization of such a controller is shown in Figure 4-9-2. The heart of the system is a *device control and timing unit* whose major function is to control the operations of a device according to commands from the CPU. The detailed design of this unit depends on the characteristics of the device being controlled. Functionally a device can be thought of as a finite state machine which transits from one specific state to another as it carries out its task. The device control unit guides the device in these state transitions and provides timing pulses for synchronization.

The device control unit also maintains the device's position in a daisy chain, i.e., it receives the INTR signal and traps it if an interrupt request has to be made. It also receives the interrupt acknowledgment signal from the CPU and resets its interrupt request flip-flop. The status of the device is stored in this unit and transmitted to the CPU upon request. Commands to the device from the CPU are decoded by the *command decoder* and transmitted to the device control unit.

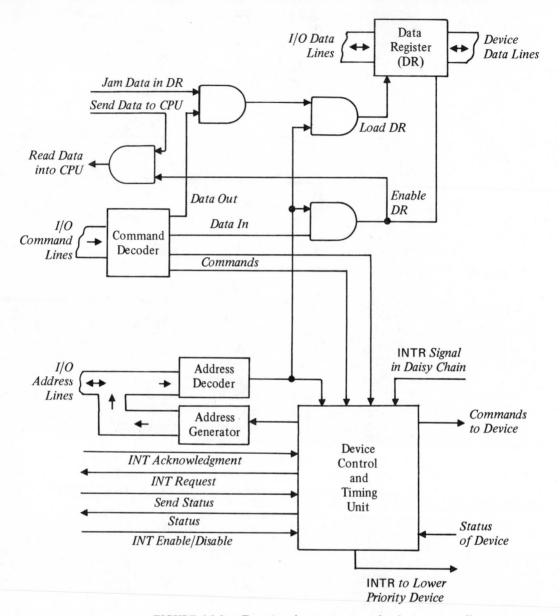

FIGURE 4-9-2. *Functional organization of a device controller.*

The *address decoder* decodes the device address on the input/output address lines and alerts the device control unit when it is addressed by the CPU. The *address generator* is used to transmit the address of the device, whenever the device needs to identify itself.

To transfer data out of the CPU and into the *data register (DR),* the CPU first sends a data-out command. Subsequently, a *jam data in DR* signal is sent by the CPU, which loads the DR from the input/output data lines. To transfer data into the CPU from the DR, the CPU sends a data-in command which enables the DR. Subsequently it transmits a *send data to CPU* signal which is transmitted back to the CPU as a *read data into CPU* signal by the device controller.

4.10 Functional Organization of a DMA Controller

The functional organization of a device controller that uses the DMA data transfer protocol is shown in Figure 4-10-1. At the start of a block transfer, the current address counter and the word counter are initialized by the program. The DMA controller maintains overall control of the device, sends cycle-steal requests to the CPU, interrupts upon termination of the block transfer, and maintains the designated position of the device on the priority chain.

An address decoder and generator is used to identify the device during DMA initialization and termination of block transfer. Data registers are used for the same purpose as in non-DMA device controllers. When a DMA controller is ready to transfer data it sends a cycle-steal request to the CPU. The cycle-steal acknowledgment signal from the CPU causes the DMA controller to enable the current address register whose contents are strobed into the CPU over the memory address bus. The resetting of this signal by the CPU causes the DMA controller to increment the current address register and decrement the word counter by one. The DMA controller then activates the control line which informs the CPU of the direction of data transfer. All these actions are carried out during one slightly lengthened instruction cycle when the CPU is executing some instruction.

At the end of this instruction cycle, the CPU is appropriately initialized to carry out a DMA transfer. It suspends execution of the next instruction and carries out a data transfer operation using the MAR and MDR registers. This data transfer operation is executed in one cycle whereupon the CPU resumes execution of the suspended program.

When the contents of the word counter reaches zero, the block transfer is terminated and the DMA controller requests a program interrupt. Upon acceptance of the interrupt, the CPU is vectored through a dedicated memory location to the proper service routine.

In some minicomputers the DMA data lines are identical to the programmed transfer data lines. This arrangement simplifies the interconnections of peripheral devices to the input/output bus but complicates the logic requirements of the CPU. The DMA data lines can also be used to transfer the DMA memory address to the processor before the data is transferred; however, this approach increases the complexity of the synchronization circuit in the CPU. Some minicomputers allow the DMA technique to be used for special memory operations, such as increment an addressed memory location or add data from the device to data stored in the memory. The increment-memory feature is used for pulse height analysis,

101

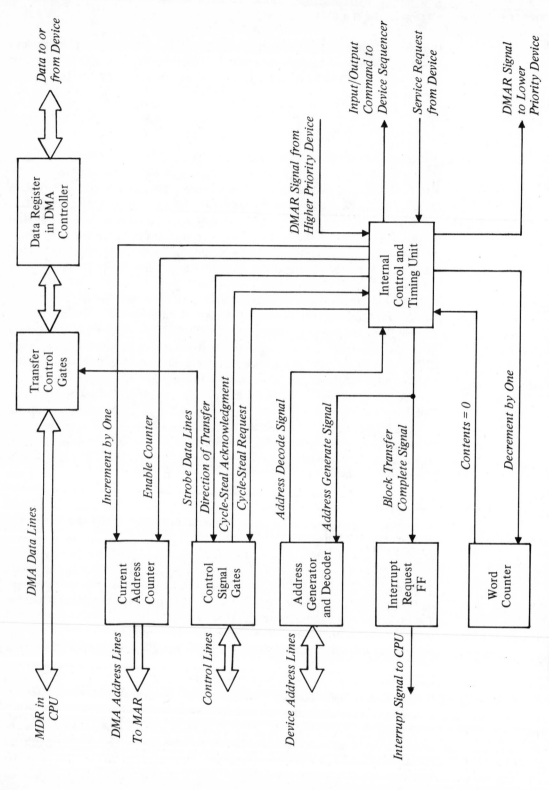

FIGURE 4-10-1. Functional organization of a DMA controller. (SR flip-flops are commonly used.)

i.e., amplitude distribution measurement. The add-to-memory feature is used for signal averaging.

SUMMARY

The hardware input/output interface of a minicomputer is described by its input/output bus. Logically the input/output bus consists of data lines, control lines, device address lines, command lines, and interrupt lines. In practice some of these lines are shared and time-multiplexed among various signals. The major input/output protocols are: programmed data transfer, program-interrupt data transfer, and direct memory access. The programmed data transfer is the simplest scheme in which the CPU is in complete command of the data transfer process. The device controller acts as a slave of the CPU and executes commands transmitted to it by the CPU. The main problem of this approach is that the CPU wastes time waiting for the device controller to finish its chore.

In the program-interrupt data transfer scheme, the CPU, after initiating a data transfer operation, continues with the execution of other tasks. The device controller, after finishing the assigned input/output operation, interrupts the CPU for service. The CPU then saves the register contents of the current program, executes a service routine, restores the register contents, and proceeds to execute the interrupted program. This saving and restoring of register contents is called interrupt overhead. In case of multiple interrupts, the CPU uses some form of priority scheme to select the device to be serviced. A commonly used method of priority assignment to the device controllers is the daisy chain. In the vectored interrupt system, every interrupting controller indirectly specifies the starting address of its service routine. The CPU can selectively or globally disable or enable interrupt systems.

The interrupt overhead becomes excessive when large blocks of data are transferred in or out of the primary memory. This overhead is eliminated by using the direct memory access technique for block transfers. The CPU initiates a block transfer by transmitting the starting address in memory and the number of words of a block to the device controller. From that point on, the device controller transfers data with the memory by using the MAR and the MDR and by stealing instruction cycles from the CPU. The CPU does not go through the save and restore operations during such cycle steals. The block transfer is terminated by the device controller using a conventional interrupt.

Device controllers are designed to interface individual devices to the common input/output bus of a minicomputer. The heart of such a controller is a control and timing unit which controls the operations of a specific device. Device controllers also incorporate data registers, command and address decoders, and interrupt daisy chain interfaces to be able to interface with the input/output bus.

PROBLEMS

1. List and explain the purpose of the different transmission lines that constitute an input/output bus.

2. What are the commonly used communication protocols with the input/output devices?

3. Discuss the differences between programmed data transfer and program-interrupt data transfer.

4. Show the execution sequence of a CPU using the interrupt mode of data transfer.

5. What is the difference between interrupt polling and vectored interrupt?

6. Explain the operations of a daisy chain.

7. Explain the technique of direct memory access. Why is it better suited for transferring blocks of data than the interrupt protocol?

8. Describe some input/output instruction formats and explain the use of their constituent fields.

9. How are data transfers synchronized in the programmed data transfer mode?

10. Explain the synchronization operations in the interrupt mode.

11. Show the flowcharts of input/output programs using the three different protocols of data transfer.

12. Explain the use of address and command decoders in a device controller.

13. Explain the use of mask flip-flops in the interrupt mode. List some conditions under which the interrupt system should be disabled.

14. Why is the building of special-purpose hardware interfaces a popular approach for minicomputer users? What are some of the problems involved? Name one minicomputer manufacturer that encourages the user to perform the interfacing task.

15. Why does the minicomputer designer design a general-purpose I/O interface?

16. Why must the end of a bus line be terminated in a characteristic impedance? What is required if the bus line is bidirectional?

17. What is a bus line driver? A bus line receiver? What properties would an ideal bus driver and receiver have? How does the deviation from "ideal" affect the length of a bus line?

18. What is the function of a device controller? What are the two functional interfaces of a controller, and what role do they play?

19. Why is the programmed I/O device controller the simplest computer interface to design? What are its basic functional components? Describe their functional operation.

20. What kind of information does the busy flag provide? Is it sufficient for all controllers?

21. Describe the state transitions of the generalized programmed I/O controller.

22. Why is the programmed I/O controller limited in its usefulness? How is this limitation corrected?

23. Describe the program interrupt sequence as viewed by the interrupt I/O controller. What three conditions must be present before an interrupt request is posted?

24. What additional functional components are necessary to convert the programmed I/O controller into the interrupt I/O controller? Describe their functional operation.

25. Using operational language, describe the functional operation of the interrupt I/O controller for the data input operation.

26. Describe the three phases of a DMA operation. What additional functional components are necessary to convert the interrupt I/O controller into a DMA controller? Describe their functional operation.

27. Describe the DMA operation sequence as viewed by the DMA controller.

28. The DMA controller has two status flags, DMA ready and busy. Describe their function.

29. How do the major time states of a DMA controller differ for the input and output modes?

30. What two important functions are performed by the peripheral interface? Why is it difficult to generalize the peripheral interface?

31. Describe the functional components added to the interrupt I/O controller to form the generalized peripheral interface. Can you think of any other components that might be added?

32. Using marks and spaces, draw a representation of the teletype character "A" (41_{16}) as it is sent over the serial transmission line. If the character is sent from the teletype to the controller, describe the operation of the controller.

33. Why is the transmission of a character between the controller and the teletype called asynchronous? What makes the transmission asynchronous? What would change if the transmission were synchronous?

34. Why is the teletype-controller interface called a current loop interface? What are some advantages of the current loop interface? How does it differ from the EIA interface?

35. Describe the functional operation of the card reader. What are some problems peculiar to its operation?

36. Describe the functional components of a card reader controller. How does it differ from the teletype controller?

37. Describe the four subcycles that form a print cycle. Does the printer automatically move from one subcycle to the next? What would happen if the print command signal goes false before the line buffer is filled?

38. Compare the card reader controller with the line printer controller. How do they differ?

39. Describe the functional operation of the line printer controller. Could you design a control sequencer with more or fewer states?

40. What is the function of the tape buffer-storage system? What two methods are used to create the buffer system?

41. Why does the magnetic head system consist of separate read and write heads? Describe the difference between the NRZI and RZ techniques of digital recording.

42. Why is the tape guide system important?

43. What is dynamic skew? Static skew? How do they differ? How is static skew corrected?

44. What is vertical parity? Horizontal parity? What kind of errors do they identify?

45. The IBG produced by the magnetic tape unit is 0.6 inch. How is it created? Is it a constant displacement? How does the controller identify the IBG? What functional component of the controller is responsible for the IBG?

46. Describe the functional components of the magnetic tape controller.

47. What is the cyclic redundancy check character? How does it differ from the parity check?

48. Describe the operation of the magnetic tape controller for the read operation. For the write operation.

49. What are the two basic types of disk systems? How do they differ?

50. How are data addressed on the surface of a disk? What is the smallest amount of data that may be retrieved in a single access?

51. How are data recorded on a disk surface? What type of transfer method is used between the controller and disk unit? Does the density at which data bits are stored vary between tracks? Why are more data bits not stored on the outer tracks?

52. What method is used to ensure synchronization between the controller and disk unit during a data transfer? How does the disk recording technique differ from that used with a magnetic tape?

53. Describe the increment memory DMA operation using the operational language.

54. Describe an add to memory DMA operation using the operational language.

55. What effect does a mismatch in word size of an external device and the I/O unit have on performance?

56. What disadvantage does a program I/O have when compared to a priority interrupt I/O?

57. Why is it necessary for the interrupt system to interrupt the CPU at the end of the current instruction? Why not at the end of the instruction fetch sequence? Or the decode sequence?

58. Is it possible to incorporate a DMA channel without the use of an interrupt mechanism? Explain.

59. How would it be possible to implement chaining of block transfers using a DMA channel in a minicomputer system?

60. What are the roles of the word count register and memory address counter in a DMA? Are they necessary?

106

61. Design a sequencer for the execution of an external I/O instruction. Assume a synchronous minicomputer? Asynchronous minicomputer?

62. Compare the control logic for programmed I/O transfers and DMA transfers.

63. What control sequences initiate and terminate operations with external I/O devices?

64. In view of the "lost" time by the CPU controlling programmed I/O transfers, why would one ever implement such a system?

65. What do you consider the main advantages and disadvantages are of the different I/O channel controls discussed?

66. What are the relative advantages and disadvantages of the different cycle-stealing input/output organizations?

67. When is it necessary for the I/O control registers to be cleared during an input(output) operation?

68. What are essential advantages of a DMA or multiplexer channel in comparison to program data transfer channels?

69. What are the primary functions of an interrupt procedure? Are they limited to I/O requests?

70. Describe the sequence of operations required by the execution of a computer interrupt.

71. How does the power fail/restart interrupt request differ from those of external I/O devices? Is the interrupt handling sequence the same?

72. What information is received by either the CPU or the external device when the program responds too late to an external request? Is there any difference between an input or output operation?

73. How are interrupts handled while the interrupt system is processing an interrupt? Is there any difference in this procedure if the requesting interrupt happens to be a power fail/restart?

PROJECTS

1. Given: **a)** 16-bit minicomputer
   b) Up to 32 I/O devices
   c) Various I/O schemes (designer's choice)
   Discuss the following in detail as they pertain to providing complete and flexible input/output operations:
   a) Design considerations
   b) Hardware - software tradeoffs
   c) Advantages - disadvantages
   d) Capabilities - limitations

2. Discuss in some detail the uses and capabilities of:
   a) UART & USART
   b) RS-232-C interface
   c) EIA 20 mA loop interface
   d) IEEE 488 or similar interface

5

Assembly Language Programming

5.1 Introduction

A minicomputer can be functionally described by its architecture, instruction set, and input/output interfaces. To be useful, a minicomputer must be programmed to process information. A program is a sequence of instructions executed by the processing unit. If the instructions in a program are selected from the instruction set of a specific minicomputer and described in a binary coded format, the program is said to be written in the *machine language* of that particular minicomputer. Such programs are often called machine language programs or *object programs*. Most computers can directly execute only object programs written in their own machine languages, and programs for a minicomputer must ultimately be executed from this machine language.

Most popular minicomputers use a single-address machine language instruction format, where the format specifies the operation code (opcode) of the instruction, the address of one of the operands, and an addressing mode (Figure 5-1-1). Furthermore, most commonly used instructions are stored in single memory words. Therefore, to write an object program, a programmer

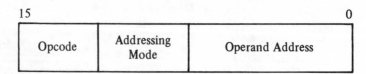

FIGURE 5-1-1. *Single-address instruction format for machine language instructions of most minicomputers.*

108

only has to specify a sequence of opcodes and operand addresses in binary coded formats following a given machine language instruction format. In practice, however, such machine language implementations of programs are difficult to achieve.

Writing of programs in a machine language is an awkward, tedious, time-consuming, and error-prone process. Since the programmer must directly specify the addresses of operands, the exact memory locations (also called *absolute addresses*) must be selected during the process of writing such a program. If a branch instruction is used in a machine language program, the programmer must also specify the address of the instruction to be executed following a successful branch. The implication is that the programmer must select the exact memory location for storing the instructions of the program. As a result, the programmer is directly responsible for carrying out the rather tedious task of keeping track of memory usage. With a large number of object programs, addressing errors in machine language instructions are almost inevitable and result in serious conflicts among programs and their memory usage. Furthermore, the specification of absolute addresses for instructions and operands constrain an object program to reside in a fixed memory region, permanently assigned, during the creation of the program.

Direct coding in a machine language makes it difficult to modify a program. Insertion and deletion of instructions into an existing program may require extensive changes in the addressing information when absolute addresses are specified in the program. Machine language programmers must also be familiar with the binary representation for opcodes and addressing modes, represent all constants and characters that are used in a program in binary codes, and think logically in terms of addresses of operands and not symbolic variables.

Obviously, efficient and error-free programming can be enhanced by using programming languages which are not as restrictive as machine languages. The next higher level of programming languages consists of *assembly languages* which free programmers from many of the clerical chores required by machine languages. Every assembly language is based on an underlying machine language and most instructions in an assembly language have one-to-one relationships with corresponding instructions in the machine language. Formats of assembly language instructions also closely resemble the formats of corresponding machine language instructions. Hence, an assembly language can be thought of as an easier-to-use symbolic version of the underlying machine language. Assembly language instructions provide the programmer with the same direct control over the hardware as provided for by the machine language instructions, yet free the programmer from many of the constraints of the latter. An assembly language program is translated into its corresponding machine language by a system program called an *assembler*. Characteristics of assemblers are discussed in the next chapter.

In every assembly language, the binary representations for instruction opcodes are replaced by *mnemonic codes* to assist the programmer in

109

remembering them. However, the most important feature of an assembly language is the *symbolic addressing* of operands and instructions. Operands are no longer specified by their absolute addresses in memory but by symbolic names. Instructions used by destinations of successful branch instructions are identified by symbolic labels. The addresses required by an object program are at least partially generated by the assembler during the process of translation. The programmer no longer needs to keep track of the memory usage of each program. Each program can be written with the assumption that it will be stored in memory starting at address zero. If such is not the case, then a system program, called a *loader*, modifies all addresses appropriately when the program is stored in the primary memory. Characteristics of loaders are also discussed in the next chapter.

The format of a typical assembly language instruction, shown in Figure 5-1-2, has four fields:

1. Labels of instructions
2. Mnemonic opcodes of instructions
3. Symbolic operands
4. Explanatory comments

Each field is separated from its neighbor by a delimiter such as one or more blank spaces. The mnemonic opcodes specify either machine language instructions, such as memory reference, register reference, input/output; or *pseudo instructions* used by the assembler to carry out the translation.

The following sections contain examples of assembly language programs for a hypothetical minicomputer. The assembly language instruction set of the hypothetical machine is kept close to those of the most popular minicomputers, so that the examples can serve as guides to the assembly language programs for specific systems. Most popular minicomputers can be approximately classified into two groups. The machines in the first group provide very few addressing modes, e.g., zero/current page mode and indirect addressing. Most of the bits in the instructions are used to directly address a reasonably large (1K) region of primary memory. Such machines provide a variety of memory reference instructions and few addressable registers in the processor. Each machine language instruction carries out

Field 0	Field 1	Field 2	Field 3
Label	Mnemonic Opcode	Symbolic Operand	Explanatory Comments

FIGURE 5-1-2. *Format of assembly language instructions.*
FIELD 0:   Labels of instructions
FIELD 1:   Mnemonic opcodes of instructions
FIELD 2:   Symbolic operands and addressing mode specifications
FIELD 3:   Explanatory comments

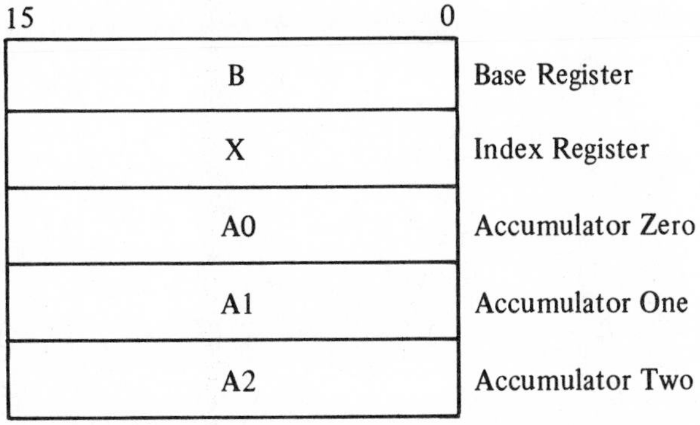

15   0

B	Base Register
X	Index Register
A0	Accumulator Zero
A1	Accumulator One
A2	Accumulator Two

FIGURE 5-1-3. Addressable registers in the processing unit of the hypothetical minicomputer.

only a few operations, frequently only one. For this reason, it is not very difficult to write assembly language programs for these machines although the programs tend to incorporate a lot of instructions. The machines in the second group use more bits to specify a variety of addressing modes and opcodes and fewer bits to directly address smaller regions (256 words) of primary memory. Such machines have a few basic memory reference instructions but more addressable registers in the processor and register-to-register instructions. Also, each instruction can carry out several complex operations. As a consequence, even though it is relatively difficult to write instructions for assembly language programs, a fewer number of instructions are required by an assembly language program to carry out the same task when compared to programs written for the first type of machines.

The hypothetical minicomputer falls somewhere in between these two groups. The processing unit has five addressable registers: B (Base) register; X (index) register; and A0, A1, and A2 (accumulators zero, one, and two). All of these registers are 16 bits wide (Figure 5-1-3) and can be directly addressed by appropriate assembly language instructions. The B-register is used for base/displacement addressing while the X-register is used for indexed addressing.

5.2 Memory Reference Instructions in Assembly Language

The hypothetical computer has five basic memory reference instructions whose mnemonic opcodes and corresponding operations are given in Table 5-2-1. The LDA and STA instructions can be applied to any one of five addressable registers (B, X, A0, A1, and A2). The formats of these assembly language instructions are shown in Figure 5-2-1. For LDA and STA, the symbol R in the operand field represents the addressable register involved in the operation. The presence of the letter I indicates indirect addressing; I is omitted for direct addressing.

111

Label	Opcode	Operand
X	LDA	R, I, SAO, AM
X	STA	R, I, SAO, AM
X	ISZ/DSZ	I, SAO, AM
X	JMP	I, SAO, AM
X	JSB	I, SAO, AM

FIGURE 5-2-1. Assembly language format of memory reference instructions.

> *X:* Optional
> *R:* Addressable register in processor
> *I:* Indirect address
> *SAO:* Symbolic address of operand
> *AM:* Addressing mode

In Figure 5-2-1, SAO represents the symbolic address of an operand used in the assembly language instruction. When the object program is loaded into the primary memory, SAO is replaced by a numeric quantity supplied by the assembler. AM describes the addressing mode used, a list of which is given in Table 5-2-2. The reader is also reminded that Section 3.4 describes the various addressing modes in detail. When indirection is used with indexed addressing, we assume that it is used in the preindexing mode, i.e., the indexed address is computed and used as an indirect address.

The instructions listed in Table 5-2-1 are about the minimum included in most minicomputer assembly languages. Those minicomputers that make extensive use of memory reference instructions may provide additional instructions, such as those listed in Table 5-2-3. However, these machines normally do not provide all of the addressing modes given in Table 5-2-2 and only a few addressable registers such as A0 and A1.

EXAMPLES:

1. STA   A0, I, POINTER, 0
   In this case the symbolic address of the operand (SAO) is called POINTER. Since AM = 0, this involves page zero addressing and EA equals the unsigned integer value of POINTER specified by the assembler. Since I is present, the contents of the memory location EA on page zero used as the final address in memory where the contents of A0 are stored.

2. LDA   A1, ARRAYBASE, 3
   Since AM = 3, we have EA = [X] + ARRAYBASE where the value of ARRAYBASE is an address in memory containing the first element of an array. Since I is absent in this case, EA is the effective address of the memory location containing the operand. The contents of the memory location EA are loaded into A1.

3. ISZ   COUNTER, 0
   COUNTER is the symbolic address of a memory location on page zero whose contents are incremented by one. If the new value at COUNTER is zero, the next instruction is skipped.

112

*TABLE 5–2–1. **Memory Reference Instructions***

Mnemonic Opcode	Operation
LDA	Load addressed register from memory.
STA	Store contents of addressed register in memory.
ISZ/DSZ	Increment/decrement the contents of a specified memory location by one. If new contents are zero, skip next instruction.
JMP	Load effective address in program counter (PC).
JSB	Transfer (PC) to A0 and load PC with address of subroutine.

*TABLE 5–2–2. **Addressing Modes***

AM	Addressing Mode
0	Page zero address; the value of SAO is treated as an unsigned integer and AM = 0.
1	Program relative address; AM = [PC] and the value of SAO is treated as a signed integer.
2	Base/displacement address; AM = [B] and the value of SAO is treated as a positive integer.
3	Indexed address; AM = [X] and the value of SAO is treated as a signed integer.

*TABLE 5–2–3. **Possible Additional Memory Reference Instructions***

Mnemonic Opcode	Operation
AND	Contents of addressed register is logically ANDed with the operand and the result stored in the register.
IOR	Contents of addressed register is logically ORed with the operand and the result stored in the register.
XOR	Contents of addressed register is exclusive -ORed with the operand and the result stored in the register.
ADD	Contents of addressed register is added to the operand and the result stored in the register.
CPA	Contents of addressed register is compared with operand. If they are not identical, the next instruction is skipped.

113

4. JMP   LOOP, 2

We have AM = 2 which implies base/displacement addressing. The value of LOOP is treated as a positive integer (displacement) and EA = [B] + LOOP. This effective address is transferred into the program counter.

5. JSB   I, SUB, 0

The symbolic address SUB represents the indirect address of the first instruction of a subroutine. The value of SUB is the address of a memory word on page zero, which contains the address of the first instruction of the subroutine. This address is loaded into the program counter after the contents of the program counter has been transferred to A0. Thus, A0 contains the return address that the subroutine must save in memory before starting other operations.

5.3 Register Reference Instructions in Assembly Language

The register reference instructions are used to manipulate and operate on the contents of the addressable registers in the processor. Since the hypothetical minicomputer has only five basic memory reference instructions given in Table 5-2-1, we need register reference instructions to perform arithmetic and logic operations on the operands stored in the registers. The general format of such an assembly language instruction is shown in Figure 5-3-1. SR and DR in the operand field are the symbolic addresses of the source and the destination registers, respectively, that are involved in the operation. For binary operations, the operands are obtained from the source and the destination registers and the result is stored in the destination register whose original contents are thereby lost. For unary operations, the source and the destination registers are identical. The set of arithmetic and logic instructions of the hypothetical minicomputer is shown in Table 5-3-1. Note that Table 5-3-1 contains more instructions than are strictly needed to carry out all the operations listed. For example, with OCM and AND we can logically generate IOR and EOR by using results from Boolean algebra. Similarly TCM can be obtained by combining OCM and INC; SUB can be generated by using TCM and ADD. However, in order to reduce programming effort all these

TABLE 5–3–1.   Arithmetic and Logic Instructions

Mnemonic Opcode	Operation
OCM	Ones complement of SR stored in DR.
TCM	Twos complement of SR stored in DR.
MOV	Contents of SR moved to DR.
INC	[SR] + 1 stored in DR.
ADD	[DR] + [SR] stored in DR.
SUB	[DR] − [SR] stored in DR.
AND	[DR] AND [SR] stored in DR.
IOR	[DR] OR [SR] stored in DR.
EOR	[DR] exclusive OR [SR] stored in DR.

114

Label	Mnemonic Opcode	SR	DR

FIGURE 5-3-1. *Format of a register reference instruction in assembly language.*
SR: Source register
DR: Destination register

instructions are assumed to be explicitly available in the hypothetical assembly language.

Recall that in Chapter 3, the concept of a link bit or carry bit was introduced in connection with the shift operations. A link bit is an extra bit which can be used to link two registers during shift operations. If a carry occurs out of the highest order bits of a parallel adder during binary addition, the value of the link bit is *complemented*. If the link bit is initially set to zero, then after a binary addition, the value of the link bit indicates whether or not a carry overflow has occurred. For this reason, it is often called a *carry bit*. The initial value of the link or carry bit can be set by appending the mnemonic opcodes given in Table 5-3-1 with special characters. These characters and the resulting values of the carry bit are listed in Table 5-3-2.

For example:

SUB   A1, A1

sets the contents of A1 to zero, but the value of the carry bit is unknown. If the carry bit was zero before SUB is executed, it becomes one after execution. On the other hand, if the initial value of the carry bit was one, then its final value becomes zero. However:

SUB0   A1, A1

sets the initial value of the carry bit to one and thus guarantees that its final value is zero. Similarly, after the execution of:

SUBC   A1, A1

the contents of A1 are zero but the carry bit retains its original value. The value of the carry bit is complemented by ADD, SUB, TCM, and INC under the conditions given in Table 5-3-3.

TABLE 5–3–2.   *Setting of the Link or Carry Bit*

Character	*Value of carry bit*
– (null)	Carry bit is not initialized.
Z	Carry bit is initialized to zero.
0	Carry bit is initialized to one.
C	Carry bit is complemented.

115

TABLE 5–3–3.   Complementation of Carry Bits

Operation	Condition
ADD	$[DR] + [SR] > 2^{16} - 1$
SUB	$[DR] \geq SR$
TCM	$[SR] = 0$
INC	$[SR] = 2^{16} - 1$

Beyond the nine arithmetic and logic instructions listed in Table 5-3-4 we need shift, rotate, and skip instructions for effective programming. A list of shift and rotate instructions is given in Table 5-3-4 although not all of these instructions are available on every minicomputer.

Internal to the processing unit, shifters and the arithmetic and logic unit (ALU) can be connected in at least three possible manners (Figure 5-3-2). Minicomputers normally do not use preshifters for reasons of economy. An independent shifter requires an extra move data operation if the result of the ALU needs to be shifted. Hence, most minicomputers use a postshifter, and combine the shift and the rotate operations with the arithmetic or logic operations.

The rotate operations in Table 5-3-1 can be carried out with the carry bit included in the process (Figure 5-3-3). In such cases, the opcodes ROL and R̄OR are appended with the letter C̄. Finally, if ROL or ROR is appended with the digit 4, the rotation operations are carried out four times. The skip instructions in the hypothetical assembly language are listed in Table 5-3-5.

Individual instructions from Tables 5-3-1, 5-3-3, 5-3-4, and 5-3-5 can be combined into a single compound instruction whenever the individual opcodes are separated by commas. For example:

ADD0, SZC   A0, A1

initializes carry bit to zero, adds A0 and A1, and stores the sum in A1; and then skips the next instruction if the new value of the carry bit is still zero.

TABLE 5–3–4.   Shift and Rotate Instructions

Mnemonic Opcode	Operation
SLA	Shift content of register left by one bit, zero the least significant bit. Sign bit unchanged.
SRA	Shift content of register right by one bit, copy sign bit into most significant bit. Sign bit unchanged.
ROL	Rotate register contents left by one bit.
ROR	Rotate register contents right by one bit.
SLL	As in SLA except that the sign bit is cleared.
SWP	The higher and lower order bytes of a register are swapped (exchanged) with each other.

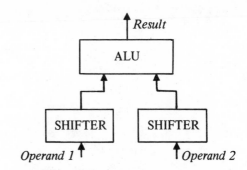

FIGURE 5-3-2a. *Preshifters with ALU.*

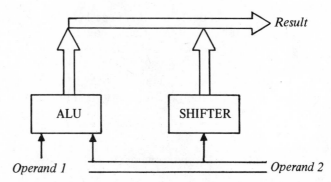

FIGURE 5-3-2b. *Independent shifter with ALU.*

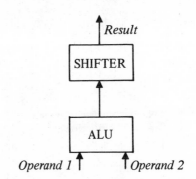

FIGURE 5-3-2c. *Postshifter with ALU.*

Similarly:

SUBZ, ROLC   A2, A2

sets the contents of A2 to +1 and:

SUB0   A1, A1

INCZ, ROLC   A1, A1

sets the contents of A1 to +2.

117

TABLE 5–3–5.   Skip Instructions

Mnemonic Opcode	Operation
SZC	Skip next instruction if carry bit is zero.
SZA	Skip next instruction if register contents equal zero.
SPA	Skip next instruction if register content is positive.
SEA	Skip next instruction if register contains an even number, i.e., least significant bit is zero.

On occasion, it is necessary to skip the next instruction on the basis of a temporary result computed by means of register reference instructions without storing the immediate result in an accumulator. In some minicomputers, a load/no-load feature is provided for this purpose. In this case it is assumed that if a compound register reference instruction ends with an **NL** (no-load), then the temporary result is discarded after use. For example:

ADD0, SZC, NL   A0, A1

acts exactly the same as:

ADD0, SZC   A0, A1

except that in the former case the sum is not stored in A1.

EXAMPLES

1. SUB   A1, A1
   OCM   A1, A1

   The first instruction clears A1; the value of the carry bit is unknown. The second instruction sets every bit of A1 to 1 including the sign bit and hence in the twos complement number system A1 = 1.

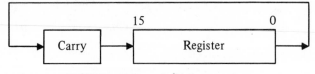

FIGURE 5-3-3a.   RORC operation.

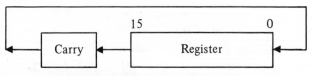

FIGURE 5-3-3b.   ROLC operation.

2.   TCM   A2, A2
     OCM   A2, A2

The instruction TCM stores the twos complement of A2 in A2 and OCM computes the ones complement of this twos complement of A2. The twos complement of a number is obtained by adding a one to its ones complement, i.e., a ones complement is one short of the twos complement. Hence, the final contents of A2 are one short of its original contents. In other words, the two instructions in sequence subtracts one from the contents of A2 without using a constant from the memory.

3.   MOV   A1, A2
     SWP   A2, A2
     SUB, SZA, NL A1, A2

The first instruction copies A1 into A2 and the second instruction swaps the two bytes of A2 with each other. The last instruction computes [A2] − [A1] and if both the bytes of A1 are identical, then this difference is zero. The SZA code of the compound instruction causes a skip of the next instruction if this difference is zero. Note that the temporary result [A2] − [A1] is not stored in A2 because of the presence of NL.

5.4 Input/Output Instructions in Assembly Language

In the hypothetical minicomputer, it is assumed that each device controller has a mask register (or flip-flop) and a flag register. When the device controller is busy, it sets the flag register and, when idle, resets it. The resetting of the flag register transmits an interrupt request signal to the processor if the interrupt circuit of the device controller has been enabled. The disabling and enabling of the interrupt request circuitry of a device controller is performed by the processor by means of the mask register. If the mask register is set, the interrupt circuit is enabled; otherwise it is disabled. Each device controller also has a 16-bit buffer register which is used during the data transfer operation.

The format of the assembly language instructions for the control and the sense operations is shown in Figure 5-4-1. The operand field contains the address of the device controller involved in the operation. Table 5-4-1 lists the opcodes and their corresponding operations.

The format of the data transfer instructions in the assembly language is shown in Figure 5-4-2. The operand field, in addition to specifying the address of the device controller, also identifies the source or destination register involved in the transfer operation. All device controllers participat-

Label	Mnemonic Opcode	Device Controller Address

FIGURE 5-4-1.   *Format of assembly language instructions for control and sense operations.*

119

Label	Mnemonic Opcode	Source or Destination Register	Device Controller Address

FIGURE 5-4-2. *Format of data transfer instructions.*

ing in input/output operations are of course specified by symbolic names and not by absolute addresses. Table 5-4-2 lists the mnemonic opcodes of the two data transfer instructions.

As with the register reference instructions, the instructions in Tables 5-4-1 and 5-4-2 can be combined to form compound input/output instructions. In such compound instructions, mnemonic opcodes are separated by commas.

TABLE 5–4–1. *Control and Sense Instructions*

Mnemonic Opcode	Operation
ENI	Enable interrupt circuitry of the addressed device.
DSI	Disable interrupt circuitry of the addressed device.
STF	Set the flag register of the addressed device.
CLF	Clear the flag register of the addressed device.
SFS	Skip next instruction if flag register is set.
SFC	Skip next instruction if flag register is clear.

TABLE 5–4–2. *Data Transfer Instructions*

Mnemonic Opcode	Operation
INP	Transfer data from device buffer to destination register.
OUT	Transfer data from source register to device buffer.

EXAMPLES

1. CLF, DSI   PRINTER
   The CLF instruction resets the flag register of the device identified by the symbolic address PRINTER and the DSI instruction disables its interrupt request circuit. The printer is, in effect, shut down; the power supply to the printer may still be on.

2.
```
        DSI    PRINTER
TEST    SRC    PRINTER
        JMP    TEST
        OUT    A2, PRINTER
```

120

The interrupt circuitry of the printer is disabled by the DSI instruction and so it cannot use the program-interrupt protocol of data transfer. However, the device controller can still reset the flag register when the printer completes its current task. The processor waits for the resetting of this register while executing the TEST loop. When the flag register is reset (cleared), the processor transfers two characters from A2 to the printer's buffer.

3.

```
        DSI, STF    TTY
WAIT    SFS         TTY
        JMP         WAIT
        INP         A1, TTY
```

The STF instruction sets the flag register of a teletype unit (symbolic address TTY) and starts a data input operation. The processor waits while testing the flag register of the TTY. When data is ready in the device, the device controller clears the flag register. The processor then transfers the data from the TTY buffer to A1 by executing the INP instruction.

5.5 Illustrative Assembly Language Programs

This section contains examples of sample programs using arithmetic computation, byte manipulation, and input/output operations in the hypothetical assembly language. In minicomputers, multiplication and division are often performed by programs and so the multiplication of two unsigned binary numbers is chosen as one of the examples. Byte manipulation forms the basis of character processing while input/output operations are of obvious importance.

5.5.1 Binary Multiplication

In the process of multiplication the multiplicand (an unsigned binary number) is multiplied by each bit of the multiplier (another unsigned binary number) to generate a set of partial products. Each partial product is shifted one bit to the left with respect to its immediate predecessor (multiplication by a power of 2), and finally all the partial products are added together. In practice it is simpler to add each partial product, after it has been shifted, to form a cumulative sum, which at the end becomes the final product. This process of binary multiplication is shown by means of an example in Figure 5-5-1. The multiplicand and the multiplier each consists of 5 bits with the product having 10 bits. The binary product of two n-bit numbers always results in a number with at most $2n$ bits.

A possible scheme for carrying out the binary multiplication in a computer is shown in Figure 5-5-2. At the start (Figure 5-5-2a) register R0 contains the multiplicand, R1 contains the multiplier, while the contents of R2 and the carry bit are zero. As long as R1 contains an even number, its

121

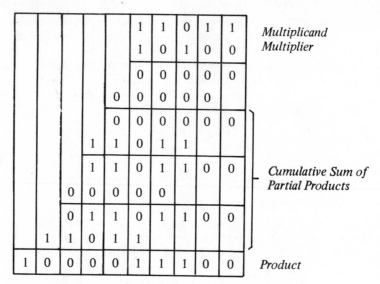

					1	1	0	1	1	Multiplicand
					1	0	1	0	0	Multiplier
					0	0	0	0	0	
				0	0	0	0	0		
				0	0	0	0	0	0	
			1	1	0	1	1			
			1	1	0	1	1	0	0	
		0	0	0	0	0				
		0	1	1	0	1	1	0	0	
	1	1	0	1	1					
1	0	0	0	0	1	1	1	0	0	Product

FIGURE 5-5-1.   Process of binary multiplication.
Multiplicand: 11011
Multiplier: 10100
Product: 1000011100

contents are rotated as shown in Figure 5-5-2*a*. When R1 contains an odd number for the first time (see Figure 5-5-2*b*), the contents of R0 are moved into R2, and the register pair [R2, R1] and the carry bit C are shifted together one bit to the right. The result is that the most significant bit of R2 is replaced by the carry bit, the least significant bit of R2 is shifted into the most significant bit of R1 and the least significant bit of R1 is lost. The resulting contents of R0, R1, and R2 are shown in Figure 5-5-2*c*.

From this point on, if R1 contains an even number, the register pair [R2, R1] and C are shifted together one bit to the right. Otherwise the carry bit is cleared, the contents of R0 and R2 are added together and the sum stored in R2, and then the register pair [R2, R1] and C are shifted together one bit to the right. The process is carried out until all the bits of the multiplier are shifted out of R1 and lost. After termination, the upper part of the product is left in R2 and the lower part in R1.

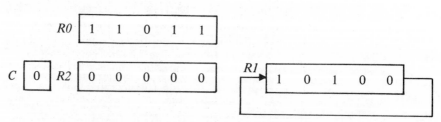

FIGURE 5-5-2a.   Rotate R1 right as long as R1 is even.

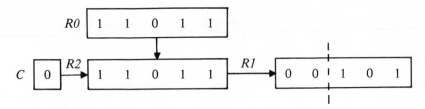

FIGURE 5-5-2b.   *Move R0 → R2 and shift C, R2, and R1 one bit to the right.*

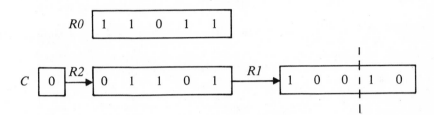

FIGURE 5-5-2c.   *Shift [R2, R1] and C one bit to the right, if R1 is even.*

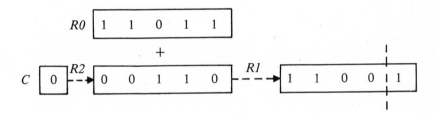

FIGURE 5-5-2d.   *[R0] + [R2] → R2, shift C, R2, and R1 one bit to the right.*

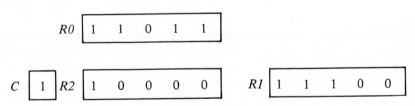

FIGURE 5-5-2e.   *Final product in R2 and R1.*

A program to carry out these operations, written in the hypothetical assembly language is shown below. It is assumed that the symbolic addresses of the multiplicand and the multiplier are MPCND and MPLR, respectively; and that the symbolic address COUNT is the indirect page zero address of a memory location containing the negative of the total number of bits in the registers (i.e., −16).

123

```
                    LDA           A0, MPCND, 2      /*LOAD MULTIPLICAND IN A0*/
                    LDA           A1, MPLR, 2       /*LOAD MULTIPLIER IN A1*/
                    SUB0          A2, A2            /*CLEAR A2 AND CARRY*/
ROTATE              MOV, ROR, SEA A1, A1            /*ROTATE A1 RIGHT AND TEST FOR EVEN VALUE*/
                    JMP           FIRSTONE          /*A1 IS ODD FOR THE FIRST TIME*/
                    ISZ           I, COUNT, 0       /*INCREMENT BIT COUNTER*/
                    JMP           ROTATE            /*A1 IS EVEN, MORE BITS TO ROTATE*/
                    JMP           DONE              /*ALL BITS ROTATED; PRODUCT ZERO; DONE*/
FIRSTONE            MOV           A0, A2            /*TRANSFER A0 TO A2; A1 ODD FOR*/
                    MOV, RORC     A2, A2            /*THE FIRST TIME, SHIFT C, A2 AND*/
                    MOV, RORC     A1, A1            /*A1 TO RIGHT BY ONE BIT*/
                    ISZ           I, COUNT, 0
                    JMP           NEXTBIT           /*MORE BITS TO PROCESS; GO TO NEXT BIT*/
                    JMP           DONE
NEXTBIT             SEA           A1, A1            /*TEST A1 FOR ODD/EVEN*/
                    JMP           ODD
                    MOVZ, RORC    A2, A2            /*A1 EVEN. CLEAR C AND SHIFT C, A2, AND*/
                    MOV, RORC     A1, A1            /*A1 TO RIGHT BY ONE BIT*/
                    JMP           LOOPCOUNT
ODD                 ADDZ          A0, A2            /*A1 ODD. STORE A0 + A2 IN A2*/
                    MOV, RORC     A2, A2
                    MOV, RORC     A1, A1
LOOPCOUNT           ISZ           I, COUNT, 0
                    JMP           NEXTBIT
DONE                —             —
```

5.5.2 Byte Manipulation

The ability to manipulate bytes of data is at the heart of all character manipulation programs. The basic operation with bytes is to fetch them from memory one at a time, and store them in a register in the processor. It is assumed that every byte contains eight bits and that every word in memory contains two bytes. A byte pointer, needed to fetch bytes from memory, is a location in memory containing the address of the next byte to be fetched. Although the operation is to fetch bytes or half-words from memory, memory can only be addressed in terms of full words. Hence, the contents of the byte pointer must be so partitioned that one part of it specifies a memory address while the other part specifies one of the two bytes at that address.

The byte addressing scheme adopted here is shown in Figure 5-5-3. Bits 0 to 7 of a memory word constitutes byte zero; byte one consists of bits 8 to 15. Bit 15 of the byte pointer selects one of these two bytes. B15 = 0 selects byte zero and B15 = 1 selects byte one. The rest of the bits in the byte pointer specify the address of the memory word containing the bytes.

Consider now a scheme for updating the byte pointer so that it will always point to the next byte to be fetched. Note that if all the bits in the byte

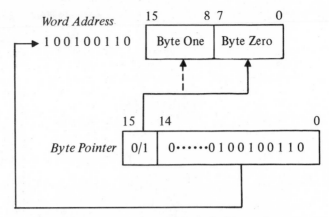

FIGURE 5-5-3. Description of a byte pointer.

pointer are ones (i.e., it has the value $2^{16} - 1$), then it points to the last possible byte that can be addressed using the scheme shown in Figure 5-5-3. In this case the following updating scheme no longer applies. Suppose the byte pointer is currently pointing to byte zero of a memory word. To make it point to byte one of the same word it need only be added to the binary number whose $B15 = 1$ and $B14 = \ldots B0 = 0$. This bit pattern can be easily generated in a register such as X by executing the following instruction:

$$\text{SUBZ, RORC} \quad \text{X, X}$$

Next assume that the byte pointer is currently pointing to byte one of a memory word. To make it point to byte zero of the next word, add to it the binary number whose $B15 = B0 = 1$ and $B14 = \ldots B1 = 0$. This bit pattern can be generated in X by following the previous instruction with:

$$\text{INC0} \quad \text{X, X}$$

which leaves a zero in the carry bit.

In the assembly language program shown below, it is assumed that BYTPNTR is the symbolic address of a memory location on page zero containing the address of the byte to be fetched. The byte fetched from memory is left in byte zero of A1. MASK is another symbolic memory location whose byte zero contains $2^8 - 1$ and byte one is zero. MASK is used to select just one byte from the two bytes which are fetched from the memory location and stored in A1.

```
LDA        A0, BYTPNTR, 0      /*PUT BYTE ADDRESS IN A0*/
SPA        A0, A0              /*TEST B15 of A0*/
JMP        BYTONE              /*BYTE ONE MUST BE FETCHED*/
LDA        A1, I, BYTPNTR, 0   /*LOAD TWO BYTES IN A1*/
LDA        A2, MASK, 2         /*LOAD MASK IN A2*/
```

125

```
              AND           A2, A1            /*BYTE ZERO LEFT IN A1*/
              SUBZ, RORC    X, X
              ADD           X, A0             /*FORM ADDRESS OF BYTE ONE OF SAME WORD*/
              STA           A0, BYTPNTR, 0    /*STORE UPDATED BYTE ADDRESS*/
              JMP           DONE
BYTONE        LDA           A1, I, BYTPNTR, 0
              SWP           A1, A1            /*BYTES ZERO & ONE ARE EXCHANGED*/
              LDA           A2, MASK, 2
              AND           A2, A1            /*BYTE ONE LEFT IN A1*/
              SUBZ, RORC    X, X
              INC0          X, X
              ADD           X, A0             /*FORM ADDRESS OF BYTE ZERO OF NEXT WORD*/
              STA           A0, BYTPNTR, 0
DONE          —             —
```

5.5.3 Master Interrupt Routine

In a simple interrupt handling system, the identity of the interrupting device is determined by polling. A program that carries out this polling operation is often called a *master interrupt routine*. Upon acknowledging an interrupt, the processor stores the contents of the program counter in a preassigned memory location, disables all interrupts and then branches to the first instruction of the master interrupt routine. This routine stores the contents of all the registers (B, X, A0, A1, and A2) in preassigned memory locations and then sequentially tests the flag registers of all the devices. The first device detected with its flag register set is then serviced and the polling resumed. After completing the polling process, the processor restores the contents of all the registers from the previously stored memory locations, enables the interrupt system, and returns to the interrupted program.

```
              STA           B, I, SAVE, 0     /*STORE [B] IN WORD POINTED TO BY SAVE*/
              ISZ           SAVE, 0           /*INCREMENT SAVE*/
              STA           X, I, SAVE, 0
              ISZ           SAVE, 0
              STA           A0, I, SAVE, 0
              ISZ           SAVE, 0
              STA           A1, I, SAVE, 0
              ISZ           SAVE, 0
              STA           AZ, I, SAVE, 0
              ISZ           SAVE, 0
              SFC           TTY               /*TEST FLAG REGISTER OF TTY*/
              JSB           I, SRVTTY, 0      /*BRANCH TO TTY SERVICE IF FLAG IS SET*/
              SFC           PRINTER
              JSB           I, SRVPRNTR, 0
              SFC           READER
```

126

```
JSB      I, SRVREADER, 0
DSZ      SAVE, 0
LDA      A2, I, SAVE, 0      /*RESTORE CONTENTS OF A2*/
DXZ      SAVE, 0             /*DECREMENT SAVE*/
LDA      A1, I, SAVE, 0
DSZ      SAVE, 0
LDA      A0, I, SAVE, 0
DSZ      SAVE, 0
LDA      X, I, SAVE, 0
DSZ      SAVE, 0
LDA      B, I, SAVE, 0
ENI      0                   /*ENABLE ALL INTERRUPTS*/
```

It is assumed that SAVE is the symbolic address of a memory location on page zero which contains the address of the first memory location where a register's contents can be stored. A block of such consecutive memory locations must be available for storing the contents of all the registers to be saved. Symbolic addresses TTY, PRINTER, and READER are used to identify a teletype unit, a line printer, and a card reader, respectively. The priorities of service of these devices are built into the master interrupt routine shown below. Note the SAVE always contains a nonnegative number, and hence the ISZ instruction merely increments it but does not skip.

5.6 Programming with a Stack

Many modern minicomputers provide a data structure, called *stack*, in hardware and assembly language instructions for operations involving a stack. As the name implies, a stack is a set of locations for storing operands and addresses, either in memory, or in registers, or in both (see Figure 5-6-1). A stack is characterized by its organization; it has a bottom element

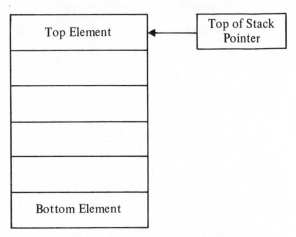

FIGURE 5-6-1.   *Structure of a stack.*

Label	Mnemonic Opcode	Source or Destination Register

FIGURE 5-6-2. *Format of assembly language instructions for operations with a stack.*

and a top element. Information can be stored or retrieved, one element at a time, only from the top of the stack. The address of the top element of the stack is stored in a location called TOP, either in memory or in a register.

In the hypothetical minicomputer it is assumed that the stack is contained in the memory and the address of its top element is stored in a special register called SP (*stack pointer*). To utilize a stack at least two special instructions are needed, called PUSH and POP. The format of these assembly language instructions are shown in Figure 5-6-2 and their operations are described in Table 5-6-1.

TABLE 5–6–1. PUSH *and* POP *Operations*

Mnemonic Opcode	Operation
PUSH	Increment SP by one. Store contents of source register in memory location addressed by SP.
POP	Load contents of memory location addressed by SP into destination register. Decrement SP by one.

EXAMPLES

1. Suppose the contents of the stack in memory and of the registers SP and A2 are as shown in Figure 5-6-3a. Then execution of:

   PUSH   A2

   results in the contents shown in Figure 5-6-3b.

2. Starting with the information contents shown in Figure 5-6-3a, execution of:

   POP   A2

   results in the contents shown in Figure 5-6-3c.

Address   Stack in Memory

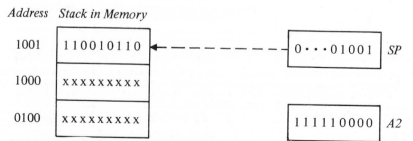

FIGURE 5-6-3a. *Memory content before execution of* PUSH *or* POP.

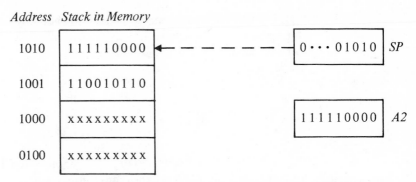

FIGURE 5-6-3b. *Memory content after execution of* PUSH A2.

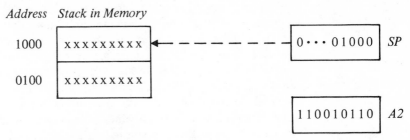

FIGURE 5-6-3c. *Memory content after execution of* POP A2.

3. Stacks in memory can be effectively used for saving and restoring register contents before and after servicing an interrupt. A master interrupt routine using a stack is given below.

```
LDA      SP, SAVE, 0        /*LOAD SP WITH CONTENTS OF SAVE*/
PUSH     B
PUSH     X
PUSH     A0
PUSH     A1
PUSH     A2
STA      SP, SAVE, 0        /*STORE CONTENTS OF SP IN SAVE*/
SFC      TTY
JSB      I, SRVTTY, 0
SFC      PRINTER
JSB      I, SRVPRNTR, 0
SFC      READER
JSB      I, SRVREADER, 0
LDA      SP, SAVE, 0
POP      A2
POP      A1
POP      A0
POP      X
POP      B
STA      SP, SAVE, 0
ENI      0
```

129

The stack operations discussed here are the most basic ones. Minicomputers that make extensive use of stacks have many more stack operations for efficient programming. These are, however, beyond the scope of the text.

SUMMARY

Programming in a machine language requires the programmer to specify opcodes in numeric forms and, more importantly, the absolute addresses of operands and instructions in memory. Modification of programs often entail extensive changes in addressing information. Assembly languages are at a higher level than machine languages and allow the programmer to address operands and instructions by means of symbols meaningful for the task. Assembly language instructions are translated into machine language instructions by an assembler and the necessary addressing information is generated partly by the assembler and partly by a loader. Each assembly language instruction has a corresponding machine language instruction. Thus, being close to the machine level, assembly languages still allow the programmer to make optimum use of the hardware.

PROBLEMS

1. What type of problems are suitable to computer solution?

2. What is an algorithm? How does it differ from a heuristic? What is a graphical representation of an algorithm?

3. What are machine language mnemonics? How is a machine mnemonic program transformed into a machine language program?

4. Why must instructions and data be kept separated in a program? How may this be accomplished?

5. Write a machine mnemonic program to order a block of ten numbers from smallest to largest. Start the program at location 0150_{16}. Draw a flowchart to describe the algorithm used.

6. Write a machine mnemonic program to evaluate the algorithm:

$$Y = \sum_{i=1}^{10} 2A_i - \sum_{i=1}^{10} 3B_i + \sum_{i=1}^{10} 5C_i$$

Start the program at location $IFC0_{16}$. Draw a flowchart to describe the algorithm used.

7. Assume each instruction requires 5 μsec to execute. Write a subroutine for a software timer that will cause a program delay of 500 msec. Use assembly language.

8. Using programmed I/O, write a program to output your name on the teletype. Pack the output name buffer with two ASCII characters per word. Use assembly language.

9. The teletype print mechanism is controlled by the computer. Hence, when a key is pressed, the character is input to the computer, but it is not printed on the paper in the carriage. To print the character, the computer must output the character back to the teletype. This is called a *character echo*. Write an assembler language program to echo any ASCII character on the teletype and to stop (halt) when the character is a $. Use programmed I/O.

10. Write a subroutine to strip the decimal digit from an ASCII numeric character and return it to the calling program.

11. Write a program to read the console data switches and print the bit pattern on the teletype in hexadecimal. Use programmed I/O for the teletype output program. Halt the program when the bit pattern $FFFF_{16}$ is entered.

12. Write a subroutine to convert a 16-bit unsigned binary integer to an ASCII character string for output. Do not suppress leading zeros. Assume the calling program provides the starting address of the number buffer.

13. Double-precision arithmetic uses double-word operands. Write assembler language subroutines to perform the following double-precision operations:
    a) Double-word load and store operation.
    b) Fixed-point double-precision addition.
    c) Fixed-point double-precision subtraction.

14. Three words in storage are labeled H, M, and S. They contain the hour, minute, and second for the present time-of-day. These locations must function as counters, advancing on demand as a time-of-day (TOD) clock. Write a subroutine that will advance the TOD clock one second each time it is called. Write a similar subroutine for a day counter.

15. Suppose a TOD clock is interfaced, and assigned the device code 14_{16}. The clock provides the TOD in binary coded decimal (BCD) using military time format: XX:YY:ZZ. The hour is read from controller register-A, the minutes from register-B, and the seconds from register-C. The BCD value resides in the rightmost 8 bits of the register. Write a subroutine to read the TOD clock and convert the BCD values into three binary integers for return to the calling program.

16. Sixteen motors are involved in controlling an industrial process. At any time, any one of the 16 motors may be on or off. Suppose a controller has been interfaced to the 16 motors and at any time the state of the motors is indicated by the values of the 16 bits in controller register-A. If the bit associated with a motor is 1, the motor is in operation; if 0, it is off. Assume the controller has the device code 20_{16}. Write a subroutine to detect the number of motors in operation, returning this number to the calling program.

17. Write a teletype I/O handler to perform both input and output operations. Allow the handler to queue both input and output requests. Make the input and output drivers interrupt driven. Use multiple entry points into the handler. This is a nontrivial problem.

18. Write the series of instructions required to inclusive OR, the contents of registers 0 and 1, with the result placed in register 1.

PROJECTS

1. In this chapter various programs were given illustrating different aspects of assembly language programming. Now, program the following:
   a) Fixed-point add and subtract to handle 16-bit signed numbers. [Hint: Use carry as required.]
   b) Fixed-point 8-bit multiply and divide.

2. If you feel brave, implement a floating-point package.

3. Write a program to accept plain text messages. Once these messages are received, count:
   a) Total vowels received
   b) Total of each vowel [A, E, I, O, U]
   c) Total number of characters received
   d) The occurrences of any other two characters
   E.g., messages:
   "The quick brown fox jumped over the lazy dogs back."
   "Now is the time for all good men."
   "Programmers do it byte by byte."

6

Minicomputer Software and Its Status

6.1 Introduction

Most minicomputer users are not experienced programmers, but rather they are researchers interested in solutions to their problems. Therefore, easy communication with their minicomputer is of paramount importance to them. This interaction takes place when they write commands to the computer in a programming language.

Although it is possible for a minicomputer user to write a program in machine language (binary machine commands), this procedure is often very difficult and time consuming. To make this interaction easier for the user, several "artificial" languages have been developed. Once again, software provided by the minicomputer vendor interacts with the user. That is, software modules are required to translate the user's *source* program into an *object* program (machine instructions) that the minicomputer can execute.

The advantages of vendor-provided software are easier development of application programs, automatic operation of the minicomputer system, and standardization between programs. Depending on the user's minicomputer configuration, a second interaction with the vendor's software may occur at the run time of the program. This interaction may require as little as a loader program or as much as an operating system (see Figure 6-1-1). The latter initiates and controls the program while it executes.

Software is usually provided by the manufacturer, while the users are responsible for their own applications programs. Minicomputer manufactur-

133

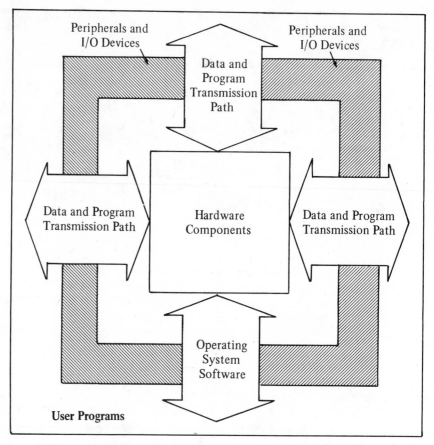

FIGURE 6-1-1.   *Interaction of hardware and software components.*

ers generally provide less software support than the manufacturer of large-scale computer systems, mostly for the following reasons:

1. The minicomputer industry is relatively new. Because of the well-known lag of software behind hardware development, application software as well as executive or operating system software is not generally available.
2. The relatively low price of the minicomputer does not encourage the manufacturers to undertake costly software developments. To keep costs low, often only the minimum amount of software required to support the basic hardware functions is provided.
3. Minicomputers are so versatile that the large number of applications makes standard application packages impossible.
4. Minicomputers are often used in special-purpose applications for which general-purpose software is not applicable.
5. Configurations ranging from 4K dedicated "controller" systems to 64K foreground-background systems with a multitude of peripheral devices would require too many software versions to achieve complete support for every possible configuration.

134

6. Small minicomputer vendors have found software not to be essential for sales.
7. The programming effort required to produce a major software component is considerably greater for a minicomputer, because of its limited instruction set, than for a large-scale computer.

Software production costs, unlike costs of minicomputers and peripheral devices, have not significantly decreased. Usually the cost of software is included in the price of the minicomputer, but some manufacturers are now separately pricing both items. Most of the software provided by the minicomputer manufacturer is in the form of binary object programs, with an extra charge for the source programs.

As the manufacturer includes software production costs in the hardware price, the minicomputer system's overall price increases. However, well-conceived system software that is needed for an individual application is much cheaper to buy from the manufacturer in the computer purchase price than for users to develop themselves. This is because manufacturers distribute their software cost over many minicomputers.

Almost all minicomputer vendors provide basic software modules that help to reduce cost for the user and permit rapid implementation. This includes software routines required by the users to develop their own application software and to be able to communicate to this minicomputer. The types of software required to implement a complete system are illustrated in Figure 6-1-2, and includes:

1. Basic support software (BSS) or program development aids for programs written in assembly language
2. High-level language translators (HLLT)
3. Utility software programs (USP)
4. Operating system software (OS)
5. Applications software, either general- or special-purpose (AS)

Development software, such as assemblers, loaders, editors, and utility routines, provides the basic software tools for producing application programs, and are provided by vendors to run on a minimum minicomputer configuration.

If the software provided by the manufacturer is not adequate, the user usually has the following options:

1. Modify the manufacturer's supplied software.
2. Write custom designed software.
3. Buy special-purpose software from software houses.

6.2 Software Categories

Software systems, as provided by minicomputer vendors, offer users an operating efficiency and an overall functional capability that reduces operating costs by greatly simplifying programming and operating procedures.

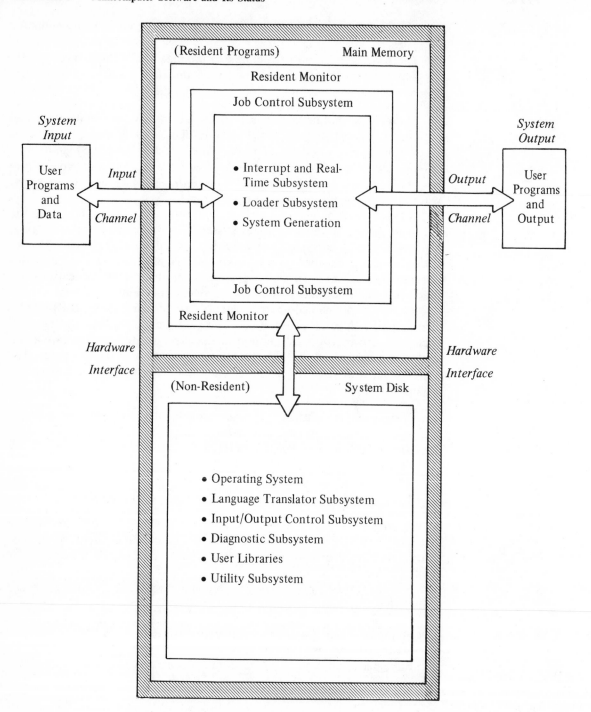

FIGURE 6-1-2.   *Interaction of the user and system software modules.*

Most software systems provided by the manufacturer are modular. That is, as the minicomputer configuration is expanded, a larger, more efficient superset or extension of the existing software can be implemented. Each software module requires some specific minimum configuration, such as memory capacity, optional hardware features, interrupt features, and peripheral devices. Clearly, software for a system with mass storage, such as drums or disks, is quite different from software for a system without such capacity.

The development and execution of programs on a small hardware configuration is more difficult than on a larger system. The reason is that smaller minicomputer systems usually lack or at best provide very poor high-level language facilities, few automatic system functions, and hence require operator intervention for every task to be performed (such as loading tapes, assembling source tapes, and linking these tapes). The availability of support software, and utility, mathematical, and diagnostic routines, although simplifying the programming tasks, may not be of any value to the user, because of their slow execution times.

Throughout the remainder of this chapter, software will be broadly treated as five distinct categories (see Table 6-2-1). All of the software provided in these categories are an aid to all computer applications rather than support to any particular application. Furthermore, the more general a given software program is, the more inefficient it is. Such inefficiency can seldom be tolerated, especially not on minicomputers. Therefore, general-purpose software is often restricted and less general on the smaller configurations than on larger configurations.

The first category, the *Basic Support Software (BSS)*, consists of a collection of standalone* programs and routines for interfacing the user and the hardware more easily and quickly, aiding in the developing of application programs. Assemblers are included in this category because they are frequently found (at their minimum configuration) in the BSS.

The second category, the *high-level language translators (HLLT)*, consists of the "artificial" programming language translators,** in particular high-level language translators. These translators can be further categorized as compilers and interpreters.

The third category, the *utility software package (USP)*, consists of data conversion programs, extended mathematical subroutines, specially developed modules for detecting and identifying hardware faults, floating-point arithmetic routines, general-purpose input/output device handlers, and various kinds of scientific subroutines.

The fourth category, the *operating system software (OS)*,*** consists primarily of programs and routines specifically required to run the overall

---

* Standalone programs perform all of their own input/output at the machine language level, requiring no linkage nor communication with other programs.

** A language processor translates functional statements into complete sets of machine instructions for carrying out specific tasks.

*** An operating system is a collection of programs that can increase productivity of the computer system, by providing common functions for all user programs.

TABLE 6-2-1.   Software Categories

Software Categories	Functional Classification	Software Components

Basic support software	Development software	Loaders
		  Absolute
		  Relocatable
		  Linking
		Assemblers
		  Basic
		  Extended
		  Macro
		Text editors
		Mathematical utilities
		I/O control subsystem
		Diagnostic utilities

High-level language translators	General-purpose software	Compilers
		  Basic FORTRAN
		  Standard FORTRAN
		  ALGOL
		  COBOL
		Interpreters
		  BASIC

Utility software	Support software	Conversion programs Diagnostic utilities Mathematical utilities Input/output utilities System utilities High-level language utilities
Operating systems		Standalone or basic OS Disk or tape OS Multiprogramming OS Real-time OS Timesharing OS
Application software	General-purpose software Special-purpose software	

computer system, allocate its resources, handle data transfers and interrupts, and allocate and protect memory among competing program functions. Such items as executives, loaders, supervisory control, sequence control, operator communication, and real-time control are included in this category.

The fifth category, the *applications software (AS)*, consists of the programs and routines designed specifically to solve user problems in user

TABLE 6-2-2.   *Software/Hardware Configurations*

Software \ Hardware	Minimum Configuration CPU 4K Memory ASR-33 TTY Single Level Interrupt	Add Options 4K Memory High-Speed Peripherals	Add Options Automatic Interrupt Expansion DMA Disks/Tapes	Add Options 8K Memory Memory Protect Real-Time Clock Multilevel Interrupt
Assemblers	X	X	X	X
Compilers		X	X	X
Interpreters	X	X	X	X
Symbolic text editor	X	X	X	X
Trace/debug system	X	X	X	X
Real-time subsystem			X	X
Resident monitor	X	X	X	X
I/O control subsystem	X	X	X	X
Basic or standalone OS	X			
DOS/TOS			X	X
Real-time OS			X	X
Timesharing OS			X	X
Loader subsystems	X	X	X	X
Mathematical libraries	X	X	X	X
Utility programs	X	X	X	X
User libraries			X	X
System editors	X	X	X	X
System generation			X	X
Diagnostic subsystem	X	X	X	X

environments. This category is the most diverse of the five categories, and examples may be found in any minicomputer application ranging from dedicated process control to general-purpose service bureau uses.

Table 6-2-2 illustrates variations of software in relationship to the different hardware configurations. The status of each software category is discussed separately in the next sections. Each software module within the category is broken down into its logical components and discussed.

6.3 Basic Support Software (BSS)

The minimum software modules provided for even the smallest configuration generally contain:

1. Assembler
2. Loaders

139

3. Mathematical utilities
4. Input/output utilities
5. Data conversion routines
6. Debugging and diagnostic routines
7. Text editor

6.3.1 Assemblers

Assembly languages follow the structure of the machine language very closely. Each function command (statement, instruction, or line) of the source program consists of a machine command and generally an operand address. The machine commands are specified by symbolic mnemonics and the operand addresses by symbolic names.

Assembly language instructions require translation before the program can be executed by the minicomputer. The program which translates the programmer's symbolic language to binary-coded language of the machine is called an assembler. The translation is generally on a one-for-one basis; that is, for each source statement written by the programmer, one machine instruction is generated by the assembler during translation.

Assembly language is used to write most software provided with the computer because it produces the most efficient code. It also uses the least number of locations in memory to solve a problem, a very important criteria for minicomputers. In addition to efficiency and space, it also provides for control of such hardware operations as input/output.

Many minicomputer manufacturers supply more than one assembler for different hardware configurations, with the assembly language for a small configuration being a subset of the assembly language designed for larger minicomputer configurations.

The capabilities of assemblers vary from manufacturer to manufacturer as well as configuration to configuration. The variations involve the following features:

1. Production of either relocatable* or absolute** object code.
2. Symbolic addressing in source language.
3. Mnemonic machine codes.
4. Octal, hexidecimal, decimal, and ASCII literals.***
5. Pseudo-operations to control the assembly process.

---

    * The program may be located anywhere in memory. All operands which refer to memory locations are adjusted as the program is loaded. Operands must be relocatable expressions; subprograms may contain external symbols and entry points, and may refer to common storage.

    ** Addresses generated by the assembler are to be interpreted as absolute locations in memory. The program is a complete entity; external symbols, common storage references, and entry points are not permitted.

    *** Binary patterns assigned to represent various signs, symbols, numbers, letters, and operations according to the American Standard Code for Information Interchange.

6. Allocation of core memory.
7. Generation of linkages to subroutines and I/O routines.
8. Provision for macro-operations.
9. Number of symbols handled in symbol table.
10. Required core size for assembler.

Compared to actual machine language, the assembly language reduces the time to write and debug programs because it is easier to learn symbolic mnemonics and to use symbolic names. The use of subroutine linkages, furthermore, permits tasks to be divided among several programmers. Because the assembler is left with the task of translating the mnemonic operation codes as well as the assignment of addresses, modifications to programs are easier.

On the other hand assembly language instructions require intimate knowledge about the hardware as well as the problem. Because of the one-to-one relationship between the assembly language and the machine language, many commands are required in the solution of even a simple problem, possibly causing errors as well as machine dependence.

There are three different kinds of assemblers provided by vendors for minicomputers, namely:

1. Basic assembler
2. Extended or symbolic assembler
3. Macro assembler

Table 6-3-1 summarizes some hardware configuration requirements as well as corresponding software characteristics of these assemblers. This table provides a basis for readily evaluating assemblers provided by vendors.

The number of times (passes) the source program needs to be read by the assembler to produce an assembled program is directly related to the memory capacity and associate peripherals of the minicomputer. Most assemblers produce absolute or relocatable code from symbolic assembly language after either one, two, or three passes of the source program. The single-pass assemblers produce output directly from the source code, often leaving many references to be resolved by the loader.

Most assemblers, however, require two or three passes of the source program through the input device, especially if its sole input/output device is an ASR-33 teletypewriter. The advantages of these assemblers are that they allow larger source programs to be assembled, as well as allow the design of the loaders to be straightforward. For larger minicomputer systems with mass storage, all passes are internal, and users need only load their source programs once.

The diagnostic messages produced by the assembler are important in the determination of assembly errors and subsequent debugging of the program. These messages can range from an indication to the user that an error occurred to explicit detection of the statement in error and its corresponding memory location.

141

TABLE 6-3-1. Variations of Assembler Capabilities with Corresponding Minimum Hardware Configurations

	Basic Assembler	*Extended Assembler*	*Macro Assembler*
Minimum configuration	4K	8K	8K
Peripherals required	ASR-33 TTY	ASR-33 TTY and/or tape, disk (whichever available)	ASR-33 TTY and/or tape, disk (whichever available)
Number of source code passes	1,2,3	2,3	2,3
Size of assembler program	2000–3000 statements	4000–5000 statements	4000–6000 statements
Size of programs that can be assembled (absolute/relocatable/ number of symbolic references)	1000/500/100	450/450/450	450/450/450
Speed of assembler statements per min.	1000–2000	3000–3500	3000–4000
Fixed binary output	Yes	Yes	Yes
Relocatable output	Yes	Yes	Yes
Diagnostic messages	Limited analysis	Detailed analysis	Detailed analysis
Pseudo-operations	8–12	10–25	25–40
Macro capability	N/A	N/A	User-defined and system-defined
Macro nesting capability	N/A	N/A	Multilevel

Fixed, binary assemblers produce absolute binary output code that must always be loaded into and executed from the same area of memory. Relocatable assemblers produce relocatable (relative to a base address) machine instructions for output. When the program is loaded for execution, the loader adds a program starting location to the base address, and, therefore, can be stored into and executed from anywhere in memory.

Pseudo-operations are directives to the assembler during the assembly stage of the program. These directives do not generate any executable machine instructions, but direct the assembler to define and allocate data, direct conditional assembly, alter the program origin, and define new operation codes, external programs, and data.

The *basic assembler* as provided by minicomputer vendors assists in program preparation by translating symbolic source language instructions into either absolute or relocatable object programs for execution on the minicomputer, usually taking care of all addressing automatically, whether it be direct, relative, indirect, or relative indirect. Variations from vendor to vendor often include the following:

1. Symbolic rather than absolute addressing of memory locations (addresses)
2. Specifications of constants in their natural form (e.g., decimal)

3.   Interspersing of comments into the program
4.   Variety of assembler directing pseudo-operations
5.   Provisions for subroutine linkages
6.   Free or fixed format source input
7.   Format of literal specifications

The *extended or symbolic assembler* is generally a fast two- or three-pass assembler which translates symbolic assembly programs into binary machine code acceptable for loading and execution. Binary object code produced may be absolute, relocatable, or a combination of both. Pseudo-operations permit the programmer to exercise control over the assembly process and generate various forms of data, including text and double-precision floating-point constants. In addition, conditional assembly features and the capabilities to generate symbolic external subprogram linkages are provided.

Source input data can be variable in length and free formatted. Extensive error checking and error documentation is provided to locate and isolate errors in assembly statements. Detecting errors does not cause processing to terminate, rather all statements are scanned in an attempt to locate other potential errors. The assembler also provides I/O capabilities for standard peripherals supported by the system. Assemblies may be complete in two- or three-source passes without reloading the assembler for each assembly. The optional third pass produces an octal or hex/symbolic printout and/or punchout of assembled programs.

The source program listing provides a side-by-side listing of the symbolic assembly statements and the generated object code. In addition to statement fields which specify the address and contents of each program location, an operand location field containing the relative program location of the operand for each memory instruction is often provided. Frequently an optional cross-reference listing of all program symbols may be obtained along with the source listing. Again, variations from vendor to vendor can be expected.

The *macro assembler* permits a programmer to use mnemonic symbols to define a set of instructions by name, along with specifying desired variables as arguments. This feature allows the inclusion of frequently used code sequences with a minimum of programming effort. A macro differs from a subroutine in that it is assembled every time it is called, and requires no execution time linkage. The programmer can direct the assembler's processing by means of a full set of pseudo-operations. An output listing, often requiring an optional third pass, produces the octal or hex/symbolic assembly program as well as the generated binary object code. Highly sophisticated macro generating and calling facilities can also be utilized within the context of the symbolic or extended assembler. Additional capabilities, that frequently vary from vendor to vendor, include:

1.   Define and call nested macros
2.   Conditional assembly statements

143

3. Assembly time branching and exits
4. Boolean and other arithmetic manipulations (e.g., double precision)
5. Text facilities
6. Use of I/O system macros
7. Facilities for linkages to separately assembled programs

The assembler takes one mnemonic source language statement, generating all instructions needed to implement the mnemonic operation, and inserting the corresponding machine instructions into the output code. Macro capabilities provide to the users the advantages of making assembly language programs shorter and easier to program. The facility for incorporating user-defined macro functions into the assembly process provides the capabilities of tailoring a language to a specific application. Frequently required functions can be programmed and incorporated into the assembler's library system and can subsequently be treated as system macros.

Nesting macros implies that one macro can use another macro in its definition. The extent to which macros can be nested of course determines the ease of programming user-defined macros.

Finally, for program preparation on other computers, most vendors supply assemblers and simulators (often called *cross assemblers*) which operate on large-scale general-purpose computer systems. These assemblers provide output in either absolute or binary format suitable for minicomputer loading and execution. The simulators incorporate all I/O operations as well as interrupt handling. Program execution time is internally tabulated and then listed. The detailed logical flow of the assemblers is presented in the next section.

6.3.2 Loaders

Corresponding to the different kinds of assemblers and their respective outputs, there exist appropriate loaders to process object code from selected input devices into core memory suitable for execution. Three separate loaders are often provided for this purpose:

1. Bootstrap loader
2. Absolute binary loader
3. Relocatable loader/linking loader

The *bootstrap loader* is a very short program used to load the absolute binary loader from a specific device into fixed locations of core memory. If the configuration of the minicomputer permits loading through a self-load feature, the bootstrap loader is frequently replaced by a self-loading bootstrap mechanism. This loader loads the absolute binary loader automatically into previously assigned memory locations. Most frequently, though, the bootstrap loader is entered into core memory through the console using the hardwired switches. Consequently, most bootstrap loaders are very short, usually 10–20 instructions long.

The *absolute binary loader* is a program used to load any absolute binary code directly into fixed or absolute memory locations. The absolute locations into which the program is loaded are previously specified at program assembly or can be optionally specified at load time. Absolute loaders are very simple programs because the absolute object programs are in a format which permits direct loading into memory. The advantages for these loaders are:

1. Size of programs that can be loaded
2. Speed of loading

On the other hand, absolute loaders have the following disadvantages:

1. Changes of addresses or program instructions require reassembly of the entire program.
2. Linking of independently assembled programs must be performed by the user.

The *relocatable loader* is used to load relocatable object programs produced by the extended assembler. The loader permits program relocation in memory to be changed or differently specified at load time without requiring the source program to be reassembled. Most relocatable loaders also permit the linking of several independently assembled programs, and are therefore known as *linking loaders*. Optional features of these loaders depend on the manufacturer but usually include the following:

1. Automatic library searching
2. Augmented memory allocation
3. Address transfer capabilities
4. Optional memory map, indicating execution time core allocations
5. Linking of associated programs and subroutine calls at load time using symbolic entry points and external references
6. Overlay capabilities
7. Optional output of symbol tables
8. Optional output of absolute version of relocatable program and subroutines
9. Retrieval and loading of implied subroutines from libraries and input/output control systems

The relocatable loader, therefore, permits the user to independently assemble program modules, then at a later time to allocate appropriate core memory and link these programs together. Frequently used subroutines can be stored and retrieved from a relocatable library.

The advantage for this kind of a loader is that changes in individual subprograms require only the reassembly of the affected subprograms. The loader then reallocates memory and recombines these new subprograms with the existing programs. The disadvantage, of course, is the computer processing time required to relocate text and link the subprograms. Furthermore, relocatable programs are much larger than absolute programs because they require relocation information for those instructions and data that depend on the load location of the program.

6.3.3 Mathematical Utilities

A number of commonly used subroutines are frequently provided by the vendor to simplify programming or to even expand their minicomputer's limited arithmetic capabilities. These routines may be in absolute or relocatable code.

   The hardware of minicomputers often does not include floating-point and double-precision arithmetic capabilities (see Chapter 3). Many applications, however, require more numerical range and precision, and therefore use software-implemented subroutines or interpreters. Unlike subroutines, the floating-point interpreter examines sequential core locations and treats their contents as floating-point instructions, thereby simulating a CPU with floating-point hardware. The only advantage of the interpreter option is that programmers can use floating-point instructions within their other program instructions and need not link to externally provided subroutines.

   In addition to increased accuracy, floating-point operations relieve the programmer of scaling problems common to fixed-point operations. The most frequent functions included in the mathematical utilities module include:

1. *Single-Precision Absolute Value:* computes absolute value of a fixed-point single-precision number.
2. *Single-Precision Signed Multiply:* computes a double-precision signed product from two fixed-point, single-precision numbers.
3. *Single-Precision Signed Divide:* divides a double-precision, fixed-point number by a single-precision, fixed-point number with single-precision quotient and remainder.
4. *Double-Precision Absolute Value:* computes the absolute value of a fixed-point, double-precision number.
5. *Double-Precision Addition:* computes the sum of two double-precision numbers.
6. *Double-Precision Subtraction:* performs a subtraction of two double-precision numbers.
7. *Double-Precision Multiply:* multiplies two double-precision fixed-point numbers to form an extended (quadruple) double-precision product.
8. *Double-Precision Divide:* divides an extended double-precision dividend by a double-precision divisor, resulting in double-precision quotient and remainder.
9. *Floating-Point Interpreter:* provides instructions that cover most floating-point operations, floating-point conversions, and transcendental functions. As a single program, the interpreter is often supplied in either absolute or relocatable machine code. Other functions frequently found

146

in this module include sine, cosine, arctangent, square root, logarithms, exponentiation, natural logarithms, and hyperbolic functions. Variations in the speed and memory size of the routines are vendor dependent.

6.3.4 Input/Output Utilities

Input/output systems provided by the minicomputer and manufacturer eliminate the need for the programmer to be concerned with the machine language detail of I/O selection, data transfer, and interrupt scheduling. The programmer is furnished with a convenient method to program and control standard peripheral devices. The set of subroutines provides the following capabilities for each available I/O device standard to the minicomputer:

1. Specification of data formats most convenient for a user's application
2. Automatic code conversion of the input data to internal representations
3. Error checking and recovery procedures

With these input/output routines, programmers can perform device-dependent I/O operations yet not be concerned with the actual machine language details regarding their control.

The most frequent input/output subroutines supplied by the vendors include control for teleprinters, paper tape readers and punches, and magnetic tapes and disks.

The input/output system often provides users with the capability to perform I/O operations that are independent of the actual physical device being used. In other words, users perform all their I/O by requesting the appropriate data transfers via logical devices by specifying the logical device address or unit, the address of the data buffer, and a word or block count of data to be transferred. The logical unit is associated with a particular physical device by the system, and can be changed to a different physical device at load time. The default correspondence of the logical units and their physical devices are usually incorporated into the I/O system routines. It is common for one or more instructions in the minicomputer's instruction repertoire to be input/output instructions, specifically tailored to the minicomputer's input/output system. A more extensive discussion on these input/output system routines and how they interface into a larger operating system is presented in Section 6.6.

6.3.5 Data Conversion Routines

Programs to convert data are needed on most minicomputers because of the variety of input formats allowed. The input, which can be in binary coded decimal (BCD), double-precision BCD, ASCII decimal, EBCDIC, floating-point, or binary, usually must be converted to be used in an application. The result may be desired in even another form, requiring yet another conversion. To facilitate these data conversions, most vendors provide utility routines that are easily interfaced between the user's program, the mathematical utilities, and the I/O utilities. These routines usually include:

1. *BCD to Binary:* converts decimal numbers (the number of digits correspond to word size) to BCD and then to its binary equivalent.
2. *Binary to BCD:* converts single-precision binary numbers to its corresponding BCD equivalent.
3. *ASCII Decimal to Binary:* converts an ASCII character string of decimal digits to its single-precision binary equivalent.
4. *Binary to ASCII Decimal:* converts a single-precision binary number to a string of ASCII characters representing its equivalent decimal value.
5. *ASCII Octal (Hex) to Binary:* converts an ASCII character string consisting of octal (hex) digits to single-precision binary numbers.
6. *Binary to ASCII Octal (Hex):* converts a binary number to a string of ASCII characters representing the octal (or hex equivalent).
7. *Floating-Point to Octal (Hex):* converts a data word expressed in floating notation to an octal (hex) representation.

Variations in the number of routines provided, the number of digits per word, as well as the option for double-precision routines are vendor and minicomputer design dependent.

6.3.6 Debugging and Diagnostic Routines

A debug module is one of the more valuable programming aids provided by minicomputer vendors. A large portion of program debugging can be performed at the minicomputer's console. However, the console is usually limited in both display capacity as well as available control functions. The online interactive (dynamic) debugger enables programmers to establish a conversational environment between their program and the minicomputer. Using the debug module, programmers can alter or display portions of the program, stop at predesignated memory locations, dump the program or selected portions of it, trace the flow of the program, and search for particular commands or data. Other options included by many vendors are:

1. Communication with the object program using either mnemonic code of the symbolic program or octal code of the binary program.
2. Modification of registers and selected areas of memory based on an event or on a periodic basis.
3. Print/punch specified areas of memory in either octal or ASCII code.
4. Symbolic disassembly of object programs from core memory.
5. Punch object program tapes via binary paper tape program that uses standard address, data and check sum format used by the assembler.
6. Real-time debugging under active supervision via TTY control, using simulated interrupts from real-time devices.

For proper operation, online programs often depend on the correctness of data being manipulated by other program functions, and consequently a real-time debugging system is essential. However, occasions can arise where alteration of a program, in order to use the debug facilities, temporarily eliminates or completely changes the problem.

The best approach is to prevent bugs in the first place either by investing in checked-out software or employing experienced personnel. The expense of the time invested in removing any residual errors will then be minimal. Program debugging for the typical minicomputer system requires many hours at the console stepping through the program instruction by instruction, while examining the console readouts and the contents of the various registers which display the binary form of the current instruction and the contents of the accumulator.

Some vendors provide debugging modules that enable the settings of halts or breakpoints which automatically initiate printouts from selected areas of memory or step the machine to help trace portions of the program. The printout can be programmed to occur each time an event occurs or on a periodic basis. While this is useful and usually decreases debugging time, it does not solve all problems. Some programs have to be changed in order to use the debug module. In the process of altering the program, the error may disappear or the error results may change.

A valuable aid in debugging online software is a debug panel which can be plugged into a minicomputer chassis. This hardware feature allows the programmer to make a variety of checks without altering the program being debugged. The programmer can halt the computer after the execution of an instruction at a given address, store a running tabulation of the last ten instructions executed, or halt the computer upon the completion of an operation storing data in a specified location.

A less obvious consideration of debugging is the use of time scales. An important goal of real-time minicomputer applications is the optimum use of time. This requires the establishment of priority interrupt systems and logical program sequencing, each making the debugging of a program more difficult. The procedure of sequentially stepping through a program is not adequate, because it is only able to check arithmetic and logic independent of time. This type of testing cannot check the possible combinations that exist at a given time. There is a need to develop dynamic tests which include the time constraint to accurately test the minicomputer programs.

These debugging routines generate indicative information reflecting the operational status of the equipment being verified, by selectively exercising every circuit of the devices. Detailed error messages are printed out identifying which instruction or bit configuration has failed. These error codes then direct attention to specific modules in which a fault condition was detected.

Included in the diagnostic module are programs which test the instruction set of the minicomputer, exercise memory, as well as perform peripheral diagnostics. These routines can often be used in either a preventive or corrective mode of operation. In the *preventive mode*, the complete

149

system is checked for operational readiness and provides an overview of the total system. In the *corrective mode* of operation, a malfunction is known to exist and separate comprehensive tests isolate this malfunction within a specific hardware segment.

Instruction diagnostics permit the user to exercise the total instruction set, and possibly data manipulation and addressing capabilities. The CPU diagnostics often isolate faults to six or fewer circuits, possibly even to individual elements. Memory diagnostics usually exercise memory for noise conditions and reliability between specified locations with fixed or dynamic patterns. Peripheral diagnostics test the operations of the I/O components, including interfaces, devices, and controllers. Other diagnostic routines frequently provided by vendors, depending on the minicomputer configuration, include the following:

1. Power shut down/restart
2. Instruction timer
3. Arithmetic tests
4. Memory allocation and protection
5. Multiply/divide tests
6. Real-time clock tests
7. Magnetic tape and disk reliability tests
8. A/D and D/A diagnostics
9. Data communications controller tests

One final debug utility routine provided is the memory dump routine. This program is often a completely modular program (absolute or relocatable) enabling the user to obtain memory dumps in either octal or mnemonic instruction formats. The memory ranges to be dumped can often be specified in absolute or octal format using any of the available input devices.

6.3.7 Text Editors

Symbolic text editors, or symbolic source update programs, simplify the correction of source programs, especially when using paper tape, by providing the capability to insert, delete, or replace characters or records from a symbolic file or source program tape. Often capabilities are provided for direct entry of source statements into memory, listing statements that have been changed, deleted, or augmented while in core, and output from memory to form a source tape.

The text editor can substantially ease the labor of writing and editing symbolic programs. It also reduces the number of assembly or compilation passes required to generate an executable object program. Programmers type their source program into memory from a teletypewriter, or load their previous source program version by way of teletype or high-speed paper tape reader into memory. The editor treats the input user source program to be processed as a continuous character stream.

A program update is controlled by commands issued from the TTY keyboard. The command structure enables the user to insert, delete, and search for strings of text. Changes may be made at both line and character levels. Variations in the capabilities and size of the text editors depend on the minicomputer configurations as well as the vendor.

6.4 High-Level Languages

High-level language translators are available with some minicomputers, usually requiring additional core memory to be of use (usually 8–12K of core memory). Some manufacturers quote the availability of compilers, such as FORTRAN (see Table 6-4-1), but limit the compilers to meet their hardware requirements. The result is compiler languages with the same name which vary greatly in memory requirements and language capabilities. Some languages have standard specifications. The American National Standards Institute (ANSI) has standards for FORTRAN, essentially FORTRAN IV, and for Basic FORTRAN (a compatible subset of FORTRAN). Many manufacturers have developed their own language, and there are, of course, no industry standards for them. COBOL and ALGOL are also available for some machines. As is true with FORTRAN, some versions of these languages meet specified standards while others do not.

Some compilers are implemented in a conversational mode, in which the user types the source statements online to the compiler and the compiler immediately executes the program. However, most compilers are designed to operate in a batch mode.

TABLE 6-4-1.   *High Level Language Translator Categories*

	Assemblers	Compilers	Interpreters
General-purpose languages	Basic Extended Macro	FORTRAN Basic Standard COBOL ALGOL RPG	Basic FOCAL
Special-purpose languages	N/A	Numerical control Graphics Simulation Civil engr. Architecture Real-time	N/A

High-level languages are structured closer to the user's language and thereby provide the following advantages:

1. Ease of programming and debugging
2. Machine independence
3. Reduction in programming effort
4. No need to understand the hardware

Programs written in these high-level languages (e.g., FORTRAN, ALGOL, BASIC, COBOL, and RPG*) consist of simple statements defining complex hardware-dependent computer operations. These commands are then translated into a series of machine-dependent instructions. However, since high-level language translators (HLLTs) are general-purpose programs, they often generate inefficient code and require more memory capacity. These disadvantages need be contrasted with the extra time required to write and debug assembly language programs. Any machine-dependent function, such as I/O device control, must be written in assembly language which can usually be accessed through standardized subroutine linkages.

High-level languages, including assembly languages, need to be translated into machine code before execution on a minicomputer is possible. There are two common techniques used to translate languages: compilation and interpretation.

Compilers translate source statements into machine code, which is then loaded into memory and executed. *Interpreters*, on the other hand, convert source statements into an intermediate language (or code). This intermediate code is then further decoded, one instruction at a time, into machine instructions and executed. This process is less efficient in the execution time of the program and in memory utilization as contrasted to compilation. Interpreters, however, require less memory space than do compilers.

High-level language translators vary from vendor to vendor, usually in the following functions:

1. Number of source tape passes for complete compilation
2. Minimum configurations required
3. Degree of standardization

The compiling process for minicomputers is very similar to the assembly of a source program. The major difference lies in the number of passes required to obtain an object program in machine language format. In addition to reloading the source program or its intermediate binary output, frequently the user may have to load that portion of the compiler program

---

* RPG is a special businessman's language useful in the preparation of reports, such as inventory records and sales analyses. Often, sequence checking, input auditing, report writing, and other processing logic is provided in the language.

which represents the next pass to be executed. An example of these compiling steps might be:

1. Load pass one of the compiler.
2. Load the source program.
3. Load next pass of the compiler.
4. Load the source program or equivalent output from the previous pass.
5. Repeat of steps (3) and (4) as required until the object program is produced.

Because of the core and time limitations of minicomputers of 8192 words (8K) of memory or less, some installations use another machine for the compiling or assembling. This machine (source computer), maybe part of a large-scale data processing system, gives the user faster compiling and assembly plus more efficient machine instructions (object code) for the minicomputer. An extension of this procedure is to directly link the source computer and minicomputer (target machine). The number of errors can be decreased because at the completion of compilation or assembly the target machine can be directly loaded with the object code. The result is fast program turnaround.

Most minicomputer manufacturers provide compilers for at least one of the three major languages. Users thereby gain a certain degree of program portability, since they can transfer their program with relatively few changes to another minicomputer system.

The most widely used standard language is FORTRAN (FORmula TRANslation), especially in the physical sciences and in engineering disciplines. FORTRAN is a desirable language to implement because of the availability of compilers, its standardization, and ease of program development. The language permits much easier communication with the minicomputer than does either assembly or machine language. This is because its form, namely the symbols, rules, grammar, and syntax, is closer to the language of the user. For example, the $+$, $-$, $*$, and $/$ symbols in this language represent the operations of addition, subtraction, multiplication, and division, respectively. Typical FORTRAN statements, such as:

$$A = (B + C)/2.0$$

reflect the algebraic origination of the language. The FORTRAN compiler, unlike most assemblers, translates a single statement into many machine language instructions.

FORTRAN statements permit programmers to express problems using words and mathematical statements similar to English. Each FORTRAN statement provided by most vendors is one of five types:

1. *Arithmetic:* defines arithmetic operations to be performed.
2. *Control:* controls the operational flow of statements to be executed within the program.

153

3. *Input/Output:* provides communication between the programmer and the system's input/output devices.
4. *Specification:* describes the form and content of data within the program.
5. *Subprogram:* defines the occurrence and form of subprograms and subroutines.

A statement and format specification list for a representative minicomputer FORTRAN is presented in Appendix B-1. Variations from vendor to vendor can be expected, especially to adapt the language to their own hardware peculiarities (see Table 6-4-2).

The need for a more flexible, powerful, and sometimes more general language motivated the development of ALGOL. As far as the user is concerned, ALGOL permits language specifications reflecting the logic of a program in a natural way. This goal is obtained by defining language elements, such as variables, constants, expressions, and procedures, as nested building blocks for a more user developed complex structure capable of representing any logical or mathematical process. Simple free-form I/O or formatted output, bit manipulation, easy manipulation of character string data, recursive and reentrant procedures, dynamic storage allocation and dynamic type conversion for full mixed-mode capability all provide major extensions in capabilities over FORTRAN. Free formatting capabilities and the use of variable names (these reflect the information they contain) make ALGOL almost self-documenting. A statement and format specification list for a representative minicomputer ALGOL is presented in Appendix B-2.

BASIC (Beginner's All-Purpose Symbolic Instruction Code)* is a very simple language designed for beginners, so that the user is able to conversationally develop programs. The user types in numbered program statements in any order, and the interpreter arranges these statements in numerical order and at the same time checks for syntactic correctness. The conversational editing and running of programs is based on the interpretation process, which is handled entirely by a self-contained system requiring no interaction of other software system components. Variations of the interpreter as provided by vendors include:

1. Minimum minicomputer configuration
2. Capability to store and access all types of mass storage devices
3. Formatted output
4. Additional statements to facilitate interaction with external data-acquisition and process control systems
5. Multiterminal systems under control of an operating or time-shared system

The statement and format specification list for a representative minicomputer BASIC is given in Appendix B-3.

A simple programming example illustrating the different languages is presented in Table 6-4-3, while a language feature chart is presented in Table 6-4-4.

---

* BASIC was developed at Dartmouth College by J. G. Kemeny and T. E. Kurtz in 1967.

TABLE 6-4-2. *Comparison of Language Specifications (Standard FORTRAN, Basic FORTRAN, and Minicomputer FORTRAN)*

	USA Standard	USA Standard Basic	Minicomputer FORTRAN
Character set			
A–Z	Yes	Yes	Yes
0–9	Yes	Yes	Yes
Blank = + − */(),.	Yes	Yes	Yes
$	Yes	No	Yes
'(apostrophe)	No	No	Yes
Statement continuation lines	19	5	5
Numeric statement label	1 to 5	1 to 4	1 to 5
Variable name	1 to 6	1 to 5	(up to 31)
Data types			
Integer	Yes	Yes	Yes
Real	Yes	Yes	Yes
Double-precision	Yes	No	Some
Complex	Yes	No	Some
Logical	Yes	No	Some
Hollerith	Yes	No	Some
Real constant			
Basic real constant	Yes	Yes	Yes
Integer constant followed by a decimal exponent	Yes	No	No
Double-precision constant	Yes	No	No
Number of array dimensions	3	2	Variable (128)
Relational expressions	Yes	No	Some
Logical operators	Yes	No	Yes
Assigned GO TO	Yes	No	Yes
Logical IF	Yes	No	Some
DO-loop range	Yes	No	Yes
READ and WRITE			
READ/WRITE (formatted)	Yes	Yes	Yes
READ/WRITE (unformatted)	Yes	Yes	Yes
Auxiliary I/O statements			
REWIND	Yes	Yes	Yes
BACKSPACE	Yes	Yes	Yes
ENDFILE	Yes	Yes	Yes
Formatted records			
First character not printed	Yes	Yes	Yes
Space before printing			
Blank One line	Yes	No	Yes
0 Two lines	Yes	No	Yes
1 First line, new page	Yes	No	Yes
+ No advance	Yes	No	Yes

155

Table 6-4-2 (continued)

	USA Standard	USA Standard Basic	Minicomputer FORTRAN
Variable dimension	Yes	No	No
Common			
Blank	Yes	Yes	Yes
Named	Yes	No	Yes
Array size declared	Yes	No	Yes
External statement	Yes	No	Yes
Type statement	Yes	No	Yes
Dimension information	Yes	No	Yes
Data statement	Yes	No	Yes
Format types			
A	Yes	No	Yes
D	Yes	No	Yes
E	Yes	Yes	Yes
F	Yes	Yes	Yes
G	Yes	No	Yes
H	Yes	Yes	Yes
I	Yes	Yes	Yes
L	Yes	No	Yes
X	Yes	Yes	Yes
Statement function must precede the first executable statement and follow the specification statements	Yes	Yes	Yes
Type specification in a function statement	Yes	No	Yes
Function may define or redefine its arguments	Yes	No	No
Transmit in a call			
Hollerith arguments	Yes	No	No
External subprogram names	Yes	No	Yes
BLOCK DATA subprogram	Yes	No	No
Specification statements			
Precede first executable statement	Yes	Yes	Yes
Must be ordered DIMENSION COMMON EQUIVALENCE	No	Yes	Yes
External function may alter variables in common	Yes	No	No

156

TABLE 6-4-3. *Comparison of High-Level Languages, Assembly Language, and Machine Language*

Machine Language		Assembly Language		BASIC	Standard FORTRAN	ALGOL
000000	0011000000001100		LDA 2,FIVE	10 LET I = 5	I = 5	I : = 5;
000001	0101000000001101		STA 2,I	20 IF I = K THEN GO	IF (I.EQ.K) GO TO 40	IF I = K THEN GO TO A;
000002	0011100000001110		LDA 3,K	TO 40	I = I + 1	I : = I + 1;
000003	1101110100001101		SUB 2,3,SNR	30 I = I + 1	40 K = I + 1	A : K : = I + 1;
000004	0000000000001001		JMP IPART	40 K = I + 1		
000005	0011000000001101	A:	LDA 2,I			
000006	1101101100000000		INC 2,3			
000007	0101100000001110		STA 3,K			
000010	0000000000001111		JMP NEXT			
000011	1101101100000000					
000012	0101000000001101	IPART:	INC 2,3			
000013	0000000001111011		STA 2,I			
000014	000005	FIVE:	JMP A			
000015	000000		I			
000016	000000		K			
NEXT	NEXT	NEXT:				

157

TABLE 6-4-4.   *Language Features*

Features \ Language	Assembly Language	Basic FORTRAN	Standard FORTRAN	ALGOL	BASIC	COBOL
Efficient utilization of memory	X					
Efficient execution time	X					
Ease of programming					X	
Most widely used			X			
Most powerful structure				X		
Machine independent		X	X	X	X	X
Machine dependent	X					
Self-documenting		X	X	X	X	X
Conversational editing					X	
Mnemonic instruction code	X					
Symbolic names	X	X	X	X	X	X
Arithmetic expressions		X	X	X	X	X
General nesting				X		
Integer arithmetic	X	X	X	X		X
Floating-point arithmetic	X	X	X	X	X	X
Double-precision	X		X			
Complex arithmetic	X		X			
Intrinsic function		X	X	X	X	X
External function	X	X	X	X	X	
Subprograms	X	X	X		X	

6.4.1 Functional Components of Assemblers

The use of assembly language in large-scale general-purpose computer systems has decreased with the development of problem oriented languages. However, the majority of programs written for minicomputer applications are still written in assembly language. This is necessitated by speed requirements, small memory capacities of minimum configurations, and lack of vendor provided compilers. In other cases where a compiler such as FORTRAN is available, assembly language may still be the best choice because of logic decisions and interaction requirements between the minicomputer and I/O devices, actuators, remote sensors, and instruments.

Essentially, minicomputer assemblers do not differ from those available on larger computer systems. However, a deeper understanding is required by the user about the minicomputer and the user interaction to the assembler and loader prior to achieving an executable program.

On a large-scale general-purpose computer the programmer submits jobs via a standard I/O device, in some cases a remote device. The user is only required to include one or more job control cards that precede programs and data. The computer, with its assembler and library of routines, produces the desired result. Most programmers are unaware of details of the assembly process, which usually requires less than a few minutes of central processing unit (CPU) time, and one or more passes to assemble the program into machine-executable steps.

On the other hand, the level of programmer involvement increases on a minicomputer. Many minicomputers have only a single teletypewriter as input device, whose slow rate increases the time required to input the source program. Additionally, the source program has to be resubmitted to the minicomputer for any subsequent pass. Important aspects of an assembler can be categorized as:

1. Ease of coding
2. Ease of debugging programs with minimum time spent in debugging
3. Efficient I/O and program language
4. Minimum housekeeping tasks
5. Core size required for the assembler
6. Capability to generate relocatable code in the memory size available
7. Number of symbols that can be handled by the symbol table

Total memory capacity of the minicomputer minus the size of the assembler determines the maximum number of symbols that can be stored in the symbol table. Symbol table size has an effect on the size of programs that can be assembled. The speed of the assembler is directly affected by the number of times the source programs need to be read by the input devices, by the memory capacity, and by the reading speed of the input devices. Assembly speed is, however, important only if the minicomputer is used extensively to assemble programs. The overview of a two-pass assembler is presented in Figure 6-4-1.

The assembler initially sets the current program location counter to some value and assembles all statements relative to this value. During pass one, the assembler reads the source tape and defines all symbols used in a symbol table because symbols in the source code may be referred to before they are defined. The user's symbol table is printed/punched at the end of pass one, possibly in alphabetical order, as well as any undefined symbols and corresponding diagnostics.

During pass two, the assembler rereads the source tape and using the symbol table from the previous pass generates the machine language code. The format of the generated machine language code is suitable for loading and execution. This object code often consists of header codes, an origin setting, actual machine instructions, a checksum* code, and a trailer code. Furthermore, during this pass, the assembler diagnoses all illegal symbolic references. If there happens to be an optional third pass, the assembler again reads the source tape and generates an assembly listing (printed/punched) from the source statements. The listing starts at the specified current location counter, and displays both the generated object code (in octal) and source code.

---

* A checksum is a summation of digits or bits used primarily for checking purposes and summed according to an arbitrary set of rules.

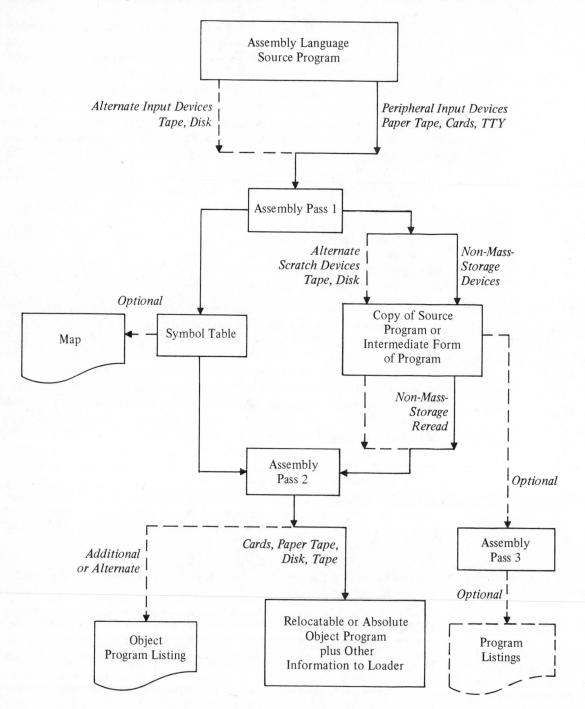

FIGURE 6-4-1.   *Overview of two-pass assembler.*

6.4.2 Functional Components of Compilers

In this section the general structure of a FORTRAN compiler will be analyzed. Other language translators work in a similar fashion. As seen in the previous sections, a compiler is a language translator that permits the user to write programs as a simple set of statements. These statements closely relate the language normally used in expressing objectives in relationship to the application. These statements are far removed from the binary coded machine language of the minicomputer.

The overall logical parts of a compiler are illustrated in Figure 6-4-2. The steps of compilation can be broken down into the following phases:

1. Scanning and conversion of source statement
2. Syntax analysis (structure)
3. Semantic analysis (meaning)
4. Code preparation
5. Code generation

The number of passes required to perform these steps and produce executable machine code depends on the memory capacity of the minicomputer, the language under consideration, and amount of optimization for the object code.

While compilers vary in the number of passes required to perform their functions, these five phases are common to most compilers, and therefore warrant a few comments:

1. *Scanning and conversion of source statements:*
   These routines scan the input characters of the source statements in order to build fixed-size symbols, used internal to the compiler processing, and to change delimiters into internal break characters for subsequent faster analysis. Often these identifiers (integers, reserved words, character symbols) are replaced by fixed-length integers for internal use.
2. *Syntax analysis:*
   The routines involved in syntax analysis decompose the source statements into their basic constituents, build an internal equivalent form of the source program, perform syntax checking, and build the symbol table. Entries in the symbol table include the identifier, its location, and corresponding attributes. Appropriate diagnostics are generated for all incorrectly specified source statements that do not adhere to the grammar or rules of the language.
3. *Semantic analysis:*
   After source language statements have been grammatically analyzed, semantic routines check for appropriate meaning and use this analysis to further enhance entries in the symbol table. In other words, these routines generate correct internal programs, as well as complete appropriate entries in the symbol table. Allocation of run time storage and

161

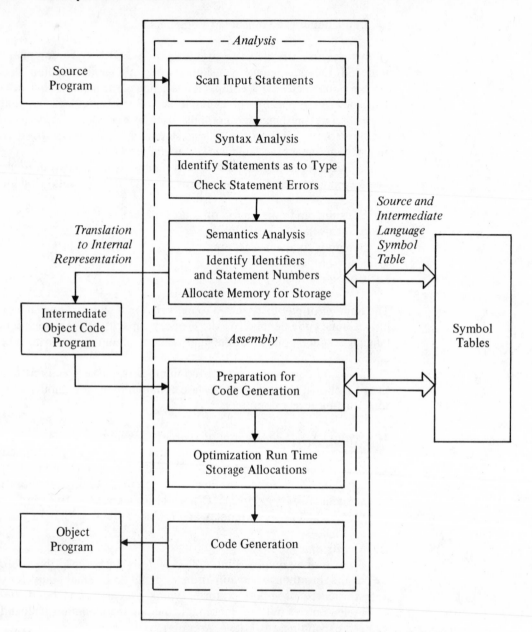

FIGURE 6-4-2. *Logical components of a compiler.*

further checking of types and classifications of all identifiers are performed.

4. *Code preparation:*

   During the code preparation phase, compiler routines are further involved in allocation of run time storage, in object code optimization, and in the elimination of redundant expressions and code. Final compile time diagnostics are generated.

5. *Code generation:*

This is the final phase of compilation. The internal form of the source program is converted (synthesized), final addressing of some instructions completed, and assembly language or machine language is generated for further processing by either an assembler or loader.

Two FORTRAN languages which are defined by USASI* or ANSI** are Basic FORTRAN (formerly FORTRAN II) and standard FORTRAN (formerly FORTRAN IV). Despite the standards proposed for FORTRAN, most minicomputer vendors provide their own renditions of FORTRAN, and therefore they become machine dependent, either lacking some features of a standard FORTRAN or including additional features not defined in a standard FORTRAN.

The variations in FORTRAN languages provided by minicomputer vendors involve the following language capabilities:

1. Different levels of subscripting
2. Function subprograms
3. Absolute or relocatable output
4. FORTRAN syntax compatible with USASI Basic and/or Standard FORTRAN
5. Subroutines
6. COMMON statements
7. Format specifications to include I, F, E, A, X, H, and Z (hexadecimal) formats
8. Multilevel array dimensioning
9. Free-form input
10. Mixed mode arithmetic
11. Generalized subscripting expressions
12. Arithmetic and trigonometric library subroutines
13. Two-branch IF statements
14. Variations in FORTRAN supplied subroutine libraries

The different capabilities provided depend on the minimum minicomputer configuration as well as the number of passes required by the compiler to analyze the FORTRAN statements (from 2 to 12 passes). These design variations range from one- to multipass compilers on 4K to 12K minicomputer systems. A 4K memory FORTRAN compilation (multipass) process is illustrated in Figure 6-4-3 and an 8K memory FORTRAN compilation (multipass) process is presented in Figure 6-4-4. The number of passes for these systems, and for systems in general, depend on the size of memory available, the storage space required by the compiler, the maximum size of the programs it is designed to compile, and the number and kind of diagnostic messages it produces for output.

---

* USASI stands for United States of America Standards Institute.
** ANSI stands for American National Standards Institute.

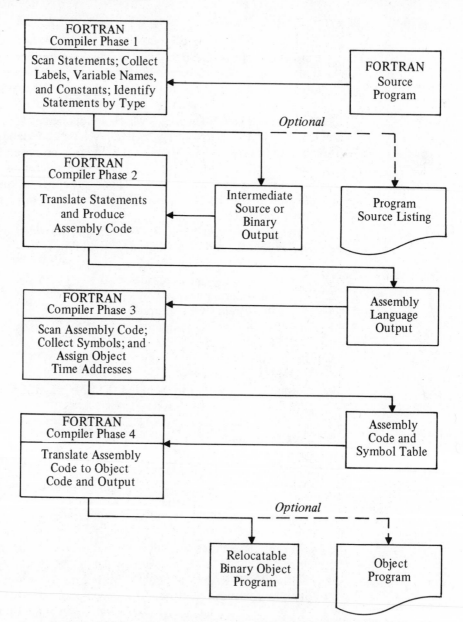

FIGURE 6-4-3.   *Multipass 4K memory FORTRAN compilation process.*

Most 4K FORTRAN compilers are provided as standalone systems with their own execution time programs that include: I/O routines or handlers, arithmetic and mathematical function utilities, and data conversion routines. Recall that in this minicomputer configuration all input/output is handled using an ASR-33 TTY. Hence, the number of times the source program needs to be read is important.

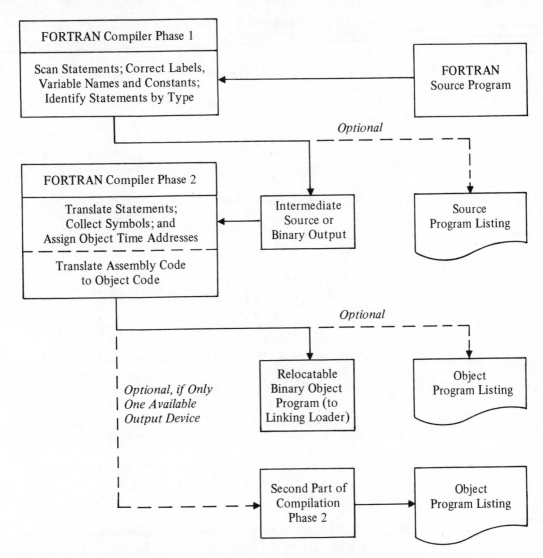

FIGURE 6-4-4. *Multipass 8K memory FORTRAN compilation process.*

The larger FORTRAN compilers (requiring 8K or more) often determine automatically the available memory size, expanding the appropriate tables, and subsequently providing faster compilation speeds. Frequent extensions provided by minicomputer vendors for these FORTRAN compilers (8–32K memory systems) include:

1. Assembly language subroutine capabilities
2. Assembly language output
3. Standard or extended precision mode
4. Complex arithmetic mode

165

5. Standard subroutine linkages for easy interface with user and/or library subroutines
6. Overlay capabilities
7. Memory map output indicating all programs and their sizes loaded in memory
8. Output of symbol table for use in online debugging
9. Reentrant FORTRAN compiler

Most general-purpose software systems, because of their generality, are inefficient in relation to single-purpose specific programs. FORTRAN compilers fall into this general-purpose software category, and thus often produce inefficient and bulky machine language programs. To overcome this inefficiency in the produced machine language, several vendors provide code optimization phases in their compilers. The optimization provided often includes:

1. Optimization in register usage
2. Elimination of redundant expressions and code
3. Complete floating-point repertoire
4. Extensive compile time diagnostics

At execution time, most FORTRAN provide run time library routines, error messages for overflow/underflow, format errors and any other execution errors. A typical FORTRAN compilation and execution flow is presented in Figure 6-4-5.

In addition to the FORTRAN compilers, most vendors include these compilers as part of their operating system software, as well as conversational and real-time FORTRAN. Conversational and real-time FORTRAN have capabilities similar to the above compilers. However, because they are real-time oriented (for such applications as data acquisition and process control) they often include: program interrupt options, in-line symbolic machine instructions, linkage to assembly language I/O routines, extended relational and binary logical operators and expressions, multitask control, and extended file capabilities. Figure 6-4-6 illustrates a typical conversational FORTRAN for interactive use. Notice in particular the interactive statement correcting capability (similar to Basic), the execution time trace debugging facility, and the optional object code for output.

6.4.3 Functional Components of Interpreters

An interpreter for a source language accepts a source program in that language as input and executes this program without producing an equivalent object program. Most interpreters provided by minicomputer vendors analyze the complete source program and convert it into some internal form (much like a compiler does). The equivalent internal form of the source program is then further decoded and executed one statement at a time. The

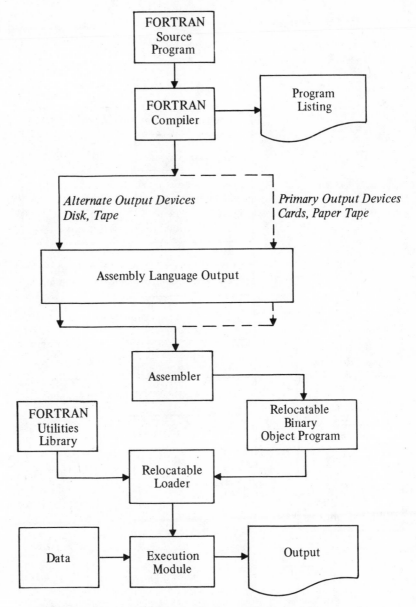

FIGURE 6-4-5. *Block diagram of FORTRAN compilation and execution.*

internal representation of the original source program is designed to minimize each decoding for subsequent execution. A block diagram illustrating the interpreter concept is presented in Figure 6-4-7.

BASIC, as was seen, is a dedicated interpretive system that permits conversational entry and execution of BASIC statements. As information is interactively entered via the input device, it is immediately examined for

167

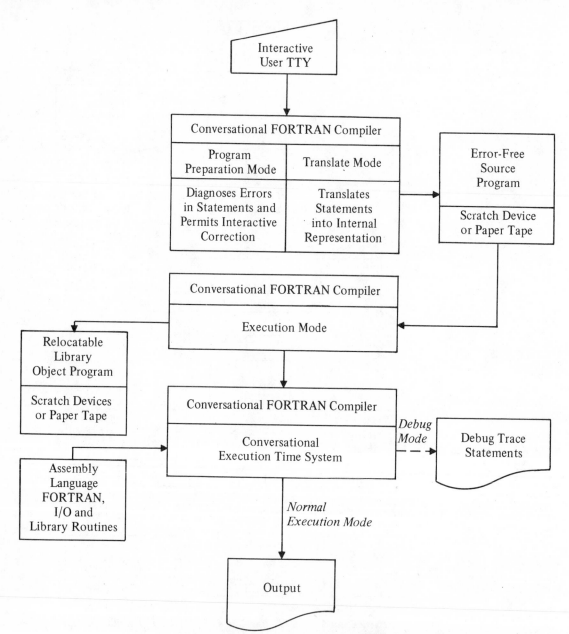

FIGURE 6-4-6. *Conversational FORTRAN in interactive use.*

syntax errors (format and specification errors) and if applicable, error messages are immediately produced. Otherwise, the statement is translated into its internal representation (see Figure 6-4-7) and included in the program. At the conclusion of statement entries into the system, BASIC switches to an interpretation mode. In this mode, the system recognizes certain problems that occur (such as division by zero), provides additional diagnostics and returns control to the user.

168

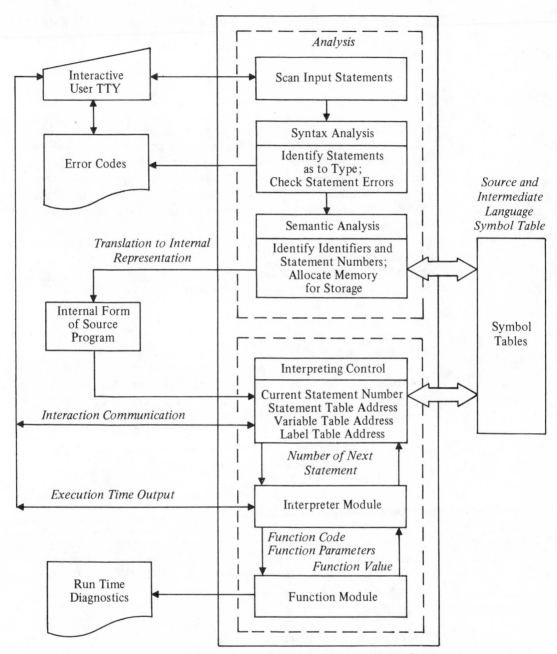

FIGURE 6-4-7. *Block diagram of typical interpreter.*

Variations of BASIC involve basic language capabilities, library support, availability as either interpreter or compiler, minimum configurations, and the capability for single or multiple user access.

Other interpreters, tailored after BASIC, and with similar capabilities, such as online interactive (conversational) modes, are often

169

provided by individual vendors. Among such vendor-dependent interpreters are Digital Equipment Corporation's FOCAL (FOrmula CALculator) and FOCAL-8.

6.5 Utility Software

Utility programs perform those tasks which cannot be accomplished by the minicomputer's hardware. Most minicomputers are built to minimize the total basic cost of the machine, and very seldom have the hardware floating-point registers required to handle floating-point operations. Consequently, utility programs are provided to handle floating-point operations. Similar comments apply to multiply/divide, double-precision arithemtic, and conversion routines.

Utility programs also assist application programmers in editing and debugging their programs. They provide for mathematical functions, system generation, sort/merge of files, hardware tests, and diagnostics programs. Many of these functions have already been discussed, but let us recall some of their capabilities.

6.5.1 Program Library

All routines in this library may be called from either Assembly language or high-level language programs. The mathematical function routines frequently meet ANSI FORTRAN standards, and include:

1. Fixed-point multiply/divide
2. Floating-point add, subtract, multiply, divide
3. Double-precision routines
4. Exponential, natural log, sine, cosine, tangent, arctangent, hyperbolic (tanh), and square root functions

In addition, some statistical subroutines (e.g., random number generator, correlation analysis), matrix multiplication subroutines, formatted I/O operations, shift routines, Boolean functions (AND, OR, NOT), and output device formatters are included.

6.5.2 System Utility Libraries

These libraries are sometimes provided by vendors of larger minicomputer systems. Included in these routines are:

1. *Sort/merge program* to sort and merge data files.
2. *System generation programs* to construct processor libraries for mass-storage-oriented systems.

3. *Minicomputer translator programs* to convert source language programs from one minicomputer's assembly language to another. These conversion programs indicate those statements that could be machine dependent and may not have been translated correctly.
4. *Memory-to-memory data conversion programs* to permit conversion of data types without using input/output routines.

Great variations in these routines because of hardware dependence exist from vendor to vendor.

6.5.3 High-Level Language Libraries

These libraries contain all the subroutines necessary to run FORTRAN, ALGOL, or COBOL compiled programs. For example, they contain implementations of string manipulation, dynamic array allocation, mode conversions, and byte manipulation.

6.6 Operating System Software

There have been two major trends in developing operating system software control and supervisory programs. The first was the development of an integrated application module. With this approach, it is extremely difficult, if not impossible, to separate the traditional elements of software (e.g., assembler, loader, control) from the basic support software and the applications software. Such modules have been available and are still the predominant type of software found on installed systems.

The second approach was the development of more general-purpose software, similar to traditional software for large-scale general-purpose computers. The growth in the number and variety of general-purpose systems is attributable to several factors, the most important of which are:

1. A large number of minicomputers have been or will be installed; i.e., there is a large market.
2. Extensive hardware to support these systems is available at a reasonable price (more core, disk, magnetic tape).
3. Much of the software has been developed for special applications by users or by software specialists under contract.

The amount of supporting software acquired with a system is dependent on the amount and type of hardware involved. A very small system cannot support and does not need a large sophisticated operating system (e.g., a communications-oriented system). However, as the size of the system grows and the number or variety of applications for which it is used increases, a more efficient and capable system is needed. At the upper end of hardware system size and sophistication, a fairly complex operating system is desirable.

A very small machine having only the main frame, 4K words of main memory, and a teletype for input normally has few or no control programs. In this size range, a system may have an absolute loader, some debug aids, and a few very basic library routines to supplement built-in hardware capability.

The addition of memory, auxiliary storage, more powerful input/ output (I/O) devices, and a more capable main frame permits a more comprehensive and powerful set of control and utility programs, such as: relocatable loaders, I/O routines (which relieve the programmer of detailed I/O programming), a batch processing (non-multiprogramming) monitor, a multiprogramming monitor, a real-time monitor, and a timesharing monitor. Various vendors give these programs different names depending on such factors as peripherals (disk operating system or tape operating system) and specific functions performed.

The facilities provided by most operating systems include:

1. Input/output control
2. Interrupt management
3. Data and program libraries management
4. Initiating, loading, and executing (sequencing) programs
5. Memory allocation management
6. Communication interfacing between the system and the user
7. Memory protection and system integrity

Additional capabilities relating to memory management and program management, such as program overlay structures, memory segmentation, memory paging, and file protection are also provided. *Overlay structures* permit programs too large for available memory resources to be segmented so that they fit into memory. Communication between segments is provided through a common storage block, similar to FORTRAN's COMMON. Two modified system programs are included in overlay segmentation, namely, a loader and an overlay monitor. A modified version of the *loader* is needed to build the appropriate overlay segments and an *overlay monitor* is needed to initiate program loading and sequencing control from one segment to the next. The interaction of the user with the operating system and its capabilities is illustrated in Figure 6-6-1.

In terms of *input/output control* functions, the central processor communicates with the user through its general-purpose I/O channels. It is pertinent to recall several important aspects of these I/O activities:

1. Individual I/O channels can connect to one or more input/output devices.
2. Hardware mechanisms are often included to uniquely identify input/ output requests from each channel.

172

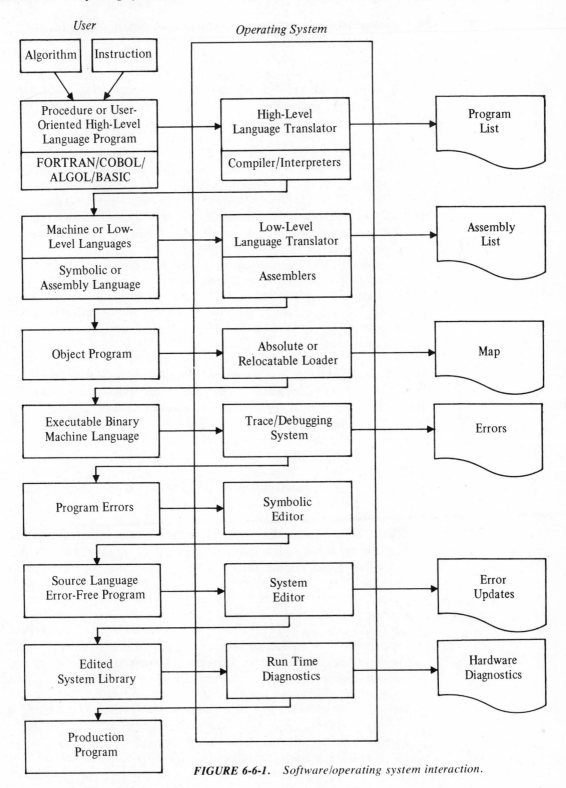

FIGURE 6-6-1. *Software/operating system interaction.*

3. All input/output occurs through common I/O instructions processed and initiated by the CPU.
4. For each input/output transfer, a device address, data or buffer address, and word or block count is set up.
5. To allow concurrent CPU processing with I/O processing, aside from the initialization sequencing, frequently an interrupt mechanism is provided.

These functions are all common to any I/O service request of a user and, therefore, are incorporated into the operating system software. The following software modules are frequently included in most operating systems:

1. *A central interrupt processor*, which routes the I/O service request to the appropriate I/O device handler, and handles all interrupts from peripheral devices requesting attention.
2. *I/O device handlers (subroutines)*, which are responsible for specific data transfers to individual I/O devices.
3. *Automatic buffering routines*, which permit users to continue application processing without regard to whether or not the data have actually been transferred to the specific device, or if the device is even available for data transfer and not already busy.

With these capabilities, the operating system provides device-independent input/output. The user specifies input/output requests using a common instruction set and logical device unit. The operating system maintains appropriate device tables containing corresponding logical and physical device assignments, as well as request queues to individual I/O devices, providing overlapped I/O and CPU processing.

In addition to the common I/O processing function, most minicomputer vendors provide variations in the following system capabilities:

1. *System Generation:*
   This module is used for the initial creation of a system tailored to a specific hardware configuration. It assembles the required I/O modules, allocates memory space for initial operations, links peripheral drivers into the system, and automatically generates the required absolute and relocatable libraries. System generation occurs only when an existing system is installed or enlarged.
2. *Operating System Organization:*
   The system organization depends on the peripheral devices and the configuration, especially for systems that include bulk memory (mass storage devices). The following organizations are representative of the systems provided (see Table 6-6-1):
   a. Basic Control System. Also known as a standalone operating system or basic operating system, this system provides loading, relocating, and linking of user programs and system library routines. In addition, all buffered input/output operations are provided on a device-independent basis. This core resident system improves

TABLE 6-6-1. *Software Features Available with Different Operating System Configurations*

Features / Operating Systems	Real-Time Operating System — Foreground/Background Operating System	Disk Operating System — Tape Operating System	Basic Operating System
Assemblers			
Basic			X
Extended		X	X
Macro	X		
Compilers			
Basic FORTRAN			X
Standard FORTRAN	X	X	
ALGOL	X	X	
COBOL	X		
Interpreters			
Basic	X	X	X
Scientific support			
programs	X	X	
Development software			
Symbolic text editor	X	X	X
Trace debug system	X	X	X
Real-time subsystem	X		
Mathematical libraries	X	X	X
Loader subsystems	X	X	X
I/O control subsystem	X	X	X
System editors	X	X	X
System generation	X	X	
System features			
Utility programs	X	X	X
User libraries	X	X	
Diagnostics	X	X	X
Checkpointing	X		
Overlay system	X	X	
Real-time clock	X		
Memory protect	X	X	
Automatic scheduling	X	X	
Time limit control	X	X	

machine utilization in assembling, debugging, and execution of application programs.

    b. Disk or Tape Operating Systems (DOS or TOS). This system, utilizing the peripheral devices, provides increased assembly, loading or compilation speeds with minimum operator intervention. In addition, this system includes comprehensive file management, buffer management for all logical I/O devices, disk or tape overlay capabilities, and extensive system libraries.

c. Foreground/Background System (F/BOS). This operating system, also known as real-time operating system (RTOS), executes programs based on assigned priority. This priority assignment includes user application area, response time, and I/O service requests. Real-time programs are incorporated as high priority foreground (I/O bound) mode while all compute bound programs are run in the background (compute bound) mode. The background jobs are assigned a priority based on the order they are received by the system (batch mode). Multitasking, timesharing, and automatic I/O transfers facilitate complete task scheduling, initiation, termination, and I/O services.

d. Timesharing Operating System (TSOS). This system assigns equal priority to all users, allocating each an equal time (time slice). TSOS is a variation of the F/BOS with timesharing users now occupying the foreground activities, while batch programs can be executed during any leftover processor time in the background.

3. *Number, Type, and Size of Foreground/Background Programs:*
System parameters, such as average memory requirements, maximum number of programs in either mode, maximum number of allowed priority levels, and type of applications that can be run in foreground or background, are considered in the determination of system hardware. System design criteria also include minimum facilities for the operating system, minimum resources for desired application programs, response time to the users, as well as I/O transfer rates or activities. Priority structures are most often software assigned and applications oriented.

4. *Operator Communication Interface:*
Most operating systems include a master scheduler which acts as interface between the operator (user) and the operating system. This module decodes messages and provides overriding capabilities.

5. *Data and Program Library Management:*
Management facilities for various data and program structures are incorporated to provide addressing, updating, and editing of any file. This file management service is often included for both the operating system's libraries, as well as the user's application programs.

6. *Memory Allocation Management:*
Most minicomputer operating systems manage memory allocations at three levels: memory resources for resident (nucleus) operating system components, resident application programs, and dynamic or temporary memory assignments for individual users. The resident program requirements, both system and user, have a direct bearing on the minimum memory configuration required by the minicomputer system. Dynamic memory space needs to be large enough so that temporary files, programs or data, can be maintained for individual users without excessive overlaying.

6.6.1 Basic Operating System

The basic operating system (BOS) is designed to permit operator-controlled loading and initiation of program execution with logical I/O services for standard peripherals. When mass storage devices are available, the capability of loading and executing programs from libraries is frequently included. BOS, therefore, provides centralized services for input/output, interrupts, clocks, and user-system communication interfaces. In general, it permits overlap of CPU and I/O processing (including automatic code conversion) by responding to and servicing all interrupts. The user is able to write programs with a high degree of device independence by simply selecting the appropriate standard peripheral I/O device handlers which perform the complete I/O functions, including peripheral interrupt processing.

The hardware configuration for this standalone operating system usually consists of the following:

1. 4–8K memory and CPU
2. ASR-33 Teletype or paper tape input/output readers
3. Possible inclusion of a magnetic tape, disk or drum peripheral device.

The standalone system software modules include the following modular subsystems (see Figure 6-6-2):

1. *System Generation Subsystem* provides a system building mechanism to generate a customized operating system to the user's particular configuration.
2. *Resident Monitor Subsystem* permits the user full access to all available peripherals for storage and retrieval of programs. The monitor accepts the appropriate commands from the user, loads these programs, saves these programs and permits their recall for subsequent execution from the system library.
3. *Loader Subsystem* provides to the user the necessary relocating and absolute loader. The appropriate loader determines the available memory capacity and loads (and relocates whenever necessary) the program into memory ready for execution. Frequently, the loader functions under BOS are restricted to only loading relocatable programs without concern for specific linkages at load time.
4. *Assembler Subsystem* interfaces with the resident monitor utilizes all available core and/or peripheral devices to maximize the assembly speed. The extended or the macro assembler capabilities are provided, depending on the minicomputer configuration.
5. *Input/Output Control Subsystem (IOCS)* provides the link between the service request for I/O, by either user or system program, and the actual I/O execution. All input/output requests to system devices are serviced by device I/O handlers, which actually move the data between the program and the I/O devices. These I/O handlers are responsible for initialization of the device and for other functions, such as interrupt

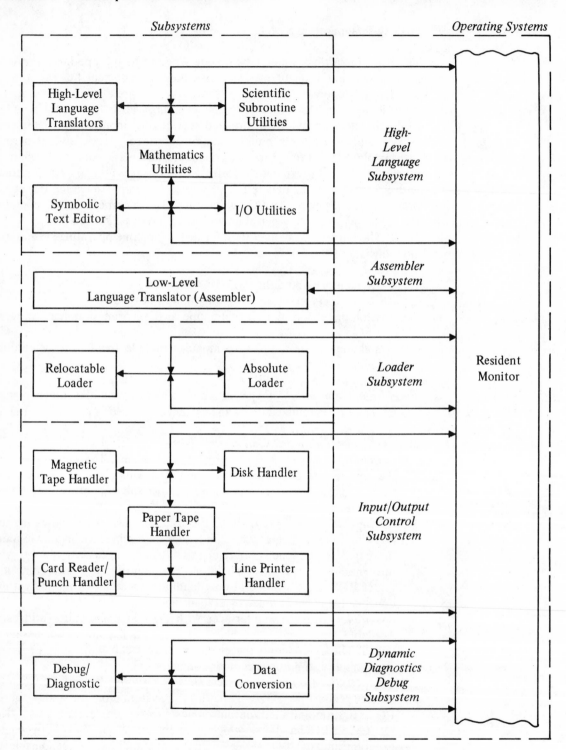

FIGURE 6-6-2.   *Basic operating subsystem components.*

servicing, peculiar to a given I/O device. Using the centralized IOCS, the user programs deal only with logical units and are therefore device-independent.

6. *Symbolic Text Editor Subsystem (STES)* provides for the generation and/or identification of source or other programs by means of keyboard commands, or information entered via magnetic tape, paper tape or teletype. The command structure of STES permits simple commands to perform updating (adding, changing, or deleting) of source text, filing of information, copying of text and/or data, editing, listing, searching, and assembling.

7. *Dynamic Debug and Diagnostic Subsystem* provides the capability to trace the operations of any portion of a program; to examine the status of any memory location, registers, or block of memory; and to dump contents of selected memory locations utilizing any of the available peripheral devices. Online interactive debugging and diagnostic sessions are provided through the resident monitor subsystem. Most services provided by this subsystem were discussed in the Basic Software Support Section.

8. *High-Level Language Subsystem* (most frequently FORTRAN) consists of three subcomponents:

    a. FORTRAN Compiler, which translates problem-oriented FORTRAN language statements into executable machine language.

    b. FORTRAN Loader, which loads FORTRAN and assembly language object programs into memory, resolving external references and linkages.

    c. FORTRAN Subroutine Library, which provides all intrinsic and basic external subroutines standard to USASI FORTRAN.

6.6.2 Disk (or Tape) Operating System

The disk or tape operating system (DOS or TOS) incorporates all of the BOS functions in addition to control functions over peripheral devices. It provides fully automatic operation, batch processing, user interaction, and full interrupt servicing. The TOS permits the user to store on line a complete operating system, which speeds the generation, checkout, and execution of user programs. The DOS, because of its rapid random access, provides more flexibility, greater operator control, and more efficient processing.

Several major functions provided by either the DOS or TOS to the user are:

1. Tutorial services regarding the capabilities of the system
2. Error diagnostics, messages, and recovery facilities
3. Standard logical-physical I/O device associations and modification capability
4. Dynamic allocation of devices at load time
5. Supervision of loading, initiation, and execution of all system and user programs, I/O device handlers, and library routines

179

In this operating system environment, a user can assemble or compile source language programs and load and execute object programs—all under the control of the executive software. This software automatically controls the loading, from either disk or magnetic tape of the appropriate assembler, compiler, loader, user library routines, or any other required programs.

Hardware configurations for DOS and TOS may require the following components:

1. 4–16K memory capacity
2. Disk for system residence (DOS)
3. Magnetic tape unit for system residence (TOS)
4. ASR-33 Teletype
5. High-speed paper tape reader/punch

This operating system (either DOS or TOS) offers extensive services for both program development and execution by including the following modular subsystems (see Figure 6-6-3):

1. *System Generation Subsystem* provides a system mechanism to initialize file and track directories and for recording the operating system and user programs onto disk (DOS), or magnetic (TOS) tape. A facility for directory and program listings is provided.
2. *Monitor Subsystem* provides the user an interface to all services of the system. The user can save and recall programs from the system-resident device (either DOS or TOS), as well as request the loading and execution of various system or user programs. The interface between the system and the user is through a command decoder which recognizes requests for system programs and loads the system loader to bring in the requested programs. Through the command decoder, device assignments can be manipulated by altering the contents of the device assignment table at load time. Actual I/O devices may, therefore, be changed without altering the logical program references to these devices.
3. *Loader Subsystem* provides for the loading of programs and any associate subroutines into memory and then completing transfer linkages between them readying the modules for execution. The loader subsystem is responsible for loading the monitor subsystem as well as for restoring control to the monitor subsystem from other system or user programs.
4. *Assembler Subsystem* permits the user to build machine language programs in a symbolic language, and also provides extended capabilities, including pseudo-operations, conditional assembly, and macro extensions.
5. *Extended I/O Control Subsystem (EIOCS)* includes data-handling subroutines, device handlers, and interrupt service routines. This subsystem permits the user to dynamically alter logical-physical unit assignments for I/O devices by means of job control commands through the monitor subsystem. Users can, therefore, write programs as if a given

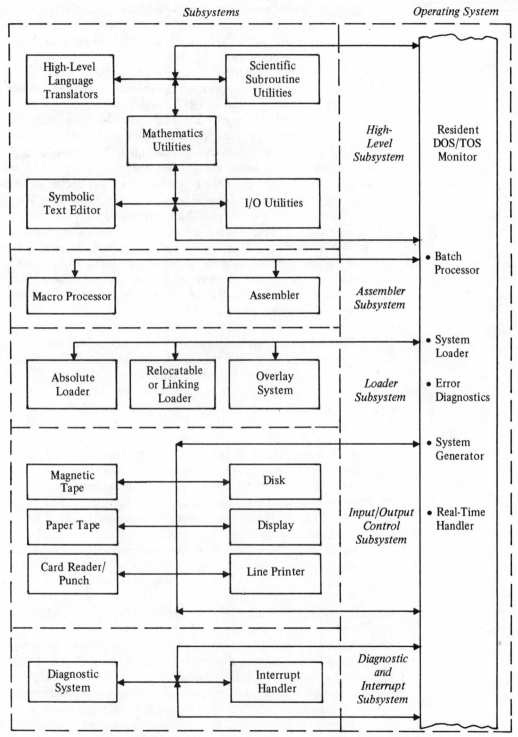

FIGURE 6-6-3.   *Disk or tape operating system components.*

I/O operation were performed on a particular type of device. In addition to device independence, users can also request:

a. Blocking and deblocking of device-oriented physical blocks into a more convenient form.

b. Physical block transfers to dynamically allocated buffers.

c. Extensive file management capabilities with comprehensive file structures for peripheral devices.

d. Automatic cataloging of files and updating capabilities.

6. *Execution Time Subsystem (ETS)* provides such miscellaneous services as system restart capabilities, dynamic memory allocation, a peripheral interchange system (used to copy files and other file-oriented functions), automatic job control for batch processing or operator sequencing, real-time clock handlers, and extensive interrupt systems. The interrupt system facilitates the design of an interrupt driven environment. (When the interrupt occurs, current processing is immediately terminated, and the requested program is loaded from either disk or tape.) The DOS or TOS conserves main memory space by permitting all software modules, except for the resident monitor, to be stored on peripheral devices, and loaded into memory on demand. An example of the procedure for the operating system in shown in Figure 6-6-4.

The modular design of these subsystems provides the user the capability to incorporate any program modules into a tailored specialized system (e.g., inclusion of different I/O device handlers).

6.6.3 Real-Time Operating System (RTOS)

The RTOS is an extremely versatile multiprogramming operating system capable of supporting services for real-time data acquisition, process control, data acquisition, and timesharing applications, concurrently with some background compilations, assemblies, and batch operations. The system controls concurrent time-shared users by protecting foreground user programs from background, batch processing user programs of low priority. The applications mentioned above all require responses from the minicomputer within some specified maximum time interval. This time interval response to the application is described as *real time*.

With RTOS the user is freed from any I/O handling, interrupt servicing, and resource allocation. Any programs in the system, whether stored in main memory or on a rotating memory device, are scheduled by RTOS giving highest priority to real-time foreground programs and lower priority to background jobs. The user can establish the priority of the programs to be executed, while the system schedules and runs programs automatically without any further operator intervention. Background programs are usually executed during the idle time intervals of the real-time operations.

Foreground programs are assumed to be checked out and may be loaded and run in response to real-time clock, external interrupts, or an

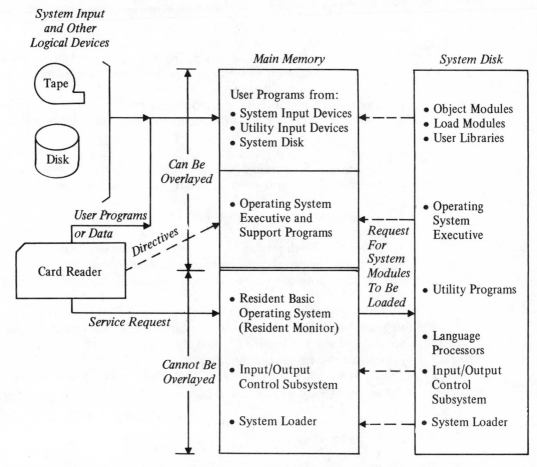

FIGURE 6-6-4. *Example of operating procedures for a basic operating system.*

operator or system command. In addition, they also have first priority to memory and I/O device resources according to their assigned priority levels.

The multiprogramming capability of RTOS performs housekeeping functions that permit general-purpose background programs to run concurrently with real-time foreground operations. The background program can be an assembly, a compilation, a debug run, a production run, an editing task, or a regular batch processing job. It can, of course, utilize only those resources not required by the foreground programs, including the idle processing time from the real-time jobs.

User programs can request scheduling in the foreground or in the background. Individual foreground programs can be loaded without interfering with the system. At any time, the operator can convert the status of the background program to a foreground program.

183

The RTOS provides the following foreground/background support functions:

1. Priority and time-oriented scheduling of programs. (Any program can request execution at a specified clock time, after a specified interval, or cyclic execution after specified intervals.)
2. Exclusive use of a particular I/O device.
3. Ability to utilize background memory when needed for real-time programs.
4. Demand linking of programs not resident in memory.
5. Initiation of background programs at the request of foreground jobs.
6. Interrupt driven programs suspending processing to await completion of I/O.
7. Temporary scratch or work files made available to the background programs.
8. Automatic batch processing without operator intervention.
9. Character-oriented data communications services.
10. Variable partitions for both foreground and background programs.

In a typical foreground/background processing environment, the foreground real-time programs are assigned individual priority levels and then automatically scheduled by the hardware. There is no further operator or operating system intervention required.

Hardware configurations for RTOS often include the following components (see Figure 6-6-5):

1. 8–16K minimum configuration
2. Real-time clock
3. Memory protect
4. Priority interrupt system
5. Disk for system residence
6. Printing terminal or a CRT
7. High-speed paper tape reader/punch
8. Power fail/restart
9. Card reader (optional)
10. Magnetic tape (optional)

A typical configuration chart, providing software components and required hardware modules, is illustrated in Table 6-6-2.

The system modules included in a RTOS, in addition to those of DOS or TOS, are the following subsystems (see Figure 6-6-6).

1. *Real-Time Scheduler (RTS)* automatically schedules core-resident programs according to the time of day, fixed time intervals (time slicing), or earliest opportunity.
2. *Processor and Relocatable Library* contains programs in core image format as well as subprograms whose locations in memory are deter-

Minicomputer Mainframe

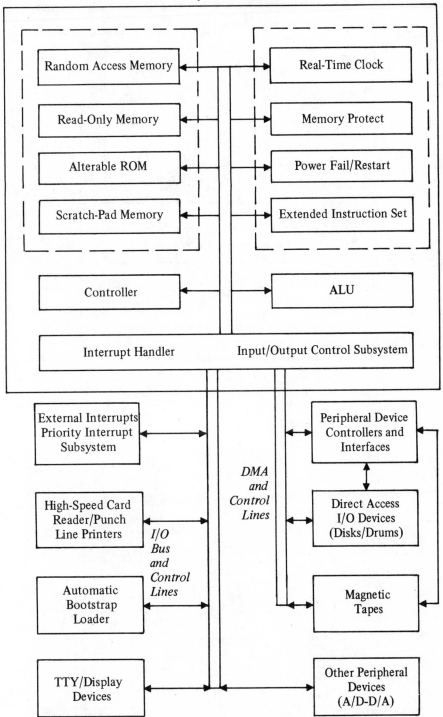

FIGURE 6-6-5. *Hardware configuration of real-time operating system (with all optional equipment).*

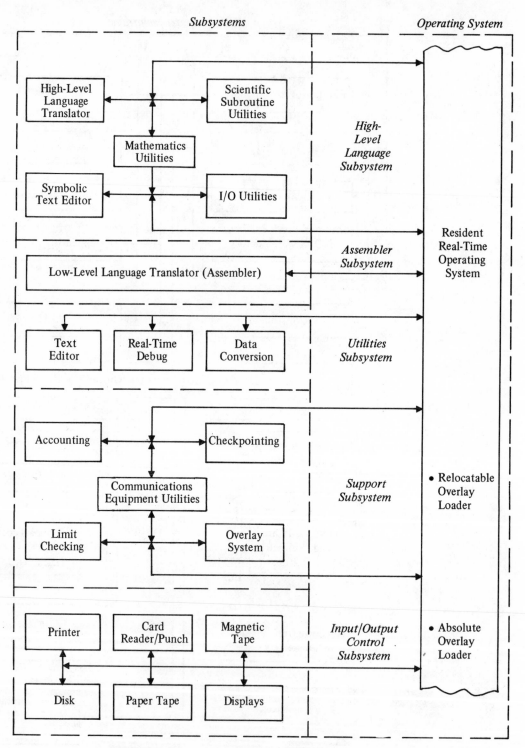

FIGURE 6-6-6. *Software module diagram for real-time operating system.*

TABLE 6-6-2. *Real-Time Operating System Configuration Chart*

Hardware → / Real-Time Operating System Software ↓	CPU · 4K Memory · Printing Terminal or CRT	CPU · 8K Memory · Printing Terminal or CRT · High-Speed Peripherals	CPU · 8K Memory · Printing Terminal or CRT · Real-Time Clock · Priority Interrupt · High-Speed Peripherals · Disks/Tapes	CPU · 12K Memory · Printing Terminal or CRT · Real-Time Clock · Priority Interrupt · High-Speed Peripherals · Disks/Tapes	CPU · 16K Memory · Printing Terminal or CRT · Real-Time Clock · Memory Protect · Priority Interrupts · Power Fail/ Restart · Disks/Tapes
High-level language subsystem					
Basic FORTRAN					
Standard FORTRAN					
ALGOL					
BASIC					
Assembler subsystem					
Basic					
Extended					
Macro					
Utilities subsystem					
Symbolic text editor					
Debug/trace					
Support subsystem					
Accounting					
Checkpointing					
Overlay system					
Real-time operating system					
Resident monitor					
I/O control system					
Math utilities					
Loader subsystem					
Automatic scheduling					
Job control subsystem					

mined by the system loader. Each library has its own directory with lists of programs and their locations on a mass storage device.

3. *Real-Time Loader* provides full overlay capability for both foreground and background. It can load programs from any suitable device and output linked load-modules to any output device. The overlay service provides segmentation into overlay tree structures for any real-time, system, or batch programs. Segments from the overlay tree are called into memory and released when no longer needed.

4. *Foreground/Background Monitor System (FBMS)* provides to both real-time and timesharing users the following functions:

a. Scheduling of processing times.

b. Memory protection of foreground/background to prevent background programs from interfering with foreground routines.

c. I/O device allocation and protection to foreground jobs.

d. Sharing of device handlers from both foreground and background jobs.

e. Automatic multilevel priority interrupt system.

f. Communication interface between foreground and background jobs which provides switching from a protect mode to a supervisor mode. Program status word instructions permit easy loading, saving or exchanging supervisor control functions. Privileged instructions can only be executed in protected memory.

g. Automatic background scheduling.

h. Dynamic memory allocation provides for variable number of foreground/background programs, as well as variable boundaries.

i. Extensive operator-system communication provides monitoring and control of program status, program priorities, and interrupt and I/O status.

j. Real-time debugging permits debugging of foreground or background programs without compromising the security of the real-time system.

k. Extensive mass storage management facilities provide for file addressing by symbolic file name in either random or sequential mode.

An example of a general RTOS flow is illustrated in Figure 6-6-7. Now consider some of the specific functions discussed above, namely the foreground and background processing, I/O service requests, load module loading, and general file maintenance.

6.6.3.1 Foreground/Background Processing.

The programs that run in the foreground partitions of the system are scheduled for execution through the RTOS at the command of the operator, real-time clock, interrupt or time interval (fixed time-slice for timesharing). In any case, the foreground programs can be split into two groups, the resident and nonresident programs.

The resident foreground programs are real-time programs requiring permanent memory as well as fast response time from the RTOS. In the case of extreme response time, interrupts may be programmed to jump directly to those interrupt handlers required, bypassing RTOS. Figure 6-6-7 illustrates a complete RTOS with foreground requirements, while Figure 6-6-8 illustrates the corresponding system submodules.

Nonresident foreground programs reside on any available peripheral devices in load module form, ready for loading through RTOS and the extended file management facilities. These load module forms are relocatable, and, therefore, can be loaded anywhere into available memory on a space available priority basis. These modules frequently require more memory space than in a typical foreground program partition. An example of foreground and background operations is illustrated in Figure 6-6-9.

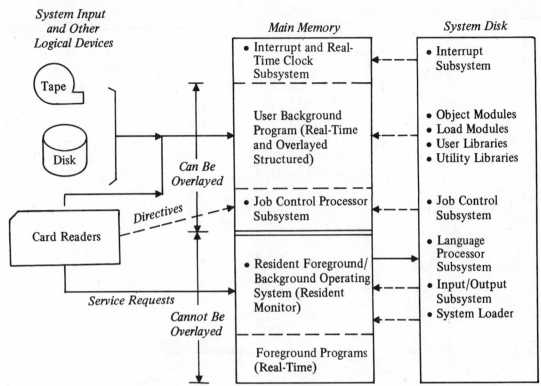

FIGURE 6-6-7. *Example of operating procedures for a foreground/ background operating system. (Programs are scheduled automatically through an operator override or internally.)*

Background jobs are used to absorb any available time from real-time processing programs. Whenever there is some idle interval time, RTOS initiates execution of a background job through a background-scheduling mechanism. Whenever a background job is preempted by a higher priority foreground job, the background program and all its associated status data are transferred to a peripheral device, and from there are automatically restored whenever processing time becomes again available (see Figure 6-6-10).

6.6.3.2 I/O Service Requests.   The IOCS system incorporated in RTOS handles all I/O requests, whether from foreground or background programs. It is responsible for device-independent I/O processing through logical devices, for queuing of I/O requests, and for the actual initiation and scheduling of the I/O device handlers. An example of I/O service request processing is illustrated in Figure 6-6-11.

6.6.3.3 Loading Procedures and the File Management.   A load module is a self-contained section of code, with or without overlays, containing all necessary information for execution. In other words, load modules have all linkages and external references resolved, but still need relocating when loaded into memory. If load modules are in overlay segment form, then an

189

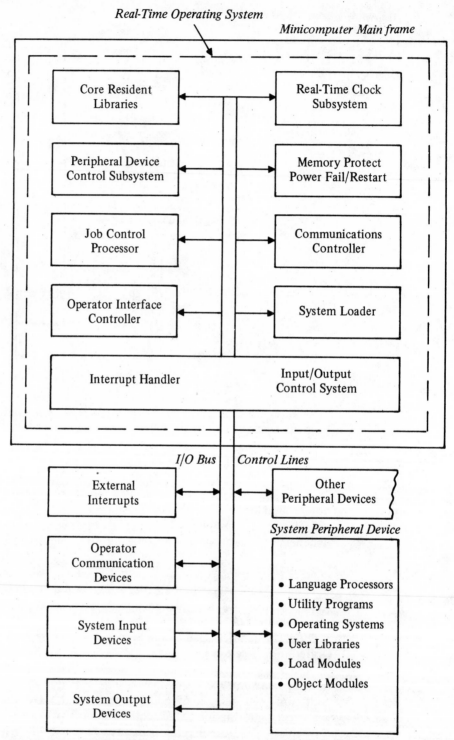

FIGURE 6-6-8. *Typical foreground system submodules.*

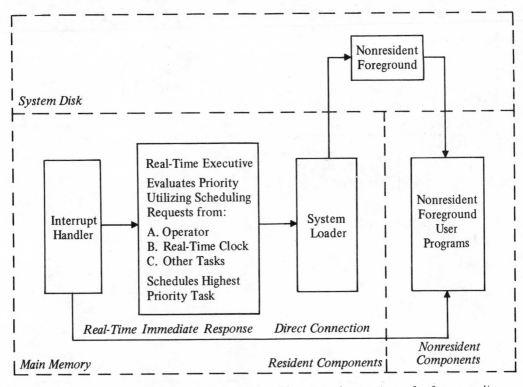

FIGURE 6-6-9.   *Scheduling of foreground operations of a foreground/ background operating system.*

overlay segment monitor must be provided to call into memory as needed, from any peripheral device, the root segment and appropriate overlay segments. At any given time, only the root segment and one overlay segment may be in main memory. An example of such a structure is illustrated in Figure 6-6-12.

File management facilities provide, to the user and to the system, capabilities for storage, access control, retrieval, and protection of data or program files. File directories provide the mechanism to access files by symbolic names in either random or sequential mode.

6.6.3.4 FORTRAN Compilation.   RTOS facilitates the use of a high-level language translator by taking the source language statements, processing them in the background mode through a compiler or assembler, and outputting the resulting object code onto an available peripheral device. From this device the object module can be automatically scheduled through a linking loader, producing a load module for subsequent execution. The input and output devices can be any of the available peripheral devices attached to the system. This concept of module passing is illustrated in Figure 6-6-13.

191

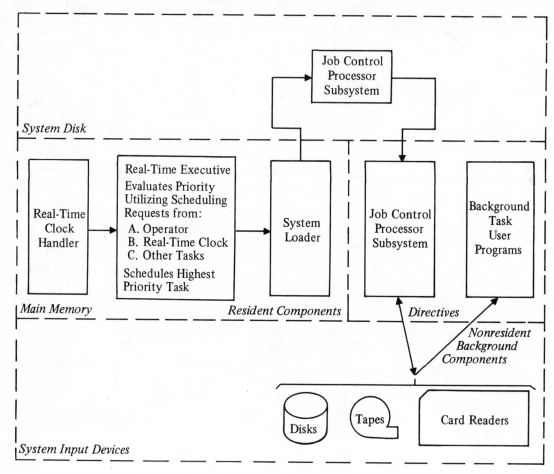

FIGURE 6-6-10. *Scheduling of background operations of a foreground/background operating system.*

6.7 Applications Software

A discussion of applications software shifts the emphasis from the equipment vendor and the attendant software necessary to produce specific minicomputer capabilities to the problems and processes of the minicomputer. Applications for minicomputers have become increasingly diverse and appear to be as limitless as the variety of user problems waiting to be solved. Minicomputers are being used for almost all applications previously dominated by large-scale general-purpose computers, in addition to many applications previously performed only by specially designed electronic monitoring and control devices.

If any aspect of applications software pervades all forms of user program development, it is the diversity of the problems encountered. Di-

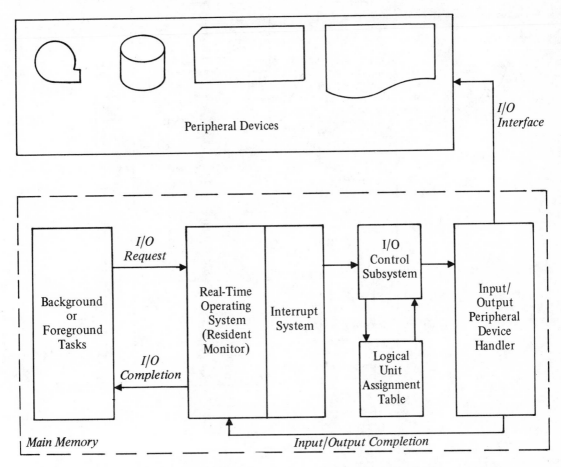

FIGURE 6-6-11.   *Input/output operations in a real-time operating system.*

versity of applications has been a cornerstone of large-scale general-purpose computer software development—large systems commonly offer a wide selection of high-level languages (and very sophisticated assemblers) to be employed in a wide variety of user environments. The smaller, more readily adaptable minicomputers seldom come to the user's doorstep fully equipped to take over this application. With a basically powerful minicomputer in hand, the user is faced with the problem of generating the application software.

Writing software requires computer programming skills, a field not necessarily related to the application problem. The software that results is limited by the equipment used (with attendant operating systems and basic support software), the application itself (as it varies from a completely dedicated computer to a general-purpose computer application), and the sources available to develop the software.

193

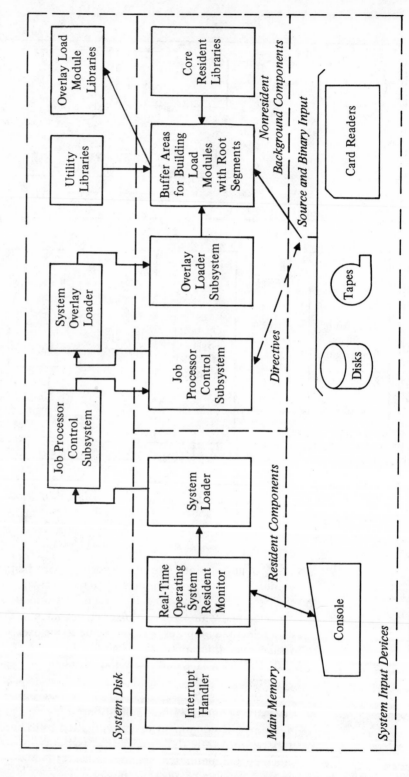

FIGURE 6-6-12. Overlay loader subsystem operations of a real-time operating system.

194

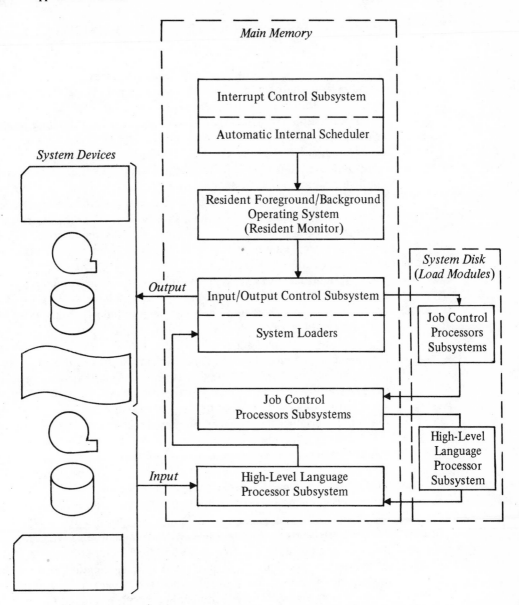

FIGURE 6-6-13. *FORTRAN compilation under the control of a real-time operating system.*

The sources available to generate applications software can be categorized into three general areas:

1. The user's in-house resources, which include time and experienced programmers.
2. The equipment vendor's resources which include general-purpose and ready-made software.

195

3. The services of a software house or computer capability "package" firm, independent of both the user and the vendor.

Large-scale general-purpose computer users usually employ the do-it-yourself method for designing and implementing applications software. The key to this approach has been the availability of substantial sophisticated basic support software that allows the user to design and program with relative ease and success. The user of a "typical" minicomputer, on the other hand, is left with the prospect of many manhours of research, instruction, and experimentation with supplied software before any reasonable application can be approached. In fact, for most applications, the user probably has neither the talent available in-house to undertake the project nor the time required before the payoff in actual processing begins. The advantages of in-house development is in the complete control that can be exercised over the development effort and the residual understanding of the intricacies of the software.

Procurement of applications software from the equipment vendor has been commonplace since the development of large-scale general-purpose computer systems. This approach has been popular with users as well. The most efficient use of the hardware (at least in the short run) could conceivably be made by the vendor-produced applications. But, this approach often leaves the user "bound" to the specific capabilities of the machine initially accepted and provides little flexibility for changes that occur as a result of either vendor alterations or application variances. In addition, the cost of such software can often escalate the basic system price considerably above that of the original minimum minicomputer system, because software development by the vendor is generally on a "one time" basis.

The most recent approach to applications software has been to employ either a general-purpose software house or systems "package" dealer. This method has not been widely used with minicomputers because of the variety of applications and the multiplicity of configurations. Packages ranging from individual programs to complete "turn key" systems usually combine most advantages of the hardware available as well as a complete treatment of the user's problem. In addition, such software is usually designed to accept changes in hardware and application parameters, with reasonable repercussions. The costs incurred are generally well defined from the beginning and software maintenance is often included in the contract. Documentation and operating instructions would probably be more complete in this approach than if generated by either the equipment vendor or the user. Finally, the user can be almost completely independent of the system development application. The most crucial factor to consider when approaching this method is the selection of the company for the software contract.

Concerning minicomputers and applications software, the user may understand the application itself better than anyone else, but may not understand it at all in terms of using the minicomputer as the problem-solving tool.

196

Users must therefore carefully weigh the possible consequences of using each method of generating applications software before placing a minicomputer in the mainstream of their activity.

Characteristics of applications software and corresponding software requirements are illustrated in Table 6-7-1, while a representative list of uses where applications software currently exists is provided in Table 6-7-2.

6.8 Limitations in Software

Many software components found on large-scale general-purpose computers can be made available on minicomputer systems. The problem encountered is in the minimum configuration size required to support such systems. Many software modules that provide efficient and easy interaction for the user to the system also require more than a minimum configuration. The expansion of the hardware configuration to support these software modules frequently is not necessary when applied to the user's application. Vendor-supplied software, even though available, may place such excessive requirements on the hardware, that the applications-oriented user is forced to become a programming expert, tolerating time and scheduling delays, to solve problems in a machine-dependent language. The limitations in existing software for a minicomputer are, therefore, not found on the larger configuration but rather on the minimum configuration system.

It is on these minimum configured systems, where users implement their application software and perform their own maintenance and hardware diagnostics, that vendor-provided software lacks convenient facilities for user-machine communication. Because of the minimum hardware configuration, programming becomes more difficult in a machine language form, more time consuming, and divorced from the user's application problem. The minimum software should provide simple applications-oriented interfaces composed of:

1. Interrupt handling
2. Simple task dispatching
3. Expansion interfaces
4. Extensive user-oriented debug facilities

In all fairness to these small systems as well as their vendors, it should be pointed out that software support for a $10,000 system is not the same as software support for a multimillion-dollar computer system. Nonetheless, the small minicomputer is highly applications-oriented and should also be oriented in its software to the user, not the professional programmer.

197

*TABLE 6-7-1. Characteristics of Applications and Corresponding
Software Requirements*

Application Class	System Characteristics	Software Requirements
Original equipment manufacturer	Cost; reliability; maintainability; addressing and indexing modes.	Assemblers; loaders; debug and diagnostics; text editors; mathematical utilities.
Communications processing data acquisition	Word length and format; execution speed; I/O processing capability; memory size; peripheral storage; byte handling.	I/O subsystem; assemblers; real-time interrupt system; mathematical utilities.
Process control	Priority interrupts; I/O flexibility; execution speed; operating system.	Real-time interrupt system; I/O subsystem; assembler.
End user	High-level language support (compilers and assemblers); large memory size.	Operating systems; high-level languages; system support subsystems.
Business data processing	Reliability; service; maintainability; peripheral devices; word length and format.	High-level languages; I/O subsystem; disk operating system.
Monitor systems	I/O structure; operating system; peripheral devices.	Basic operating system; I/O subsystem; interrupt systems.
Scientific standalone processing system	Maximum memory size; multiply/divide instructions; addressing and indexing flexibility; peripheral devices.	Standalone operating system; assemblers; loaders; debug and diagnostics; text editor.
Dedicated processor	Execution speed; I/O processing capability; memory size; peripherals.	Assembler; I/O subsystem; interrupt subsystem; standalone operating system.
Time-shared systems	Compilers; debugging support systems; instruction repertoire.	Real-time operating system; compilers; I/O subsystem.
System component	Priority interrupt; execution speed; memory size; byte handling capability.	Real-time operating system; assembler interrupt subsystems; I/O subsystems.

TABLE 6-7-2. *Current Minicomputer Applications*

Categories	Typical Applications
Process control	Refineries, manufacturing plants, assembly units, fluids, reactors, power plants
Communications	Telecommunications switching, editing, network, modem/multiplex, A/D collection
Adjuncts to other computers (system components)	I/O functions, conversions, pre-/postprocessing, terminals, on-/offline subsystems
Timesharing	Multiple general-purpose or multiple dedicated functions
Reservation/scheduling	Transportation, hotels, airline systems, rental cars
Diagnostic aids	Multitude of problem identification, resolution, repair for computers and processes
General business	Established large-scale general-purpose computer business applications, billing, accounting, inventories
Others	Hospitals, banks, tracking systems, simulation systems, real-time systems, traffic control systems, navigation aids, typesetting and print control, pollution sensing, protection systems

SUMMARY

Vendor-provided software offers the advantages of easier application program development, automatic operation of the minicomputer system, and standardization between programs. However, vendor-provided software availability has been limited for the following reasons:

1. Minicomputers are a relatively new industry, and there is a lag between hardware development and software development.
2. The development of software would increase the cost of the minicomputer.
3. The versatility of the minicomputer makes standard application packages impossible.
4. The special-purpose applications of some minicomputers prohibit the use of general-purpose software.
5. The wide variation in minicomputer configurations necessitates too many versions of the software programs.
6. Availability of software is not a prerequisite for sales.
7. The limited instruction set of minicomputers necessitates a large programming effort in order to develop software.

Furthermore, software costs have not decreased significantly in recent years as have the costs of minicomputers and peripheral devices.

Most vendor-provided software systems are modular which allows the user at a future time to implement a larger, more efficient superset or extension to existing software. The basic categories of software are basic support software, high-level language translators, utility programs, operating system software, and application software (both general- and special-purpose).

Basic support software (BSS) consists of standalone programs and routines for interfacing the user and the hardware and for promoting the development of programs for particular applications. The minimum BSS package normally includes a loader, an assembler, mathematical utilities, input/output utilities, data conversion routines, debug and diagnostic routines, and a text editor.

High-level language translators consist of both assembly and high-level languages translators. These can be further subdivided into assemblers, compilers, and interpreters.

Utility programs consist of data conversion programs, extended mathematical routines, programs for detecting and identifying hardware faults, floating-point arithmetic routines, general-purpose input/output device handlers, and various scientific subroutines.

Operating systems software includes programs that are required to run the overall computer system, allocate its resources, handle data transfers and interrupts, and allocate and protect memory. Operating system software is composed of such items as executives, loaders, supervisory control, sequence control, operator communication, and real-time control.

Application software comprises programs designed to solve user problems in user environments and is by far the most diverse of the five categories. Application software is developed at any of three sources: in-house, by equipment vendors, or by software houses.

Finally, note that the software provided by the various vendors varies greatly, not only in what is normally supplied with a minicomputer but also in the capability of common components, such as a FORTRAN compiler. The amount of memory, the number and type of peripherals, and the anticipated applications of a minicomputer determine the amount and type of software needed for a given minicomputer.

PROBLEMS

1. What are the advantages/disadvantages in software development when utilizing:
    a.   Vendor-produced generalized software packages
    b.   Software houses
    c.   In-house programming staff

2. Even though minicomputer vendors provide less general-purpose software support than their large-scale general-purpose computer manufacturer counter-

parts, this support often may not be needed. Argue the pros and cons of this assertion.

3. Discuss the development of minicomputer software in relationship to their specialized application areas, limited instruction repertoire, and minimum configuration.

4. Compare and contrast program development software with general-purpose support software.

5. What kind of software is provided by the minicomputer vendors? If not provided, how is missing software developed?

6. Why is it necessary to provide an assembler, a loader, a tape editor, mathematical packages, and utility routines in a minimum 4K minicomputer? Is it possible to provide less software?

7. Distinguish between a relocating and an absolute loader. List advantages of one over the other.

8. What effects do minimum minicomputer configuration, slow input/output devices, lack of mass storage devices, and limited instruction repertoire and addressing capability have on the development of software?

9. What advantages/disadvantages are there in developing input/output software?

10. Why are debug packages on minicomputers as important as the actual language translators? Why are they not so important on large-scale computer systems?

11. Discuss why any software should be provided by the minicomputer vendors for systems that are of a minimum configuration.

12. Compare and contrast the role of the operator by a user on a minicomputer with the role of the user in a large-scale computer system.

13. Describe the five distinct software categories presented in the chapter. Include in your discussion the individual software components and their modular construction.

14. What is a standalone program?

15. Differentiate between assemblers that require one, two, or even three passes. What effect does the number of passes for the assembler have on the loader?

16. If the minicomputer is highly application- and user-oriented, why is the assembler provided with a minimum configuration, and not a high-level language translator?

17. Discuss the advantages/disadvantages of high-level language translators as opposed to assemblers.

18. Discuss each of the extended assembler capabilities enumerated in the chapter.

19. Differentiate among executing, interpreting, and translating (compiling).

20. Why is it advantageous for minicomputer vendors to provide translators for use on large-scale computer systems?

21. Differentiate among standalone, disk, tape, and real-time operating systems.

22. Compare and contrast the three different kinds of assemblers provided by

vendors for minicomputers, namely: basic assembler, extended assembler, and macro assembler.

23. How is the number of passes the source program makes through the assembler related to the memory capacity and associate peripherals of the minicomputer?

24. What advantages do multipass assemblers have over single-pass assemblers?

25. What determines the maximum number of assembly instructions in a program that can be assembled?

26. Discuss what is meant by a cross assembler. How is it used?

27. Differentiate among a bootstrap loader, an absolute binary loader, and a relocatable loader. How do these loaders relate to corresponding assemblers?

28. What is the difference between a relocating loader and a linking loader? Is it necessary to have both?

29. How is a floating-point interpreter used on a minicomputer? What advantage does this interpreter have over externally provided subroutines?

30. The hardware of minicomputers seldom includes floating-point and double-precision arithmetic capabilities. How then are these features made available?

31. How can a minicomputer user perform device-dependent I/O operations and yet not be concerned with the actual machine language details regarding their control?

32. Describe the capabilities most frequently provided by debug packages, and justify their need.

33. Under what circumstances would a real-time debugging system be essential to a minicomputer user?

34. Compare and contrast the preventive mode to the corrective mode of operations of diagnostic packages.

35. What is a text editor? What are its uses?

36. What mechanism does the text editor use to facilitate the updating of the symbolic text strings?

37. Differentiate between conversational and batch mode compilers.

38. What aspects of a compiler would make the language translator minicomputer-dependent, and vary from the USASI standard.

39. What are the advantages and disadvantages of each of the following:
    a. FORTRAN
    b. ALGOL
    c. BASIC
    d. Assembly Language

40. Describe what advantages a macro processor has over a basic assembler. What can this processor be used for?

41. Draw a flow diagram and describe all the salient features of a typical two-pass minicomputer assembler.

42. Discuss the five major phases of a language translator, indicating peculiarities applicable to minicomputer systems.

43. To overcome inefficiencies in produced machine language code from the high-level language translator, several optimization techniques are included in the compilation procedure. Discuss three optimization techniques.

44. Differentiate between the functional components of a compiler and those of an interpreter.

45. Discuss the major facilities provided by a typical minicomputer operating system, especially including the function of:
    a. Overlay system
    b. Input/output control
    c. Interrupt management
    d. Data management

46. What is meant by a central interrupt processor? What effect does it have on the operations of the operating system?

47. Compare the designs and specific functions of a foreground/background operating system and a timesharing operating system.

48. What is the primary function of a basic operating system and how does BOS help in the operation of a minicomputer?

49. How does the additional overhead in space and time of a DOS/TOS compare to the benefits derived for the minicomputer user?

50. Are there any differences between a real-time operating system and a foreground/background operating system? If so, what are they?

51. Explain the different approaches for development of applications software. In particular emphasize the utilization of resources, including costs, manpower, and equipment.

52. What software limitations are indeed in store for a minicomputer user? Can these limitations be removed without extensive resource investments? Would the tradeoffs be favorable?

PROJECT

For the minicomputer of your choice, write one of the following:

1. A text editor

2. A FORTRAN cross-assembler

3. An assembler

4. A storage and retrieval system to handle one of these:
   a. Mailing labels
   b. Checking accounts
   c. Parts inventory

5. A floating-point package

6. A chess player

7. A checkers player

8. A company checkbook package

7

Microprogramming, Minicomputers, and Microprocessors

7.1 Introduction

The impact of large-scale integration (LSI) in computer design is reflected by significant improvements in the price/performance ratio of all components of the computer main frame (i.e., processors, memories, interfaces). In addition, production of very small, low-priced processors with relatively unsophisticated architecture, utilizing microprogrammed control as an alternative to the hardware design of the control unit, have significantly increased. The flexibility of changing or extending a computer's instruction set, the implementation of special-purpose functions, the replacement of existing instructions, the need for emulating all or parts of other computer systems and the flexibility for correcting design errors all have made it practical as well as desirable for computer vendors to implement microprogrammed systems.

7.1.1 Structure of Digital Computers

Computers can be partitioned into four distinct functional modules, the Memory Unit (MU), the Arithmetic and Logic Unit (ALU), the Control Unit (CU), and the Input/Output Unit (IOU). The logical relationship of these functional modules, common to most conventional computer organizations, is illustrated in Figure 7-1-1. Figure 7-1-2 is used to illustrate these various

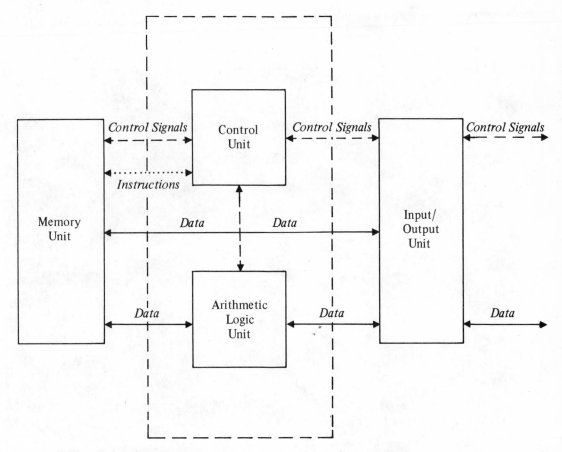

FIGURE 7-1-1. *Functional representation of a computer.*

components on the Mostek MK 3870 Single-Chip Microcomputer. There are several observations that can be made from this diagram:

1. In the stored program concept, a program's instruction as well as its data reside in the same functional, dynamically alterable memory module.

2. The paths that connect these different functional modules are known as buses, obviously requiring a source module and a destination module. A bus is thus characterized by the triplet: (S, P, D)—source module, path identifier, and destination module. Furthermore, design consideration for the bus structure needs include bus width, memory width, size of information transferred, and register width.

3. To increase the speed of the machine, one can either speed up the basic clock cycle, or perform operations in parallel. To perform operations in parallel implies the existence of multiplicity in bus structure. The multiplicity in the bus structure may require a bus controller which regulates bus access, bus connection, and sequence control.

FIGURE 7-1-2. *Microphotograph of Mostek's MK 3870 Chip. (Reprinted by permission of MOSTEK–Photo Copyright Mostek Corporation 1979.)*

7.1.2 Control Module

Any design implementation of these functional modules requires the transfer of data as control signals from one set of logic elements to another. These control signals, in a conventional computer, are usually implemented by way of a hardwired control unit. In this type of a control unit, the control portion is designed to accommodate each machine language instruction that is part of the computer's repertoire. The control unit consists of a combination of hardware and specific fixed, hardwired combinatorial and sequential logic sequences with many cross-connections. This results in a complex control unit that becomes difficult to understand, to maintain, and to modify.[9,12,37,41,46,53,56,57]

The functions of such a control unit (see Figure 7-1-3), whose logical structure is given in Figure 7-1-4, are:

1. To fetch a machine instruction.
2. To decode this instruction.
3. To establish appropriate data paths to perform the correct operation.
4. To prepare for processing the next machine instruction.

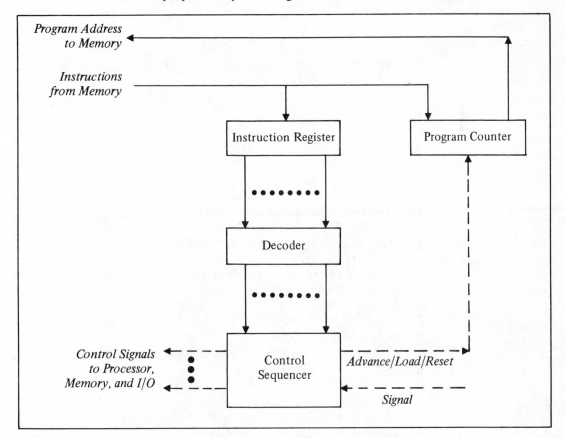

FIGURE 7-1-3.   Fixed control unit organization.

207

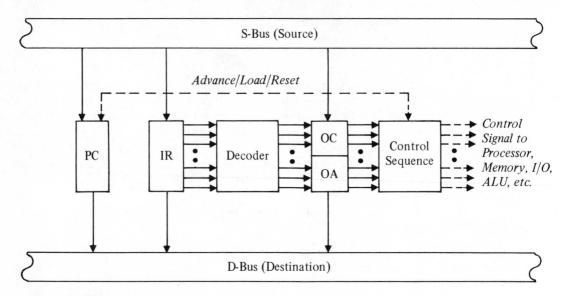

S-Bus (Source)

Advance/Load/Reset

PC   IR   Decoder   OC   OA   Control Sequence   *Control Signal to Processor, Memory, I/O, ALU, etc.*

D-Bus (Destination)

PC: Program Counter
IR: Instruction Register
OC: Operation Code
OA: Operand Address

FIGURE 7-1-4.   *Logical building blocks of a hardwired control unit.*

The design of such a control unit, because of its hardwired control sequences, is frequently optimized for a particular subset of the machine's instructions, and consequently for a particular class of applications. Alternatively, such a design might be generalized to a large class of instructions with the accompanying inefficiency in all of but a few operations.

7.1.3 Microprogrammed Control Units

Professor M. V. Wilkes, in seeking a systematic alternative to the usual procedures of designing the control unit, suggested replacing most of the combinatorial and sequential logic of the hardwired control unit by a simple programmable control unit in conjunction with a memory in which to store this control information.[5,38-40,45,47,54] The result of such a control unit would be a more structured organization of the hardware logic, providing design alternatives at a later date.

The description of such a control unit, illustrated in Figure 7-1-5 is as follows:

1.   By rearranging the structure of the control unit, a machine instruction can be specified as a sequence of subcommands.
2.   The control unit can be viewed as a matrix consisting of *one* vertical line for each control gate and a set of horizontal lines having access to all

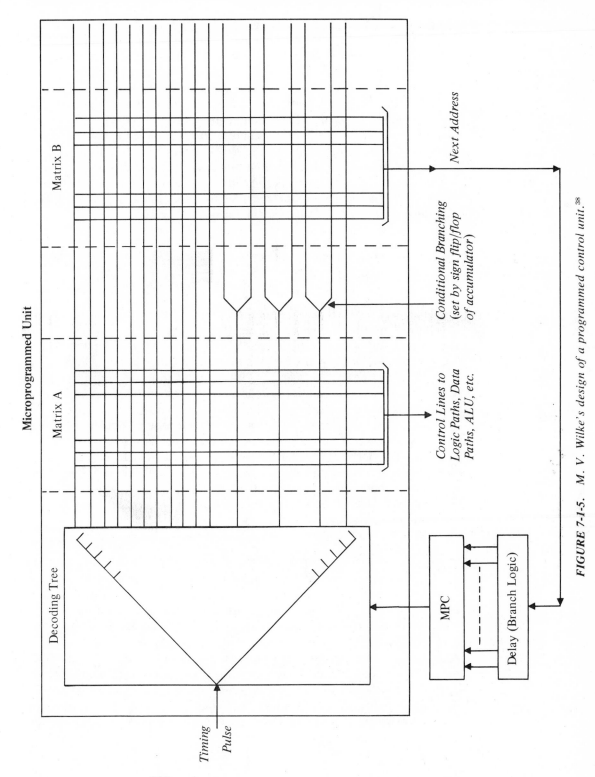

FIGURE 7-1-5. *M. V. Wilke's design of a programmed control unit.*[38]

possible control gates at the intersections. This assumes that there are as many vertical lines to as many control elements/paths/logical elements/functions that need be accessed for proper functioning of the system.

3. A machine instruction can then be specified as a set of horizontal lines, each of which is connected to the specific combination of gates it wishes to pulse to control the paths over which data flows. The connections of a horizontal to a vertical line having been set by way of a programmable switch, the settings (i.e., the switch control) for all of the horizontal and vertical lines can be stored in a control storage (CS), in terms of a binary bit pattern, from which it can be retrieved on demand.

4. Conditional branching could provide for the next address logic which controls the branches of the decoding tree such that only *one* horizontal line would receive the next clock pulse.

The sequence performed for a typical decoded machine language instruction is as follows (see Figure 7-1-6):

1. The machine language instruction is fetched from main memory and loaded into the instruction register (IR) as before.

2. The content of the instruction register (IR) is decoded, in parallel, by the decoder, and broken into its constituents: operation code (OC), operand addresses (OA).

3. The binary representation of the operation code (OC) is used as an address to control storage, from which to fetch the bit pattern that is used to set the horizontal/vertical switches for the particular horizontal lines (that represents this machine language operation).

4. Once the horizontal/vertical switches are placed (latched), a control pulse is sent down the appropriate horizontal line causing the required control operations to be performed. An automatic delay in the control sequence, due to the physical placements of the vertical lines, is built into the control unit.

The number of vertical control lines could potentially be very large, and thus impact the design through the required control storage size, bus width, control store registers, and drivers (Figure 7-1-6). As a result of this cost/design tradeoff, a machine language instruction is represented not just by one horizontal line setting, but a number of horizontal line settings. However, because the binary representation of the operation code was used as an address into control storage, as well as to address a specific horizontal line, the control words from control storage that make up the machine language operation code frequently cannot be sequentially ordered, and thus an address needs to be included to point to subsequent control storage words (i.e., the control words that are required to completely represent the operation code).

210

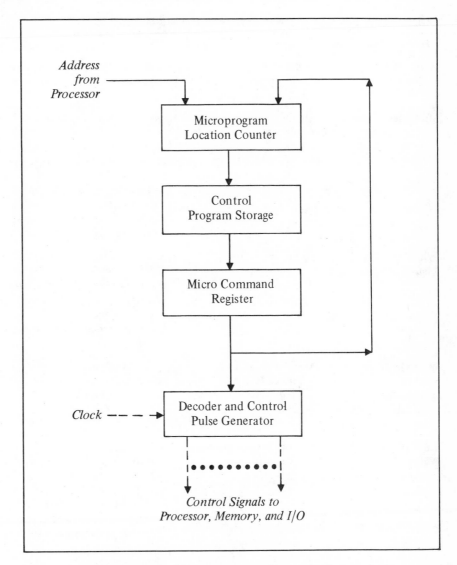

FIGURE 7-1-6. *Microprogrammed control unit organization.*

In addition, the bit patterns in the control words are often partially encoded to minimize the width of the control storage elements, the width of the connecting paths, and any control registers. This requires that the control storage words be placed into a decoding buffer (perhaps called a microcommand register) and decoded, prior to being used in the control elements. Thus, an additional tradeoff between control storage words decoding (i.e., delay time as a function of the level of encoding) and the cost of the functional elements (i.e., widths) must be considered. A brief summary of these tradeoffs is given in Table 7-1-1.

211

TABLE 7-1-1.   *Summary of Several Design Components and Associated Impacts*

Design Component	Component Function	Design Impact
Width of bus	Amount of information fetched per cycle	Multiple fetches with associated delays if width is not adequate.
Multiplicity in bus structure	Amount of parallelism and concurrency	Impacts the instruction format in terms of instruction width, instruction encoding, and interrelationship of control functions (microcommands). Speed is attained by allowing many operations to proceed simultaneously, impacting the number of buses and independent paths. The greater the degree of simultaneity, the fewer the number of mutually exclusive gating operations and the wider the control storage words.
Width of control storage words	To minimize storage, the microinstruction words should be as short as possible.	The width of control storage words impacts encoding the maximum information into the minimum number of bits. However, some flexibility can be lost unless all encoded signals are mutually exclusive, and additional hardware to decode maximally encoded microinstructions adds unwanted gate propagation delays.
Multiple control storage words/machine language instructions	Amount of control storage fetches required per machine language instruction	Impacts the design by requiring capabilities, such as subroutining, indexing, parameterization, and conditional branching.
Encoding of microinstruction (complete/partial/none)	Amount of information per control storage word	Encoding of microinstructions impacts the width of control storage, connecting paths, registers, and drivers, versus the additional circuitry and buffers with associated decoding and delay times. One way to control the data paths in a system is to have one control bit for each data path or data path option. However, since many of the microoperations are mutually exclusive, grouping mutually exclusive operations reduces the number of bits required.

TABLE 7-1-1. (continued)

Design Component	Component Function	Design Impact
		Minimal encoding • Each bit is allowed to actuate a logic-control line. • No decoding hardware. *Direct (single-level) encoding* • Mutually exclusive signals are encoded into fields of a microinstruction. • Reduces the width of the microinstruction word. *Indirect (two-level) encoding* • Meaning of the field is defined by another field of the microinstruction (i.e., mode or type field). • Reduces size of the microinstruction word.
Instruction formats	The variety of microcommands and addressing capability of the machine.	Tradeoff between control storage size, bus width, control storage registers, and drivers, impacts the instruction formats in terms of the number of microcommands per instruction. *Vertical (monophase*) microinstruction design* • Short instructions • Many instructions per macrooperation • More elemental microorders • Small repertoire • Longer execution time per macrooperation *Horizontal (polyphase*) microinstruction design* • Wide instructions • Few instructions per macrooperation • Many simultaneous microorders • Large repertoire • Fast execution time per macrooperation

* Monophase and polyphase refer to the length of time, in clock pulses, that each microinstruction operates the control logic during a macrooperation.

7.1.4 Summary

In the subsequent sections of this chapter, the following terminology applies:

1. *Microcommands (or microoperations)*—The operation making up a single step, i.e., one of the horizontal lines.
2. *Microinstructions*—A collection of microoperations executed in one basic machine cycle (e.g., it might tell the hardware to move data from one register to another via a functional subassembly such as an adder or a shifter).
3. *Microprogram (or firmware*)*—The sequence of microinstructions or steps for one machine language instruction.

Changing the microprogram (MP) implementation of the machine language (ML) instructions changes the way the computer executes these machine language instructions and, therefore, changes the nature of the computer. The implications of a microprogrammed control unit (MCU) are twofold, namely:

1. The underlying structure of the control unit is independent of the actual machine instruction set which was implemented.
2. It is possible to select an instruction set much later in the development of the hardware by changing the contents of the control store instead of redesigning and revising the control unit.

Two levels of control are, therefore, available on the system:

1. Machine instructions of the programmer.
2. Microoperations of the logic designer.

In addition to providing a systematic alternative to hardwired control, the MCU design also provides for flexibility and reliability. This flexibility applies not only to internal operations, but also to external I/O and control functions.

7.2 A Simple Microprogrammed Computer

7.2.1 Programmable Control Unit

Most computers essentially use similar system architecture, differing primarily in how much microprogramming they contain (if any), and how these microprograms are used (when available).

---

* While microprograms contain information that controls hardware at a primitive level, these controls are stored in a memory and executed as stored programs. This gives microprograms a software as well as a hardware flavor, and was, therefore, called firmware by Opler.[37]

As an example, let us consider a simple computer, illustrated in Figure 7-2-1. This elementary computer employs a stored program element for the control unit rather than a hardwired control unit. These microprograms essentially cover fixed programming tasks, which seldom, if ever, need modifications, and are usually stored in a read-only memory (ROM). It should, however, be pointed out that the ROM (used as a control storage element) and the microprogramming capability are *not synonymous*.[2,14,19,21,33,45,48]

Assume that the control portion of this simple system generates the signals specified in Table 7-2-1. Each of these signals, called a microoperation or microcommand, performs an elementary operation, and is executed in *one* basic computer clock cycle.

Words from ROM are read in sequence under control of an address register, sometimes called microprogram location counter (MLC) or program counter (MPC), unless a branch or jump command occurs. This is similar to a machine instruction fetch. The general description of this microprogrammed control unit, illustrated in Figure 7-2-2, is as follows:

1. Fetch an ML instruction from main storage.
2. Decode this instruction into an operation code and operand(s).
3. Establish the appropriate data paths to perform the correct operation. The MCU uses the decoded operation code as a starting address for the required microprogram:
   a. Fetch an MI from control store (ROM) and load into microinstruction register (MIR).

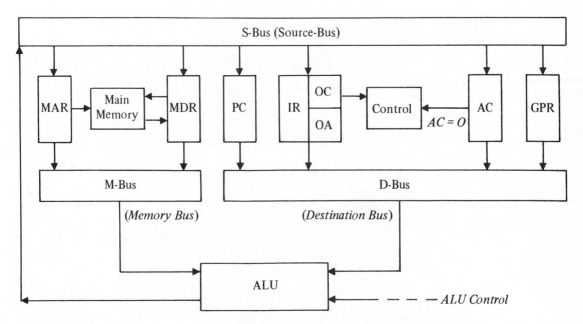

FIGURE 7-2-1.   *Simple computer configuration.*

Microprogrammed ROM Device

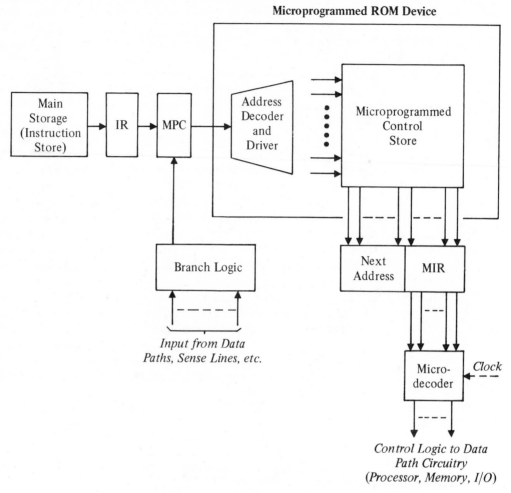

FIGURE 7-2-2.   *Programmable control unit (PCU).*[5]

    b.   Decode the MI through the microdecoder resulting in the following outputs:

        —Control data paths to processor, memory, I/O units.

        —Determination of the next address of the microprogram. This address can be determined from parts of the current MI itself, from status information, from data paths (i.e., sense lines), and from branch logic.

    c.   Branch to **a)** until the current MP is completed.

  4. Prepare for processing the next ML instruction.

    A time sequence of control signals capable of controlling the data paths in the system is generated by executing a series of microcommands from the control storage. By combining these, complete ML instructions can

TABLE 7-2-1.   Microoperations or Microcommands

Mnemonic	Meaning
R	Read memory into MDR
W	Write memory with content of MDR, addressed by MAR
SMAR	Gate S-Bus into MAR
SMDR	Gate S-Bus into MDR
SPC	Gate S-Bus into PC
SIR	Gate S-Bus into IR
SAC	Gate S-Bus into AC (Accumulator)
SGPR	Gate S-Bus into GPR(s)
MARM	Gate MAR onto M-Bus
MDRM	Gate MDR onto M-Bus
PCD	Gate PC onto D-Bus
OAD	Gate OA onto D-Bus
ACD	Gate AC onto D-Bus
GPRD	Gate GPR(s) onto D-Bus
DALUS	Gate D-Bus through ALU to S-Bus
MALUS	Gate M-Bus through ALU to S-Bus
ADD1	Gate D-Bus through ALU to S-Bus, and add one
MDS	Add M-Bus to D-Bus in ALU and phase on S-Bus
JMP	Unconditional jump to address field of MI
JACZ	Unconditional jump to address field of AC-0
JOC	Jump to address of op-code field

be formed. For each microinstruction (MI), each microcommand (MC) combination must complete a full logic implementation requiring the transfer of data or control signals from one set of logic elements to another. Examples of representative functions of these elementary operations (via control data paths) are:

1. Gate data from various registers into the ALU.
2. Select the function the unit will perform on the data.
3. Gate the result into the selected register.

Gating functions which can be used to control the data paths include:

1. Data into adder to be complemented.
2. Data into adder to be transmitted uncomplemented.
3. Data into adder shifted right or left.

From a grouping of all microcommands that utilize the same functional or logical components of the system (see Table 7-2-2) it becomes apparent that only those MCs that utilize nonoverlapping control or logic elements can be performed at the same time.[35]

217

TABLE 7-2-2.   *Grouping of Microcommands*

Memory Control	ALU Control	JMP Instructions	M-Bus Control	D-Bus Control	S-Bus Control	Jump Address Field
R W ADD1	DALUS MALUS MDS	JMP JACZ JOC	MARM MDRM	PCD OAD ACD GPRD	SMAR SMDR SPC SIR SAC SGPR	
NOP	NOP	NOP	NOP	NOP	NOP	NOP
Number of operations for each group in subfield						
3	5	4	3	5	7	2
Number of bits to specify each group in subfield						
2	3	2	2	3	3	As large as is required to specify the next MP address

The number of bits to specify each group in a subfield can be determined from the number of operations that are within each of these groups. Consider the memory control subfield. The available operations in this subfield are Read (R), Write (W), and No Operation (NOP). These operations can be arbitrarily assigned the values of 01, 10, and 00, respectively, and therefore require but 2 bits to be specified.

7.2.2 Example Microprogram

To illustrate the MCU concept, consider a simple ML instruction sequence, such as:

ADD M

STORE M′

These two instructions are intended to add the content of memory location M to the accumulator, leaving the result in an accumulator, and then to store the result into a different memory location M′. The sequential operations for the above two ML instructions are given in Table 7-2-3, while the sequence of microinstructions for these operations is illustrated in Table 7-2-4. The number of microcommands that can be performed in parallel is clearly determined by the availability of separate buses in the machine's architecture, and is reflected by the mutually exclusive set of microcommands given in Table 7-2-2.

Several additional comments should be made about Table 7-2-4:

1. To provide flexibility to the MCU design, the use of subroutining, indexing, and parameterization has been incorporated into micropro-

TABLE 7-2-3.   Sequential Operations for ADD M, STORE M'

Sequential Operations (Mnemonics)	Meaning
Instruction Fetch (ADD)	
[PC]→ MAR	Content of PC transferred to MAR.
R { [M$_{[MAR]}$]→ MDR	Instruction read from memory into
[MDR]→ M$_{[MAR]}$	MDR (read-regeneration cycle).
[MDR]→ IR	Instruction from MDR transferred to IR.
Instruction Decode (ADD)	
IR→ decode→ OC, OA (i.e., ADD M)	Address to control store is determined by OC of the instruction (i.e., ADD).
Instruction Execution (ADD)	
[OA]→ MAR	Content of address portion of instruction register transferred to MAR (i.e., M).
R { [M$_{[MAR]}$]→ MDR	Desired data read into MDR.
[MDR]→ M$_{[MAR]}$	
[MDR] + [AC]→ AC	MDR added to AC; result stored
[PC] +1→ PC	in AC, update program counter.
Instruction Fetch (STORE)	
[PC]→ MAR	Content of PC transferred to MAR.
R { [M$_{[MAR]}$]→ MDR	Instruction read from memory into
[MDR]→ M$_{[MAR]}$	MDR (read-regeneration cycle).
[MDR]→ IR	Instruction from MDR transferred to IR.
Instruction Decode (STORE)	
IR→ decode→ OC, OA (i.e., STORE M')	Address to control store is determined by OC of the instruction (i.e., STORE).
Instruction Execution (STORE)	
[OA]→ MAR	Content of address portion of instruction register transferred to MAR (i.e., M').
[AC]→ MDR	Data from AC transferred to MDR.
[MDR]→ M$_{[MAR]}$	Write data into memory at M'.
[PC] + 1→ PC	Update program counter.

TABLE 7-2-4. MP Instruction Sequence to ADD M, STORE M'

		Memory Control	ALU Control	JMP Instruction	M-Bus Control	D-Bus Control	S-Bus Control	Jump Address
Instruction Fetch	1		DALUS			PCD	SMAR	
	2	R						
	3		MALUS		MDRM		SIR	
Decode	4			JOC				
Execute	5		DALUS			OAD	SMAR	
	6	R						
	7		MDS		MDRM	ACD	SAC	
Update	8		ADD1			PCD	SPC	
Instruction Fetch	9		DALUS			PCD	SMAR	
	10	R						
	11		MALUS		MDRM		SIR	
Decode	12			JOC				
Execute	13		DALUS			OAD	SMAR	
	14		DALUS			ACD	SMDR	
	15	W						
Update	16		ADD1			PCD	SPC	START
Return	17			JMP				

MP for ADD M (spans rows 1–8); MP for STORE M' (spans rows 8–17)

Micro-command — Microinstruction

gramming. *Subroutining* implies sections of microprograms that can be used by other routines to accomplish specific or common purposes (e.g., instruction fetches); *indexing* is required to locate data within arrays of lists, or to keep track of the operations that are performed (e.g., counters); *parameterization* is a technique used to store parameters which characterize the status of the program, and which can be tested for triggering selective actions or responses.[3,4,45] For example, microinstruction cycles (1–4) and (9–12) are identical, and could easily be incorporated as a microprogram subroutine.

2. Although a certain amount of microinstruction optimization could be achieved by combining microinstructions (e.g., instructions 8 and 4), this fusing of instructions can only be done to instructions that utilize independent functional elements, and are independent of results achieved by intervening instructions. For example, instruction 8 could only be fused with instruction 4 if the machine were a fixed length instruction machine. In other words, if the decode cycle needs to determine, by whatever means, the value required to add to the update cycle

(8), the two instructions could obviously not be combined. Instruction optimization via instruction fusion is possible, but note its complexity.

3. The grouping of microinstructions has resulted in a partial encoding, with corresponding savings in instruction width, bus width, and control register width, as a consequence of a larger decoding delay in the decoding buffer. The tradeoff between the two designs must be carefully analyzed.

4. Each microinstruction cycle in Table 7-2-4 represents an *asynchronous* basic clock cycle. That is, the sequential nature of microinstructions does not represent the continuous real-time clock. The most obvious example is microinstruction 2, which represents a READ from main memory. Thus, although microinstruction 3 is the third basic clock cycle given to the MCU for this microprogram, it does not necessarily represent the third contiguous (sequential) real-time clock cycle.

7.3 Microinstruction Design

7.3.1 Microinstruction Encoding

One way to control the data paths in a microprogrammed computer system is to have one (ROM) control bit for each data path or data path option. However, since many of the microinstructions are mutually exclusive, grouping these mutually exclusive operations reduces the number of bits required per microinstruction. Two kinds of encoding schemes are used:[23,41]

1. In the *minimally encoded MI* each bit is allowed to actuate a logic control line and, therefore, little additional decoding hardware logic is required.

2. To minimize control storage, the MI words should be as short as possible, implying encoding the maximum information into the minimum number of bits. This *maximally encoded MI* requires additional hardware logic to decode and activate the logic-control lines and, therefore, add unwanted gate propagation delays. Two types of encoding formats for microinstructions are:

   a. *Direct encoding.* Mutually exclusive signals are encoded into fields of the MI, reducing the size of the word.

   b. *Indirect encoding.* The meaning of the field is defined by another field of the MI (i.e., by a mode or type field), thereby reducing the size of the MI word. This type of encoding is also known as *bit steering* or *format shifting* depending on whether the field is determined by the value of a control field in the MI or by the content of status registers.

If too many mutually exclusive functions are encoded together, the cost of the decoding network at the output of the control storage and the delay through the network are prohibitively large.

221

7.3.2 Addressing and Branch Logic

Control storage, implemented via ROM, is typically accessed, to fetch an MI, *once* for each basic control cycle of the system (e.g., 150–400 ns). It is, therefore, desirable to have the ROM read cycle (i.e., the time required to fetch the MI from ROM and to load it into an MIR) as small a fraction as is possible of the basic machine cycle. This provides the system with the maximum amount of time to select the address for the next microinstruction (see Figure 7-3-1 for a typical ROM access timing outline).

Different addressing techniques used to determine the next MI address include the following:[23,41]

1. For short length control storage (about 4096 words) each MI could contain 12 bits for an address of the next instruction, passing the output

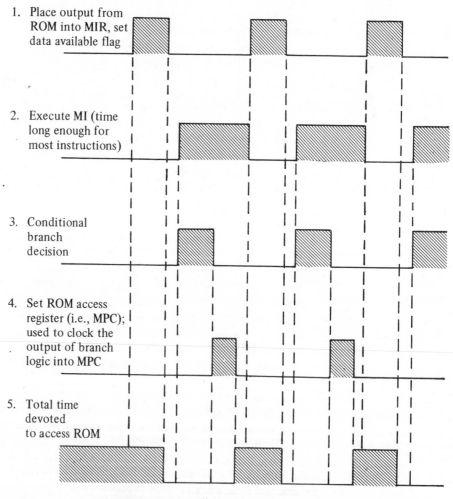

1. Place output from ROM into MIR, set data available flag

2. Execute MI (time long enough for most instructions)

3. Conditional branch decision

4. Set ROM access register (i.e., MPC); used to clock the output of branch logic into MPC

5. Total time devoted to access ROM

FIGURE 7-3-1.   ROM access timing requirements.

from ROM directly into the microprogram address register (MPAR) to select the next instruction. This eliminates the use of the MPC. However, whenever the address is part of the control storage word, the additional time to decode this address could be too long in response to input stimuli (e.g., status lines). This concept is discussed in subsequent sections.

2. Microprogram systems that use an MPC for automatic sequential execution, unless overridden by way of jump instructions, require more external circuitry to interpret the next MI address. An example of an MCU utilizing this kind of addressing is illustrated in Figure 7-3-2.

3. Using a short address field (e.g., 4–6 bits in length) can specify the next sequential MI, with other instructions required to branch outside of this restricted range.

4. Introduction of the full starting address of the response routine from a second ROM completely eliminates the need for jump tables.

Each of these different addressing techniques results from appropriate design tradeoffs. For example, the longer the MI, the more expensive the ROM and the simpler the machine logic, and vice versa.

7.3.3 Microinstruction Design

7.3.3.1 Instruction Execution Time.[23,41] Two principal designs for microinstructions (MIs) are: vertical and horizontal. A *horizontal* (or polyphase) microprogram uses MIs that are not encoded, controlling resources in parallel. Maximum flexibility for MIs is provided because each function (or operation) is available in every MI (or control word). Maximum speed is achieved by reducing the number of MIs required for each macrooperation (or ML instruction). This method makes efficient use of the hardware requiring little control logic but wide control words (e.g., 30–150 bits/control word).

A *vertical* (or monophase) microprogram uses MIs that are partially encoded, controlling resources serially. With this technique the control system loses some flexibility due to the decoding but efficiently utilizes small control words (e.g., 12–24 bits/control word). An MI can trigger only a single issue of control signals to a system function, because of its serial nature, so that no other system function can be active at the same time. Consequently, each macrooperation may be slower (requiring several cycles/instruction), yet easier to write and modify. Table 7-3-1 compares these two MI formats, while Figure 7-3-3 diagrams them.

The MI execution times, in both of these techniques, are usually selected to be long enough to permit the most basic MI execution to take place. Longer operation execution times, requiring *two or more* MI times, can be implemented by any of the following schemes:

1. Executing the same MI twice, storing the data only after the second instruction has been completed.

223

Microprogrammed ROM Device

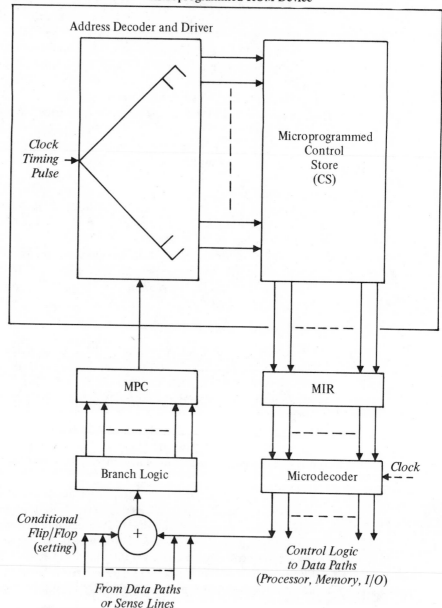

FIGURE 7-3-2. *Block diagram of an MC with sequential access and conditional branching.*[5,19]

2. Utilizing a bit or bits within an MI to extend the MI execution time.
3. Designing the MI execution time using the longest execution MI time as the basic clock.
4. Using the concept of residual control, which combines both vertical and horizontal MIs. With this technique there are several "set up" registers

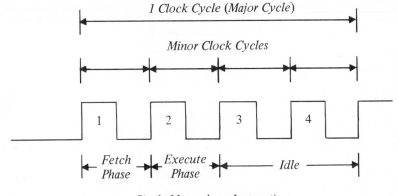

a.   Single Monophase Instruction

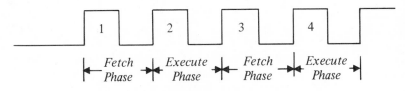

b.   Overlapped (double sequential) Monophase
     Instruction, requiring even number of clock
     pulses/clock cycle

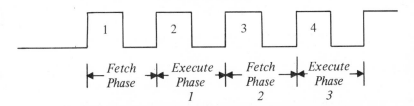

c.   Polyphase Instruction with single instruction
     fetch and three (3) sequential execution phases

FIGURE 7-3-3.   *Vertical versus horizontal microinstructions.*

which contain static information (i.e., information which may remain unchanged during the execution of several MIs), which can be selected and manipulated by vertical MIs. The content of these registers then controls several resources by the horizontal method.

7.3.3.2 Instruction Access Time.   The components of an MI fetch, decoding, and execution time frame are given in Figure 7-3-4. For example, if a conditional branch is to be made on an overflow register from some ALU operation, the information will probably not be developed until it is too late for this branch decision to be made within this instruction cycle. Consequently, one MI and *one* MI execution time is lost because the branch

TABLE 7-3-1.   Comparison Between Vertical and Horizontal MI Designs[23,41]

Vertical (Monophase)	Horizontal (Polyphase)	
Short instructions (16–20 bits long—may be packed two or more per memory word for access efficiency)	Wide instructions (word lengths of 40–120 bits)	
Many instructions/macrooperation (typically 2 or 3 operand addressing)	Few instructions/macrooperation (multiple operand specifications)	
Flexibility—more elemental microinstructions (highly decoded fields in microinstruction words)	Complexity—many simultaneous microorders (relatively simultaneous execution of microorders with little internal sequencing)	*A d v*
Many ROM accesses (relatively long microinstruction execution times)	Few ROM accesses (relatively short microinstruction execution times)	*a n t*
Long execution time per macrooperation	Fast execution time per macrooperation	*a g*
Microinstructions sufficiently complex that several internal clock cycles are needed to complete the microinstruction's execution	Fields in the microinstruction word utilized with relatively little decoding	*e s*
Microinstructions can be classified into several major functions	Little classification into functions	
Most bit combinations meaningful	Most bit combinations are not meaningful	
Requires large ROM (although short word)	Requires large ROM (wide microinstruction word)	*Dis- advan- tages*
Simplicity	Complexity/shorter	

NOTE:
Monophase: • There are no distinct subcycles of the basic clock cycle.
                • Each microinstruction is effected by a single simultaneous issue of control signals.
Polyphase: • Each major clock cycle comprises multiple minor clock cycles.
               • The hardware generates control signals at each minor clock cycle.

decision must be delayed until the next microinstruction. Therefore, the shorter the access time is to ROM (in proportion to the complete MI cycle time), the more time is available for branching decisions. Since a high percentage of MIs contain conditional branches, many instructions and instruction times can be saved by making this access time as small as possible.

There are two basic techniques involved in accessing ROM for MIs: parallel and serial (illustrated in Figure 7-3-5). In the *parallel* operations, the address of the next MI may be obtained and accessed while the present MI is being executed. The address may be from a field of the present MI, from the MPC, or from status sense lines (flip-flops). In the *serial* operation, the

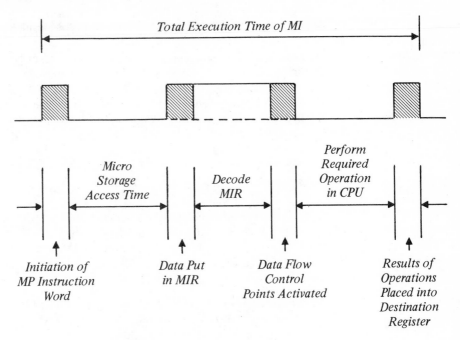

FIGURE 7-3-4.   *Execution time frame for MIs.*

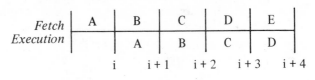

a.   Parallel Operation

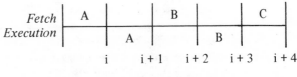

b.   Serial Operation

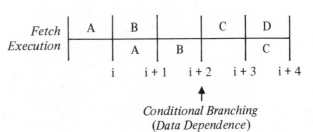

c.   Combined Serial-Parallel Operation

FIGURE 7-3-5.   *Microinstruction accessing from ROM.*

address of the next MI is obtained and accessed at the completion of the current MI. A variation of this latter technique incorporates a combination of *serial-parallel* operations in which the next address depends on conditions of the current MI.

In all of these different operations, the parallel operation is much faster in execution because of the overlap between accessing an instruction while executing the previous instruction, incurring no delay due to MI access times.

7.3.4 Control Storage

Microprogramming control denotes a design technique based on the use of control words stored in control storage having characteristics and costs of a suitable storage technology. Aside from ROM control storages, other suitable control storages that have been used in microprogrammed systems include:

1. pROMs (low-cost high-speed programmable ROM)
2. RAM (random access memory) or WCS (writable control storage)
3. A mixture of ROMs with RAMs

The advantages of low-cost high-capacity semiconductor ROMs are the substantial increase in performance and capability of the MP system, with accompanying lower costs and reduction in space. Diagnostic routines and debugging aids can be readily implemented, and the system can be easily adapted for special tasks. Field changes can be made by simply changing ROM boards. The biggest disadvantage of ROMs is that the desired bit pattern (representing the MP) must be inserted by the ROM manufacturer (which takes from 4–6 weeks). ROM bit patterns must be accurate the first time to avoid mask changes with attendant loss of time and money.

Field-programmable ROMs (pROMs) similar to semiconductor ROMs, can also only be programmed once, which implies that many will be discarded before a correct MP is developed. However, because the desired bit patterns (representing the MP) can be established and set in the field, without the 4–6 week delay times of the semiconductor ROMs, a reduction of development time results.

Writable control storage are read/write memories (volatile) that are used in the control portion of a microprogrammed system. This enables the system designer to change the external characteristics of a system, to easily correct errors in the microprogrammed implementation, and to load a large library of control programs on demand. This type of control storage is, however, more expensive, volatile, and requires a memory loader.

The advantages of microprogramming can be lost if time must be spent accessing core for constants and for temporary data storage. A solution, most often encountered, is to use ROMs for MP instruction and RAMs for the temporary storage of data. This design provides flexibility to the system designer in that only a small amount of ROM need be used, storing the more frequently used MPs in ROM, while overlaying other MPs and data into RAMs.

ROMs are usually *p*-channel metal-oxide semiconductors (PMOS), dynamic or static, with better than 1 μsec access times. Most popular ROM organizations are 256 (or 512) × 8. RAMs are also PMOS, dynamic or static, with under 1 μsec access times and 256 × 1 bit organization. Programmable ROMs (pROMs), which are electronically programmable control storage memories are frequently used for prototyping.

7.3.5 Software Aids

Control storage for MP minicomputers is realized ranging from the inflexible ROM through fast WCS. The microprogrammability of these systems range from *not user accessible* (in which users are not given the facilities for placing MPs into control storage), to *user programmable,* and to *dynamically programmable.*[1,21] For both user microprogrammable systems, vendors often provide such assistance as:

1. Translators that transform high-level language representations into microprograms (MPs) ready for loading into control storage.
2. Simulators that assist in the detailed debugging of MPs.
3. Online debugging systems to monitor executing programs.

This range of available supporting modules is illustrated in Figure 7-3-6.

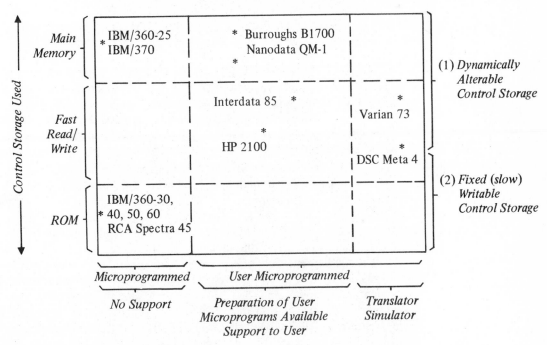

FIGURE 7-3-6.   *System microprogrammability support for the user.*[1]

7.3.5.1 Microprogramming Languages.

The different levels of available microprogramming languages can be classified as follows:[1,21]

1. Microlanguages
2. Assembler and flowchart languages
3. Register transfer languages
4. Macro register transfer languages
5. Procedure-oriented machine-dependent languages
6. Procedure-oriented machine-independent languages

Microlanguages are sequences of machine language MIs, each MI, a series of bits, that is interpreted by the control unit to control machine operation. The formats of MIs are largely determined by design decisions concerning the hardware characteristics.

Assembler microprogramming languages provide the capability to express MIs in a mnemonic and symbolic form similar to assembly language formats. Some MIs can even contain references to the predecessor and successor MI.

Flowchart microprogramming languages are networks of boxes representing the microprogram. Each box in this network represents *one* MI, and flow lines connecting boxes indicate possible subsequent MIs. Each of the lines in a box represents an operation or a field in the MI. The flowchart microprogramming language is most often used for horizontal microprogrammed computers.

Register transfer microprogramming languages are sequences of MIs, in a format similar to the basic assembly languages, in which subcommands represent primitive machine operations. Programming in this language requires detailed knowledge of the system hardware configuration and characteristics, with a one-to-one correspondence to machine instructions. These languages are often used where the assembler and flowchart languages are inappropriate because of the large number of field in an MI word.

Macro register transfer languages are basically the same as register transfer MP languages with the addition of equivalence and macro facilities. In other words, the facilities for mnemonic representations of register, subcommands, MIs, and parametric substitution are provided.

Procedure-oriented machine-dependent MP languages and *procedure-oriented machine-independent MP languages* provide all the facilities of the macro register transfer languages, plus additional statements for flow of control, compound expressions, data structure definitions, and description capabilities of computer design languages.

The implementation of assembler, flowchart, and register transfer languages are by way of a software cross-translator (i.e., MPs are translated on a separate computer and the resulting MIs loaded into control storage for execution), with translation in a one-to-one form to microlanguages. The implementation of higher level language translators varies from direct transla-

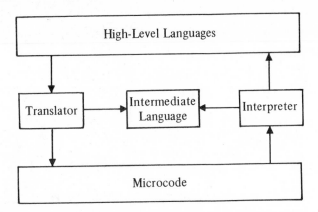

FIGURE 7-3-7. *Various language levels as implemented by using Microcode and HLLS.*[1]

tion to microprograms, to translation via software into some intermediate language (directly interpreted; see Figure 7-3-7).[1,21]

7.3.5.2 Debugging Aids. Debugging a microprogrammed system can be challenging and time consuming if not approached in a systematic fashion with proper design aids. The designer of a microprogrammed system during the debugging phase should have available the following:

1. A way to store and modify the ROM MPC
2. A way to monitor the contents of the MIR
3. An ROM control storage simulator

The ability to store and modify the ROM MPC provides a convenient way to identify the location of errors, as well as individual MP changes. An ROM control storage simulator enables the designer to make many changes during the debugging of the MP, saving the expense in mask changes (to ROMs or pROMs) or in discarded pROMs. A control storage simulator can be implemented by either hardware, software, or as a combination of both. The logical building blocks of such a simulator, illustrated in Figure 7-3-8, speed system debugging by providing:[1,36]

1. A way to store and modify the ROM MPC
2. The capability to single step the system clock
3. A way to set the contents of the ROM address register
4. A way to lock this address register (i.e., to be unaffected by jump and test instructions)
5. A starting address to any points in the MP
6. A single step execution phase for a locked microinstruction
7. A complete trace of the MP in execution

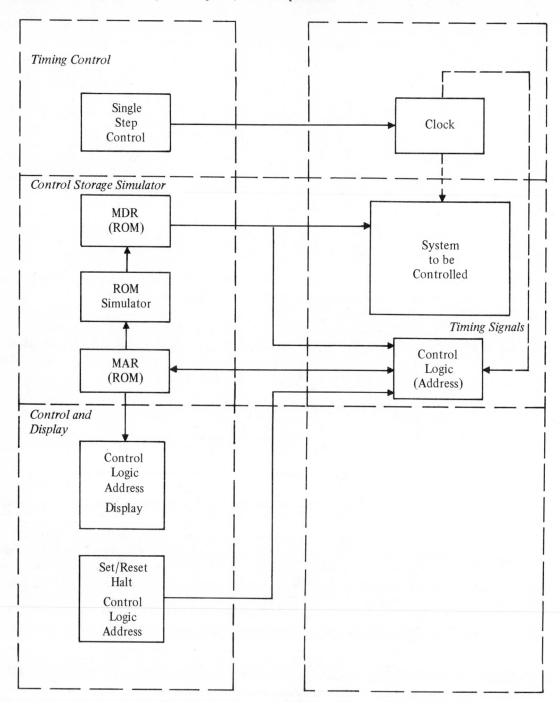

FIGURE 7-3-8.   *Logical components of a control storage simulator.*

7.4 Characterization of System Requirements

A system considered for MP implementation must be analyzed in terms of appropriateness regarding hardware or software tradeoffs. These tradeoffs include the required systems functions, the systems operations, response time, and expansion. Several system characteristics and tradeoffs are given in Table 7-4-1. The selection of an appropriate MP computer system includes considerations of architectural features, performance, and cost and, therefore, must include:

1. Width of a control word
2. Interrelationship of control functions
3. Encoding of control words
4. Branching logic and addressing modes

7.4.1 Microprogramming Versus Hardware

Microprogramming allows modifications to a general-purpose hardware without hardware modifications, and can, therefore, be useful to meet unanticipated requirements, to upgrade functional capabilities, and to use a minicomputer system for more than a single purpose. For each of these modifications, microprogramming adapts an existing general-purpose minicomputer system to a tailor-made configuration. Appropriate capabilities are incorporated without any hardware modifications. Furthermore, microprogrammed adaptations reduce time and cost for custom designed needs, maintenance costs, costs for changes/additions, and costs by replacing several hardware components with a single general-purpose microprogrammed reliable component. In terms of operating (execution) speed, hardwired computer systems can be made to operate at main frame memory (often core memory) cycle times, while for their speed microprogrammed

TABLE 7-4-1. *System Characteristics and Implications for Microprogrammed Computers*

Control Unit Design	*Desirable Characteristics*
Random logic (i.e., hardware)	Small set of simple control functions
MP control unit	Complexity Flexibility Expansion
MP control unit w/ROM, RAM Some random logic	Interrelated logic control Decision making Extensive emulation

233

computer systems depend on the amount of parallelism, the width and scope of data paths, and the ratio of control storage cycle time to main memory cycle time.

7.4.2 Microprogramming Versus Software

Microprogramming can enhance the performance and the efficiency of a system which otherwise would be software implemented whenever a single MI performs the function of many software instructions, whenever such MIs reduce the number of memory accesses for fetching and storing data, and whenever the MIs make it possible to achieve more efficient algorithms. Therefore, the software conducive for MP replacement includes functions that are characterized as:

1. Compute (CPU) bound
2. Highly repetitive
3. Awkward in assembly language implementation
4. Instructions with high overhead (i.e., fetch time, address computation, operand calculations)

To use microprograms as a replacement for software requires detailed knowledge of MI timings, available parallelism between operations, branch logic timings, transfer address calculations, conditional data transfer timings, and intimate debugging procedures. Such systems, once designed, add capabilities not achievable, in a practical sense, through software (e.g., a bootstrap loader),[20] and provide functions that make the software production a simpler process.

Reliability is greatly enhanced through automatic protection (ROM), microdiagnostics, and standardization in design of computer systems.

7.4.3 Implications

Computer system designers can, depending on the complexity of the system, save development and production costs, space and power consumptions by utilizing microprogrammed control logic. An exact analysis of the tradeoffs would include analysis of duplicate conventional and microprogrammed designs of a number of varying complex systems.[5,16,28]

For the most elementary type of systems, random (hardwired) control logic will be the most economical design. This is because a microprogrammed system has a base cost associated with the addressing sequencing, the conditional branch logic, and the memory selection circuitry. Figure 7-4-1 illustrates the relative costs of both types of designs for growing system complexity. The cost of MP control increases more slowly with increasing complexity because each additional sequencing cycle adds only a word to the control storage. On the other hand, the faster cost increase of the

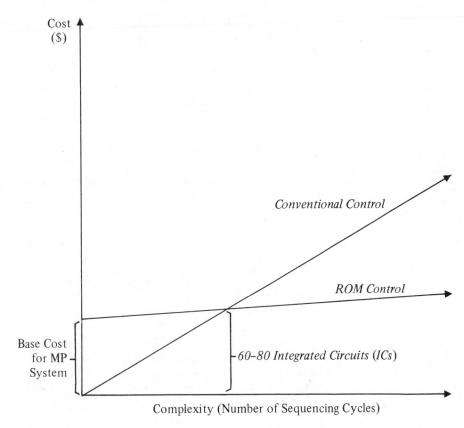

FIGURE 7-4-1.   *Relative costs of conventional and microprogrammed systems with increasing system complexity.*[4,5,19]

conventional control is due to the additions of gating functions, and gates, or some type of storage element per additional control cycle.

The decreasing cost, with the increasing flexibility offered by MP hardware technology, has increased the tendency for MP design architecture, having the following advantages:[3,4,5,7,8]

1. Reduction of random logic results in a more structured control organization with accompanying design adaptations.
2. Implementation of MP diagnostic routines and service aids increase reliability and ease of maintenance.
3. System definitions and designs are postponed to a later time in the design cycle.
4. Economical expansions and modifications to the MP design, including field changes.
5. Emulation of other instruction sets of general-purpose systems (with some loss in execution speed). Optimum operand manipulation, shift controls, can be achieved through implementations of variable word length instructions and data formats under MP control. A very sig-

235

nificant speed tradeoff occurs in favor of MP emulations whenever problem-oriented requirements are added to a basic instruction set (e.g., multiple-precision arithmetic, byte manipulations).

6. Simplification of most I/O interface requirements. The timing and buffering can be accomplished internally without additional hardware or software (i.e., eliminating the need for I/O software routines).

The effects of an improperly managed or controlled microprogrammed system include problems with software transferability, changes in code generation from the language translators, and the support of a variety of instruction sets or modes, all due to changes in the MP architecture.

7.4.4 Application Areas

Microprogrammed systems, because of flexibility, versatility, and cost reductions (throughout the design, development, and maintenance) extend across large product and application areas ranging from simple control functions to complex real-time control systems.

Aside from the more common applications, such as emulation of other systems, and upward/downward compatibility among minicomputer systems of a series, MP control units (because of their cost effectiveness) can be applied to functions previously performed only by special circuits or custom-made devices. A description of some representative applications follows.

1. *Process control system.* A process control system performs real-time data acquisition and online control while performing status reporting as a background function. Some of the control functions include preprocessing for the data acquisition, control interfacing, dedicated real-time data processing, management data reporting, and executive functions. Examples of such systems include data sensing, environmental monitoring, factory-automation systems, and component manufacturing.[52]

2. *Instrumentation Systems.* Microprogrammed instrumentation systems automatically relieve operator interaction with complex instrumentation in laboratory activities. Examples include signal generators, synthesizers, thermocouple recorders, and complex pulse generators.[43]

3. *Intelligent Terminals.* These microprogrammed systems perform offline editing, compiling, processing, and communications activities. Example systems include point-of-sale and supermarket checkouts, terminals for investment houses, automated bank tellers, and portable data terminals.[44]

4. *Real-Time Data Processing.* This processing activity can be characterized by large volumes of data, an efficiency in processing this data, repetitive computational operations on the data, and array data calculations. Examples include multisensor correlations, spectral analysis, pattern recognition, filtering of digital signals, and fast Fourier transforms.[59]

236

5. *Data Communications Systems.* Convenient functions controlled by MP systems include polling activities, multiplexing, buffer management, scheduling tasks, code conversions, reformatting, routing and addressing messages, generating transmission codes, error detection/correction, editing, and data compressions. Example systems include programmable front-end processors, communication processors, line interface units, multiplexers, concentrators, and intelligent terminals.[24,30]

Applications of microprogrammed systems are virtually unlimited because of their high performance/cost implementations. In addition, systems applicable for MP implementation include the following types of equipment:

1. Calculators (programmable, or fixed function)
2. Process control equipment
3. Numerical control equipment
4. Traffic controllers
5. Computer peripherals
6. Terminals (intelligent, point-of-sales)
7. Medical equipment and instruments
8. Monitoring equipment
9. Data communication equipment
10. Source data automation equipment
11. Educational equipment and devices

7.4.5 Example Microprogrammed Minicomputer Systems

In the following sections representative microprogrammed minicomputers are illustrated. These systems are intended only as representative systems of a much larger group.

7.4.5.1 Digital Scientific Meta 4.   The Digital Scientific Meta 4 is a general-purpose microprogrammed computer with no standard machine language instruction set. Rather, the user has the capability to prepare the microprogram in control storage (ROM) aided by the vendors' translator and simulator. The block diagram structure is given in Figure 7-4-2.[1,10]

The microinstruction format (32 bits wide) consists of an operation code, defining one of four microinstruction types, and several operand specifications. The basic format contains several bits which are used as modifiers, which in addition can indicate the following:

1. Shift the output of the ALU (right or left).
2. Utilize the carry bit of the ALU to add the carry from the previous operation.
3. Autodecrement and test specified registers.
4. Conditional transfer (on zero) as specified in a register.
5. Initiate read/write operations.

237

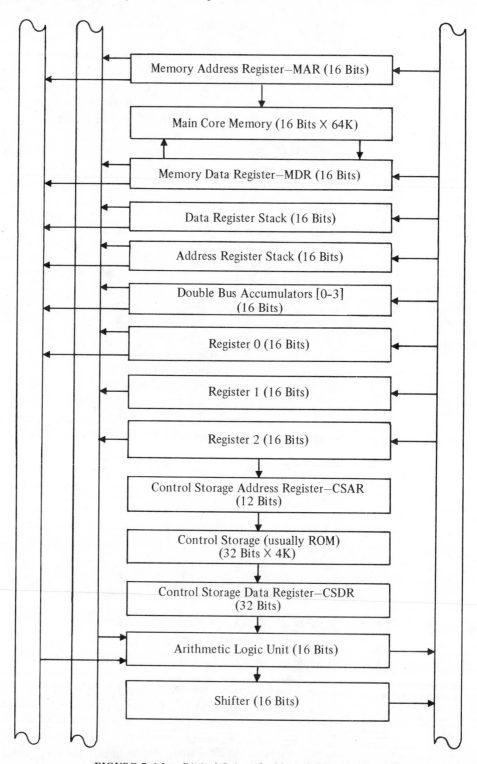

FIGURE 7-4-2. *Digital Scientific Meta 4 Organization.*[1,10]

7.4.5.2 Hewlett-Packard HP 2100. The Hewlett-Packard HP 2100, illustrated in Figures 7-4-3 and 7-4-4, is a general-purpose microprogrammable computer supporting a machine language instruction set of about 80 instructions. The control storage, with a capacity of 4096 words and a 60-μsec access time, partially implemented as an ROM and partially as a writable control storage is used to implement part of the basic instruction set, with the remainder of the instruction set hardwired. Other microprograms may be loaded into WCS via a system editor. A microprogrammed supplied assembler and debugger facilitate microprogram preparations making the HP 2100 a dynamically used MP minicomputer system.[1,15,50]

The HP 2100 processor includes a set of sixteen registers, two of which are non-user-accessible accumulators, another a program counter, and one a switch register. With twelve and possibly fourteen registers available to the user for storing intermediate or temporary results, fewer memory references result in faster program execution.

The HP 2100, using minimally encoded vertical MI formats with a 24-bit control word divided into six subfields, permits an MI to specify more parallel machine operations than is possible with a 16-bit machine language instruction. The MIs, using basically a three-address instruction format, utilize single-level encoding for most of the microcommands in the subfield, although two-level encoding is possible. The HP 2100 MI format is illustrated in Figure 7-4-5.

7.4.5.3 Interdata Model 85. The Interdata Model 85 is a general-purpose microprogrammable minicomputer with a read-only memory (custom-alterable by the vendor), as well as a user-alterable control storage, supporting about 130 standard machine language instructions. The architecture of the system utilizes two buses for source and destination address instructions, as well as provides two 24×16-bit register stacks. These register stacks are paralleled, providing 16 registers as general-purpose registers, with the other 8 registers dedicated to the microprocessor. The basic Interdata 85 organization, illustrated in Figure 7-4-6, uses the manufacturer-supplied ROM-resident microprograms to effect the standard machine language instruction set, while the WCS can be loaded from main memory under the control of the machine instruction set or other microprogrammed routines. To aid in the microprogramming preparation, Interdata provides an assembler, a debugger, and a dynamic simulator.[1,22]

The basic microinstruction format (given in Figure 7-4-7) is 32 bits long with three addresses, utilizing two-level encoding of subfields based on the operation code (i.e., vertical format).

7.4.5.4 Microdata 3200. The Microdata 3200 is a general-purpose microprogrammable computer utilizing 32-bit, field encoded microinstructions (eight 4-bit fields), and 16-bit registers and data paths. Control storage, both read-only and/or read/write, are accessed for loading and checking through a Monobus. Up to 4096 words of control storage are available with 60 μsec access time and 135 μsec microinstruction execution time. The architecture

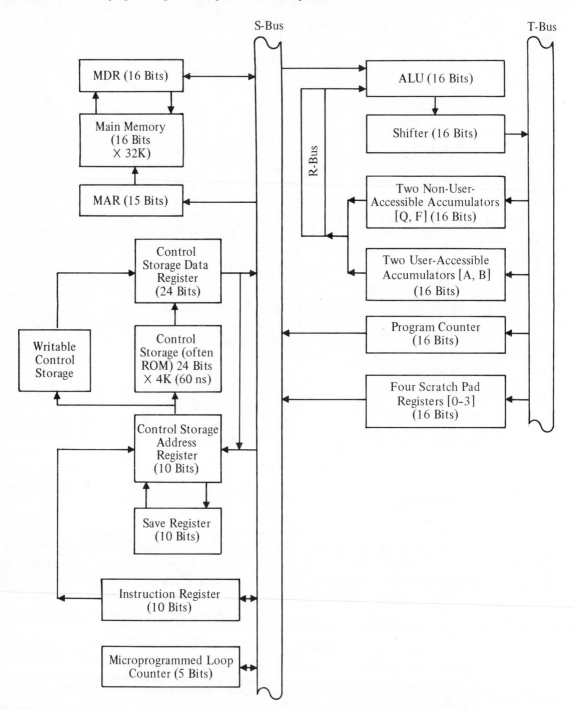

FIGURE 7-4-3. *Hewlett-Packard HP 2100 Organization.*[1,15,50]

FIGURE 7-4-4. *Hewlett-Packard 21MX-Series user-microprogrammable minicomputers with semiconductor main memory. (Reprinted by permission of Hewlett-Packard.)*

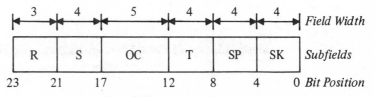

R — Specifies the register whose content is to be placed onto the R-bus (input to ALU)

S — Specifies the register whose content is to be placed onto the S-bus (input to ALU)

T — Specifies the register whose content is to be placed onto the T-bus

OC — Operation function of the ALU/shifter

SP — Used to indicate I/O operations, core memory, accesses, counter manipulations, etc.

SK — Skip field to control sequencing of control storage

FIGURE 7-4-5. *Example of HP 2100 microinstruction format.*

241

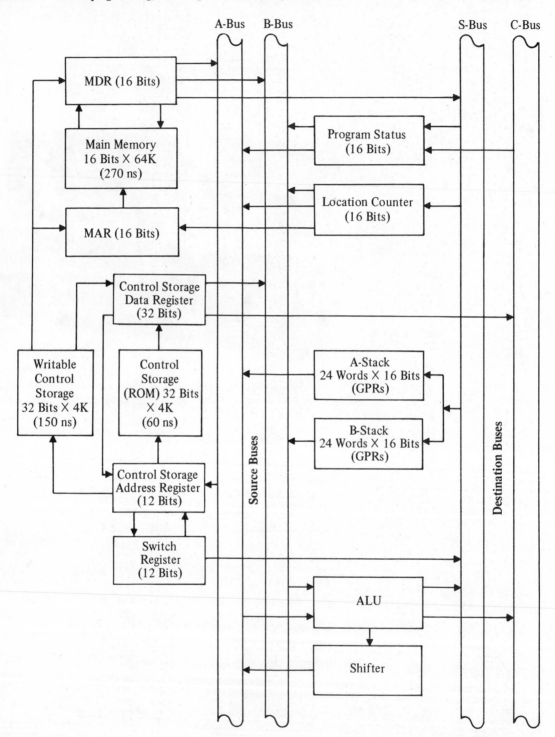

FIGURE 7-4-6.   Interdata Model 85 Organization.[1,22]

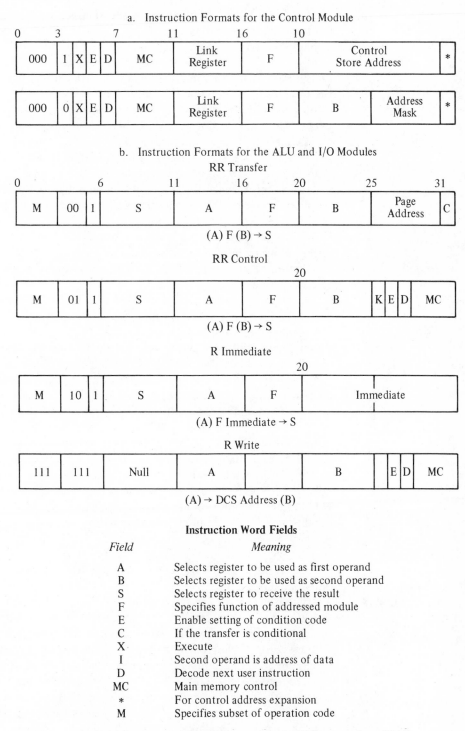

a. Instruction Formats for the Control Module

0	3				7	11	16	10	
000	1	X	E	D	MC	Link Register	F	Control Store Address	*

| 000 | 0 | X | E | D | MC | Link Register | F | B | Address Mask | * |

b. Instruction Formats for the ALU and I/O Modules

RR Transfer

0		6	11	16	20	25	31
M	00 1	S	A	F	B	Page Address	C

(A) F (B) → S

RR Control

						20	
M	01 1	S	A	F	B	K E D	MC

(A) F (B) → S

R Immediate

					20
M	10 1	S	A	F	Immediate

(A) F Immediate → S

R Write

111	111	Null	A		B	E D	MC

(A) → DCS Address (B)

Instruction Word Fields

Field	Meaning
A	Selects register to be used as first operand
B	Selects register to be used as second operand
S	Selects register to receive the result
F	Specifies function of addressed module
E	Enable setting of condition code
C	If the transfer is conditional
X	Execute
I	Second operand is address of data
D	Decode next user instruction
MC	Main memory control
*	For control address expansion
M	Specifies subset of operation code

FIGURE 7-4-7. *Microinstruction format of the Interdata 85.*[1,22]

243

of the computer is organized as a set of modules that are connected to a common high-speed bus (Monobus). Any number of modules, up to 256 kilobytes of addressing space, and any mix of modules is possible.[1,6,18,32,36]

Transfer on the bus is asynchronous, with transfer rates limited only by the logic in the two modules involved. Bus allocation is overlapped with the transfer time such that during one bus cycle, a data transfer is occurring in parallel with the device selection to control transfer during the next bus cycle. Although the Monobus treats all modules in common, the modules can be classified as processor, memory, and I/O modules.

The processor modules, illustrated in Figure 7-4-8, contain three working registers, a program pointer register, and a register file of 16 general-purpose registers (optimally expandable to 32). The ALU operates on bytes or words, and on resulting 8- or 16-bit operands with negative, zero, overflow, and perhaps carry outputs.

Instructions, at the machine language level, are fetched as a byte string, utilizing hardware instruction look-ahead. There is an overlap of the instruction fetch and execution, with no execution time penalty for the microprogram.

MOS memory modules utilize a read/write cycle of 400/300 μsec, respectively. The memory module has a byte parallel read/write capability. The semiconductor memory module, 4–132K (16 bit words), requires refreshing every 30 μsec during normal operations, while only 2 μsec during standby operations. Memory modules can be of almost any speed or capacity, with or without buffer registers. Cache buffers can be added to the system without changing the architecture of the computer system.

I/O modules are addressed via the Monobus at the register level. Because each I/O module could serve as a bus controller or master, the upper 16-kilobyte bus addresses are used to address each I/O device, providing for at least 1024 devices (using 16-byte addresses for each device).

The microinstruction format (32 bits wide) consists of seven 4-bit fields, one 3-bit field, and one 1-bit field (see Figure 7-4-9). The field encoded MI contains the address of the next MI, as well as fields that are defined or conditioned by the contents of other fields.

7.4.5.5 Nanodata QM-1. The organization of the microprogrammed Nanodata QM-1, illustrated in Figure 7-4-10, uses a nanoprogram (residing in a writable nanostore) to fetch and interpret an 18-bit vertical microinstruction stored in control store. The paths between functional subassemblies are programmable by way of horizontal nanoinstructions, 360 bits defining five 72-bit vectors. The rearrangement of the system is established through programmable interconnections of the machine's facilities (twelve buses, three register banks, a three-level storage hierarchy, an ALU, and a shifter), and thus their functions. The system permits both control store and nanostore to be loaded under user program control, with the vendor providing an assembler and a simulator for both the micro- and nanoprograms. Because the control store is both readable and writable under nanoprogram control, it

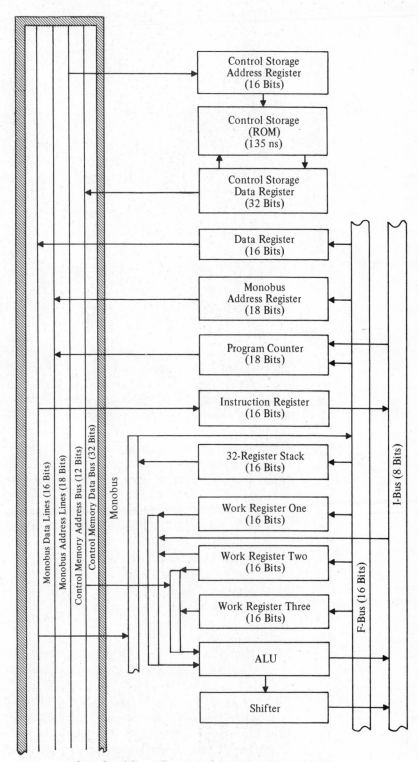

FIGURE 7-4-8. *Microdata 3200 Organization.*[1,8,17]

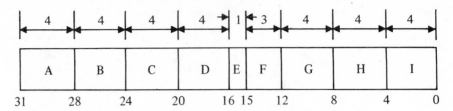

A – ALU operations functions
B – Source field and/or shift end conditions
C – File register address and control
D – Destination field
E – Expanded destination field indicator
F – Jump addressing mode
G – Next MI address constant
H – Jump condition extension
I – Jump condition

FIGURE 7-4-9.   *Microinstruction format of the Microdata 3200.*

can be used to store information other than microinstructions (e.g., control information for local store addresses of buses).[1,8]

The format of the microinstruction is given in Figure 7-4-11. The K-vector defines conditions that point to local store, defining connections and functions of local registers that remain in effect during the execution of the microinstruction, with some residual control. The T-vectors, executed serially and circularly, indicate several other operations (e.g., selection of another nanostore word, test, conditional branch, ALU and shift operations, register transfers, and conditional sequencing) which are executed in parallel.

As an example of an operation, illustrating the use of these vectors, consider the contents of these vectors for a typical ADD operation:

K = ALU operation of ADD.
T_1 = Move A-field into register associated with left input to ALU.
T_2 = Move B-field into register associated with right input to ALU. (T_1 and T_2 establish a 2-bus connection.)
T_3 = Operation to send A parameter to ALU output side, and fill ALU hold register.
T_4 = Gate contents of ALU hold register to wherever the A output data address indicates. Fill status register and terminate.

7.4.5.6 Varian 73.   The Varian 73, illustrated in Figure 7-4-12, is a general-purpose microprogrammable minicomputer supporting a machine language instruction set of about 150 instructions. Control storage exists for both ROM, used to supply the basic machine instruction set, and a CWS that can

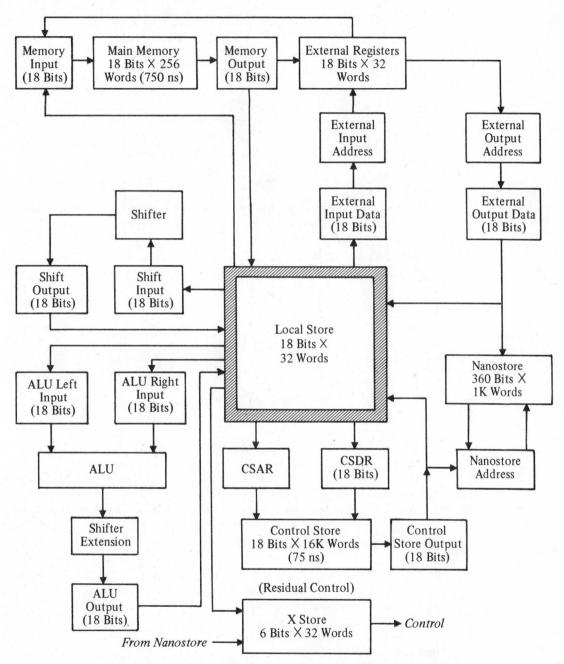

FIGURE 7-4-10.   *Nanodata QM-1 Organization.*[1,11]

be loaded from main memory. A vendor supplied assembler, debugger, and interactive simulator is provided to facilitate microprogram preparation.[1,55]

Utilizing a horizontal highly encoded MI format, with a 64-bit control word divided into 25 subfields (most of which use two- and three-level

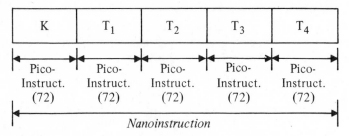

$$K + (i)T = \text{nano-machine instruction (40 ns)}$$

FIGURE 7-4-11. *Microinstruction format of the Nanodata QM-1.*[1,11]

encoding), permits the Varian 73 an unusually high parallelism. The MI format includes microcommands to indicate such operations as ALU functions, operand shifting, memory accesses and operations, register transfers, condition testing, I/O control, and control storage accessing and sequencing.

7.5 Future Trends

Microprogramming has proven to be important because it is effective as a design tool and has a favorable performance/cost ratio. In addition, microprogramming has provided a viable alternative for enhancing software efficiency, both for the vendor-supplied software, as well as the specialized dedicated user tasks. In addition to the traditional applications (i.e., emulation, architectural adaptations, and custom tailor made instruction sets), microprogramming is also used for implementations of language interpreters,[27,31] operating system control functions, replacements of support software, and microprocessors.[40]

7.5.1 Direction of Future Systems[5,46,58]

In the past, programming languages have been heavily supported with extensive language translators (such as compilers) which require significant permanent and temporary storage space and which consume considerable processing capacity while translating. *Direct interpretation* of either high-level languages or intermediate languages can be implemented in terms of primitive operations through microprogramming. This approach eliminates the storage requirements of the language translators, and significantly reduces processing time for programs in a debugging phase.

Operating system modules are a major component of most minicomputer systems. Microprograms of certain operating system control functions offer a convenient mechanism to reduce conventional storage requirements, as well as to provide enhanced performance. As an example, consider the

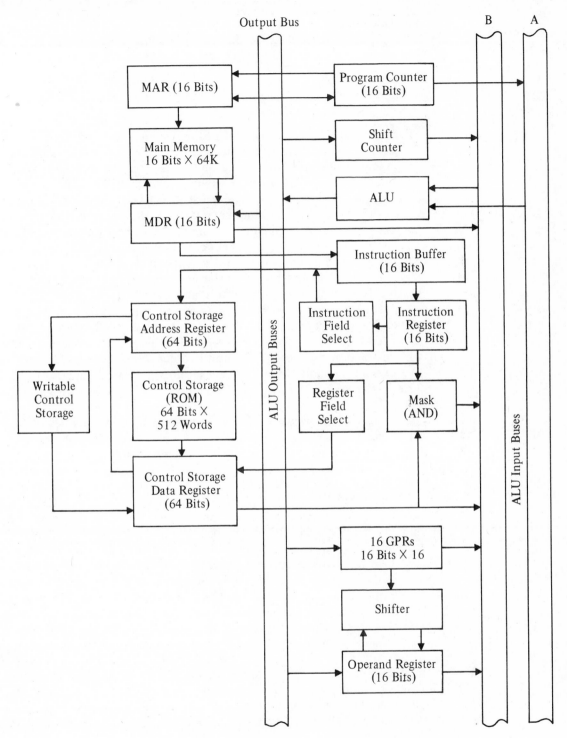

FIGURE 7-4-12. *Varian 73 Organization.*[1,55]

implementations of such control functions as loading, I/O interfacing, interrupt response, scheduling, accounting, and CPU timing controls.[20]

7.5.2 Microcomputers

Microprocessors, an outgrowth of LSI technology, are processors on chips or circuitry cards. Most minicomputers and some microprocessors use microprogrammed control units because they are easy to implement and very cost effective. Versatility is enhanced by the fact that all basic operations are programmed into a control storage (most often ROM), which may be altered to suit various application requirements. To build a minicomputer utilizing microprocessor chip technology requires a microprocessor, the addition of memory for its control storage, input/output controls to interface peripheral equipment, and finally a clock and timing module.

Microprocessors may be classified as 4-bit, 8-bit, or bit-slice processors depending on the architecture and technology used.[6,13,25,26,29,49,51]

Four-bit processors can serially process 4-bit words with BCD arithmetic. Based on *p*-channel MOS (PMOS) technology, they are pin-limited (24 or less) and slow. They can, however, be designed into microcomputers with instruction execution times on the order of milliseconds. Representative examples include Intel's MCS-4 (4040) shown in Figure 7-5-1, Intel's 8008 in Figure 7-5-2, as well as Teledyne's TDY-52A, Rockwell's PPS-4, Fairchild's PPS-25, and National's IMP-4.

Eight-bit processors, by switching to *n*-channel MOS (NMOS), bipolar or complementary MOS (CMOS) technologies, have increased performances, with instruction execution times comparable to those of some minicomputers (1–5 μsec). Examples of such 8-bit processors include Intel's MCS-8 (8080), Rockwell's PPS-8, Signetics 2650, National's IMP-8, and Motorola's M6800. Compared to PMOS devices, NMOS and CMOS systems demonstrate representative improved speed, gate densities, increased number of pins (typically on the order of 40), and parallel address/data transmission (e.g., Intel's 8085 and 8086 in Figures 7-5-3 and 7-5-4).

Bit-slice processors can be used to design computer organizations with variable size words, utilizing 2- or 4-bit slices. Thus, microcomputers with 8-, 12-, 16-, 24-, or 32-bit parallel bits/word can be designed. Typical 16-bit processors, constructed from these bit-slice components, include National's GPCIP and Raytheon's RP-1600.

The slice architecture implies that slices of the CPU contain multiple registers, various status registers, and an ALU. The registers and the logic modules are organized usually in a conventional parallel bus architecture. Parallel arrangement of the slices create word-size processors under microprogrammable control logic. Examples include National's IMP-16, Computer Automation's Naked Mini LSI-1, Interdata's 6/16, and Fairchild's 9400 (Figure 7-5-5).

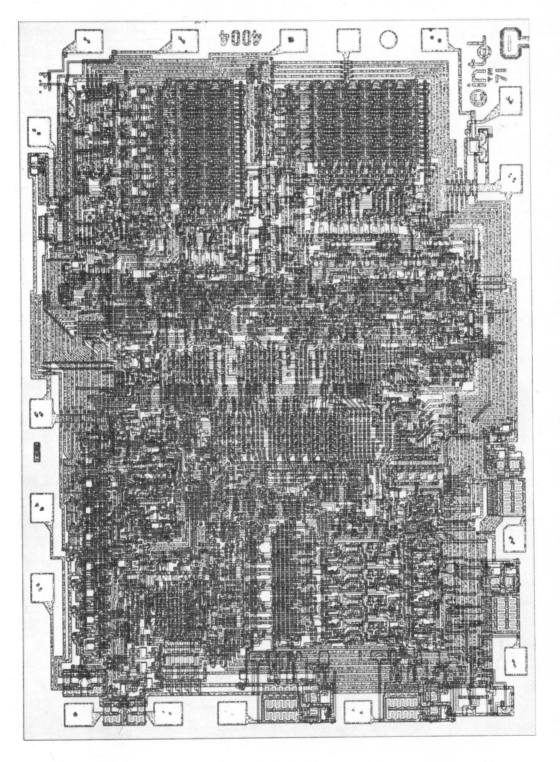

FIGURE 7-5-1. Intel's 4004 four-bit processor. (Courtesy Intel Corporation.)

251

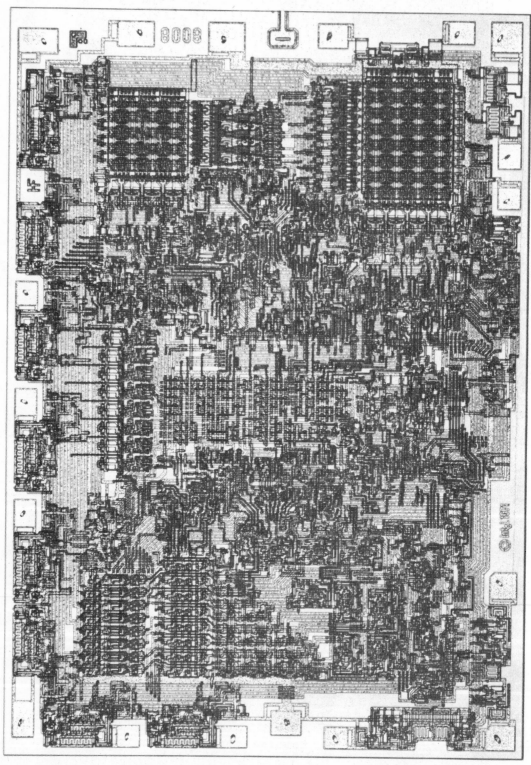

FIGURE 7-5-2. Intel's 8008 eight-bit processor. (*Courtesy Intel Corporation.*)

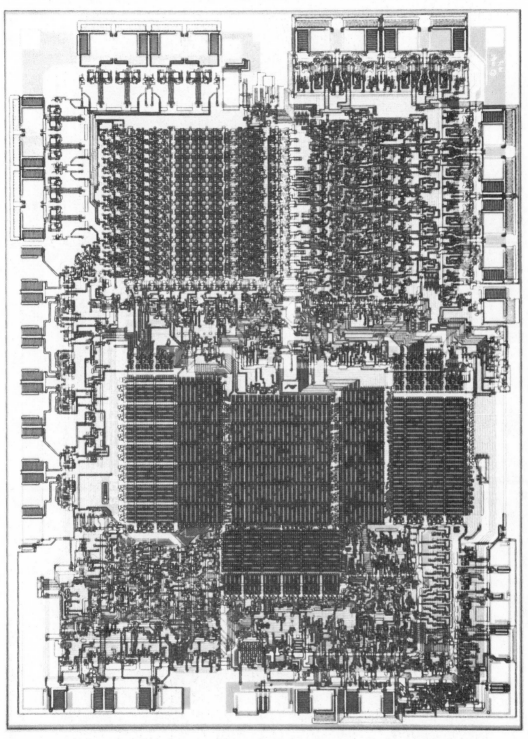

FIGURE 7-5-3. *Intel's 8085 eight-bit processor. (Courtesy Intel Corporation.)*

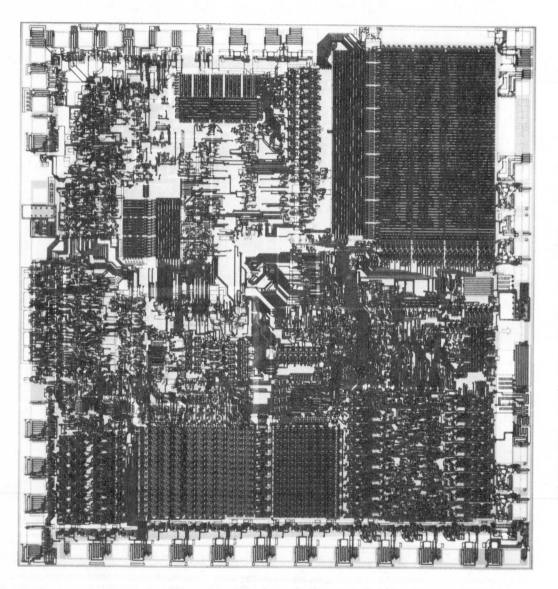

FIGURE 7-5-4. *Intel's 8086 eight-bit processor. (Courtesy Intel Corporation.)*

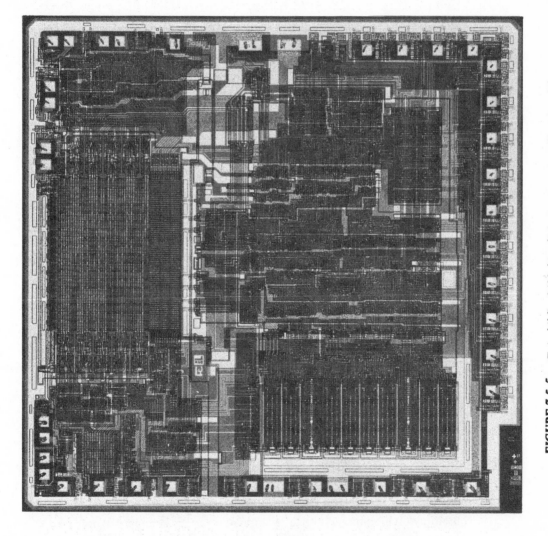

FIGURE 7-5-5. *Fairchild's 9400 bit slicing processor. (Reprinted by permission of Fairchild Camera and Instrument Corporation.)*

TABLE 7-5-1.   Representative Microcomputer Characteristics

Characteristics	Range
Data word size	4–32 bits
	(4 × 25 for PPS-25)
Instruction set	40–120 instructions
Instruction format	8–24 bits
	(LSI-11 with 5 × 16 bits)
ROM control storage	400 (23 bits)–16K (8 bits)
RAM	Up to 65K (16 bits)
GPR	1–16
Cycle time (fetch/execute)	0.54–62 μsec
Stack depth	2–32 levels
	(8080, 6800, and LSI-11 have 64K)
Interrupt handling capability	None/full
Chip size	Typically 180 mils/side
Power dissipation	≃ 1W at 70°C

The microcomputer (MC), distinguished by the use of an LSI-CPU, costs approximately an order of magnitude less than a minicomputer, while at the same time being also an order of magnitude slower (see Table 7-5-1).

The main component of a microcomputer—the microprocessor—is composed of one or more LSI chips that perform the basic functions of a processing unit (e.g., accept data from input devices, modify the data through the ALU, or output the data to external devices). Microcomputers differ in their system architecture by the number of internal registers, microprogrammed control units, I/O interface capabilities, and their address/data bus organization. Representative characteristics of such microcomputer systems are given in Table 7-5-1.

The distinguishing characteristics of a microcomputer system (Table 7-5-2) include equivalent word lengths, slower relative speed to minicomputers, fewer addressing modes, with less sophisticated interrupt-handling capabilities. On the other hand, microcomputer systems provide better price/performance ratios, lower power consumptions/heat dissipation, in addition to smaller size, and higher reliability in comparison to minicomputers. The main recognized difference between a microcomputer and a minicomputer appears to be cost (see Table 7-5-3).

Expected characteristics of evolving microcomputers are given in Table 7-5-4. A larger number of bits (resolution), higher speeds, more extensive and powerful instruction sets, and elimination of non-LSI components are certain. In addition, most minicomputer features, including hardware multiply/divide, bit and byte manipulations, are standard features; e.g., Texas Instruments' TMS 9900 (Figures 7-5-6 and 7-5-7), Zilog's MCZ-1 Microcomputer Systems (Figures 7-5-8 and 7-5-9), Digital Equipment Corporation's PDP-11 (Figure 7-5-10), and Data General's MicroNOVA (Figure 7-5-11).

TABLE 7-5-2.   *Generation of Microcomputer Characteristics*[25]

Technology	*PMOS* *(p-channel MOS)*	*CMOS or NMOS* *(Complementary* *MOS/n-channel MOS)*	*SOS or Bipolar Logic* *(Silicon on saphire* *NMOS, PMOS,* *CMOS)*
Instruction Set Execution Speed	Pre-minicomputer and primitive 50–100 times slower than average minicomputer	Pre-minicomputer 3–10 times slower than average computer	Minicomputer equivalent
System Architecture	• Fixed hardware, variable software (e.g., TMS-1000) • Microprogrammable instruction set • 400 kHz moderate 1-chip organization	For 8-bit Processors: • Variable hardware/variable software (e.g., TMS-8080) • Fixed second generation instruction set • 2 MHz moderate multichip organization For 16-bit Processors: • Variable hardware/variable software (e.g., TMS-9900) • Fixed third generation instruction set • 3 MHz fast multi-chip organization	For Bit-slicing Processors: • N-bit bipolar bit slice (e.g., SBP 0400) • Variable hardware/variable software • Microprogrammable to emulate existing machines and software • 10 MHz fast multi-element organization
Comments	• First generaton CPU chips are most accurately visualized as a low-cost replacement for discrete logic	Comparable to slow minicomputers	Low-end minicomputer replacements

TABLE 7-5-2. *(continued)*

Technology	PMOS (p-channel MOS)	CMOS or NMOS (Complementary MOS/n-channel MOS)	SOS or Bipolar Logic (Silicon on saphire NMOS, PMOS, CMOS, HMOS)
Relative Time Frame	1971	1973-present	1976-present
Representative examples	4-bit CPU: Intel 4004 Rockwell PPS-4 Teledyne TDY-52A National IMP-4 Fairchild PPS-25 Texas Instruments TMS-100	8-bit CPU: Intel 8080A Intel 8048 Intel 8085 Intel 8086 Motorola 6800 Signetics 2650 Zilog Z-80 Mostek 6502	RCA-COSMAC Zilog Z800 Zilog Z8 Motorola 6809 Motorola 68000 Intel 8086 Intel 8085 Mostek 3870 Motorola 6802
	8-bit CPU: Intel 8008 Mostek 5065 National SCAMP Rockwell PPS-8 National IMP-8	16-bit CPU: General Instruments CP 1600 Western Digital MCP 1600 Texas Instruments TMS 9900	
	16-bit CPU: National IMP-16 National PACE	8-bit CPU: RCA 1801 RCA 1802 Intersil ISD-8	
	Bit-slicing CPU(TTL/ ECL/I²L): Fairchild 9400 Intel 3002 Motorola 10800 Texas Instruments SPP0400		

TABLE 7-5-3. *Comparisons of Microcomputers and Minicomputers*

Microcomputer	Minicomputer
• Started as an outgrowth of calculators	• Started as a modularized approach of small computers
• Ideal for low-medium computational performance tasks	• Ideal for high performance scientific and business applications

Advantages	
• Modularized component organization	• High computing power
• Fast design time	• Backed by system-oriented suppliers
• High flexibility	• Availability of a large number of hardware/software aids
• Small size and weight	• Allows the use of core or semiconductor memory
• Low power consumption	
• Relatively inexpensive	• Availability of large word lengths
• Useful for high-volume applications	

Disadvantages	
• Limited software support	• More expensive than microcomputer
• Restricted execution speed	• Requires mating of minicomputer and semiconductor or core technology
• Lower overall performance	
• Limited instructions	
• Promoted by computer-oriented supplier	• Available in word lengths of 8 bits or more
• More difficult interfacing	• Oriented to small or medium sales volume

Examples	
• LSI-11	• PDP-11 Family
• Intersil 1600	• PDP-8 Family
• μNova	• Data General Nova Family

TABLE 7-5-4.   *Characteristics of Evolving Microcomputers*

Density	Larger (300 miles max) and denser (200,000 devices/chip) chips
Packaging	24–64 pin DIPs (dual-in-line packages)
Resolution	• MOS (8–16 bits on single chip) • Bipolar (2–4 bit slice)
Speed	• MOS ($\leq$ .4 μsec cycle time) • Bipolar ($\leq$ 0.2 μsec cycle time)
Memories	RAMs (64K—50 μsec) ROMs (256K—100 μsec)
Interfacing	Special I/O and peripheral interface circuits, one-chip clock and timing circuits
Technology	SOS and CMOS predominance
Instruction Set	Extensive, in excess of 512
Power	10 nW/gate—CMOS
Clock rate	10 MHz

FIGURE 7-5-6.   *Texas Instruments' TMS 9900 Microprocessor. A 16-bit single-chip processor features minicomputer instruction power and MOS n-channel silicon-gate technology. (Reprinted by permission of Texas Instruments–Photo Copyright Texas Instruments 1979.)*

FIGURE 7-5-7. *Compatibility-Texas Instruments' TMS 9900 Micro-processor. Shown as the largest component on the circuit board. Serves as the heart and brains of the single-circuit-board computer, the 990/4. The 990/4 is shown in configurations for rack mounting and as a complete system with operator control panel. (Reprinted by permission of Texas Instruments–Photo Copyright Texas Instruments 1979.)*

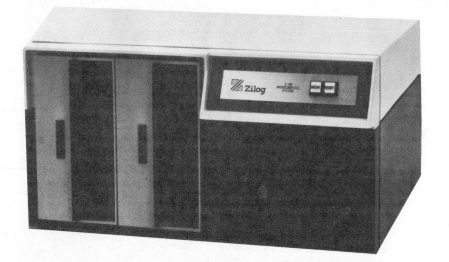

FIGURE 7-5-8. *Zilog's MCZ-1/20 Microcomputer System. Includes a single, desk-top enclosure that houses the power supplies, floppy disk drives, and a nine-position card cage. A z-80 CPU and 60K bytes of memory are standard. (Reprinted by permission of ZILOG.)*

FIGURE 7-5-9. *Zilog's MCZ-1/25 Microcomputer System. A rack-mountable version of the MCZ-1/20 ideal for use in desk configuration's, cabinets, or freestanding equipment racks. (Reprinted by permission of ZILOG.)*

FIGURE 7-5-10. *Digital Equipment Corporation's PDP-11/03. (Reprinted by permission of Digital Equipment Corporation.)*

FIGURE 7-5-11. *Data General's microNOVA®. Family is available on a chip, in a board, or in a box. (Reprinted by permission of Data General Corporation. Copyright © 1977, 1978 Data General Corporation, Westboro, Massachusetts.)*

263

SUMMARY

Microprogramming offers users an effective design tool and a favorable performance/cost ratio. Furthermore, microprogramming has provided a viable alternative for enhancing software efficiency, both for the vendor-supplied software, as well as the specialized dedicated user tasks. In addition to the traditional applications (i.e., emulation, architectural adaptations, via a programmable bus structure, and custom-made instruction sets), microprogramming is also used for implementations of language interpreters, operating system control functions, replacements of support software, and microprocessors.

Microprogramming provides capabilities otherwise not available to a high-level language or assembler language programmer. These capabilities include the design of specialized functions, replacing existing functions, interfacing to special purpose devices, and most importantly, a standardized hardware design.

All of these functions can be implemented using microprogramming regardless of the multiplicity in the bus structure, the width of the buses, and the microinstruction design. On the other hand, capabilities such as optimization, concurrency for speed, and the speed at which the system must respond to input signals are directly effected by how many different control functions can be specified in a single control word (concurrency); how the different control functions are interrelated; whether the different control functions are performed sequentially (monophase MP), concurrently (polyphase MP), or as a combination of both; how the control words are encoded; how the address of the next control word is derived; and how much multiplicity exists in the bus structure.

These large variations in capabilities (speed, hardware gate level control, interfacing) should be the primary motivating factors in designing and selecting a specific bus architecture, and not just the fact that microprogramming was used as a design alternative for the control unit.

PROBLEMS

1. Briefly describe each of the following concepts:
   a. Microprogramming
   b. Microinstructions
   c. Read-Only Memory
   d. Writable Control Storage

2. Differentiate the basic functions of the control section of a hardwired control unit and a microprogrammed control unit.

3. Describe how machine language instructions are implemented by microinstruction sequences of a microprogrammed computer system.

4. What similarities and differences exist between:
   a. A computer program and a microprogram
   b. A computer instruction and a microinstruction
   c. An operation and a microoperation

5. Describe the cost/performance tradeoffs that can be made when implementing an algorithm by way of microprogramming.

6. How is conditional branching implemented in a microprogram? What special considerations must be available?

7. List and discuss the merits of various memories that can be used for a microprogrammed control storage.

8. Why can a microinstruction not be executed out of core memory?

9. Why bother with writable control storage when a microprogrammed minicomputer already has ROM?

10. What effect do each of the following have on system design of a microprogrammed minicomputer?
    a. ROM access time
    b. Cost of the ROM control
    c. Microinstruction format
    d. Number of microcommands/microinstruction

11. Under what circumstances is it advantageous to use a microprogrammed control storage over the traditional minicomputer design? Be specific by using an example application.

12. Why are timing considerations, especially access time to the control storage, critical in microcontrol design?

13. Discuss several variations in defining fields within the microinstruction formats.

14. How does microprogramming add flexibility and reliability to a minicomputer?

15. Discuss briefly each of the following design questions:
    a. How are control words to be encoded?
    b. How is the address of the next control word determined?
    c. How many different control functions are to be specified in a single control word? How are these to be formulated?
    d. How can the execution time of a microcommand exceed the basic clock cycle?

16. Why is a machine language instruction often faster on a hardwired control unit than on a microprogrammed control unit.

17. Discuss some of the limiting factors in the use of microprogrammed control storage.

18. What is meant by emulation? How is this made possible by way of microprogramming?

19. Devise schemes for implementing subroutine, indexing, and parameterization in microprogrammed control store.

20. Differentiate between minimally and maximally encoded microinstructions.

21. What is meant by residual control?

265

22. Discuss the importance of control cycle speed, and relate this time to the machine language instruction time.

23. How does vertical microprogramming differ from horizontal microprogramming? How are they the same?

24. Discuss the availability of software support of microprogrammed minicomputers.

25. What is the impact of parallelism on the design of a microprogrammed computer system? What role does the ROM word size and the ROM memory organization have on this design?

26. Discuss the need of a control storage simulator. What are some of its operating characteristics?

27. Enumerate several applications which would have performance improvements if microprogrammed.

28. In what way can I/O interfaces be simplified, assuming microprogrammed facilities?

29. Describe several techniques that are used in decoding microinstructions.

30. Consider serial and parallel accessing of microinstructions. What is meant by each? Illustrate advantages of one over the other.

31. Describe at least four different microprogramming languages and how they are implemented.

32. What are some of the desirable characteristics of a control storage?

33. What kind of software algorithms are conducive to microprogrammed replacement?

34. Elaborate on at least five specific functions of a data communication system that can be implemented on a microprogrammed minicomputer.

35. What are some of the negative effects of an improperly managed or controlled microprogrammed system?

36. Compare any two microprogrammed minicomputers described in this chapter.

37. What characteristics differentiate the Nanodata QM-1 from any other microprogrammed minicomputer?

38. What is meant by direct interpretation of microprogramming (higher level) languages?

39. Discuss distinguishing characteristics of a microcomputer.

40. How does a microcomputer differ from a microprogrammable minicomputer?

41. Why is a microprocessor not a computer on a chip?

42. Under what circumstances would a microcomputer be used over a microprogrammed minicomputer?

43. Describe the software development phase for a microprogrammed computer system.

44. What are the three major differences between a microprocessor and a conventional processor?

45. What is a microcomputer?

PROJECT

1. Pick at least one minicomputer family and one microcomputer family and compare, contrast, and discuss:
   a. Architecture
   b. Programming model
   c. Instruction sets
   d. Technical specifications
   e. Typical systems
   f. Interrupt structures
   g. I/O structures

Sample Systems:
Minicomputers
  Texas Instruments' 990 through 9900
  DEC PDP-11/2 through 11/30
  Data General's Nova® Series
  National's 1600 Series
Microcomputers
  Motorola 6800 through 6809 Family
  Intel 8008 through 8086 Family
  Zilog Z80 through Z8000 Family
  MOS Technology 6501 through 6505
  Signetics 2650 Family
Be accurate and detailed.

REFERENCES

1. Agrawala, A. K., and T. G. Rauscher, "Multiprogramming: Perspective and Status," *IEEE Trans. on Comp.*, Vol. C-23, No. 8, August 1974, pp. 817–837.
2. Amdahl, L. D., "Microprogramming and Stored Logic," *Datamation*, Vol. 10, No. 2, February 1964, pp. 24–26.
3. Boutwell, E. O., Jr., "The PB-440," *Datamation*, Vol. 5, No. 2, February 1964, pp. 30–32.
4. Burns, R., and D. Savitt, "Microprogramming, Stack Architecture Ease Minicomputer Programmer's Burden," *Electronics*, Vol. 46, No. 4, February 15, 1973, pp. 95–101.
5. Callahan, B. L. J., "The State-of-the-Art: Microprocessors and Microcomputer," *Modern Data*, Vol. 7, No. 5, May 1974, pp. 28–31.
6. Callahan, B. L. J., "Microprocessors and Microcomputers: The State of the Art," *Modern Data*, Vol. 7, No. 6, June 1974, pp. 30–32.

7. Davidow, W. H., "General-Purpose Microcontrollers, Part 1: Economic Considerations," *Computer Design,* Vol. 11, No. 7, July 1972, pp. 75–79.

8. Davidow, W. H., "General-Purpose Microcontrollers, Part 2: Design and Applications," *Computer Design,* Vol. 11, No. 8, August 1972, pp. 69–75.

9. Davies, P. N., "Readings in Microprogramming," *IBM Systems Journal,* Vol. 11, No. 1, 1972, pp. 16–40.

10. Digital Scientific Corporation, *Meta 4 Computer System,* San Diego, California, 1970.

11. Electronics Review, "Computer Alters Its Architecture Fast via New Control," *Electronics,* Vol. 47, No. 17, August 8, 1974, pp. 39–40.

12. Flynn, M. J., and R. F. Rosin, "Microprogramming: An Introduction and a Viewpoint," *IEEE Transactions on Computers,* Vol. 20, No. 7, July 1971, pp. 727–731.

13. Forney, G. D., and J. E. Vander May, "8-bit Microprocessors can control data networks," *Electronics,* Vol. 49, No. 12, June 24, 1976, pp. 110–113.

14. Grasselli, A., "The Design of Program—Modifiable Micro-Programmed Control Units," *IEEE Transactions on Electronic Computers,* Vol. EC-11, 1962, pp. 336–339.

15. Hewlett-Packard, *2100 Computer Microprogramming Guide,* Hewlett-Packard Co., Cupertino, California, 1972.

16. Holt, R. M., and M. R. Lemas, "Current Microcomputer Architecture," *Computer Design,* Vol. 13, No. 2, February 1974, pp. 65–73.

17. House, D. L., and R. A. Henzel, "The Effect of Low Cost Logic on Minicomputer Organization," *Computer Design,* Vol. 10, No. 1, January 1971, pp. 71–102.

18. House, D. L., "Micro Level Architecture in Minicomputer Design," *Computer Design,* Vol. 12, No. 10, October 1973, pp. 75–80.

19. Hovik, K., "Microprogramming," *Electronic Products,* Vol. 14, No. 4, April 19, 1971, pp. 82–86.

20. Howard, J. A., and L. Pfeifer, "An ROM Bootstrap Loader for Small Computers," *Computer Design,* Vol. 9, No. 10, October 1970, pp. 95–97.

21. Husson, S. S., *Microprogramming: Principles and Practices,* Prentice-Hall, Inc., Englewood Cliffs, New Jersey, 1970.

22. *Interdata Model 85 Microprogramming Ref. Manual,* Interdata Publication No. 29-021.

23. Jaeger, R., "Microprogramming: A General Design Tool," *Computer Design,* Vol. 13, No. 8, August 1974, pp. 150–157.

24. Kallas, S. A., Jr., "Considerations in Selecting Minicomputers for Data Communications," *Data & Communications Design,* Vol. 3, No. 6, June 1974, pp. 17–19.

25. Klingman, E. E., "Comparisons and Trends in Microprocessor Architecture," *Computer Design,* Vol. 15, No. 9, September 1977, pp. 83–91.

26. Lane, A., "Microprocessor-System Design," *Digital Design,* Vol. 5, No. 8, August 1975, pp. 62–66.

27. Lawson, H. W., and B. K. Smith, "Functional Characteristics of a Multilingual Processor," *IEEE Transactions on Computers,* Vol. C-20, No. 7, July 1971, pp. 732–742.

28. Lewis, D. R., "Microprogramming: More 'In' Than Ever," *Electronic Design,* Vol. 21, No. 17, August 16, 1973, pp. 58–63.

29. Liccardo, M. A., "Architecture of Microcontroller System," Proc. National Computer Conference, 1975, pp. 75–84.

30. Maholick, A. W., and H. H. Schwarzell, "Integrated Micro-programmed Communication Control," *Computer Design*, Vol. 8, No. 11, November 1969, pp. 127–131.

31. Melbourne, A. J., and J. M. Pugmire, "A Small Computer for the Direct Processing of FORTRAN Statements," *Comput. J.*, Vol. 8, 1965, pp. 24–27.

32. Microdata, *The Micro 800*, Microdata Corp., Santa Ana, California, 1969.

33. Microdata, *Micro 812 Programmable Data Communications Processor*, Microdata Corp., Santa Ana, California, April 1970.

34. Microdata, *Micro 1600 Computer*, Microdata Corp., Santa Ana, California, 1970.

35. Microdata, *Microprogramming Handbook*, Microdata Corp., Santa Ana, California, 1970.

36. Micro Systems, Inc., *Introduction to Microprogramming*, Technical Notes, Santa Ana, California, April 18, 1969.

37. Opler, A., "Fourth Generation Software," *Datamation*, Vol. 13, No. 1, January 1967, pp. 22–24.

38. Rakoczi, L. L., "The Computer Within the Computer, A Fourth Generation Concept," *Comp. Group News*, Vol. 2, 1969, p. 14.

39. Redfield, S. R., "A Study in Microprogrammed Processors: A Medium Sized Microprogrammed Processor," *IEEE Transactions on Computers*, Vol. C-20, No. 7, July 1971, pp. 743–750.

40. Riviere, C. J., and P. J. Nichols, "Microcomputers Unlock the Next Generation," *Data Communications*, Vol. 2, No. 5, September/October 1974, pp. 21–28.

41. Rosin, R. F., "Contemporary Concepts of Microprogramming and Emulation," *Comput. Surveys*, Vol. 1, No. 12, December 1969, pp. 197–212.

42. Rostky, G., "Focus on Semiconductor Memories," *Electronics Design*, Vol. 19, No. 19, September 16, 1971, pp. 50–63.

43. Rudd, W. G., "Microcomputers in Instrumentation and Control," *Instruments & Control Systems*, Vol. 47, No. 4, April 1974, pp. 63–66.

44. Schiller, W. L., *et al.*, "A Microprogrammed Intelligent Graphics Terminal," *IEEE Transactions on Computers*, Vol. C-20, No. 7, July 1971, pp. 775–782.

45. Schultz, G. W., "Designing Optimized Microprogrammed Control Sections for Microprocessors," *Computer Design*, Vol. 13, No. 4, April 1974, pp. 119–124.

46. Schultz, G. W., R. M. Holt, and H. L. McFarland, Jr., "A Guide to Using LSI Microprocessors," *Computer*, Vol. 6, No. 6, June 1973, pp. 13–19.

47. Snyder, F. G., "The Microprocessor Shake Out," *Digital Design*, Vol. 4, No. 9, September 1974, pp. 20–22.

48. Sobel, H. S., *Introduction to Digital Computer Design*, Addison-Wesley Publ. Co., Reading, Massachusetts, 1970, pp. 277–315.

49. Staff-Electronics, "Microprocessors: A Special Issue," *Electronics*, Vol. 49, No. 8, April 15, 1976, pp. 74–174.

50. Stedman, J., "Microprogrammability Lets User Tailor New Minicomputer to His Requirements," *Electronics*, Vol. 47, No. 9, May 2, 1974, pp. 87–93.

51. Teener, M., "Minicomputers and Microcomputers: Microcomputers—Part 2," *Mini-Micro Systems*, Vol. 9, No. 6, June 1976.

52. "The Universal Controller," *Computerworld*, April 19, 1972, p. 1.

53. Tucker, A. B., and M. J. Flynn, "Dynamic Microprogramming: Processor Organization and Programming," *Communications of the ACM*, Vol. 15, No. 4, April 1971, pp. 240–250.

54. Vandling, G. C., and D. E. Waldecker, "The Microprogram Control Technique

for Digital Logic Design," *Computer Design,* Vol. 8, No. 8, August 1969, pp. 44–51.

55. Varian Data Machines, *Varian 73 Computer Handbook,* Irvine, California, 1973.

56. Ward, B., *Microprocessor/Microprogramming Handbook,* Tab Books, Blue Ridge Summit, Pennsylvania, 1975.

57. Wilkes, M. V., "The Growth of Interest in Microprogramming: A Literature Survey," *Comput. Surveys,* Vol. 1, No. 9, September 1969, pp. 139–145.

58. Wolf, H. F., "Microcomputers—Revolution or Evolution," *Digital Design,* Vol. 4, No. 6, June 1974, pp. 42–47.

59. Wolf, R., "Multiple Minicomputers Go to Work for Large Time-Sharing Applications," *Data Processing,* Vol. 12, No. 9, September 1970, pp. 33–37.

8
Techniques for Selecting Minicomputers

8.1 Introduction

Minicomputers offer the potential user a large, flexible array of equipment at very attractive prices. The attractive prices result from several major technological improvements in the design and performance of logic elements (ICs, MSI, and LSI) and memory systems, economies of scale, and competition among many minicomputer manufacturers. The improvements in both cost and performance have resulted in two main impacts on the potential user:

1. Users who could not economically afford a large-scale general-purpose computer can now implement a minicomputer dedicated to their applications.
2. Several entirely new application areas are now made feasible and economical.

It should be noted that the validity of any minicomputer evaluation may be affected by limitations that exist in the minicomputer industry concerning standardization of nomenclature and minicomputer specifications. Frequently, different names are used for the same equipment and the same name is used for different equipment. Consequently, the task of selecting the best minicomputer from the ever-increasing number of minicomputer models available for the wide range of applications becomes complex and difficult.

271

In this chapter, guidelines and evaluation techniques are presented to aid the potential user in selecting a minicomputer for a specific application. The selection procedure includes:[7]

1. Defining the application.
2. Specifying requirements.
3. Considering minicomputer characteristics:
   a. Main Frame Design
      —Central Processor
      —Memory
      —Input/Output Structure
      —Interrupt System
   b. Interface design and standard peripheral devices
   c. Software
   d. Manufacturer's experience and support
4. Performing a preliminary screening.
5. Applying techniques for final evaluation.

Each minicomputer application area has a particular set of hardware and software requirements. These requirements must be identified and correlated to a minicomputer's performance. Constraints or limitations imposed by the user often include cost, delivery date, I/O requirements, peripheral capabilities, software support, and reliability of the minicomputer system. The upper bound on cost frequently provides an easy elimination mechanism.

Performance of a minicomputer system, on the other hand, is a complex interaction of memory cycle time, instruction execution times, word length, instruction repertoire, parallel data transfer capabilities, DMA cycle stealing (if available), interrupt latency time, and I/O overhead (see Chapter 4). Because of this complex interaction of various components within a minicomputer system, the measurement of performance differs for the same minicomputer when considering different applications.

The definition of the user's application provides limitations imposed by the user and is presented in Section 8.2. The performance of a minicomputer system, a direct consequence of the system's hardware and software characteristics, is analyzed in Section 8.3. The remainder of the chapter provides selection techniques that permit selection of a minicomputer system that maximizes overall performance subject to the constraints of the user's application and economic limitations.

8.2 Definition of Application

The first phase in the selection of a minicomputer is a thorough systems analysis of the task under consideration for computerization. The success or failure of an entire computer application can be traced to this stage, since a desirable selection cannot be realistically obtained for a dedicated application without a clear and precise understanding of the task.

The definition phase of the system selection must include a description of the minicomputer system's function, an identification of the system's components and interfaces, and the functional requirements of the system.

1. *Description of the system's function:* The user must develop a set of weighted selection criteria reflecting the needs of the user's application area. The specifications must be application-oriented rather than machine-oriented. The weights applied to each criterion must reflect the importance of that criterion for the particular application. The basic application requirements should include task specifications, critical time responses and load factors regarding communication rates, input/output transfers, and interrupt processing. The specification of the system's function should also include a processing characteristic for the minicomputer. Most applications can be described by one of the following characteristics:

   a. Data manipulation which requires significant volumes of input/output processing as well as actual central processing.

   b. Computational processing which is highly central processor bound (little input/output processing).

   c. Control or real-time processing which is critical in terms of interrupt handling and response time.

   d. System components which require control processing capabilities to sense physical quantities (e.g., analog voltages and current signals), perform logical and/or arithmetic operations, and response times to control the physical devices.

2. *Identification of system's components and interfaces:* System components, which are a direct consequence of the processing characteristic of the application, should be specified. Using the description of the system's function, a block diagram can be established indicating existing and new equipment, as well as any interface between the two. The interface area should be characterized by its responsibility, not necessarily by its definition. Interface areas for future expansion capabilities should also be included. The result should be a highly modular block diagram, with each module composed of a system component and an appropriate interface.

3. *Functional requirements of the system:* The last stage of the definition phase consists of specifying the functional requirements of the system. This should include:

   a. Module or component function

   b. Software requirements of the module

   c. Frequency or usage of module

   d. Hardware requirements of the module

   e. Critical time or load factors of the module

   f. Interface requirement of the module to the entire system

   g. Peripheral requirements

273

TABLE 8-2-1.   *Selection Factors for Minicomputers*

	Minicomputer Characteristics	
Application Class	*Important Factors*	*Selection Criteria*
Standalone system	Software	Flexible input/output
	Memory size	Multilevel priority interrupt
	Asynchronous	Real-time clock
	Aids for debugging	High reliability
Real-time control system	Cost	Speed/structure
	Efficient I/O handling	I/O flexibility
		Maximum I/O rate
	Buffering	Power failure protect
		Automatic restart
	Asynchronous	Real-time clock
		Multilevel priority interrupt
Scientific computation	Software	Hardware multiply/divide
	Speed	Addressing and indexing mode
	Throughput	ROM/memory size
		Reliability/protection
	Man-computer interaction	I/O communication
		Interface/peripherals
Communication system	Word structure	Byte handling instructions
	I/O transfer rates	DMA
		Multilevel priority interrupt
		Memory size
System component	Preprocessing	Hardware cost
		Reliability
		Deliverability
		Maintainability
	Data communication	Interface flexibility
		Multilevel priority interrupt

With the block diagram of phase two and the above specification list, a hierarchical program structure should be made. This program structure now includes:

1. Hierarchical flow
2. Frequency or usage of each program
3. Approximate memory requirements
4. Communication interfaces

5. Critical time or input/output factors
6. Indication of software availability of each program module

Although many of the specifications from the definition phase can be directly translated into required hardware components, it is desirable to delay this correspondence until later stages of the selection procedure. For example, real-time clocks, power failure protection, and automatic restart options are generally required in real-time control applications for unattended operation. However, at this stage of system selection, it is more desirable to retain the application characteristic "unattended real-time operation" and not the common corresponding hardware characteristics. This will preclude eliminating alternative minicomputer systems too soon.

Table 8-2-1 summarizes important factors in the selection of minicomputers for various application categories. Table 8-2-2 illustrates the typical description checklist for the definition phase of the selection procedure, while Figure 8-2-1 provides an outline of the selection procedure in block diagram form.

The prospective user must consider the relative type of processing required by the particular application when estimating the impact of minicomputer programming and software characteristics. The relative importance of individual minicomputer characteristics depends largely on the application under consideration. In addition to the hardware specification and costs, software requirements and applications must also be accurately specified. Software may frequently cost as much or more than the hardware components, and if inaccurately specified, may nullify any advantages obtained by careful minicomputer selection.

TABLE 8-2-2. *Descriptive Checklist for Definition Phase*

Definition of application	Descriptive checklist
Statement of problem	
Description of system function	Primary system function Secondary system function
Task specification Critical responses Load factors	Communication rates I/O transfer rates Real-time acquisition Real-time processing Interrupt processing
Processing characteristics	Data manipulation Computational processing Control or real-time processing System component

TABLE 8-2-2. (continued)

Definition of application	Descriptive checklist	
Identification of system components (hardware)	Central processor	Instruction repertoire Addressing and indexing mode Double-precision arithmetic Instruction word size I/O mechanism Number of registers Acquisition cost Acquisition time Reliability Service support Expandability
	Random access memory	Capacity Cycle time Word size Expandability Service support
	Additional memory storage	Capacity Offline vs. online Transfer rates Acquisition cost Acquisition time Random/sequential Compatability
	I/O peripheral hardware	Required I/O functions cost Data transfer rates Acquisition time/cost Peripheral type
	Interface require-ments	Acquisition time/cost Priority interrupts Parallel input/output Asynchronous vs. synchronous Real-time clocks Service support Expandability
Functional re-quirement of system (software)	Programming requirements	Language File handling Programming time Real-time constraints Peripheral device requirements Compatability Acquisition time/cost

TABLE 8-2-2. (continued)

Definition of application	Descriptive checklist	
	Program and data size estimates Expandability Operating system requirements	Memory requirements Ease of use Accessibility Diagnostics I/O support
	General support programming	Languages Libraries Diagnostics
	Acquisition time/ cost Reliability (documentation) Maintenance and support	
Data base description	Kinds of data Capacity Expandability	Bits/bytes/words
Expansion requirements	Random access memory	Availability Addressability Size Ease of modification
	Peripheral storage	Maximum size Speed Access time Ease of addition
	Interface	Availability Ease of modification
	Software	Modification to support Hardware
	CPU	
General support	Maintenance Emergency service Documentation Training Software development/support Custom design	

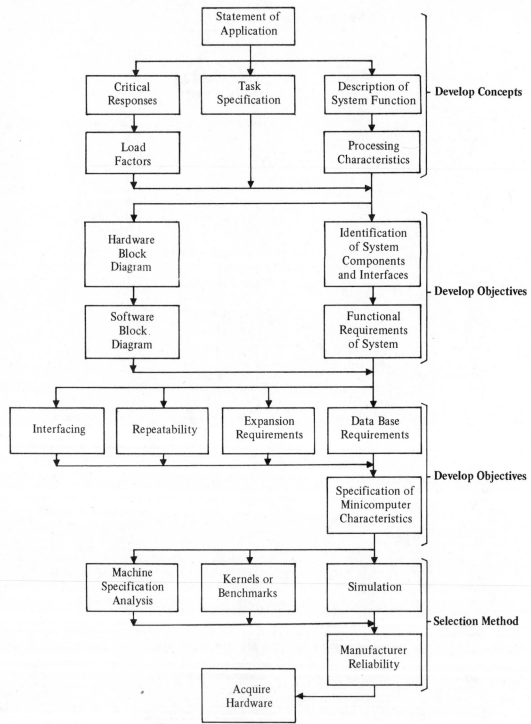

FIGURE 8-2-1. PERT chart for a minicomputer system selection procedure.

The application analysis should define a functional specification which includes both hardware and software requirements at a component level. This specification will also provide a basis for decisions regarding subsequent expansions, interfacing and modifications.

The next phase in the selection process consists of a specification of the user's limitations or constraints:

1. The *cost* of the new hardware, system design, software, and documentation needs to be specified.
2. Acquisition, *delivery,* and installation dates must be scheduled and could be used as constraint factors.
3. Service, *maintenance,* training, and installation are generally not included in the price of a typical minicomputer. The support that can be expected from the vendor for each of these must be carefully examined.
4. *Environment* in which the system is to be used must be considered.

8.2.1 Data Base

The functional specification of the definition phase provides the system designer with a block diagram flowchart indicating the interrelationship of the hardware and software modules. This interrelationship may be further expanded by considering the type of data the minicomputer must maintain in support of the specific application under consideration. The types of data should include:

1. Required input/output parameters
2. Permanent or historical values
3. Parameters or arguments required for the control programs
4. Temporary variables used by the control programs
5. Permanent file or record requirements

Associated with each type of data there should be an identification or estimate regarding size, number, retention, and responsiveness characteristics. Documentation of old or related systems and supporting hardware reference material can be sources for this information. Using this information, an estimate of the memory requirements* can be determined, indicating the types of hardware needed as well as the extent to which peripheral devices will be required to support the minicomputer system.

Accuracy and flow of data must be considered at this point. The data flow, possibly in graphic display format, should reflect information from which the flow can be readily analyzed, eliminating redundancy and duplication of program steps, and simplifying programming. The detailed flow, in conjunction with the functional specification of the definition phase, pro-

---

* Memory requirements can be estimated by using the number of variables of each type multiplied by the storage per variable.

279

vides the system designer with logical conditions to be applied to the data being processed. These logical conditions should include data editing, required calculations, input/output processing, interrupt processing, updating and deletion of data, and required outputs (e.g., reports and master files).

For large data storage requirements, indicating the use of peripheral mass memory devices (e.g., drums, disks, and magnetic tapes), additional analysis regarding access frequency, device speed and capacity, transfer rates, and responsiveness must be included. For this type of data base, particular enphasis should be placed on expansion capabilities and their incorporation into the system design. For example, will the addition of a disk require extensive hardware modifications in the form of an additional controller, interface, and expansion chassis, or can it be added without further hardware modification?

8.2.2 Expansion Requirements

The functional capabilities included at various phases of the design should include expansion provisions. It is important to define these expansion requirements in terms of more hardware, more software functions or services, and more data handling capabilities. The consequences of these expansion estimates must be analyzed in terms of their effect on the configured software and hardware modules, and on their respective interfaces.

Frequently, a change in the size of the data base has a pronounced effect on execution times, memory requirements, response time, and data rates from peripheral devices. Minicomputer systems designed in a modular form provide ready expandability without extensive changes in the main frame configuration. Memory expansions, additional peripherals, or additional hardware options to the main frame should be readily interfaced to existing components with little or no effect on the application software.

Additional consideration must be given to the proposed modular software system such that expansion capabilities, in either additional hardware or data bases, can be made without extensive software changes.

8.2.3 Repeatability

The approach to system design and definition phase is affected by the economies of a one-of-a-kind design versus the repeated use of a design. Repeatability applies to both hardware and software components and affects the design by its influence in the following areas:

1. One-of-a-kind system should use standard vendor products.
2. Repeated systems should consider tailored components designed to specific needs which are purchased in quantities.
3. The interfacing of components can be provided by the vendor for standard modules, or specially designed for tailored components.

280

4. Similar comments apply to software modules. One-of-a-kind systems should consider generalized software at the expense of core memory and speed, while repeated systems should consider assembly or machine-language-oriented optimized software.

8.2.4 Interfacing

Most systems need some type of interface between the minicomputer and the physical process being controlled, regulated, monitored, or measured. The different signals involved in this communication include analog and digital inputs and outputs. Most vendors provide a complete and compatible line of interface modules for standard data communication devices, analog/digital and digital/analog devices, and to sense signal and control modules. Software to support this interface equipment is also available, as long as the interface requirements are somewhat standard.

If the application requires special-purpose devices, the design cost of the interface may be several times that of the initial minicomputer cost itself. The important considerations in designing a system must, therefore, include the basic requirements of the interface, software control, and any special-purpose devices. The following criteria should be included in the interface specification:

1. Requirements for signal conditioning
2. Noise conditioning for analog signals
3. Availability of input/output interfaces to such devices as analog signal readers, tape readers and punches, card readers and punches, line printers, data communication devices, plotters
4. Requirements for signal levels and structure of input/output equipment

All interfaces that connect external devices to the minicomputer make use of the I/O system. It is therefore important for the system designer to include in the interface specification:

1. What parts of the I/O system partake in the operations of the interface.
2. The data rates anticipated.
3. Connection of the interfaces to the minicomputer without modifications.
4. A hardware-oriented or software-oriented interface solution utilizing the I/O subsystem of the minicomputer.

A summary of the design factors for interfaces is presented in Table 8-2-3. The design of any interfaces should also adhere to the following guidelines:

1. System expansion should be considered.
2. The interface should not be overdesigned in terms of demands and frequency of the I/O facilities.
3. Diagnostic and maintenance programs should be developed.
4. Preventive maintenance features should be included in the design.

281

TABLE 8-2-3. *Design Factors for Interfaces*[11]

	Data transfer	Design factors
Program-controlled data transfer	Low cost because of little hardware Software capability to examine each data word	Simplicity of design Software overhead reduces other available processing time
	Used for relatively low data rates Software has active interface role	Double buffering required Software can examine data for limit conditions
Hardware-controlled data transfer (DMA)	High data rate accommodation Little software overhead	No need for double buffering Little software attention required
	Higher cost because of more complex hardware	Special comparison circuitry necessary for limit detection
	Data block transfers	Programmed transfer necessary for interrupts and status information

8.2.5 Examples of Analysis[5]

This section presents a step-by-step definition phase for the following hypothetical application.

Statement of the problem: Intensive-care nurses are continuously in short supply, with forecast manpower trends indicating little relief. To alleviate this pending personnel shortage with minimal cost, a minicomputer system is planned. Computerized monitoring of patient vital life functions with centralized alerting and patient status reports are mandatory capabilities. The system should eliminate the requirements of nurses recording routine data (every 15 minutes) and enhance life-saving probabilities.

Description of the system's function: This system provides automatic monitoring of variables that could change rapidly. It routinely collects and processes analog inputs for the following variables:

1. ECG
2. Respiration or respiration rate
3. Blood pressure
4. Temperature
5. Pulse or pulse pressure
6. Central venous pressure
7. Heart sounds
8. Electroencephalogram
9. Other signals

The reasons for automatically recording these variables are:

1. Physiological variables that fluctuate quite rapidly and widely must be measured frequently, or even continuously.
2. Frequent measurements by nurses can subject patients to constant disturbances that could prejudice their chances for quick recovery.
3. Human bias is eliminated.
4. During particular danger periods, continuous measurements must be made if change is to be sensed in time to institute therapy.
5. Continuous recording has demonstrated brief episodes, previously unobserved and of unknown clinical significance, which recur sporadically and affect heart rate, pulse pressure, and mean arterial and venous pressures.

Task specification: Biomedical monitoring depends on sensing *changes* in life functions. Any sudden change is considered to be a bad sign and calls for further investigation. The minicomputer system should detect sudden changes in vital life functions, ignoring gradual changes except when they violate specified limits. The analog input is to be compared with a time average of the preceding wave forms, causing interrupt signals for sudden changes in analog signals outside tolerances. Four vital signs per patient are inspected: ECG and blood pressure are in analog signals, while respiration and temperature are not.

Critical responses:
1. The use of catheter electrodes eliminates many of the motion artifacts common to surface ECG, thereby improving reliability of the alarm system.
2. Miniature pressure transducers mounted on the catheter tip provide more reliable heart-action measurements.
3. The use of semiconductor implantable pressure gauge in end of catheter measures blood pressure directly.
4. Respiration can be measured using electrodes across the chest of the patient.
5. Real-time clock to initiate interrupt processing and life function alarm system is needed.
6. Sampling rates of A/D channels and appropriate conversions.

Load factors:
1. The critical time for the system is that required to gather and process all 16 A/D data channels. This time is estimated to be 4.8 milliseconds, permitting an interval of only 5 milliseconds between ECG samples.
2. Storage limitations preclude extensive automated record keeping and retrieval system.

Processing characteristics: This system can be classified as a control or real-time processing system because of its critical interrupt-handling requirements.

283

Identification of system components and interfaces: The following are the major items of equipment (Figure 8-2-2):

1. Minicomputer CPU (12–16 bit; memory to be specified later).
2. A teleprinter for loading system and printing.
3. Interrupt subsystem for priority interrupt control to support individual patient monitoring.
4. Real-time clock with selectable timing intervals 1 μsec, 10 μsec, and 100 μsec.
5. Power fail/restart option because of real-time monitoring requirement.
6. CRT display to convert and display life functions related and user entered information.
7. Analog scope control with character buffer, 2 channel intensity and 2 channel D/A converters.
8. Analog input subsystem:
   a. 16 inputs.
   b. Speed requirements are 16 channels within 5 milliseconds (69 kHz conversion rate).
   c. A low-level voltage input ($\pm$ 4–5 mV) for the four sensors is expected. Some form of noise filtering is required.
   d. A 10-bit accuracy, sample and hold, with differential preamplifiers are required.

Functional requirements of system: In Figure 8-2-3, the functional modules or programs are listed with selected comments.

Program Module	Word Estimate
Keyboard routine	500
Display initiation routine	500
Display building routine	1600
Coordination (monitor) routine	3700
Real-time sample routine	1400
TOTAL	7700 words

The purpose of the *keyboard routine* is to decode the input from the CRT and TTY keyboards; to modify selected areas of core on the basis of this decoding; to request display of a particular format on the CRT or TTY; and to request display back of keyboard input. The purpose of the *display initiation routine* is to provide a standard linkage between requests for output and the actual display builder, thus saving code and conceptually simplify the system architecture. The purpose of the *display builder routine* is to move standardized output (e.g., names and labels) from minicomputer to CRT, and to convert 10-bit histogram entries into a form suitable for CRT display. The purpose of the *coordinator or monitor routine* is to maintain control over all system activities; to serve as communication line between all routines; to decide priorities of interrupts and routine requests; and to maintain queues of interrupted tasks. The purpose of the *real-time sample*

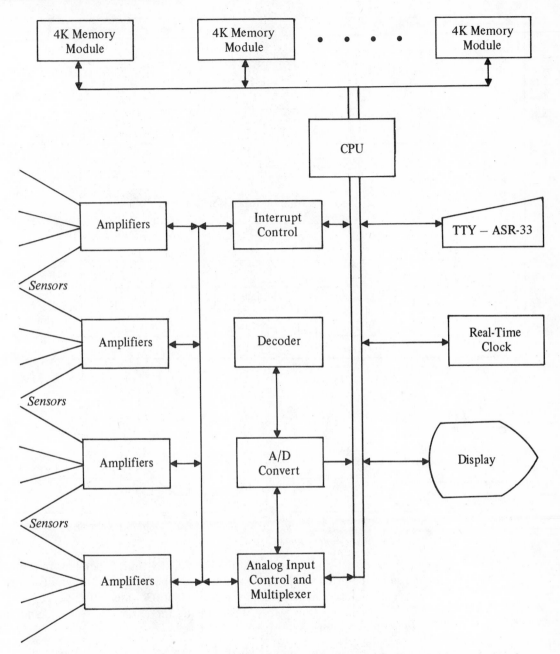

FIGURE 8-2-2. *Identification of system components and interfaces of hypothetical automatic patient monitoring system.*

routine is to collect data and initiate record output; to initiate life function alarms; and to test probes.

The two interrupt lines alert the minicomputer to a critical situation that requires immediate response. Neither user initiated analysis programs, nor diagnostic routines have been considered in this functional analysis.

285

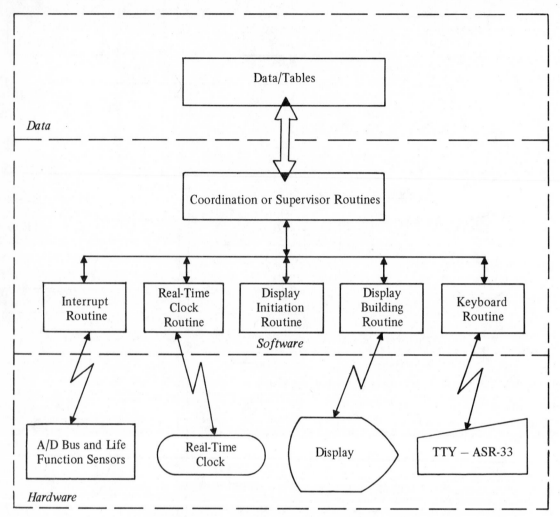

FIGURE 8-2-3. *Function requirements of the patient monitoring system (software components).*

The real-time sample routine is critically time-dependent in terms of the sampling process. Sixteen samples must be processed in 5 milliseconds, i.e., each sample must be processed in about 330 μsec (10^{-6} sec).

Data Base Description: The analog inputs are converted, and subsequently are composed of:

Instantaneous value	1 word
Conversion constants	2 words
Limits	2 words
Multiplex address	1 word
Engineering units	2 words
Spare	2 words
	$10 \times 16 = 160$ words

Total estimate for data is 160 words per sample period. Internal tables for histogram plotting require:

ECG	200 words
Respiration	4 words
Blood pressure	100 words
Temperature	1 word
	305 words/patient

The total estimate is 1220 words for tables, 160 words for analog sample, 7700 words for programs—for a total of 9080 words. Core memory requirement is therefore in the range of 8–12K.

Expansion Requirements:

1. *Size*. Analog inputs from automatic patients monitoring can be expected to increase from 4 patients to 12–20 patients. An increase beyond the initial design of 300–500%. The increase in analog signals will place a great constraint on the real-time sample routine, and consequently on the A/D sample rate and the basic machine cycle time for processing samples.
2. *Scope*. Future applications, beyond the increase in size, might include user-initiated analysis programs, extensive automated record keeping, and retrieval systems. Diagnostic routines might also be run. Direct access devices or some peripheral mass storage should be considered for expansion purposes.

Repeatability: The initial design is for automatic monitoring of patients in the intensive care units. This system, if shown to be economically practical, might be expanded to cover other automatic monitoring functions throughout the entire hospital (e.g., nursery).

8.3 Minicomputer Characteristics

Once the application area has been defined, the functional capabilities must be translated into hardware characteristics useful in the selection procedure. The task specification, the constraints on critical variables, the load factors, and the processing characteristics define the minimum system requirements in terms of minicomputer specifications. Selection of a minicomputer should therefore consider the compatibility between the architecture of the minicomputer and the functional demands of the given application. A match up of application demands and minicomputer characteristics is illustrated in Table 8-3-1.

Some of the more common minicomputer characteristics to be evaluated for the establishment of requirements are:

1. *CPU Capability:* This minicomputer characteristic describes primarily the logical and arithmetic operations; various data and file handling

TABLE 8-3-1.   *Application Demands and Related Minicomputer Characteristics*

Application demands	Characteristics
Arithmetic calculations	Size of computer word
Logical operations	Word structure and format
Frequency of operations	Memory cycle time
Arithmetic accuracy	Word length/double-word instructions/subroutine software (decrease in speed)
Multiply/divide operations	Hardware capability (extra cost) Software capability (slow/extra core)
Addressing capability	Word size and operand size
Real-time processing	Processing speed/interrupt capability
Input/output processing	Channel capacity/byte handling instructions/number and type of I/O channels

instructions; single- and double-precision arithmetic; floating-point arithmetic; and multiply/divide instructions. These characteristics can be related to a particular application by noting that performance (or work throughput*) is defined as the amount of work per instruction multiplied by the number of instructions per second.

a. *Word length:* This characteristic describes the number of bits in the minicomputer word, and often indicates the speed and efficiency of the minicomputer.

b. *Data/instruction format:* A description of the operation code along with modifying and addressing fields provides a good indication of the instruction repertoire of the minicomputer, execution time for effective processing estimates and program storage requirements.

c. *I/O capability:* The amount of data transfers and the manner in which peripheral devices communicate with the CPU and memory is an indication of the flexibility and expansion capability of the minicomputer system. A further consideration is the tradeoff between the number and configuration of the I/O channels to the system needs; the number of peripherals versus the minicomputer's ability to process and accept the load.

The number of instructions executed per second is related to memory cycle time, instruction execution time, interrupt system, and interface system.

---

* Throughput could also be defined as the amount of effective work the minicomputer can do in a given time.

     a. *Speed:* This characteristic describes the average time required for a CPU to execute an instruction, to access memory, or to perform an I/O operation. It is indirectly affected by the number and type of instructions, addressing modes, interrupt and I/O facilities.

     b. *Interrupt system:* Interrupt latency time, as well as the type of interrupt system available on the minicomputer, has a direct relationship to its applicability for application areas.

     c. *Interface:* The mechanical complexity of interfacing, the requirements for either standard or special purpose interfacing, and the availability of software support for these interfaces indicate expansion capabilities and timing information for particular applications.

2. *Bus Organization:* This characteristic describes the manner in which data are transferred between external devices and memory, as well as the transfer of information internal to the minicomputer. The common transmission modes are parallel or serial, and synchronous or asynchronous.

3. *Memory Capacity:* This characteristic describes the total storage capacity of a basic minicomputer and relates to the size of either program or data available to an application.

4. *Peripheral Availability:* The type of standard or "off-the-shelf" peripherals and controllers available provide interface requirements and expansion capabilities. The data transfer rates, the compatibility with controller and interfaces, and the availability of fully integrated software drivers have a direct relationship to the selection procedure.

5. *Vendor Support:* This characteristic relates to the maintainability of the minicomputer. The availability of programs for maintenance support, the response time of a vendor in terms of repair and service facilities, the extent of documentation for hardware and software indicate the effort required to repair and maintain the minicomputer.

Depending on the individual application area, some of these characteristics and features are more important than others, and should therefore be weighted accordingly. Even though minicomputer architecture can be a decisive factor in the selection process, there are tradeoffs concerning the application, software factors, vendor support and proximity, and total system cost. Examples of such tradeoffs include the optimization of memory usage versus the cost of software; speed versus processing capabilities and data transfer loads; hardware priority interrupt systems versus software identification schemes and real-time response.

The following sections present the importance of each of these factors and the mechanism for determining individual needs. Table 8-3-2 illustrates the ranges of minicomputer characteristics under consideration.

8.3.1 Internal Memory

Most important internal memory characteristics are readily available from minicomputer manufacturers. These characteristics include cycle time,

TABLE 8-3-2.   Ranges of Minicomputer Characteristics

Characteristics	Features available		
	Minimum	*Average*	*Maximum*
Memory			
Word length (bits)	8	8 or 16	32
Size (words)	1024 to 4096	4096 to 32,768	1024 to 65,536
Increment size (words)	1024	4096	8192
Cycle rate (kHz)	125	571 to 1000	2000
(cycle time μsec)	10.0	(1.0 to 1.75)	(0.5)
Parity check	No	Optional	Standard
Memory protect	No	Optional	Standard
Direct addressing (words)	256	256 to 4096	All of core
Indirect addressing	No	Single/multilevel	Multilevel
Central processor			
General-purpose registers	One	1, 2, 3, or 4	128
Index registers	None	1	15
Hardware multiply/divide	No	Optional	Standard
Immediate instructions	No	Half yes	Yes
Double-word instructions	No	Mostly yes	Yes
Byte processing	No	Half yes	Yes
Input/output			
Programmed I/O channel	1	1	1
I/O word size (bits)	8	8 or 16	32
Priority interrupt lines	1	1 standard, up to 64 optional	2 standard, up to 256 optional
Direct memory access	No	Optional	Optional
I/O maximum transfer rate (DMA)	125K	400–600K	1000K
Other features			
Real-time clock	No	Optional	Standard
Power fail/restart	Optional	Optional	Standard
Largest disk (megabits)	No	2.1 to 9.0	183.6
Assembler	Yes	Yes	Yes
Compiler	No	Basic FORTRAN	Basic FORTRAN, standard FORTRAN, ALGOL
Operating system	No	No	Real-time, foreground/background

word length, maximum memory capacity, memory parity, and memory protection.

Memory cycle time is a major factor determining the effective speed (instruction cycle time) of a minicomputer, as well as the maximum instruction and I/O throughput rate.

The speed of processing information is particularly important in real-time and teleprocessing applications where the CPU must respond in a short enough time interval to control the operation. It is also important in applications where the minicomputer is part of a larger system and must perform tasks within a specified time. In other applications, processing time may not be a significant factor.

Memory cycle time. When combined with memory capacity, word length can be used as a prime measure of minicomputer performance. Shorter word length often indicates slower processing speed, lower cost, poorer performance, and limited instruction repertoire. There are, however, application areas in which the use of a shorter word length is as fast and efficient as the use of the larger word length (e.g., data communication).

Word size also determines the *accuracy* and efficiency of operations. The optimum word size should be chosen so that the word size is equal to the unit of information to be processed. This length is dependent on specific application areas, as well as the suitability of the type of data to be manipulated.

The *precision* required in the application determines the data word length, while the instruction word length is a function of the number of instructions necessary to fully utilize the capabilities of the CPU, the addressing requirements, and special features such as index register designators. It is desirable to have the data word length and the instruction word length the same so that data and instructions can be treated in a uniform manner. If higher precision is required for an application, such as scientific calculations, double-word-length operations are fully provided, as an option, by minicomputer vendors. For many applications, such as monitoring functions, communications processing, message switching, or character manipulation, smaller-word-length minicomputers may be adequate. But, for operations requiring some degree of accuracy in computation, larger word length minicomputers are more desirable.

Some consideration of additional memory features, such as memory protection and memory parity, must be made. For many application areas, enhanced reliability of random access memory has minimized or entirely eliminated the need for parity checking. Applications dealing in process control and communications that require fast memory cycle times or high I/O data transfer rates are more susceptible to system noise and consequently require the availability of memory parity checking capabilities.

Memory protection is a minicomputer memory feature that prevents access to certain restricted regions of memory, except by special instructions. This feature can be implemented using hardware, software, or a combination of both and should be considered a desirable characteristic whenever more than one program is placed simultaneously in memory (see Table 8-3-3).

8.3.2 Central Processing Unit Features

The features of the central processing unit (CPU) are major factors in determining the speed and efficiency with which an application can be

TABLE 8-3-3.   Summary of Memory Characteristics and Their Selection Criteria

Characteristics	Selected Criterion
Type of memory	Availability of random access, read only, semiconductor, and scratch-pad
Size (words)	Basic size/maximum size/ incremental size
Cycle time (μsec)	Memory word length/bits per cycle/ memory cycle time
Direct addressing capability (words)	Depends on address length of instruction operand
Indirect addressing (levels)	Single or multilevels
Access to memory	DMA—Cost/maximum word transfer rate/data path width I/O channel (programmed)—cost/ maximum word transfer rate/data path width I/O channel (interrupt driven)— cost/maximum word transfer rate/ data path width
Memory options	Memory protection/memory parity Power failure/restart

performed. Some of the CPU features that should be examined are the number of basic instructions, instruction execution speeds, the number of address modes, the number of accumulators, the number and type of index registers, and hardware registers.

When comparing minicomputers it is important to consider the instruction repertoire and instruction speeds. The required repertoire will depend on the application and it may be important that certain instructions are performed within a certain time frame due to frequency of use or due to the particular requirement of the application.

One major trend in CPU design is the use of more general-purpose hardware registers and/or accumulators providing programming versatility and efficiency. This reduces the required number of memory references in any given program but increases hardware costs. General-purpose registers can be used for indexing and other operations not normally handled by the accumulator, but a general-purpose register may also be used as an accumulator. In this approach, a full set of inter-register instructions, grouped into a special instruction word format, are frequently used to manipulate arithmetically and logically the contents of these registers.

8.3.3 Addressing and Indexing

Techniques for accessing memory are related directly to the speed and efficiency of a minicomputer, as well as the instruction word length, memory size, and minicomputer architecture.

As an example, consider a minicomputer with the following characteristics:

1. 65K of random access memory
2. 16-bit word length
3. Four general-purpose registers
4. Instruction repertoire, including register-register and register-memory instructions
5. Instruction and data fetch width of 16 bits

Utilizing *direct addressing,* two words would be required for register-memory instruction—16 bits for operand addresses, and 16 more bits for the operation code and register indicator. As a result of fetching two words per instruction, the processing time is decreased, and memory utilization per program cut down.

For *indirect addressing* the format of an instruction word would consist of 6 bits for the operation code, 2 bits for the register indicator, and 8 bits for the operand address. The 8 bits for the operand address provides only direct addressing to 255 words, and other "indirect" techniques need to be used to address all of memory.

If the application requires direct "fast" addressing of large memory, the former technique must be considered. If, on the other hand, memory space is limited and at a premium, then the latter technique is indicated.

8.3.4 Input/Output and Interrupts

Many minicomputer applications require data transfer at high rates and in large quantities between memory and external devices. Whenever either one or both of these requirements are present, the input/output structure of the minicomputer becomes a critical characteristic that must be thoroughly evaluated to ensure that the minicomputer matches the application. Each characteristic of the I/O structure needs to be examined separately to determine its interaction with the application. Special emphasis should be given to the data transfer method because of its great influence on the overall performance of the I/O structure. Tradeoff considerations between cost and performance should be made whenever necessary to keep within the objectives stated in the application definition.

For I/O-oriented applications the following characteristics should be given serious consideration: types of I/O channels, interrupts, response time to interrupts, maximum word transfer rates, I/O data bus width, interfacing, I/O instruction size, and type of priority controls. Considering the two basic types of I/O channels (see Chapter 4), a channel under hardware control (direct memory access—DMA) is extremely efficient compared to a channel under program control. The difference in efficiency is primarily due to the number of external interrupts required to transfer data and the response time to service each interrupt.

Because of the large range of word lengths (8–32 bits/word) for minicomputers and because of their effect on the maximum transfer rates, minicomputers should be compared on the basis of effective throughput or effective transfer rates. Two computers may have the same maximum word transfer rate, however the computer with an I/O data bus width of 24 bits will effectively transfer three times as much data as a computer with an I/O data bus width of 8 bits. In addition to throughput considerations, the I/O data bus width should also match, for programming convenience, the word length of the external device.

The selection criterion for a particular channel must include considerations for the required interface. Basic interfacing requirements are quite similar for most minicomputers, but the selection should be made very carefully because cost and packaging vary. Whenever an application requires a large number of external devices, the size of the device code field of the I/O instruction should be examined to determine the number of device codes available. Another consideration, when a number of external devices are connected together on a common bus, is the type of priority control. If all of the I/O data being transferred are highly structured, program control may be satisfactory. However, if the I/O data are unstructured, priority may need to be controlled by some type of interrupt technique. Again, as with the DMA channel, additional consideration should be given to interfacing each external device. Finally, if the number of external devices is exceptionally large, the requirement for an additional controller power supply should be included. Table 8-3-4 summarizes the most important input/output characteristics.

8.3.5 Data Rates

Available data formats affect the versatility of the minicomputer, while the completeness of the instruction repertoire determines its overall performance and throughput. Bit handling capabilities are useful in control system and process monitoring applications; byte (8 bits treated as an information entity) handling capabilities enhance data rates for I/O-oriented applications. Extra precision requirements can be satisfied by using extra words as well as special instructions.

Minicomputer performance is strongly related to not only which instructions are available in the instruction repertoire, but also how the instructions perform such functions as arithmetic operations, conditions for branching, bit/byte manipulations, adequate logical operations, and logical compares. If the instruction repertoire does not include a specific function, such as floating-point arithmetic, software routines must perform the operations, at the cost of memory space and longer execution times.

The more powerful the instruction repertoire is, the higher program efficiency becomes, and throughput and effective computer power increases. A tradeoff to this versatility in the instruction repertoire is an

TABLE 8-3-4.   *Summary of I/O Characteristics*

Characteristics	*Selection Options*
Number	Number of I/O channels supported by basic minicomputer
Type of I/O channel	Programmed I/O channel (I/O bus): Direct Memory Access
I/O word size (bits)	Matches data word of external devices
Priority interrupt lines or levels	Single or multilevel, hardware priority and programmable priority mechanism
I/O maximum transfer rates	50K words/sec: 1 million words/sec (1/memory cycle time)
Transfer width (bits/word)	Matches memory word size
Device priority structure	Number of external priority interrupt lines
Interrupt identification	Hardware; software
Interrupt response time (latency)	Critical in terms of determining input/output rates
Parallel input/output	Synchronous; asynchronous
Multiplexer	Number of channels supported
Speed of service	Depends on I/O instruction and facilities for isolating device requiring service
I/O and control instructions	Single- or double-byte instructions; automatic and block transfer instructions; interrupt returns; individual or block enable/disable instructions

accompanying increase in the word size, decrease in effective memory capacity, and longer individual instruction execution times.

Data rates of the CPU are also affected by the data transfer rates from peripheral devices, as well as the word length of these devices. A common word length for internal RAM, data paths, and peripheral devices should be considered mandatory. The word length and the instruction repertoire affect the minicomputer's capability to process data, to respond to interrupts, and to perform input/output functions, and therefore relates to performance, required memory size, and arithmetic precision.

8.3.6 Software

For practical reasons, vendor-supplied software can be subdivided into two categories: program development aids and general-purpose support software. Program development software, usually included in the price of the minicomputer, provides users with tools for producing application programs. This software usually consists of assemblers, loaders, text editors, and arithmetic and utility routines. General-purpose support software, often offered at additional cost beyond that of the minicomputer, is oriented more toward the user by providing procedure libraries, utility libraries, functional libraries, high-level language compilers, special-purpose application packages, and various kinds of operating systems (see Chapter 6).

For each type of vendor software module under consideration, the following criteria must be established:

1. Software efficiency
2. Minimum hardware and configuration requirements for the software module
3. Software documentation, including availability of manuals, program source, and identification of program originators
4. Software libraries, including utilities, mathematical and diagnostic support programs
5. Software support, including training, maintenance, updates and corrections, and custom design services

Individual software modules should be analyzed with the following tradeoffs in mind: speed of assembly or compiling, the availability of debugging aids, and the efficiency of program organization, compared to the programming and debugging time, the core utilization, operating speed, and the type of language used. Table 8-3-5 contains a summary of representative application areas and appropriate software modules.

TABLE 8-3-5.   Application Areas and Corresponding Software Modules[4,10]

Application	Software module	Reasons for choice of software module
Scientific computation	High-level compilers FORTRAN, ALGOL, BASIC	Numerical calculations Diagnostics and special features of language
Examples: Matrix inversions, numerical integration, structural design, optimization problems	I/O device handlers Operating system Editors	Ease of programming/debugging/ maintenance relatively independent of the computer used Possible real-time functions

TABLE 8-3-5. (continued)

Application	Software module	Reasons for choice of software module
Business or commercial problems	High-level languages COBOL, PL/I, BASIC	Ease of programming/debugging/ maintenance relatively independent of the computer used
Examples: Established LSGP computer business applications, billing, accounting, inventories, project scheduling, project control systems	I/O device handlers Operating system Editors	
Communication systems	Assembly language	Handling of data communications among terminals requires byte addressing and logical instructions
Examples: For telecommunications switching, editing, network, modem/multiplex, A/D collection, data concentration systems, intercomputer data transmission	Loader Debug package I/O device handlers	High transfer rates Buffering and interrupt capabilities
System component	Assembly language	High transfer rates, buffering, and interrupt handling
Examples: I/O functions, conversions, pre-/postprocessing, terminals on-/off-line subsystems	Loader Debug package I/O device handlers	Handling of data communications among terminals requires byte addressing and logical instructions
Standalone system	Assembly language	Execution times Ease of programming/debugging maintenance
Examples: University and research laboratories, laboratory and monitoring applications, instrumentation control	Loaders Debug package I/O device handlers Editors Operating system (for larger systems)	Flexible I/O command structure Man-machine communication High reliability
Real-time control systems	Assembly language or	Memory space limitations Critical response time Small machines with limited core memory

TABLE 8-3-5. *(continued)*

Application	Software module	Reasons for choice of software module
Examples: Real-time data collection/ reduction systems. Telemetry, spectra analysis, reactor control	Assembly language high-level language mixture Loader Debug package I/O device handlers	Real-time constraints and interrupt service Dependent on specific computer used as well as device controlled Special purpose I/O device control and conversion
Process control Examples: For refineries, mfg. plants, assembly units, fluids, reactors, power plants, monitoring and control applications	Assembly language or Assembly language high-level language mixture	Small machines with limited core memory used in feedback loop Provision for speed of real-time operations used in controlling special purpose I/O devices Feedback mechanism to system under control
Timesharing systems Examples: For multiple general-purpose or multiple dedicated functions	Timesharing monitor Assembly or high- level language	Response time for each user Ease of programming/debugging Fast input/output transfer rates Priority interrupt structure Real-time response possibility
Diagnostic aids Examples: Multitude of problem identification, resolution, repair for machines and processes	Machine language	Permits minor changes without reassembling or recompiling

Other supporting software essential to minicomputer utilization includes debugging and diagnostic programs, interface controllers, and peripheral device support in the form of I/O handlers. Specific considerations regarding I/O handlers must include capabilities for the following:

1. Using standard devices of the minicomputer vendor
2. Library provisions
3. Overlay provisions
4. Diagnostics for I/O devices
5. Programs providing easy access to I/O equipment

Interface controllers are frequently structured to a specific minicomputer design. Expansion provisions must, however, be identified. Diagnostic programs should provide adequate maintenance and error isolation indications; and debugging programs should provide adequate error messages to minimize time lost in debugging application programs. Table 8-3-6 summarizes a minicomputer software selection checklist. A detailed discussion of the software available on a minicomputer was presented in Chapter 6.

TABLE 8-3-6.   Checklist for Minicomputer Software Selection

Software components	Descriptive checklist
Assembler system	Features and minimum configuration required
	Availability of relocatable code
	Device independence
	Input/output device required
	Macro capability, if available
	Modular expansion
	Required number of passes
	Minimum storage requirements
	Speed of assembler and size of symbol table
	Availability of pseudo-operations and conditional-assembly
	Software maintenance
High-level language translators	Language version
	Minimum computer and peripheral configuration
	Device independence
	Modular expansion capabilities
	Minimum storage requirements
	Efficiency of produced output code
	Compatibility of output code with assembler system
General support subsystems	Availability of subroutine libraries
	Availability of utility libraries
	Availability of function libraries
	Availability of maintenance programs
	Operational procedures for the use of these support libraries
	Functions supplied, execution times, and minimum code requirements for each of the support libraries
Operating systems (standalone or batch/DOS–TOS/ RTOS/TSS)	Ease of use (operating procedure)
	Ease of modification (documentation)
	Diagnostic/debug capability
	Storage requirements
	Data/program protection
	I/O handlers and support
	Scheduling
	Coordination of I/O devices with user programs

8.3.7 Additional Hardware Characteristics

There are several additional hardware components which should be considered when evaluating a minicomputer system. A real-time clock is necessary if data are to be collected and analyzed with respect to real-time. To minimize loss of data or information, a power failure, auto-restart hardware system, supported by vendor software, should be considered.

Maintenance and diagnostic capabilities should include considerations for online versus offline testing of circuit boards, isolation of functional hardware modules through encompassing diagnostic systems, and the availability of spare components with ease of interchange.

8.3.8 Manufacturer Criteria

Each potential vendor should be evaluated to determine their reputation for service, engineering support, and stability within the computer industry. In examining service, past performance should be considered in terms of on-time delivery of new equipment and turnaround maintenance on their customers' equipment. Engineering support should be considered in terms of available software, documentation, training manuals, and technical assistance offered to implement their minicomputer. Stability should be considered in terms of number of years in the computer industry; number of minicomputers sold, especially the model that is currently being considered; financial position; and if a manufacturer, production capacity and expansion programs.

Because of the economics of minicomputer systems, vendors frequently provide neither maintenance *nor* service as a standard feature. It is therefore important to consider the technological reliability of the evaluated minicomputer system from the standpoint of design and production. Technology has been able to produce extremely reliable components as well as reduce the number of components and internal corrections required for a minicomputer system.

For critical applications, reliability and maintainability becomes an overriding selection criterion, given that the system meets the minimum functional needs. The use of integrated circuits and careful design reduces the number of components and power consumption required for a system. Reliability therefore is related to the number of circuit cards, the interconnecting techniques, the assembly techniques, and inspection procedures.

8.3.9 Environmental Considerations

Because of the diverse application areas considered for minicomputer systems, some consideration must be given to the environmental conditions in which these systems are to exist. Extreme temperatures, vibrations, power fluctuations, and electrical noise all impact the day-to-day operation of

300

minicomputer systems. Additional considerations should include requirements for extra power supplies for memory expansion modules and upgrade
capabilities for interface controllers.

8.4 Methods of Selection

Once the characteristics of the particular application area have been defined
in the definition phase, it becomes necessary to determine decision criteria
for evaluation purposes. These decision criteria reflecting system capabilities, include hardware, software, application areas, and general support. They are used in preliminary evaluation of minicomputer systems by
attaching values and indicating importance of individual criteria (see Table
8-4-1). Identifying mandatory as well as desirable characteristics (identified
by an asterisk in Table 8-4-1) permits immediate elimination of systems that
do not provide requirements crucial to that particular application.

Subsequent to this preliminary screening, the vendors of the remaining minicomputer systems are requested to submit proposals for detailed
evaluation of their configurations. This detailed evaluation is outlined in
Table 8-4-2.

The first step consists of determining specific selection criteria for
hardware and software components (Tables 8-4-3 and 8-4-4) as well as
manufacturer criteria (Table 8-4-5). The relative importance of each of these
specific criteria is identified by a weight, and a scoring basis is established.
The specific selection criteria included in these tables are the result of the
analysis from Section 8.3. In the final analysis (item number 9 of Table 8-4-2)
the selection of a minicomputer will depend on the evaluated overall performance* in relationship to the effective cost.**

In establishing a scoring basis, remember that many of the specific
criteria have values which depend on the application area. The criteria most
significant in terms of the application definition and measurement of performance are throughput, speed of processing, availability, cost, and expansion.

Throughput, often used synonymously with performance, may be
defined as the steady-state work capacity of the minicomputer system.
Turnaround, another measure of performance, is defined as the time interval
between the job presented to the minicomputer as input and the receipt of
the output. Throughput is seen as a function of the job mixture over some
finite time interval, while turnaround is a function of a selected application.
Both of these performance measures are highly dependent on the internal
processing speed of the minicomputer and therefore are inversely related to

---

* Performance is defined as the weighted sum of the hardware and software components,
as well as vendor capabilities. The individual hardware, software, and vendor capabilities are
the weighted sums of discrete characteristics evaluated by some uniform scoring basis.
** Effective cost is the weighted sum of hardware, software, and implementation costs,
and frequently includes other support and maintenance costs.

301

TABLE 8-4-1. *Decision Criteria for Minicomputer Characteristics, Importance Values, and Examples of Corresponding System Components*

System capability	Value score	Weight	Example of system components
Hardware	(20):		
Reliability		2	Control units
Availability		2	Direct-access devices
Throughput/cost		6*	Processors
Communication-orientation		2	Storage devices
			Peripheral devices
Compatibility		1	Terminals
Expansion		2	Channels
Modularity		1	Unit record devices
Support		2	
Maintenance		2	
Software	(30):		
Reliability		2	Batch processing
Availability		6*	Multiprocessing
Multiprogramming		1	direct-coupled
Data management		6*	dual-processors
Overhead requirements		1	Multiprogramming multitasking
Compile times		2	telecommunication
Execution times		2	multiaccess
Industry standards		2	Timesharing
Ease of use		6*	
Documentation		2	
Application	(25):		
Availability		6*	Compilation
Scope		1	Data acquisition
User's library		2	Simulation
Modularity		4	Business processing
Language		1	Telecommunications
Ease of modification		6*	Control and monitoring
Sophistication		1	Scientific computation
Documentation		4*	Data management
General support	(25):		
Education		6*	
Consulting		5*	
Responsiveness		4*	
Proximity		2	
Sales relationship		2	
Training		6*	
Total	(100)	100	

* Mandatory

TABLE 8-4-2. *Outline of Selection Procedure*[7]

Outline of selection procedure

1. Establish specific selection criteria for:
   A. Hardware components
   B. Software components
   C. Vendor components

2. Identify desirable and necessary criteria, with corresponding minimum specifications.

3. Establish relative importance of these selection criteria (i.e., weights).

4. Identify scoring criteria and scoring basis. A zero score on any one of the critical selection criteria results in immediate disqualification of that specific system.

5. Separate pricing costs for software, hardware, application programs, and supporting services, broken down for each logical function or identifiable module.

6. Establish relative risk in selection (security index).

7. Techniques for rating each vendor:
   A. Literature survey and analysis
   B. Application benchmarks or kernels
   C. Test programs
   D. Simulation

8. Establish cost versus performance criteria for both hardware and software components.

9. Establish performance evaluation criteria.
   A. Best performance with effective cost less than constraint cost.
   B. Lowest cost with performance criteria above minimum standard.
   C. Highest performance/cost ratio within specified cost and performance standards and constraints.

each other. In other words, an increase in throughput is usually obtained at the expense of turnaround time, and vice versa.

Availability and modularity are also measures of performance. The *availability* of the minicomputer deals with the technology of the product (reliability) as well as the maintenance support. It is a measure of the percentage of time the minicomputer needs maintenance and the duration of the time that the system is not available for application processing. The *modularity* in the components of a minicomputer system provides a measure for expansion as well as ease of interfacing.

Aside from these general comments, performance was shown (Section 8.3) to be sensitive to frequency of execution of individual operation codes, the extent of overlapping among subsystems, the number of hardware registers, the addressing modes, instruction formats, instruction capabilities, word size, data path width, and memory cycle time, among a number of other parameters. Most of the parameters vary in importance from one application to the next, and the scoring basis should, therefore, reflect the individual importance to a particular application.

303

TABLE 8-4-3.   *Specific Selection Criteria for Hardware Components*

Selection criteria	Weight	Suggested scoring basis
Word size	10	4: 32 Bits 3: 18 Bits 2: 16 Bits 1: 12 Bits 0: 8 Bits or less
Cycle time	4	4: <0.75 μsec 3: 0.99–0.75 μsec 2: 1.50–1.00 μsec 1: 2.00–1.50 μsec 0: 2.00 μsec or above
Memory size	4	4: 132K and above 3: 64–132K 2: 32–64K 1: 16–32K 0: <16K
Index registers	5	4: >8 3: 5–8 2: 2–5 1: One 0: None
Number of interrupt levels	4	4: >64 3: 32–64 2: 16–32 1: 8–16 0: 0–8
Response time to interrupts	6	4: <1 μsec 3: 1–4 μsec 2: 4–8 μsec 1: 8–12 μsec 0: >12 μsec

Arithmetic features	4	4: Hardware multiply/divide
		   Double-precision
		   Floating-point arithmetic
		3: Hardware multiply/divide
		   Double-precision
		2: Hardware multiply/divide
		   or fast subroutines
		1: Fast subroutine multiply/
		   divide
		0: Little arithmetic capability

Instruction set	5	4,3: Extensive 2: Adequate 1,0: Primitive

TABLE 8-4-4.   *Specific Selection Criteria for Software Components*

Selection Criteria	Weight	Suggested Scoring Basis
Operating systems (Standalone or Batch/DOS-TOS/ RTOS/TSS)	10	Award points for core requirements, ease of use, ease of modification, input/output support, data protection in power failure, data management facilities.
General support	8	Award points for availability of: A) Procedure libraries B) Function libraries C) Utility libraries D) I/O handlers E) Loaders F) Diagnostic routines
Application languages Assembly language	6	Award points for number of passes, relocatability, ease of use, ease of modification, execution times, ease of debugging, macro capabilities, size of assembler, and availability of pseudo-operations.
High-level languages	6	Award points for level, special features, diagnostics, ease of modification, availability, hardware configuration required, size of program that can be compiled, and core size required for compiler.

It is possible to perform controlled executions of representative tasks to establish instruction distributions and aid in the scoring selection. Unfortunately, typical measurements for job mixtures are difficult to accurately identify and establish, especially because of instruction set incompatibilities, I/O interfaces and variations, and monitoring of execution times. It is much less expensive and sufficiently accurate to use the techniques of Section 8.3 to establish the scoring basis.

A score of zero on any one of the critical selection criteria should result in immediate disqualification of that system. With this procedure it is possible to validate the scoring basis of each criterion by simply obtaining the average score for the minicomputers under consideration for that criterion. If an excessively large number of criteria have low scores, a review (and possibly a redefinition) of the scoring basis should be made.

The next step in the selection procedure consists of establishing separate pricing costs for the software, hardware, application programs, and supporting vendor services, broken down for each of the logical functions or

305

TABLE 8-4-5.   Specific Selection Criteria for the Manufacturer

Selection criterion	Weight	Scoring basis
Delivery time	7	4: Less than 30 days ARO 3: 30–45 days ARO 2: 45–60 days ARO 1: 60–75 days ARO 0: Over 75 days ARO
Past performance	5	4: On time delivery/good service 3: On time delivery/intermittent service 2: Late delivery/good service 1: Late delivery/intermittent service 0: Known for late deliveries and poor service
Maintenance (service)	5	4: 24-hour turnaround on CPU, and on call maintenance 3: Location of service center 2: Maintenance service available 1: Slow response to service request 0: No maintenance experience
Location of manufacturer	3	4: Locally 3: — 2: Local representative 1: — 0: Distant
Alternative sites of same system	1	4: Locally available 3: — 2: Locally present but not available 1: — 0: No alternate site
Number installed	4	4: >100 3: 75–100 2: 50–75 1: 10–50 0: <10
Documentation	5	4: Excellent hardware/software manuals 3: — 2: Adequate interface/ programming manuals 1: — 0: Little or no documentation

TABLE 8-4-5. (continued)

Selection criterion	Weight	Scoring basis
Training	4	4: Full operation and maintenance training 3: Limited number of personnel trained 2: On-site training only 1: Training through manuals only 0: No training
Engineering support (interfacing)	4	4: Full interfacing support 3: Support for all devices 2: Support only for vendor's devices 1: Only guidelines 0: No support
Field upgrade policy	1	4: Full customer engineering upgrading 3: — 2: Upgrading/own implementation 1: — 0: No upgrading
Warranty	1	4: Full warranty/fast service 3: Full warranty/intermittent service 2: Partial warranty 1: Partial warranty/intermittent service 0: No warranty
Compatibility	1	4: Compatible with existing system 3: — 2: Reprogramming required 1: — 0: Retraining required

identifiable modules of Section 8.2. The *software cost* includes system software, programming for individual tasks of the application, and any hardware add-ons made necessary by desirable software functions. The *hardware cost* includes the vendor's base price of the minicomputer, expansion requirements, interfacing, and documentation. Add-on costs, frequently not considered, include training, service or maintenance, documentation, and implementation. Table 8-4-6 illustrates the various elements of the effective costs for a minicomputer system.[5]

The next selection criterion establishes a security index indicating the relative risk each vendor provides as to any inability to provide the selected system or services. Table 8-4-7 illustrates the various factors necessary to

TABLE 8-4-6.   *Elements of Effective Cost Determination*

Category	Detailed considerations
Software cost	Programming Modifications Source copies Documentation
Hardware	Basic components Modifications Interfacing Expansion Engineering support Field upgrades
Add-on cost	Training Service Maintenance Implementation Documentation

establish this security index. The selection criteria are ranked in the order of importance to the overall minicomputer system.

The capability for the system to grow is an important consideration and should be analyzed in some detail. Modular computer systems are designed to enable the user to arrange his configuration with expansion in mind. Modularity in design also encompasses compatibility in architecture, instruction sets, interfaces, software, and application programs.

Once the application requirements are established in terms of the hardware, software, and vendor criteria, individual techniques for obtaining performance evaluation values need to be considered. There are three basic evaluation methods that can be used to rate individual minicomputer systems:[9]

1. Simulation
2. Kernels or benchmark programs
3. Analysis of machine specifications

Each of these evaluation techniques is discussed in the next sections.

Having obtained scores for each of the selection criteria by one or more of the above evaluation methods, multiply these values by their corresponding weight factors and sum them (see Tables 8-4-3 through 8-4-5). Then, calculate the cost of each system (using Table 8-4-6), and prepare a cost/performance chart. This chart (see Figure 8-4-1) indicates the various options and ranges of possibilities available to a prospective buyer. It indicates which minicomputers are below the minimum overall performance level, which minicomputers are above the maximum acceptable cost, and what other cost/performance tradeoffs are available. With the established performance evaluation criterion, the prospective buyer can objectively select the desired system, as well as maintain alternate options.

TABLE 8-4-7.   Methods for Determining Vendor Security Index (lowest negative value represents smallest relative risk)[8]

Security indicators	Value	Score	Weight
1. Late delivery (delivery schedule)	20		
2. Excessive downtime (hardware performance)	18		
3. Insufficient support (manufacturer support)	16		
4. Insufficient software support (availability of software)	10		
5. Intermittent software operation (quality of software)	10		
6. No supporting application programs (availability of application programs)	10		
7. Exceeded original cost (cost of minicomputer system)	8		
8. Incompatibilities between components of the system (capability of system expansion)	7		
9. Architectural complications in interfacing (compatibility of minicomputer systems)	5		
10. Little or no documentation (documentation)	5		
Total	100 -	Score	

8.4.1 Simulation

Simulation, as used in computer evaluation, is defined as testing the cost/ performance ratio of a user's requirements, established in the definition phase, on a variety of computer systems. It is the newest, most sophisticated, and most expensive vendor evaluation technique, and therefore should be used only if a large number of minicomputers are to be bought.

The basic input to the simulation process is the system configuration specifications pertaining to the input/output, peripheral devices, storage memories, and processor characteristics of each application. Also, the mode of operation, reflecting the system response time, throughput, and availability is provided. The simulation system then processes the data against the specified model using the available computer resources. The result consists of the cost of the various configurations, the optimum configuration, and result-

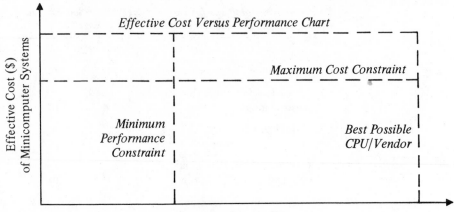

Performance is defined as:

$$P_s = \sum_{i=1}^{N} W_i * S_i$$

where: N = total number of selection criteria

s = particular minicomputer system

i = selection criterion for particular application

W = criterion weight

S = implementation value

FIGURE 8-4-1.   *Effective cost versus performance chart.*

ing evaluation criteria for the various application areas. An outline of such a simulation process is illustrated in Figure 8-4-2.

An example of such a simulation system is SCERT, systems and computers evaluation and review technique.[6] This system consists of a set of computer programs used to simulate the performance of various minicomputers and to compare these results to the user's specification. The SCERT simulator consists of five phases, as illustrated in Figure 8-4-3.

The *first phase* is a detailed input description of either the current or the proposed system configuration, including work loads. This information is utilized to tailor-design a mathematical model of the current and proposed work loads. The *second phase,* using the previously generated component data base, provides the mechanism to model the hardware and software system under consideration. The *third phase* merges the work load model with the hardware/software model to determine the required I/O and processing activities. These data indicate the specific operations required for each of the components simulated, having taken into account internal processing requirements, memory requirements, data management, file structures, etc. The *fourth phase* integrates all of the previously developed data

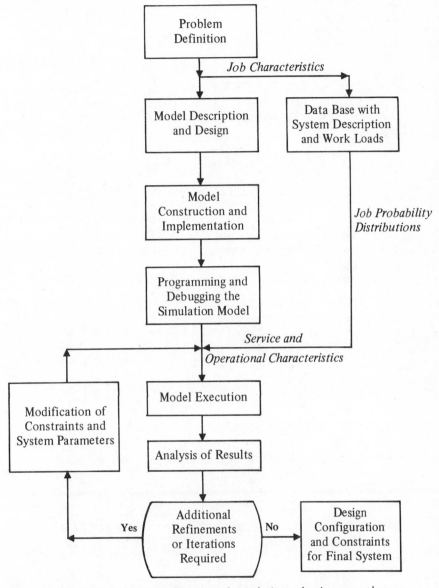

FIGURE 8-4-2. *Block diagram of simulation selection procedure.*

and models into an encompassing simulation process. This processor is then used to fully develop the final throughput performance and configuration analysis. The *last phase* is the generation of the various output reports, including:

1. System specifications
2. Internal analysis of each minicomputer using the various programs
3. Central processor utilization

311

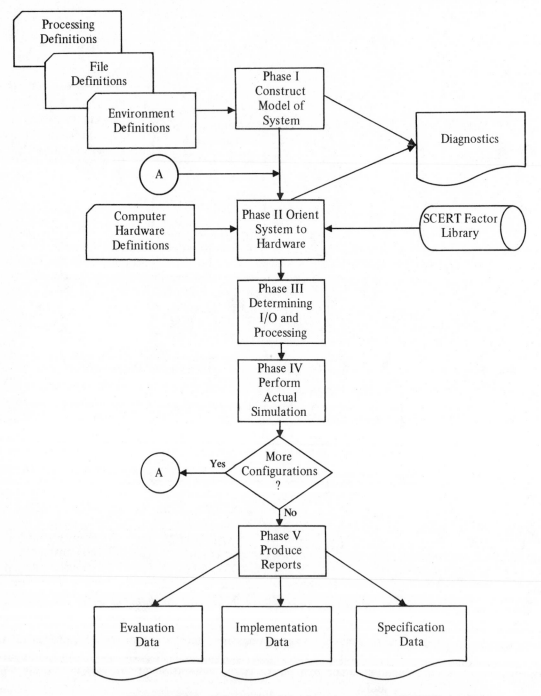

FIGURE 8-4-3. *Flowchart of the five phases of the SCERT simulation program.*[6]

4. Cost to implement each minicomputer system
5. Computer capabilities in critical hardware areas
6. Real-time analysis for real-time processing systems

The advantage of the simulation technique is its accuracy in simultaneously providing detailed information for many systems. When properly used, a good simulation program, such as the one described above, can be one of the best predicting mechanisms regarding system performance. However, in the final analysis, the results are no better than the many assumptions that are incorporated in the model design and construction.

8.4.2 Kernels or Benchmark Programs

Kernels (small programs consisting of a few instructions) and/or benchmark programs, when properly written, do not simulate the behavior of the entire system under consideration, but rather the desirable application programs themselves. The results of test programs or kernels are selected measures of the minicomputer capabilities, while the result of benchmark programs are selected measures of various functional capabilities (application-oriented) of the minicomputer.

Both of those selection procedures are rather limited because of the selection of representative job loads which need be assigned to measure the different aspects of the minicomputer's capabilities before any comparisons can be made. Selections of typical work loads for the benchmark programs are equally subjective, and can therefore be biased. The major problems are whether the benchmark programs selected are representative, and whether the evaluation is weighted (or biased) too heavily by the capabilities of the programmers assigned to the benchmark programs, and not the minicomputer's capabilities. To maintain objectivity, the benchmark programs to be tested should all be assigned to the same system evaluator (programmer). This, of course, implies that the programmer is equally proficient on all minicomputer systems under consideration, and does not favor any one system.

The second problem, aside from objectivity, is the assignment of objective weights to the results of using two or more kernels. Benchmark programs should be related to the proposed minicomputer applications, and should be representative of the expected work loads. Suggested benchmark programs for various application areas are presented in Table 8-4-8.

8.4.3 Machine Specifications

Minicomputer characteristics published in data processing literature, which report performance, costs, expansion capabilities, and software support of the various minicomputers, represent the most frequently used guides to system and vendor selection. Whenever published evaluation reports (e.g.,

313

TABLE 8-4-8. Examples of Benchmark Programs for Representative Applications

Application areas	Suggested benchmark programs
Data manipulation processing	1. Interchange contents of two arrays in memory. 2. Generalized byte handling program. 3. Counting the number of one-bits in a register or memory location, with the results left in another register or location.
Computation processing	1. Add two random core locations, storing the results into a third location. 2. Perform a fixed-point multiplication routine utilizing software. 3. Compare arithmetically the contents of two registers or memory locations and branch to one of three locations, depending on the result of the comparison. 4. Perform a double-precision right shift of two registers or memory locations (the lower bits of one register or location shift into the upper bits of the other) with the number of shifts being specified in a third location.
Control processing	1. Search a list of values whose starting address is in a core location, to determine the address of the list value which is equal to a specified value. 2. Branch to one of four different arbitrary addresses, depending on the value of two adjacent bits in a register or a location. The bits should be neither low-order nor high-order bits.

Auerbach Reports[1]) for the hardware, software, or application components are available, they should certainly supplement any of the previously mentioned techniques.

The information obtained through the available literature should be qualified by conducting, if possible, a survey of other installations using similar system components. Performance specifications, even if available from the literature, require either simulation or benchmark programs for confirmation of evaluation.

8.4.4 Example of a Selection Procedure

The selection procedure outlined in Section 8.4 has been applied to the application defined in Section 8.2.5. The maximum cost constraints were set at $55,000, while the minimum acceptable standards for the system were specified as:

Hardware:

1. 12–16-bit word size
2. At least 12K memory

314

3. 1.0–2.0 μsec cycle time
4. Availability of memory parity
5. At least two index registers
6. At least 16 automatic interrupt levels
7. Real-time clock
8. Automatic power failure/restart
9. Interrupt latency time of 8 μsec or less

Software:

1. Availability of assembler
2. Availability of FORTRAN compiler
3. Real-time clock programs
4. Interrupt control subsystem

The data for the minicomputer systems and cost figures were taken from Reference 2. The primary scoring basis, chosen for the selection criteria is given in Table 8-4-9. The results of the selection procedure are presented in Table 8-4-10 and in Figure 8-4-4, indicating that two minicom-

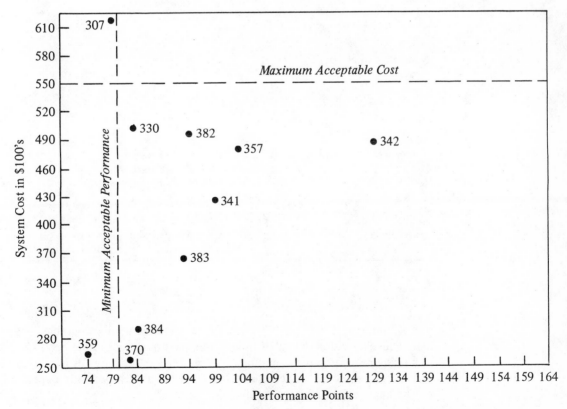

FIGURE 8-4-4. *Cost/performance ratios for the example in section 8.4.4.*

315

TABLE 8-4-9.   Primary Scoring Basis for Selection Criteria

Selection criterion	Weight	Scoring basis
Word size	10	4: 32 Bits 3: 18 Bits 2: 16 Bits 1: 12 Bits 0: 8 Bits
Memory size	2	4: >132K 3: 64–132K 2: 32–64K 1: 16–32K 0: <16K
Cycle time	4	4: <0.75 μsec 3: 0.99–0.75 μsec 2: 1.50–1.00 μsec 1: 2.00–1.50 μsec 0: >2.00 μsec
Index registers	5	4: >8 3: 5–8 2: 2–5 1: 1 0: 0
Number of interrupt levels	4	4: >64 3: 32–64 2: 16–32 1: 8–16 0: 0–8
Response time to interrupt	10	4: <1 μsec 3: 1–4 μsec 2: 4–8 μsec 1: 8–12 μsec 0: >12 μsec
Availability of assembler	6	Award points for number of passes required, macro capability, and relocatability.

puters, numbered 307 and 359, do not meet the minimum acceptable performance levels, with number 307 above the maximum acceptable cost. Of the remaining minicomputers, number 342 has the best cost/performance ratio, and therefore should be selected. Other selections can be made depending on the final selection criterion chosen.

316

TABLE 8-4-10.   *Results of the Selection Analysis of Section 8.4.4*

Selection criteria	Machines										
	Weight	384	383	382	370	359	357	342	341	330	307
Word length	10	10	10	20	10	10	10	40	10	20	40
Memory size	2	2	2	2	6	6	6	2	2	2	2
Cycle time	4	4	12	4	12	4	12	12	12	8	8
Index registers	5	0	0	0	0	0	15	20	15	5	5
No. of interrupt levels	4	16	16	16	16	16	12	16	16	12	8
Response time to interrupts	10	40	40	40	20	20	30	20	20	30	10
Assembler	6	12	12	12	18	18	18	24	24	6	6
Total		84	92	94	82	74	103	134	99	83	79
Cost (in $100)											
Basic computer		54	105	100	190	190	135	200	100	180	155
Additional core to 32K		161	175	315	0*	0*	280	240	280	280	336
4 ASR-33 Teletypes		72	72	72	60	60	60	32	32	39	100
Real-time clock		3	5	3	8	8	5	10	10	0	15
Automatic restart		3	5	3	0	15	0	5	5	0	9
Total cost		293	362	493	258	273	480	487	427	499	615

* Not needed

SUMMARY

Techniques for selecting minicomputer systems vary greatly because of the numerous and wide range of application possibilities available for minicomputer usage. It is important that a systematic and uniform approach, such as described in this chapter, be taken in the selection and evaluation of minicomputer systems. The selection technique should include some form of cost/performance criterion while at the same time be flexible and inexpensive. The cost of the selection procedure cannot overshadow the cost of the actual minicomputer system itself.

In addition to the definition of the application, the minicomputer characteristics, and the evaluation technique, particular attention must be given to the expansion (and upgrading) capability, reliability, and deliverability of the minicomputer systems. The manufacturer's reputation must be considered, and finally, the terms of the contract should include arrangements for maintenance, spare parts, warranty, and service.

PROBLEMS

1. Outline a selection procedure for minicomputer evaluation. Discuss each step in detail.

2. Describe the importance that the definition of the application plays in the selection procedure for minicomputers.

3. The definition phase of system selection includes a description of the minicomputer system function, an identification of the system's components and interfaces, and the functional requirements of the system. Describe each of these topics, and discuss their relationship.

4. Discuss why individual minicomputer characteristics depend largely on the application under consideration.

5. Describe the PERT chart for a minicomputer system selection procedure. What advantage does a PERT chart mechanism present?

6. Develop concepts, objectives, and selection methods for a minicomputer application of your choice.

7. What role does the specification of the data base play in a selection procedure?

8. Why is it important to consider expansion requirements when evaluating a new minicomputer system?

9. Describe several criteria that need to be considered in the interface specification.

10. Present a complete analysis of the definition phase for an application of your choice.

11. Relate the number of instructions executed per second to other pertinent characteristics of the CPU.

12. Describe the more common transmission modes that data can use between peripheral devices and main memory.

13. Discuss the tradeoffs between processing speed, data transfer rates and application under consideration.

14. Define throughput and discuss how it differs from turnaround time.

15. Word size determines accuracy and efficiency of operations. Relate word size, type of data, and application area.

16. Discuss the role of addressing, indexing, and interrupt mechanism required for data communication applications.

17. What considerations must be made for I/O-oriented applications in terms of I/O accessing techniques, interrupt mechanisms, and response times?

18. Discuss how data formats affect the versatility of minicomputers. What effect does this have on data rates and transfer rates?

19. Describe how an appropriate scoring basis might be established for specific applications.

318

20. Discuss measurements of performance.

21. What importance does cost play in the minicomputer evaluation procedure?

22. Outline how the simulation evaluation technique differs from benchmark programs.

23. Differentiate among simulation, kernels or benchmark, and machine specification analysis through the use of literature.

24. Differentiate between kernels and benchmark programs.

25. How could simulation be used in the analysis, design, and selection phase of a minicomputer system?

26. What specific selection criteria must be investigated to determine the correct configuration of a communications oriented minicomputer system?

27. Briefly discuss the advantages of benchmark techniques in vendor selection.

28. Which of the vendor selection techniques do you feel is the best technique for minicomputer selection? Why?

29. Identify and briefly discuss the steps of a minicomputer selection procedure.

30. Discuss what factors should be considered in a minicomputer selection.

PROJECT

A few years ago (1967) a company, call it Apex Electronics (APE), had under its dynamic Chief Executive Officer, David A. Mnemonic, built an impressive conglomerate. This conglomerate consisted of:

Aerospace Division
Electronics Division
Control Division

In 1970 the Electronics Division consisted of a series of decentralized organizations which included:

Division Hdqtrs.—Dallas, Texas
Widgit Division—Arlington, Virginia
Transistor Division—Las Vegas, Nevada
Electro-Data Division—Houston, Texas
Electro-Systems Division—New York, New York

The company operated on a project manager basis for the design, installation, and repair of a variety of systems. Among the divisions' many capabilities was the maintenance and repair of major electronic equipment. The company's competitive edge was its quick turnaround. Also one of its capabilities was its ability to design, develop, and successfully install one-of-a-kind special-purpose electronic equipment.

While engaged in this repair of electronic equipment, it was necessary to maintain a rather extensive inventory control and reporting system. Essentially, reports from the warehouse were converted into a listing of parts according to federal stock number. There was no method to check on the availability of a particular part except by reading the listing. The listing required 4 hours to compute, 12 hours to print, and filled 20 boxes of paper reports. The information was stored on computer hardware, but the time of the report was still a week late.

319

The inventory growth pattern was projected as:

Year	Number of Items	Dollar Volume
1965	60,000	6,000,000
1966	70,000	7,000,000
1967	125,000	12,500,000
1968	160,000	16,000,000
1969	170,000	17,000,000
1970	180,000	18,000,000
1971	185,000	18,500,000

The need to reduce the volume and control the number of items in stock was obvious.

Your job, if you decide to accept this mission, is to design an integrated management system, utilizing what you have learned in this text plus any other appropriate knowledge you know about today's technology of distributed processing using minicomputers, interactive systems with minicomputers, etc.

HINT: It would seem appropriate to justify the computer(s) system chosen utilizing Chapter 8 information.

REFERENCES

1. *Auerbach Minicomputer Reports,* Auerbach Publishers Inc., Philadelphia, Pennsylvania, 1970.
2. Bartik, J. J., "Minicomputers Turn Classic," *Data Processing,* Vol. 12, pp. 42–48, January 1970.
3. Calingaert, P., "System Performance Evaluation, Survey, and Appraisal," *Comm. ACM,* Vol. 10, pp. 12–18, January 1967.
4. Corsigilia, J., "Matching Computers to the Job—First Step Towards Selection," *Data Processing,* Vol. 12, pp. 23–27, December 1970.
5. Hare, Van Court, Jr., *Systems Analysis: A Diagnostic Approach,* Harcourt, Brace & World, Inc., New York, pp. 1–20, 1967.
6. Herman, D. J., "SCERT: A Computer Evaluation Tool," *Datamation,* Vol. 13, pp. 26–28, February 1967.
7. Pooch, U. W., "Minicomputer System Selection and Evaluation," Proc. Fourth Texas Conference on Computing Systems, Austin, Texas, November 17–18, 1975.
8. Schneidewind, N. F., "The Practice of Computer Selection," *Datamation,* Vol. 13, pp. 22–25, February 1967.
9. Schwartz, E. S., "Computer Evaluation and Selection," *Data Management,* Vol. 6, pp. 58–62, June 1968.
10. Theis, D. J., and L. C. Hobbs, "Minicomputers for Real-Time Applications," *Datamation,* Vol. 15, pp. 39–61, March 1969.
11. Vachon, B., and W. Weiske, "Interfacing: A Balancing Act of Hardware and Software," *Electronic Design,* Vol. 19, pp. 58–63, May 1971.

Appendixes

APPENDIX A.1

Rules of Boolean Algebra

Boolean algebra provides a method whereby complex logic statements can be manipulated in order to rigorously determine their validity.

Rules	AND	OR
Laws of Identity	$A=A$	$\overline{A}=\overline{A}$
Commutative Law	$A \cdot B = B \cdot A$	$A+B=B+A$
Associative Law	$A \cdot (B \cdot C)=(A \cdot B) \cdot C$	$A+(B+C)=(A+B)+C$
Indempotent Law	$A \cdot A = A$	$A+A=A$
Distributive Law	$A \cdot (B+C)=A \cdot B+A \cdot C$	$A+B \cdot C=(A+B) \cdot (A+C)$
Absorption Law	$A+A \cdot B=A$	$A \cdot (A+B)=A$
Expansion Law	$A \cdot B+A \cdot \overline{B}=A$	$(A+B) \cdot (A+\overline{B})=A$
DeMorgan's Law	$\overline{A \cdot B}=\overline{A}+\overline{B}$	$\overline{A+B}=\overline{A} \cdot \overline{B}$
Consistency Properties	$A+B=B$ if $A \cdot B = A$	
Zero Element	$A \cdot 1=A$	$A+0=A$
Unit Element	$A \cdot 0=0$	$A+I=I$
Complement	$A \cdot \overline{A}=0$	$A+\overline{A}=I$
Involution (Double Negation)	$(\overline{\overline{A}})=A$	
Logical Manipulation	$(\overline{A}+B) \cdot (A+\overline{B})=\overline{A} \cdot A+\overline{A} \cdot \overline{B}+A \cdot B+B \cdot \overline{B}$	

APPENDIX A.2

Logic Symbols Used in Logic Design

This appendix shows the most important functions of *two* inputs by a simple truth table as well as the more commonly used symbols for the corresponding logic gates.

A *gate* is defined to be a logic element which performs a basic logic operation.

(1) *AND Function*

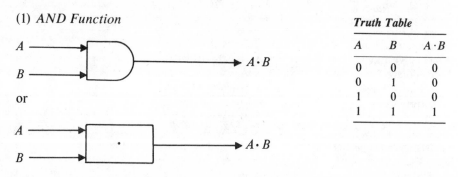

Truth Table

A	B	A·B
0	0	0
0	1	0
1	0	0
1	1	1

(2) *OR Function*

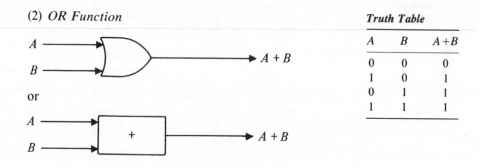

Truth Table

A	B	A+B
0	0	0
1	0	1
0	1	1
1	1	1

(3) *NAND Function*

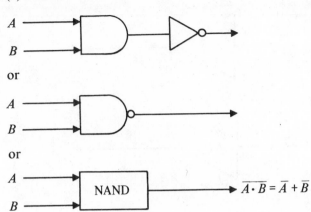

Truth Table

A	B	NAND
0	0	1
0	1	1
1	0	1
1	1	0

or

or

$\overline{A \cdot B} = \overline{A} + \overline{B}$

(4) *NOR Function*

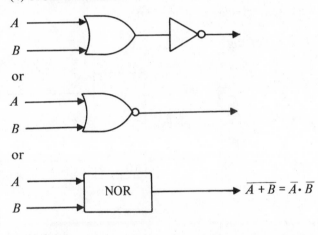

Truth Table

A	B	NOR
0	0	1
1	0	0
0	1	0
1	1	0

or

or

$\overline{A + B} = \overline{A} \cdot \overline{B}$

(5) *XOR (Exclusive OR) Function*

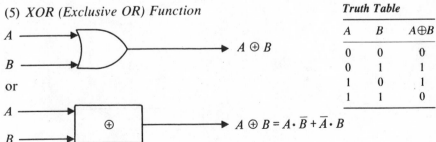

Truth Table

A	B	A⊕B
0	0	0
0	1	1
1	0	1
1	1	0

$A \oplus B$

or

$A \oplus B = A \cdot \overline{B} + \overline{A} \cdot B$

325

(6) *NOT (Inversion) Function*

A	$\bar{A}$
0	1
1	0

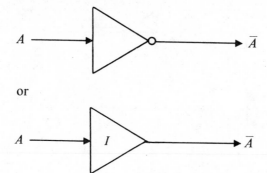

or

Functional Subunits consist of some storage elements and/or combinational logic to perform a particular logic or arithmetic operation.

Flip-Flops remain in a fixed state (stable) until a change in its input occurs which causes it to change its state.

(1) *SR (Set-Reset) Flip-Flop*

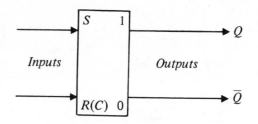

Transition Table

S	R	$Q(t)$	$Q(t+1)$
0	0	0	0
0	0	1	1
0	1	0	0
0	1	1	0
1	0	0	1
1	0	1	1
1	1	0	Ind.
1	1	1	Ind.

Characteristic Equation (Next State Equation)

$$Q(t+1) = S + Q(t)\,\bar{R}$$

326

(2) *JK Flip-Flop*

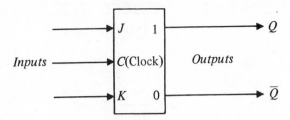

Transition Table

J	K	$Q(t)$	$Q(t+1)$
0	0	0	0
0	0	1	1
0	1	0	0
0	1	1	0
1	0	0	1
1	0	1	1
1	1	0	1
1	1	1	0

Characteristic Equation (Next State Equation)

$$Q(t+1) = \overline{K}\, Q(t) + J\, \overline{Q(t)}$$

(3) *T (Trigger or Complement) Flip-Flop*

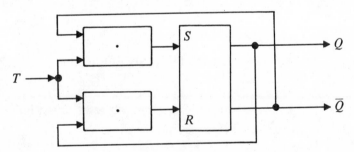

Transition Table

T	$Q(t)$	$Q(t+1)$
0	0	0
0	1	1
1	0	1
1	1	0

Characteristic (Next State) Equation

$$Q(t+1) = Q(t)\, \overline{T} + \overline{Q}(t) \cdot T$$

327

(4) *SRT (SRFF with trigger input) Flip-Flop*

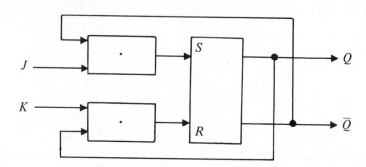

Transition Table

S	R	T	Q(t)	Q(t+1)
0	0	0	0	0
0	0	0	1	1
0	0	1	0	0
0	0	1	1	0
0	1	0	0	0
0	1	0	1	0
0	1	1	0	Ind.
0	1	1	1	Ind.
1	0	0	0	1
1	0	0	1	1
1	0	1	0	Ind.
1	0	1	1	Ind.
1	1	0	0	Ind.
1	1	0	1	Ind.
1	1	1	0	Ind.
1	1	1	1	Ind.

Characteristic (Next State) Equation

$$Q(t+1) = S + T\,\overline{Q}(t) + \overline{R\ T}\,Q(t)$$

(5) *D(Delay) Flip-Flop* will reset or set upon state of D input and a clock pulse,

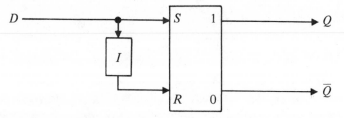

Characteristic (Next State) Equation

$$Q(t+1) = D(t)$$

I.e., the input to the flip-flop at any clock interval will appear at the output *one* clock pulse later.

APPENDIX A.3

Binary Arithmetic

(1.) Binary Number System

The binary number system is the base two number system which uses only two digits, 0 and 1. The weight assigned to a binary digit or bit is a power of two and depends on the position of the bit in a bit string. Table A-1-1 shows examples of bit strings, weights attached to each position and the equivalent decimal number.

TABLE A-1-1. *Examples of Binary Numbers.*

$2^8 = 256$	$2^7 = 128$	$2^6 = 64$	$2^5 = 32$	$2^4 = 16$	$2^3 = 8$	$2^2 = 4$	2	1	Decimal Value
1	0	0	1	1	0	0	0	1	305
0	1	0	1	0	0	1	1	0	166
1	0	1	0	1	0	1	0	1	341
0	1	0	1	0	1	0	1	0	170

The decimal equivalent of any binary number, such as 010101010, is obtained as:

$$0 \times 2^8 + 1 \times 2^7 + 0 \times 2^6 + 1 \times 2^5 + 0 \times 2^4 + 1 \times 2^3 + 0 \times 2^2 + 1 \times 2 + 0$$
$$= 128 + 32 + 8 + 2$$
$$= 170$$

In general, if $b_n, b_{n-1}, \ldots, b_0$ is a bit string, i.e., $b_i = 0$ or 1 for $i = 0, \ldots,$ n, then the equivalent decimal number is given by:

$$d = b_n \times 2^n + b_{n-1} \times 2^{n-1} + \ldots + b_0 \times 2^0$$

(2.) Binary Addition

The block diagram of a general binary addition is shown in Figure A-2-1. A_i and B_i are the two binary digits being added, C_i is a carry bit from a previous addition. S_i denotes the sum bit and C_{i+1} the carry bit for the next binary sum. The rules of binary addition, i.e., the rules for computing S_i and C_{i+1} from A_i, B_i, and C_i are given in Table A-2-1.

Table A-2-1.   Rules for Binary Addition.

C_i	A_i	B_i	S_i	C_{i+1}
0	0	0	0	0
0	0	1	1	0
0	1	0	1	0
0	1	1	0	1
1	0	0	1	0
1	0	1	0	1
1	1	0	0	1
1	1	1	1	1

EXAMPLES

```
CARRY    0 0 0 1 0 1 0 0     IN DECIMAL
AUGEND   1 1 0 0 1 0 1 1        203
ADDEND   0 0 1 0 1 0 1 0         42
SUM      1 1 1 1 0 1 0 1        245

CARRY   10 0 1 1 1 0 0 0     IN DECIMAL
AUGEND   1 0 0 0 1 1 0 0        140
ADDEND   1 1 0 1 0 1 0 1        213
SUM      0 1 1 0 0 0 0 1        353
```

The last example demonstrates a case of *carry-overflow*. The sum is too large to be represented by eight bits and a carry digit is generated out of the last column of bits. In a computer, the registers involved in a binary addition can store a finite number of bits. If the sum becomes too large to be stored in a single register, a *register overflow* occurs. The carry bit that overflows is stored in a separate flip-flop, often called a link bit or an extend bit.

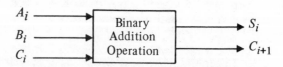

FIGURE A-2-1.   *Block Diagram of Binary Addition Operation.*

(3.) Negative Binary Integers

In most minicomputers, negative binary integers are represented in sign/twos complement form. The most significant bit, in most cases bit fifteen, is used to represent the sign of the number. If the number is positive, this bit is zero; otherwise it is one. The magnitudes of negative numbers are represented in twos complement form. If B is a n-bit binary integer, then its twos complement, denoted by B' is $B' = 2^n - B$. The ones complement of B is obtained by complementing every bit in B. The twos complement is obtained by adding a one to the ones complement. Table A-3-1 shows a sequence of binary integers in the sign/twos complement system using four bits. Note that when a negative integer is represented in the sign/twos complement system, its most significant bit becomes 1 automatically, indicating that it is a negative number.

TABLE A-3-1. *Examples of Binary Integers in Sign/Twos Complement System.*

	Binary Integer				Decimal Equivalent
	0	1 1 1			+7
	0	1 1 0			+6
	0	1 0 1			+5
S	0	1 0 0	M		+4
I	0	0 1 1	A		+3
G	0	0 1 0	G		+2
N	0	0 0 1	N		+1
	0	0 0 0	I		0
B	1	1 1 1	T		−1
I	1	1 1 0	U		−2
T	1	1 0 1	D		−3
	1	1 0 0	E		−4
	1	0 1 1			−5
	1	0 1 0			−6
	1	0 0 1			−7
	1	0 0 0			−8

(4.) Arithmetic Operations in Twos Complement System

In the sign/twos complement number system, binary integers are added by using the same rules of binary addition discussed in section A.2 and the sign bit is treated like all the other bits during addition.

EXAMPLES

		IN DECIMAL
AUGEND	0 1 0 1 0 1 1 0	+86
ADDEND	0 0 0 1 1 1 1 1	+31
SUM	0 1 1 1 0 1 0 1	+117

AUGEND	0 0 1 1 1 0 0 1	+57
ADDEND	1 1 1 0 1 0 1 1	−21
SUM	0 0 1 0 0 1 0 0	+36
OVERFLOW 1		
AUGEND	1 1 0 0 0 0 0 0	−64
ADDEND	0 0 0 1 0 0 1 1	+19
SUM	1 1 0 1 0 0 1 1	−45
AUGEND	1 1 0 0 1 0 0 1	−55
ADDEND	1 1 0 0 0 0 1 0	−62
SUM	1 0 0 0 1 0 1 1	−117
OVERFLOW 1		

The last example demonstrates a case of an *arithmetic overflow* out of the sign bit column. However, the sum is still correct in the sign/twos complement system.

In the sign/twos complement system, integers are subtracted by *adding* the twos complement of the subtrahend to the minuend.

EXAMPLES

		IN DECIMAL
MINUEND	0 1 0 1 0 1 1 0	+86
SUBTRAHEND	1 1 1 0 0 0 0 1	+31
DIFFERENCE	0 0 1 1 0 1 1 1	+55
OVERFLOW 1		
MINUEND	0 0 1 1 1 0 0 1	+57
SUBTRAHEND	0 0 0 1 0 1 0 1	−21
DIFFERENCE	0 1 0 0 1 1 1 0	−78
MINUEND	1 1 0 0 0 0 0 0	−64
SUBTRAHEND	1 1 1 0 1 1 0 1	+19
DIFFERENCE	1 0 1 0 1 1 0 1	−83
OVERFLOW 1		
MINUEND	1 1 0 0 1 0 0 1	−55
SUBTRAHEND	0 0 1 1 1 1 1 0	−62
DIFFERENCE	0 0 0 0 0 1 1 1	+7
OVERFLOW 1		

Note that although there have been several arithmetic overflows out of the sign bit column, the corresponding differences are all correct in the sign/twos complement system.

(5.) Arithmetic Overflows

Whenever a carry digit is generated out of the column of the sign bits, an arithmetic overflow is said to have occurred. An arithmetic overflow does not automatically imply that the result is incorrect. However, in some cases such an overflow is accompanied by an incorrect result. In other cases, incorrect results are obtained even without an arithmetic overflow. One example of each case is shown below.

EXAMPLES

		IN DECIMAL
AUGEND	1 0 0 1 0 0 1 0	−110
ADDEND	1 0 1 0 0 1 0 0	−92
SUM (INCORRECT)	0 0 1 1 0 1 1 0	−202
OVERFLOW 1		
AUGEND	0 1 0 1 1 0 1 0	+90
ADDEND	0 1 1 0 1 0 1 1	+107
SUM (INCORRECT)	1 1 0 0 0 1 0 1	+197

Let C_s and C_D denote the carry digits out of the sign bits and the most significant bits respectively. Inspection of the above examples indicates that whenever $C_s = C_D$, the result is correct regardless of whether $C_s = 1$ or $C_s = 0$. The result is incorrect whenever $C_s \neq C_D$. An overflow bit is defined by $C_{ov} = C_s \oplus C_D$; whenever $C_{ov} = 1$, the result is incorrect. Some minicomputers provide a separate flip-flop for storing C_{ov} aside from the link bit or extend bit. In such systems, verification of the accuracy of the result can be easily done by testing this overflow flip-flop.

APPENDIX B.1

Statement and Format Specification List of FORTRAN

Statement	Form	Example	Comments
ARITHMETIC ASSIGNMENT	$v = e$	$A = B * C$	Variable name=expression.
CALL	CALL $name(a_1,\ldots,a_n)$	CALL PLOT(X,Y,PEN)	a_i=actual arguments or expressions.
COMMENT	C in column 1		Columns 2–80 ignored.
COMMON	COMMON $a,b,\ldots,z$	COMMON A,B,C	$a\ldots z$ are nonsubscripted variable names.
CONTINUE	CONTINUE	CONTINUE	Control passes to next statement.
DATA	DATA/$v_1,v_2/a_1,a_2$	DATA/A,B/6.0,3.0	Constants a_1,a_2 are assigned to variables v_1,v_2 at compile time.
DIMENSION	DIMENSION $a_1(k_1),\ldots,a_n(k_n)$	DIMENSION A(120), B(3,4)	a=array names. k=maximum subscript number.
DØ	DØ $n\ i=m_1,m_2,m_3$	DØ 10 I=3,12,3	Repeat execution through statement n with $i=m_1$; increment m_3 as long as $i \le m_2$. (m,i) may not be subscripted; $m_3=1$ could be omitted.
END	END	END	Informs compiler that there are no more program statements.
EQUIVALENCE	EQUIVALENCE $(v_1,\ldots,v_n)$ $\ldots(v_m,\ldots,v_n)$	EQUIVALENCE (A,B), (X,Y,Z)	v=variables or subscripted array names. Equivalenced names in parentheses refer to same memory location.
FORMAT	FORMAT $(k_1,\ldots,k_n)$	FORMAT (I6,F8.2,A3)	k=format specifications used in conjunction with I/O statements.
FUNCTION	FUNCTION $name\ (a_1,\ldots,a_n)$	FUNCTION PLOT (X,Y,IPEN)	a=dummy arguments; name defined as variable containing value of function.
GØ TØ	GØ TØ n GØ TØ $(n_1,n_2,\ldots,n_m),i$	GØ TØ 10 GØ TØ (10,20,30),I	n=statement number. $1 \le i \le m$ and control passes to n_i, i is a nonsubscripted integer variable.
IF	IF(E) n_1,n_2,n_3	IF(A) 10,20,30	Control passes to n_1,n_2,n_3 if $E \le$, $=$, ≥ 0.
PAUSE	PAUSE PAUSE a	PAUSE PAUSE 20	Temporary halt; hit continue key. Octal equivalent of n is displayed.
READ	READ $(d,f)l$ READ $(f)l$ READ f,l	READ (5,10) A,B,C READ (10) A,B,C READ 10, A,B,C	d=device number. f=format statement. l=list variables.
RETURN	RETURN n	RETURN RETURN 10	*For subroutine:* Control returns to statement following call. *For statement:* Evaluation of expression in calling program is resumed using value of function.

Statement	Form	Example	Comments
STOP	STOP STOP n	STOP STOP 10	Used to halt execution. Octal equivalent of n is displayed.
SUBROUTINE	SUBROUTINE $name$ $(a_1, \ldots, a_n)$	SUBROUTINE PLOT (X,Y,JPEN)	a=dummy arguments; name need not appear anywhere else in subroutine.
WRITE	WRITE $(d,f)l$ WRITE $(f)l$ WRITE f,l	WRITE (6,10)A,B,C WRITE (10)A,B,C WRITE 10,A,B,C	d=device number. f=formal start number. l=list variables.
COMPLEX	COMPLEX $n_1, n_2, \ldots$	COMPLEX A,B,C	n_1, n_2 are variables assigned memory locations to store complex quantities.
DOUBLE PRECISION	DOUBLE PRECISION $n_1, n_2, \ldots$	DOUBLE PRECISION A,B,C	n_1, n_2 are variables assigned memory locations to store double-precision quantities.
EXTERNAL	EXTERNAL $name$ 1, $name$ 2	EXTERNAL PLOT	name 1, --- are names of subprograms that appear in the argument list of a function or subroutine programs.
INTEGER	INTEGER $n_1, n_2, \ldots$	INTEGER A,B	Declares $n_1, n_2, \text{-----}$ to be integer variables.
LOGICAL	LOGICAL $n_1, n_2, \ldots$	LOGICAL A,B,C	Defines n_1, n_2---- that the names n_1, n_2 are logical quantities.
REAL	REAL $n_1, n_2, \ldots$	REAL I,J,K	$n_1, n_2,$-- are defined as real variables in memory locations.
BACKSPACE	BACKSPACE i	BACKSPACE 6	Backspace one unit record for unit i.
ENDFILE	ENDFILE i	ENDFILE 6	End-of-file indicator for unit i.
REWIND	REWIND	REWIND	Causes rewinding of unit i.
INTEGER	rIw	FORMAT (5I3,I7)	r=repetition count. w=total width in characters.
FLOATING PT (DECIMAL)	rF$w.d$	FORMAT (5F7.3,F4.1)	w=total width includes sign, decimal point. d=characters to right of decimal point.
EXPONENTIAL	rE$w.d$	FORMAT (5E7.3,E5.3)	d=number of characters in exponent.
ALPHANUMERICS	rAw	FORMAT (6A4,A2)	
H(HOLLERITH OR LITERAL)	nH $characters$	FORMAT (4HHELP)	n=number of characters: parentheses must be balanced.
PARENTHESES	n ($specs$)	FORMAT (A3,3(A3,I5))	Format specs in parentheses is repeated n times.
CARRIAGE CONTROL			Indicates beginning of a new data record.

336

Statement and Formation Specification List of ALGOL

Statement	Form	Example	Comment
STATEMENT BRACKETS	*begin....end*	*begin....end;*	Services to enclose and bind together a sequence of separate ALGOL statements that are to be executed together as one unit.
COMPOUND STATEMENT	*begin* $s_1;s_2;s_3;....$ $...s_n$ *end*		Where $s_1,s_2,....s_n$ are ALGOL statements.
BLOCK			A compound statement containing at least one declaration after *begin*.
TYPE DECLARATION			A declarator followed by a list of identifiers separated by commas.
ARRAY DECLARATION	*array* $a_1,a_2,....,a_n$;	*array* A[5,5]	*array* may be preceded by *integer* or *real* according to the type of elements composing the array.
ARRAY	I[A:B,A:B,A:B....A:B]	NAME[-5:0,1:6]	I is the array identifier and the B's are the upper and the A's the lower bounds of the subscripts.
SWITCH DECLARATION	*switch* $S:=L_1,L_2,...$ $..L_n$;	*switch* A:=a,b,c,7;	S is the switch identifier and $L_1,L_2,L_3.... L_n$ are labels.
DESIGNATIONAL EXPRESSIONS	S[AE]	GO TO A[i]; A[i]	A-LABEL or S[AE] where S is the switch identifier and AE is an arithmetic expression.
GO TO	*go to* L;	*go to* 30;	L is a designational expression.
CONDITIONAL ARITHMETIC EXPRESSION	*if* A *then* B *else* C;	*if* a≠b *then* a:=b *else* a:=c;	Where A is an arithmetic comparison, B a conditional or unconditional arithmetic expression.
ARITHMETIC ASSIGNMENT STATEMENT	V:=A;	I:=J-4; A:=NAME(Y);	V=variable. A=arithmetic expression.
MULTIPLE ASSIGNMENT STATEMENT	$V_1:=V_3:=A$;	i:=j:=k:=x-4;	$v_1,v_2,v_3,....$are variable names of same type, A is an arithmetic expression.
FOR CLAUSE	*for* $v_i:=A$ *do* *for* $v:=A_1,A_2,A_3,.....$ $A_n do$	*for* a:=5,10,15,20 *do*	v is a variable (loop variable) and A is a list element. $A_1,A_2,....A_n$ are list elements.
FOR LIST ELEMENT	A *step* B *until* C A *while* D A		A,B,C are an arithmetic expression or number, or a series of arithmetic expressions or numbers separated by commas. D is an arithmetic comparison.

Statement	Form	Example	Comment
FOR STATEMENT	*for* V:= A *do* B; *for* V:= A₁, A₂,....Aₙ *do* B;	*for* j:=1,25,300 *do* A[i,j]:=B[j];	Where B is an unconditional statement.
IF CLAUSE	*if* A *then*	*if* a ≠ b *then*	A is an arithmetic comparison.
CONDITIONAL STATEMENT	*if* A *then* B; *if* A *then* B *else* C;	*if* a≠b *then* a:=b; *if* a≠b *then* a:=b *else* a:=c;	A is an arithmetic comparison; B, an unconditional statement; and C may be a conditional or unconditional statement.
READ STATEMENT	*read* a,b,c,....n;		Take the next n numbers from the input device and assign their value to the variables named, respectively.
PRINT STATEMENT	*print* a,b,c,....n;		Prints the next n numbers from the output device.
COMMENT			Any text between *comment* and the next semicolon that follows it is comment. Any text between *end* and the next semicolon or *end* or *else* that follows it is comment.
PROCEDURE DECLARATION	*procedure* A(B); *value* V;SP;S;		A is the name of the procedure; B is the list of formal parameters, each separated by a comma; V is a list of formal parameters, SP specifies the kinds and types of the formal parameters. S is the procedure body.
PROCEDURE CALL	P(A)		A is a list of the actual parameters, separated by commas.
REAL OR INTEGER PROCEDURE DECLARATION			As for procedure declarations, real or integer declaration must occur before the procedure declaration. The procedure identifier is itself used as a variable and the procedure body must contain an assignment statement which assigns a single numerical value (*real* or *integer*) to this variable.

APPENDIX B.3

Statement and Format Specification List of BASIC

Statement	Form	Example	Comments
LET	LET $v = f$	LET A(5)=B(5)=10	Assign the value of the expression f to the variable v.
READ	READ $v_1, v_2, \ldots, v_n$	READ A,B,C,N,X(N)	Variables v_1 through v_n are assigned the value of the corresponding numbers in the DATA string.
DATA	DATA $n_1, n_2, \ldots, n_n$	DATA 10,15,.25,'ABC'	Numbers n_1 through n_n are to be associated with corresponding variables in a READ statement.
PRINT	PRINT $a_1, a_2, \ldots, a_n$	PRINT 'A =' A,SQRT(X)	Print out the values of the specified arguments. These arguments may be variables, text, or formatted control characters.
GOTO	GOTO n	GOTO 10	Transfer control to line n and continue execution from there.
IF-GOTO	IF f_1 r f_2 GOTO n	IF A3>X+2 GOTO 100	If the relationship r between the expressions f_1 and f_2 is true then transfer control to line n; if not, continue the execution in the regular sequence.
IF-THEN	IF f_1 r f_2 THEN n	IF A3>X+2 THEN 100	Same as IF-GOTO
FOR-TO	FOR $v = f_1$ TO f_2 STEP f_3	FOR J=100 TO 1 STEP=3	Used to implement loops; the variable v is set equal to the expression f_1. From this point the loop cycle is completed following which v is incremented after each cycle by f_3 until its value is greater than or equal to f_2. If STEP f_3 is omitted, f_3 is assumed to be a one.
NEXT	NEXT v	NEXT I	Used to tell the compiler to return to the FOR statement and execute the loop again, until v is greater than or equal to f_2.
DIM	DIM $v(s)$ DIM $v(s_1, s_2)$	DIM A(5),B(100,2)	Enables the user to create a table or array with the specified number of elements where v is the variable name and s is the maximum subscript value any number of arrays can be dimensioned in a single DIM statement.

Statement	Form	Example	Comments
GOSUB	GOSUB n	GOSUB 230	Permits the user to enter a subroutine at several points in the program. Control transfers to line n.
RETURN	RETURN	RETURN	Must be at the end of each subroutine to enable control to be transferred to the statement following the last GOSUB.
INPUT	INPUT $v_1, v_2, \ldots, v_n$	INPUT 10,20,.25,'ABC'	Causes typeout of A ? to the user. Waits for the user to supply the values of the variables $v_1, v_2, \ldots, v_n$.
REM	REM	100 REM 200 REM	When typed as the first three letters of a line allows typing of remarks within the program.
RESTORE	RESTORE	RESTORE	Sets pointer back to the beginning of the string of DATA values.
STOP	STOP	STOP	Equivalent to transferring control to the END statement.
DEF	DEF FNB(x) = f(x) DEF FNB(x,y) = f(x,y)	10 DEF FNA(X) = SIN(X) . . 50 PRINT FNA(7)	The user may define his own functions to be called within his program by putting a DEF statement at the beginning of a program. The function name begins with FN and must have three letters. The function is then equated to an expression $f(x)$ which must be only one line long. Multiple variable function definitions are allowed.
END	END	END	Last statement in every program, signals completions of the program.

APPENDIX C

BCD and ASCII Character Set

MSB\LSB	0	1	2	3	4	5	6	7	8	9	A	B	C	D	E	F
0	NUL	SOH	STX	ETX	EOT	ENQ	ACK	BEL	BS	HT	LF	VT	FF	CR	SO	SI
1	DLE	DC1	DC2	DC3	DC4	NAK	SYN	ETB	CAN	EM	SUB	ESC	FS	GS	RS	US
2	SP	!	"	#	$	%	&	'	(	)	*	+	,	-	.	/
3	0	1	2	3	4	5	6	7	8	9	:	;	<	=	>	?
4	@	A	B	C	D	E	F	G	H	I	J	K	L	M	N	O
5	P	Q	R	S	T	U	V	W	X	Y	Z	[	\	]	↑	←
6	`	a	b	c	d	e	f	g	h	i	j	k	l	m	n	o
7	p	q	r	s	t	u	v	w	x	y	z	{			}	~	DEL

AMERICAN STANDARD CODE FOR INFORMATION INTERCHANGE (ASCII)

For example, the letter "A" is HEX 41 and the character "(" is HEX 28. (Read MSB/LSB) the entries 00 through 1F and 20 and 7F are nonprinting. In some devices, rows 6 and 7 are printed as if they were rows 4 and 5. The entries shown are without parity, that is, without the high order bit set for either even or odd parity.

Number and Code Comparisons

8-Bit Binary	Decimal	HEX	BCD	EBCDIC	ASCII
0000 0000	0	00		NUL	NUL
0000 0001	1	01		SOH	SOH
0000 0010	2	02		STX	STX
0000 0011	3	03		ETX	ETX
0000 0100	4	04		PF	EOT
0000 0101	5	05		HT	ENQ
0000 0110	6	06		LC	ACK
0000 0111	7	07		DEL	BEL
0000 1000	8	08			BS
0000 1001	9	09			HT
0000 1010	10	0A		SMM	LF
0000 1011	11	0B		VT	VT
0000 1100	12	0C		FF	FF
0000 1101	13	0D		CR	CR
0000 1110	14	0E		SO	SO
0000 1111	15	0F		SI	SI
0001 0000	16	10		DLE	DLE
0001 0001	17	11		DC1	DC1
0001 0010	18	12		DC2	DC2
0001 0011	19	13		TM	DC3
0001 0100	20	14		RES	DC4
0001 0101	21	15		NL	NAK
0001 0110	22	16		BS	SYN
0001 0111	23	17		IL	ETB
0001 1000	24	18		CAN	CAN
0001 1001	25	19		EM	EM
0001 1010	26	1A		CC	SUB
0001 1011	27	1B		CU1	ESC
0001 1100	28	1C		IFS	FS
0001 1101	29	1D		IGS	GS
0001 1110	30	1E		IRS	RS
0001 1111	31	1F		IUS	US
0010 0000	32	20		DS	SP
0010 0001	33	21		SOS	!
0010 0010	34	22		FS	"
0010 0011	35	23			#
0010 0100	36	24		BYP	$
0010 0101	37	25		LF	%
0010 0110	38	26		ETB	&
0010 0111	39	27		ESC	'
0010 1000	40	28			(
0010 1001	41	29			)
0010 1010	42	2A		SM	*
0010 1011	43	2B		CU2	+
0010 1100	44	2C			,
0010 1101	45	2D		ENQ	-
0010 1110	46	2E		ACK	.

345

Number and Code Comparisons (Continued)

8-Bit Binary	Decimal	HEX	BCD	EBCDIC	ASCII
0010 1111	47	2F		BEL	/
0011 0000	48	3Ø			Ø
0011 0001	49	31			1
0011 0010	50	32		SYN	2
0011 0011	51	33			3
0011 0100	52	34		PN	4
0011 0101	53	35		RS	5
0011 0110	54	36		UC	6
0011 0111	55	37		EOT	7
0011 1000	56	38			8
0011 1001	57	39			9
0011 1010	58	3A			:
0011 1011	59	3B		CU3	;
0011 1100	6Ø	3C		DC4	<
0011 1101	61	3D		NAK	=
0011 1110	62	3E			>
0011 1111	63	3F		SUB	?
0100 0000	64	4Ø		SP	@
0100 0001	65	41			A
0100 0010	66	42			B
0100 0011	67	43			C
0100 0100	68	44			D
0100 0101	69	45			E
0100 0110	70	46			F
0100 0111	71	47			G
0100 1000	72	48			H
0100 1001	73	49			I
0100 1010	74	4A		¢	J
0100 1011	75	4B		.	K
0100 1100	76	4C	□)	<	L
0100 1101	77	4D	[	(	M
0100 1110	78	4E	<	+	N
0100 1111	79	4F	≢	|	O
0101 0000	8Ø	5Ø	&+	&	P
0101 0001	81	51			Q
0101 0010	82	52			R
0101 0011	83	53			S
0101 0100	84	54			T
0101 0101	85	55			U
0101 0110	86	56			V
0101 0111	87	57			W
0101 1000	88	58			X
0101 1001	89	59			Y
0101 1010	9Ø	5A		!	Z
0101 1011	91	5B	$	$	[

Number and Code Comparisons (Continued)

8-Bit Binary	Decimal	HEX	BCD	EBCDIC	ASCII
0101 1100	92	5C	*	*	\
0101 1101	93	5D	]	)	]
0101 1110	94	5E	;	;	↑
0101 1111	95	5F	△	¬	→
0110 0000	96	6∅	-	-	`
0110 0001	97	61	/	/	a
0110 0010	98	62			b
0110 0011	99	63			c
0110 0100	1∅∅	64			d
0110 0101	1∅1	65			e
0110 0110	1∅2	66			f
0110 0111	1∅3	67			g
0110 1000	1∅4	68			h
0110 1001	1∅5	69			i
0110 1010	1∅6	6A			j
0110 1011	1∅7	6B	,	,	k
0110 1100	1∅8	6C	%(	%	l
0110 1101	1∅9	6D	γ	—	m
0110 1110	11∅	6E	\	>	n
0110 1111	111	6F	⧸⧸⧸	?	o
0111 0000	112	7∅			p
0111 0001	113	71			q
0111 0010	114	72			r
0111 0011	115	73			s
0111 0100	116	74			t
0111 0101	117	75			u
0111 0110	118	76			v
0111 0111	119	77			w
0111 1000	12∅	78			x
0111 1001	121	79			y
0111 1010	122	7A	₺	:	z
0111 1011	123	7B	#=	#	(
0111 1100	124	7C	@'	@	{
0111 1101	125	7D	:	'	}
0111 1110	126	7E	>	=	-
0111 1111	127	7F	~	"	DEL
1000 0000	128	8∅			
1000 0001	129	81		a	
1000 0010	13∅	82		b	
1000 0011	131	83		c	
1000 0100	132	84		d	
1000 0101	133	85		e	
1000 0110	134	86		f	
1000 0111	135	87		g	

Number and Code Comparisons (Continued)

8-Bit Binary	Decimal	HEX	BCD	EBCDIC	ASCII
1000 1000	136	88		h	
1000 1001	137	89		i	
1000 1010	138	8A			
1000 1011	139	8B			
1000 1100	14Ø	8C			
1000 1101	141	8D			
1000 1110	142	8E			
1000 1111	143	8F			
1001 0000	144	9Ø			
1001 0001	145	91		j	
1001 0010	146	92		k	
1001 0011	147	93		l	
1001 0100	148	94		m	
1001 0101	149	95		n	
1001 0110	15Ø	96		o	
1001 0111	151	97		p	
1001 1000	152	98		q	
1001 1001	153	99		r	
1001 1010	154	9A			
1001 1011	155	9B			
1001 1100	156	9C			
1001 1101	157	9D			
1001 1110	158	9E			
1001 1111	159	9F			
1010 0000	16Ø	A0			
1010 0001	161	A1			
1010 0010	162	A2		s	
1010 0011	163	A3		t	
1010 0100	164	A4		u	
1010 0101	165	A5		v	
1010 0110	166	A6		w	
1010 0111	167	A7		x	
1010 1000	168	A8		y	
1010 1001	169	A9		z	
1010 1010	17Ø	AA			
1010 1011	171	AB			
1010 1100	172	AC			
1010 1101	173	AD			
1010 1110	174	AE			
1010 1111	175	AF			
1011 0000	176	BØ			
1011 0010	177	B1			
1011 0010	178	B2			
1011 0011	179	B3			
1011 0100	18Ø	B4			

Number and Code Comparisons (Continued)

8-Bit Binary	Decimal	HEX	BCD	EBCDIC	ASCII
1011 0101	181	B5			
1011 0110	182	B6			
1011 0111	183	B7			
1011 1000	184	B8			
1011 1001	185	B9			
1011 1010	186	BA			
1011 1011	187	BB			
1011 1100	188	BC			
1011 1101	189	BD			
1011 1110	19Ø	BE			
1011 1111	191	BF			
1100 0000	192	CØ	?		
1100 0001	193	C1	A	A	
1100 0010	194	C2	B	B	
1100 0011	195	C3	C	C	
1100 0100	196	C4	D	D	
1100 0101	197	C5	E	E	
1100 0110	198	C6	F	F	
1100 0111	199	C7	G	G	
1100 1000	2ØØ	C8	H	H	
1100 1001	2Ø1	C9	I	I	
1100 1010	2Ø2	CA			
1100 1011	2Ø3	CB			
1100 1100	2Ø4	CC			
1100 1101	2Ø5	CD			
1100 1110	2Ø6	CE			
1100 1111	2Ø7	CF			
1101 0000	2Ø8	DØ	!		
1101 0001	2Ø9	D1	J	J	
1101 0010	21Ø	D2	K	K	
1101 0011	211	D3	L	L	
1101 0100	212	D4	M	M	
1101 0101	213	D5	N	N	
1101 0110	214	D6	O	O	
1101 0111	215	D7	P	P	
1101 1000	216	D8	Q	Q	
1101 1001	217	D9	R	R	
1101 1010	218	DA			
1101 1011	219	DB			
1101 1100	220	DC			
1101 1101	221	DD			
1101 1110	222	DE			
1101 1111	223	DF			
1110 0000	224	EØ	∓		
1110 0001	225	E1			

Number and Code Comparisons (Continued)

8-Bit Binary	Decimal	HEX	BCD	EBCDIC	ASCII
1110 0010	226	E2	S	S	
1110 0011	227	E3	T	T	
1110 0100	228	E4	U	U	
1110 0101	229	E5	V	V	
1110 0110	23Ø	E6	W	W	
1110 0111	231	E7	X	X	
1110 1000	232	E8	Y	Y	
1110 1001	233	E9	Z	Z	
1110 1010	234	EA			
1110 1011	235	EB			
1110 1100	236	EC			
1110 1101	237	ED			
1110 1110	238	EE			
1110 1111	239	EF			
1111 0000	24Ø	FØ	Ø	Ø	
1111 0001	241	F1	1	1	
1111 0010	242	F2	2	2	
1111 0011	243	F3	3	3	
1111 0100	244	F4	4	4	
1111 0101	245	F5	5	5	
1111 0110	246	F6	6	6	
1111 0111	247	F7	7	7	
1111 1000	248	F8	8	8	
1111 1001	249	F9	9	9	
1111 1010	25Ø	FA			
1111 1011	251	FB			
1111 1100	252	FC			
1111 1101	253	FD			
1111 1110	254	FE			
1111 1111	255	FF			

APPENDIX D

Glossary of Terms

A

Abend: Abnormal end (termination)

Access Time: Refers to the amount of time required to reach a specific record located on some auxillary memory device.

Accumulator: A general-purpose register that can perform all functions within the computer instruction set.

Adder: A device that forms as an output, the sum of two or more numbers presented as inputs. These may be organized as bit, binary, serial, or parallel.

Address: A character or group of characters that identifies a register, a particular part of storage, or some other data source or destination.

ALGOL: ALGOrithmic Language.

Application Program: A program written to accomplish a specific task as opposed to supervisory, general purpose, or utility program.

Architecture: A term commonly used to denote the organization, design, and interconnection of components of digital computers.

Arithmetic and Logic Unit: The CPU chip logic that actually executed the operations requested by an inputted command.

ASCII American Standard Code for Information Interchange.

ASR/KSR: Automatic Send Receive/Keyboard Send Receive.

Assembler: A translator that converts symbolically represented instructions into their binary equivalents.

Auxillary Memory: Memory not under direct control of the central processing unit. Synonymous with auxillary memory.

B

Background: The automatic execution of lower priority programs or procedures when higher priority programs are not using the system resources. Contrast with foreground.

Base: Refers to the radix of a number system.
   Refers to the control grid in a vacuum tube.
   Refers to the support material on a printed circuit board upon which the pattern is placed.

BASIC: Beginners All-Purpose Instruction Code developed by Dartmouth College.

Benchmark: A program or set of routines used to test the performance of a computer system.

Bidirectional: Generally refers to interface ports or bus lines that can be used to transfer data in either direction, e.g. to or from a minicomputer.

Binary: A characteristic property, or condition in which there are but two possible alternatives.

Bit: Abbreviation for binary digit. Most commonly a unit of information equalling one binary decision, or the designation of one of two possible and equally likely values or states.

BSS: Basic System Support

Buffer: A device designed to be inserted between some other machines or program elements to match impedances, peripheral equipment speeds, and to prevent mixed interactions.

Buffer Storage: An input device in which information is assembled from external or secondary storage and stored ready for transfer to internal storage.

Bus: One or more conductors used as a path over which information is transmitted. A bus may interconnect many sources to many destinations.

Byte: An IBM-developed term used to indicate a specific number of consecutive bits treated as a single entity. A byte is most often considered to consist of eight bits, which as a unit, can represent one character or two numerals.

C

Card Reader: A typical computer input device that accepts punched cards containing computer instructions, data, or system control language.

Carry: Refers to the signal or expression which may arise when the sum of two digits in the same place equals or exceeds the base of the number system being used.

Central Processing Unit (CPU): A unit of a computer that includes the circuits controlling the interpretation and execution of instructions.

*CMOS: C*omplementary *M*etal-*O*xide *S*emiconductor

*COBOL: CO*mmon *B*usiness *O*riented *L*anguage. A data processing language that makes use of English-like language statements.

Compiler: A computer coding system that generates and assembles an assembly program from instructions written in some high-level language.

Complement: A number which is derived from the finite positional notation of another by one of the following rules:
  a. True complement
  b. Ones complement

Controller: An element or group of elements that operates automatically to regulate a controlled device, variable, or system.

Control Lines: Refers to those lines that perform control functions such as flag, sense, enable, INTA, OPREQ, etc. These may either emanate from or input to a computer.

Control Unit: That component of a digital computer which directs the sequence of operations, interrupts, coded instructions, and sends the proper signals to other computer components and circuits to carry out the instructions.

*CPM: C*ards *P*er *M*inute
        *C*ritical *P*ath *M*ethod

Cycle Stealing: The ability to delay the execution of a program some specified amount of time during which some other function is accomplished.

D

Daisy Chain: An organization of bus lines and devices such that the signal passes from one unit to the next in serial fashion.

Data: A general term used to denote any or all facts, numbers, letters, and symbols that can be processed or produced by a computer.

Data Channels: Refer to memory addressed space that is used to hold data to be used by some I/O device. These spaces require a unique address, some data pattern or bit string, and some form of control, usually called a DMA controller.

Debugging: The process of isolating and removing unwanted errors from a computer program.

Dedicated Processor: A processor that performs one and only one set of functions.

Destructive Memory: Refers to memory material and design that changes (destroys) its contents when read (usually magnetic core). Contrast with nondestructive.

Digital: Refers to the use of discrete integral numbers in a given base to represent all the quantities that occur in a problem or calculation.

Disk: A computer auxillary memory device capable of storing information magnetically. Similar in appearance to a phonograph record. Disc is an alternative spelling.

*DMA: D*irect *M*emory *A*ccess. Sometimes called data break. This is the preferred form of data transfer for use with high-speed devices. Causes transfer directly from a device to memory.

Dynamic RAM: Data is stored capacitively, and must be recharged (refreshed) periodically or it will be lost.

E

EBCDIC Code: An acronym for *E*xtended *B*inary *C*oded *D*ecimal *I*nterchange *C*ode.

Editor: A general-purpose text editing program used to produce or prepare source programs.

Effective Address: Refers to the final computed address of the next instruction or data to be fetched. The effective address is computed utilizing the base address, indexing value, displacement, etc. as appropriate.

*EIA: E*lectronic *I*ndustries *A*ssociation

Emulate: A procedure designed to initiate one system with another. Contrast with simulate.

Enabled: Refers to a state of the central processing unit that allows the occurrence of certain types of interruptions.

Enable Signal: Refers to that signal that conditions some device to either accept data or to write data off the data bus. The enable signal normally takes the device out of the tri-state condition.

Exponent: Refers to the power value to which a number is to be raised.

F

Fetch: A particular portion of a computer cycle during which the location of the next instruction is determined. The fetch may consist of only an operation code from which other fetches may be necessary.

Fixed-Point Arithmetic: A method of calculation in which operations take place in an invariant manner, and in which the computer does not consider the location of the radix point.

Flag: Refers to a bit used to store one bit of information.

Flip-Flop: A circuit device having two stable states with usually two input terminals corresponding to each of the two states. Usually acts as a temporary storage device (latch).

Floating-Point Arithmetic: Arithmetic used in a computer where the computer keeps track of the decimal point, exponent, etc.

Flowchart: A programmer tool for determining a sequence of operations as charted using sets of symbols, directional marks, and other representations to indicate stepped procedures of computer operations.

Foreground: Refers to the environment in which high priority programs are executed. All command processor programs operate in foreground.

*FORTRAN: FOR*mula *TRAN*slator. A computer programming language.

Front End: Refers to minor processors that are used to interface to a host data processing system.

Full Adder: Perform full addition which includes both sum and carry out of one position into the next higher bit position.

G

Garbage: A slang computer term for unwanted and meaningless information carried in memory or storage.

Gate: A circuit having one output and several inputs. The output remains unenergized until certain input conditions are met.

H

Half Adder: Refers to a circuit with two input and two output channels for binary signals. Compare with full adder.

Handshaking: A descriptive term often used interchangeably with buffering or interfacing, implying a direct connection or matching of specific units or programs. Refers also to the exchange of predetermined signals when a connection is established between two data set devices.

Hardware: Refers to the "hard" or metallic components of a computer system in contrast to the "soft" or programming components.

Hardwire Logic: Refers to logic designs for control or problem solutions that require interconnection of numerous integrated circuits formed or wired for specific purposes and relatively unalterable.

Heuristic: Pertaining to exploratory methods of problem solution in which solutions are discovered.

Hexadecimal: A positional numbering system using 16 as the radix.

*HLLT: H*igh-*L*evel *L*anguage *T*ranslator.

I

*IC: I*ntegrated *C*ircuit refers to sets of discrete circuit components fabricated onto a single piece of substance called a chip. The integrated circuit is fabricated into three major categories:

   a. *SSI: S*mall-*S*cale *I*ntegration, refers to circuits containing 12 gates or less.

   b. *MSI: M*edium-*S*cale *I*ntegration, refers to circuits having more than 12 gates and less than 100 gates.

   c. *LSI: L*arge-*S*cale *I*ntegration, refers to circuits having more than 100 gates per chip.

*IEEE: I*nstitute of *E*lectrical and *E*lectronics *E*ngineers.

Index: A technique for addressing modification that is often implemented by means of index registers.

Index Register: A register designed to modify the operand address by addition or subtraction, yielding a new effective address.

Indirection: Refers to the procedure of addressing a memory location that contains the address of data rather than the data itself.

Information Bit: The fundamental unit of measurement for information.

Instruction: Information that, when properly coded and introduced as a unit into a digital computer, causes the computer to perform one or more of its operations.

Instruction Cycle: The amount of time required to

execute a program instruction and then be prepared for the next instruction.

Instruction Format: Refers to the organization of the bit pattern of each instruction presented to the computer.

Instruction Register: A register that is used to hold the instruction currently being executed.

Instruction Set: Refers to the total structured group of characters recognized by the computer and upon which the computer will perform specified actions.

Integer: Refers to a number in which there is no radix point or exponent modifier.

Interface: Refers to the specifications of the interconnection between two systems or units.

Interpreter: An interpreter is a program that operates directly on a source program in memory. The interpreter transfers the instructions of the source program one by one, as encountered, and executes them immediately.

Interrupt: Refers to the suspension of normal operations in favor of some other occasional routine, such as I/O.

J

JCL: Job Control Language

Job: Usually refers to an externally specified unit of work for the computing system. A job may consist of one or more job steps.

K

Kilo: One thousand.

KSR: Keyboard Send/Receive. A combination teletypewriter transmitter and receiver with transmission capability from keyboard only.

L

Language Interpreter: A general term for any processor, assembler that accepts statements in one language and produces equivalent statements in another language.

Library: Refers to a collection of standard and proven routines and subroutines by which problems and/or parts of problems may be solved.

Line Printer: A type of high-speed printer capable of producing an entire line at a time.

Link Bit: Refers to a specific one-bit diagnostic register which contains an indicator for overflow from the accumulator.

Linking Loader: Allows users to load and execute programs anywhere in memory.

Loader: A program that operates as or on input devices to transfer information from offline memory to online memory.

Load Signal: The control signal that signifies that a loading operation is to take place.

Logic: The systematic scheme that defines the interactions of signals in the design of an automatic data processing system.

Loop: A self-contained series of instructions in which the last instruction can modify and repeat itself until a terminal condition is reached.

LSI: Large-Scale Integration refers to a component density of more than 100 active elements per chip, usually, LSI implies the grouping of more than one function (e.g., microinstruction decode, control, registers) into a single piece of real estate.

M

Macro: Refers to code that is translated prior to the assembly process. This code is then inserted into the main body code upon each call for the macro code.

Mantissa: Refers to the string of significant digits with its sign and decimal point on the left of the floating point number.

MAR: Memory Address Register.

Mask: Refers to a machine word that specifies which parts of another machine word are to be operated on.

Master Clock: The primary source of timing signals. Used to control the timing of pulses.

Matrix: A rectangular array of data or information.

MDR: Memory Data Register.

Memory: The main storage media for a computer and one of the main components of a computer.

Memory Cycle: A computer operation consisting of reading from and writing into memory. The time required to complete the process.

Memory Cycle Times: With respect to memory cycle times, we can speak of access time and cycle time. Access time is the time required to read out randomly selected word from memory. Cycle time is the minimum time interval required between the initiation of two successive, independent, memory operations.

Memory Mapped I/O: Refers to the fixing of a specific address in memory to be utilized as an I/O port.

Memory Project: Refers to that technique of protecting sections of memory selectively from destruction or modification.

Microcomputer: A general term referring to a complete computing system, consisting of hardware and software whose main processing blocks are made of semiconductor integrated circuits.

Microinstruction: A bit pattern that is stored in a microprogram memory word and specifies the operation of the individual LSI computing elements and related subunits, such as main memory and input/output interfaces.

Microprogram: A program of analytic instructions which the programmer intends to construct from the basic subcommands of a digital computer.

Microsecond: A measurement of time equivalent to 10^{-6} seconds.

Millisecond: A measure of time equivalent to 10^{-3} seconds.

Minicomputer: Characterized generally by higher performance than microcomputers, richer instruction sets, high level languages, etc.

Mnemonic: Refers to the technique to assist the programmer, usually in the form of symbolic characters.

MSI: *M*edium *S*cale *I*ntegration.

N

NAND: Abbreviation for not; logical gate.

Nanosecond: A measurement of time equivalent to 10^{-9} seconds.

Nibble: An IBM-coined term referring to 4 bits of any byte.

NMOS: *N*-channel MOS circuit use currents made up of negative charges.

NOR: NOT or circuit. Circuit has an output when all inputs are down.

NOT: A logic operator having the property of inversion or negation.

O

OCTAL: A numbering system using 8 as the radix.

Opcode: Operation Code. That code decoded which instructs the computer what operation to perform.

Operand: The fundamental quantity upon which an operation is performed.

Operating System (OS): A basic group of programs with operation under control of the Data Processing Execution or monitor program.

Overhead: Pertains to the distribution of operating time of the checking, monitoring, scheduling, etc. portions of the executive system over all jobs or tasks related to the total cost of the complete system.

P

Parity Bit: Refers to a bit used to check that data has been transmitted correctly and accurately.

Page: The subdivision of a program that can be moved into or out of memory by an operating system or hardware device.

Peripheral: Refers to I/O and other devices not under direct control of the computer.

PERT: *P*rogram *E*valuation *R*eview *T*echnique

Polling: Refers to the technique by which each of the terminals having a communications line is periodically interrogated to determine whether it requires service.

Port: A place of access to a system or circuit. Usually related to input or output. Entrance to memory.

Precision: Refers to the number of base digits contained in the mantissa.

Priority Assignments: Refers to the assignments of references of one media or device over another. Mostly this type of requirement stems from the requirement to allocate resources in an effective and efficient manner.

Priority Interrupt: Refers to the capability to give precedence relationships to different I/O devices, such that high priority devices receive preferential treatment.

Program: A set of instructions arranged in the proper sequence for directing a digital computer in performing a desired job.

Program Counter: Contains the address of the next instruction byte or word to be fetched from memory.

Program Interrupt: The program interrupt system may be used to initiate programmed data transfers in such a way that the time spent waiting for device status is greatly reduced.

PROM: *P*rogrammable *R*ead *O*nly *M*emory.

Protocol: Essentially a set of conventions between communicating processes on the format and content of messages to be exchanged.

R

RAM: Random Access Memory.

Random Access: Access to a computer storage under conditions whereby there is no rule for predetermining the position from where the next item of information is to be obtained.

Real-Time: Refers to the solution of a problem in sufficient time to respond within the problem time.

Relocation: Refers to the ability to move code or data into or out of memory or within memory.

ROM: Read Only Memory.

Rotate: Refers to the process of moving in a circular manner each bit in a register either right or left.

RS-232-C: Recommended Standard 232 (Version C). Refers to a serial communications transfer bus.

S

Scratch Pad: A nickname for CPU memory. It pertains to information that the CPU holds only temporarily.

Shift: A displacement of an ordered set of computer characters one or more places to the right or left.

Single Phase: Refers to ac power supplies, in which one outward and one return conductor are required for transmission.

Software: The term invented to distinguish computer programs, etc. from the hardware components required for the computer.

Stack: Generally a block of contiguous memory locations that are accessible only from one end.

Strobe: General term for detailed examination of a designated phase or epoch of a recurring waveform or phenomenon.

SSI: Small-Scale Integration

Symbol: A letter representing a particular quantity. May be a label, address, value, etc.

Symbolic Address: A character pattern that, when translated, defines an address.

T

Tape Drive: A mechanism for controlling the movement of magnetic tape.

Tape Operating System (TOS): An operating system for smaller systems without any disk drives.

Time Sharing: A technique by which many users may share the same system simultaneously.

Translate: To change computer information from one language to another without significantly changing the meaning.

Trap: A programmed or unprogrammed (Abend) conditional jump to some known location.

TSO: Time Sharing Option.

TTL: Transistor-Transistor Logic.

TTY: TeleTYpewriter.

Twos Complement: Refers to the method of representation of binary bit pattern numbers. Positive numbers are represented as normal, but negative numbers are represented using the reverse pattern plus 1.

U

UART: Universal Asynchronous Receiver Transmitter

USART: Universal Synchronous/Asynchronous Receiver Transmitter

Utility Programs: Refers to programs or routines that may be used by many programs (systems and application). These are usually of a general nature.

V

Vector: The term for a symbol which denotes a directed quantity

Vectored Priority Interrupt: An Interrupt Control Unit (ICU)-implements eight levels of vectored priority interrupt.

Vendor: Refers to the manufacturer of equipment of software.

W

Word: A group of characters occupying one storage location in a computer.

APPENDIX E

Frequently Used Acronyms

AC—Accumulator
A/D—Analog-to-Digital Converter
AI—Address Information
ALU—Arithmetic and Logic Unit

BCD—Binary Coded Decimal

CMOS—Complementary Metal-Oxide Semiconductor
CSAR—Control Storage Address Register
CSDR—Control Storage Data Register
CPU—Central Processing Unit
CRT—Cathode Ray Tube
CU—Control Unit

D/A—Digital-to-Analog Converter
DMA—Direct Memory Access

EA—Effective Address

FA—Full Adder

HLLT—High Level Language Translation
HOB—High-Order Bit

IC—Integrated Circuit
I/O—Input/Output
IOU—Input/Output Unit
IR—Instruction Register

LOB—Low-Order Bit
LSI—Large-Scale Integration

MAR—Memory Address Register
MC—Microcommand
MCU—Microprogrammed Control Unit

MDR—Memory Data Register
MI—Microinstruction
ML—Machine Language
MLC—Microprogrammed Location Counter
MOS—Metal Oxide Semiconductor
MP—Microprogram
MPAR—Microprogram Address Register
MPC—Microprogrammed Program Counter
MIR—Microinstruction Register
MRI—Memory Reference Instruction
MSI—Medium-Scale Integration
MU—Memory Unit

NMOS—N Channel Metal-Oxide Semiconductor

PC—Program Counter
PMOS—P Channel Metal-Oxide Semiconductor
pROM—Programmable Read-Only Memory

RAM—Random Access Memory
ROM—Read-Only Memory

SOS—Silicon On Sapphire
SSI—Small-Scale Integration

TTY—Teletypewriter

VLSI—Very-Large-Scale Integration

APPENDIX F

Bibliography

Altman, L., (Ed.), Electronics Book Series, *Micro Processors,* McGraw-Hill, Inc., New York, NY, 1975.

Barden, W., Jr., *How to Buy and Use Minicomputers and Microcomputers,* Howard W. Sams & Co., Inc., Indianapolis, IN, 1976.

Barna, A. and D. I. Porat, *Introduction to Microcomputers and Microprocessors,* John Wiley & Sons, New York, NY, 1976.

Bell, C. G., J. Grason, A. Newell, *Designing Computers and Digital Systems,* Digital Press, Digital Equipment Corporation, Maynard, MA, 1972.

Bibbero, R. J., *Microprocessors in Instruments and Control,* John Wiley & Sons, New York, NY, 1977.

Booth, T. L., *Digital Networks and Computer Systems,* John Wiley & Sons, Inc., New York, NY, 1971.

Burton, D. P., and A. L. Dexter, *Microprocessor Systems Handbook,* Analog Devices, Inc., Norwood, MA, 1977.

Chattergy, R. and U. W. Pooch (Eds.), *Microprocessors, Microprogramming and Minicomputers,* Western Periodicals Company, North Hollywood, CA, 1977.

Cohn, D. L. and J. L. Melsa, *A Step by Step Introduction to 8080 Microprocessor Systems,* Dilithium Press, Forest Grove, OR, 1977.

Data General Corporation, *How to Use the Nova Computers,* Data General Corp., Southboro, MA, 1972.

Digital Equipment Corporation, *Small Computer Handbook,* Digital Equipment Corp., Maynard, MA, 1972.

Digital Equipment Corporation, *Introduction to Programming,* Digital Equipment Corp., Maynard, MA, 1973.

Digital Equipment Corporation, *OS/8 Handbook,* Digital Equipment Corp., Maynard, MA, 1974.

Digital Equipment Corporation, *PDP-11 Processor Handbook,* Digital Equipment Corp., Maynard, MA, 1976.

Digital Equipment Corporation, *Microcomputer Handbook,* Maynard, MA, 1977.

Eckhouse, R. H., Jr., *Minicomputer Systems: Organization and Programming (PDP-11),* Prentice-Hall, Englewood Cliffs, NJ, 1975.

Foster, C. C., *Programming a Microcomputer: 6502,* Addison-Wesley Publishing Co., Reading, MA, 1978.

General Automation, Inc., *The Value of Micropower—A Microcomputer Handbook,* Anaheim, CA, 1974.

Graham, N., *Microprocessor Programming for Computer Hobbyists,* Tab Books, Blue Ridge Summit, PA, 1977.

Gruenberger, F. and D. Babcock, *Computing with Minicomputers,* Melville Publishing Co., Los Angeles, CA, 1973.

Hewlett-Packard, *A Pocket Guide to Interfacing HP Computers,* Hewlett-Packard, Palo Alto, CA, 1969.

Hewlett-Packard, *A Pocket Guide to Hewlett-Packard Computers,* Hewlett-Packard, Palo Alto, CA, 1970.

Hilburn, J. L. and P. N. Julich, *Microcomputers/Microprocessors: Hardware, Software and Applications,* Prentice-Hall, Inc., Englewood Cliffs, NJ, 1976.

Katzan, H., Jr., *Microprogramming Primer,* McGraw-Hill Book Co., New York, NY, 1977.

Kligman, E. E., *Microprocessor Systems Design,* Prentice-Hall, Inc., Englewood Cliffs, NJ, 1977.

Korn, G. A., *Minicomputers for Engineers and Scientists,* McGraw-Hill Book Co., New York, NY, 1973.

Leventhal, L. A., *8080A/8085 Assembly Language Programming,* Osborne & Associates, Inc., Berkeley, CA, 1978.

Lewis, T. G. and M. Z. Smith, *Applying Data Structures,* Houghton Mifflin Co., Boston, MA, 1976.

Lewis, T. G. and J. W. Doerr, *Minicomputers: Structure & Programming,* Hayden Book Company, Inc., Rochelle Park, NJ, 1976.

McMurran, M. W., *Programming Microprocessors,* Tab Books, Blue Ridge Summit, PA, 1977.

Microdata, *Microprogramming Handbook,* Microdata Corp., Santa Ana, CA, 1971.

Osborne, A., *An Introduction to Microcomputers—Vol. 1. Basic Concepts,* Adam Osborne and Associates, Inc., Berkeley, CA, 1976.

Osborne, A., *An Introduction to Microcomputers—Vol II. Some Real Products,* Adam Osborne and Associates, Inc., Berkeley, CA, 1976.

Osborne, A., *8080 Programming for Logic Design,* Osborne and Associates, Inc., Berkeley, CA, 1976.

Osborne, A., *An Introduction to Microcomputers—Volume 0—The Beginner's Book,* Osborne and Associates, Inc., Berkeley, CA, 1977.

Osborne, A., *An Introduction to Microcomputers—Volume II—Some Real Products* (1977 Revision), Osborne and Associates, Inc., Berkeley, CA, 1977.

Osborne, A., J. Kane, R. Rector, S. Jacobson, *Z-80 Programming for Logic Design,* Osborne and Associates, Inc., Berkeley, CA, 1978.

Osborne, A., *6800 Programming for Logic Design,* Osborne and Associates, Inc., Berkeley, CA, 1977.

Pooch, U. W. and R. Chattergy, *Design of Microcomputer Systems for Engineers and Hobbyists,* Hayden Book Company, Inc., Rochelle Park, NJ, 1979.

Sippl, C. J., *Microcomputer—Dictionary and Guide,* Matrix Publishers, Inc., Champagne, IL, 1976.

Sloan, M. E., *Computer Hardware and Organization,* Science Research Associates, Inc., Palo Alto, CA, 1976.

Souček, B., *Minicomputers in Data Processing and Simulation,* Wiley-Interscience, New York, NY, 1972.

Souček, B., *Microprocessors and Microcomputers,* John Wiley & Sons, New York, NY, 1976.

Stone, H. S. and D. P. Siewiorek, *Introduction to Computer Organization and Data Structures: PDP-11 Edition,* McGraw Hill, New York, NY, 1975.

Tanenbaum, A. S., *Structured Computer Organization,* Prentice-Hall, Inc., Englewood Cliffs, NJ, 1976.

Texas Instruments, Inc., *Microprocessor Handbook,* TI Learning Center, Texas Instruments, Inc., Dallas, TX, 1975.

Texas Instruments, Inc., *990 Computer Family Systems Handbook,* Texas Instruments, Inc., Dallas, TX, 1975.

Torrero, E. A. (Ed.), *Microprocessors—New Directions for Designers,* Hayden Book Company, Inc., Rochelle Park, NJ, 1975.

Varian Data Machines, *Varian 620/L Computer Handbook,* Varian Data Machines, Irvine, CA, 1971.

Ward, B., *Microprocessor/Microprogramming Handbook,* Tab Books, Blue Ridge Summit, PA, 1975.

Weitzman, C., *Minicomputer Systems: Structure, Implementation and Application,* Prentice-Hall, Inc., Englewood Cliffs, NJ, 1974.

Weller, W. J., A. V. Shatzel and H. Y. Nice, *Practical Microcomputer Programming: The Intel 8080,* Northern Technology Books, Chicago, IL, 1976.

Index

361

†